Sociology
Basics

Sociology
Basics

Volume 1

Anomie and Deviance—
Microsociology

Consulting Editor
CARL L. BANKSTON III

SALEM PRESS, INC.
Pasadena, California
Hackensack, New Jersey

Essays originally appeared in *Survey of Social Science: Sociology*, 1994; new material has been added.

∞ The paper used in these volumes conforms to the American National Standard for Permanence of Paper for Printed Library Materials, Z39.48-1992 (R1997).

Library of Congress Cataloging-in-Publication Data

Sociology basics / consulting editor, Carl L. Bankston, III.

    p.   cm. — (Magill's choice)

Includes bibliographical references and index.

Selected articles previously published in: Survey of social science. Sociology series, 1994, in 5 vols.

    Contents: v. 1. Anomie and deviance—microsociology—v.2. Modernization and world-system theories—workplace socialization.

    ISBN 0-89356-205-X (set : alk. paper). — ISBN 0-89356-206-8 (v. 1 : alk. paper). — ISBN 0-89356-207-6 (v. 2 : alk. paper)

    1. Sociology—Encyclopedias. I. Bankston, Carl L. II. Survey of social science. Sociology series. III. Series

    HM425.S63   2000

    301'.03—dc21   00-036775

                                    CIP

First Printing

PRINTED IN THE UNITED STATES OF AMERICA

PUBLISHER'S NOTE

Sociology Basics, the latest title in Salem Press's popular Magill's Choice series, is a distillation of the articles of broadest interest that appeared in Salem's five-volume *Survey of Social Science: Sociology Series* (1995). That series was designed to provide general readers with insights into sociology topics that often are accessible only to academicians and experts in the field. By supplying information in a quickly retrievable format and easy-to-understand style, the *Survey of Social Science* series provides nonspecialists with views of essential areas that have become important to laypersons, as well as specialists. *Sociology Basics* takes this process one step further by selecting from the original set's 338 articles 90 topics that cover the most fundamental issues and concepts in sociology.

Articles in *Sociology Basics* follow the familiar Magill format. They begin with ready-reference information, identifying the type of sociology and fields of study to which each topic belongs. A brief summary then describes each topic's significance, and key terms are listed and defined. The body of each article is then divided into three sections. The "Overview" sections introduce and explain the topics. "Applications" sections describe how the topics are put into practice, with examples from sociological studies, and show how the principles involved may be applied to everyday life. "Context" sections locate the subjects within the field of sociology as a whole, relating them to historical and cultural currents, and noting their implications. Annotated bibliographies—which have been updated in *Sociology Basics*—follow these sections; they direct readers to other sources that have been selected for their accessibility to students and general readers. Finally, "Cross-References" sections list related articles that appear elsewhere in the *Sociology Series*.

Like sociology itself, *Sociology Basics* is broad in scope. Its 90 articles examine topics from fourteen fields, which are summarized in the Category List at the back of volume 2. Under the heading of "Culture," for example, readers will find articles on "Cultural Norms and Sanctions," "Culture and Language," "Culture: Material and Expressive Culture," "Subcultures and Countercultures," and "Values and Value Systems." Twenty-three articles fall under the heading of "Major Social Institutions." they include topics on capitalism, class, democracy and politics, economics, education, family, and religion.

Special care was taken to ensure that the articles of greatest interest to students and readers new to sociology are in *Sociology Basics*. Many readers may wish to refer first to "History of Sociology" and "Sociology Defined." Other topics of special importance to newcomers to the field include "Conflict Theory," "Functionalism," "Knowledge," and "Microsociology." Of particular interest to those considering deeper study of sociology will the nine articles on sociological research. These include topics on hypothesis testing, qualitative and quantitative research, sampling techniques, surveys, and reliability in measurement.

Readers can locate information in several ways. Articles are arranged alphabetically by title, and cross-references at the ends of articles direct readers to related topics. Addition help can be found in the Category List and comprehensive index in volume 2. The glossary in volume 2 defines more than 470 important terms.

Salem Press is pleased to be able to acknowledge the many scholars who contributed the articles appearing here. A list of their names and affiliations can be found on the following pages. We also wish to thank Héctor L. Delgado of the University of Arizona for his services as Consulting Editor to the original series, and Carl L. Bankston III, of Tulane University, who selected the articles used in *Sociology Basics* and wrote the new introduction.

CONTRIBUTORS

Olusoji A. Akomolafe
LeMoyne-Owen College

Bryan C. Auday
Gordon College

James A. Baer
Northern Virginia Community College

Bruce E. Bailey
Stephen F. Austin State University

Alan J. Beauchamp
Northern Michigan University

Ralph Bell
Governors State University

Jon L. Berquist
Chalice Press

Richard A. Dello Buono
Rosary College

David P. Caddell
Seattle Pacific University

Malcolm B. Campbell
Bowling Green State University

Michael Candelaria
Community Unitarian Universalist Church

Richard K. Caputo
Yeshiva University

Arlen D. Carey
University of Central Florida

H. B. Cavalcanti
University of Richmond

Jiajian Chen
Wright State University

Denise Kaye Davis
Independent Scholar

Jackie R. Donath
California State University, Sacramento

Charlotte Chorn Dunham
Texas Tech University

Sharon Elise
California State University, San Marcos

Susan Ellis-Lopez
Heritage College

James H. Fisher
Wright State University

Karen Anding Fontenot
Southeastern Louisiana University

Donald R. Franceschetti
University of Memphis

Roberta T. Garner
DePaul University

Gerald R. Garrett
University of Massachusetts at Boston

Roy Neil Graves
University of Tennessee at Martin

Larry D. Hall
Spring Hill College

Dean Harper
University of Rochester

Arthur W. Helweg
Western Michigan University

Howard M. Hensel
Air War College

Joseph E. Jacoby
Bowling Green State University

Charles L. Kammer III
College of Wooster

Terry J. Knapp
University of Nevada, Las Vegas

Nathan R. Kollar
St. John Fisher College

Jerry M. Lewis
Kent State University

Richard D. McAnulty
University of North Carolina at Charlotte

Salvador Macias III
University of South Carolina at Sumter

Susan Mackey-Kallis
Villanova University

John Markert
Cumberland University of Tennessee

Grace M. Marvin
California State University, Chico

A. R. Maryanski
University of California, Riverside

Linda Mealey
College of Saint Benedict

Laurence Miller
Western Washington University

Diane Teel Miller
Liberty University

Donald R. Ortner
Hampden-Sydney College

Nis Petersen
New Jersey City University

Gregory P. Rich
Fayetteville State University

Lanzhen Q. Rich
Fayetteville State University

Hernán Vera Rodríguez
Pontifical Catholic University of Puerto Rico

Andrew L. Roth
University of California, Los Angeles

Sunil K. Sahu
DePauw University

Robert C. Schehr
Colgate University

Rejoice D. Sithole
University of Wisconsin Centers, Waukesha

Charles Vincent Smedley
Charleston Southern University

William L. Smith
Georgia Southern University

M. F. Stuck
State University of New York College at Oswego

Shengming Tang
Western Illinois University

Curt Tausky
University of Massachusetts at Amherst

Leslie V. Tischauser
Prairie State College

Daniel E. Vasey
Divine Word College

Milton D. Vickerman
Bloomfield College

Bruce H. Wade
Spelman College

Theodore C. Wagenaar
Miami University

Jichuan Wang
Wright State University

M. C. Ware
State University of New York College at Cortland

Ira M. Wasserman
Eastern Michigan University

Ann L. Weber
University of North Carolina at Asheville

Mark W. Weigand
University of Colorado, Denver

Karen M. Wolford
State University of New York College at Oswego

Clifton K. Yearley
State University of New York at Buffalo

TABLE OF CONTENTS
Volume 1

Publisher's Note v
Contributors vii

Introduction 1

Anomie and Deviance 7

Bureaucracies 14

Capitalism 21
Caste Systems 28
Causal Relationships 34
Churches, Denominations, and Sects 40
Civil Religion and Politics 46
Class Consciousness and Class Conflict 52
Collective Behavior 59
Conflict Theory 65
Cultural and Structural Assimilation 71
Cultural Norms and Sanctions 77
Cultural Transmission Theory of Deviance 83
Culture: Material and Expressive Culture 89
Culture and Language 95
Culture of Poverty 101

Democracy 107
Demographic Factors and Social Change 116
Demography 122
Deviance: Analysis and Overview 129
Deviance: Functions and Dysfunctions 135
Dramaturgy 141

Education 147
Education: Conflict Theory Views 154
Education: Functionalist Perspectives 160
Ethnicity and Ethnic Groups 166

Ethnography 173
Ethnomethodology 179

Family: Functionalist Versus Conflict Theory Views 186
Functionalism 193

Gender Inequality: Analysis and Overview 199
Gender Inequality: Biological Determinist Views 205

History of Sociology 211
Horticultural Economic Systems 217
Hunting and Gathering Economic Systems 223
Hypotheses and Hypothesis Testing 229

Immigration and Emigration 235
Industrial and Postindustrial Economies 242
Industrial Sociology 249

Knowledge 255

Labeling and Deviance 262
Legitimacy and Authority 268
Looking-Glass Self 273

Marriage Types 280
Marxism 286
Medical Sociology 293
Microsociology 298

Volume 2

Modernization and World-System Theories 305

Political Sociology 312
Poverty: Analysis and Overview 319
Power Elite 326
Prejudice and Discrimination: Merton's Paradigm 332
Prejudice and Stereotyping 338
Protestant Ethic and Capitalism 345

Qualitative Research 351
Quantitative Research 357

Race and Racial Groups 363
Race Relations: The Race-Class Debate 369
Racial and Ethnic Stratification 375
Religion 381
Religion: Functionalist Analyses 388
Religion: Marxist and Conflict Theory Views 394
Role Conflict and Role Strain 400

Samples and Sampling Techniques 406
Secularization in Western Society 412
Significant and Generalized Others 419
Social Change: Sources of Change 425
Social Groups 432
Social Mobility: Analysis and Overview 438
Social Stratification: Analysis and Overview 444
Social Stratification: Functionalist Perspectives 450
Social Stratification: Marxist Perspectives 457
Social Stratification: Weberian Perspectives 463
Socialization: Religion 470
Socialization: The Family 476
Socialization: The Mass Media 483
Sociobiology and the Nature-Nurture Debate 489
Sociology Defined 496
Statuses and Roles 503
Structural-Strain Theory of Deviance 508
Subcultures and Countercultures 515
Suicide 521
Surveys 527
Symbolic Interaction 533

Technology and Social Change 539

Urbanization 546

Validity and Reliability in Measurement 553
Values and Value Systems 559

War and Revolution 566
Workplace Socialization 574

Glossary 580
Category List 603
Index 605

Sociology
Basics

INTRODUCTION

Sociology is one of the youngest academic disciplines. As Terry J. Knapp points out in this set's article on the history of sociology, French philosopher Auguste Comte coined the term "sociology" in the early nineteenth century. It was only in the late nineteenth century, however, that the discipline began taking definite shape and was beginning to be taught widely in universities and secondary schools. Despite its comparative youth as an academic discipline, sociology has become an established and accepted social science. Most universities and colleges now have departments of sociology, and there are few, if any, institutions of higher education that do not teach the subject. Many high schools offer sociology courses, in addition to courses in the broader area of social studies.

Although it has become a common part of our modern educational system, many people, even among the well educated, remain unsure just what it is that sociologists do. Further, sociology has produced terms and concepts that are unfamiliar or unclear to students and general readers. While there are many introductory textbooks on sociology and some good dictionaries of sociology, there are few works providing convenient access to key sociological ideas and terminology in handy one- or two-volume formats. The present reference work attempts to fill this need.

Sociology as a Field of Study. Former British prime minister Margaret Thatcher once declared that there is no such thing as "society," there are only individuals. If this were true, then sociology—the study of society—would be meaningless. People could be understood by looking only at individual biological and psychological characteristics, such as genetic makeups or life histories. However, sociologists are committed to the view that there is such a thing as society, and that a society is not simply the sum of the individuals in it.

Mortality is one of the unavoidable facts of human existence. All human beings are born and all human beings eventually die. If social relations were only relations among individuals, then these relations would be in a state of constant, radical change as new people enter the world and older people depart. Indeed, some change does occur. Younger generations do not feel or behave exactly as older generations have done. Changes, however, are never complete. While there are changes, there is also continuity over generations.

By looking around, sociologists can identify two kinds of continuity. The first is continuity in the ways that people shape their world. Virtually every community contains buildings that are older than the oldest people living within it. Even the newer buildings, moreover, have been influenced by inherited styles. To use another example of continuity over generations, airplanes are a relatively new technology, and the airplanes of today are quite different from those of fifty or seventy-five years ago. Still, today's airplanes could not have been developed without building on the designs of the earlier types.

Buildings and airplanes are material objects. Society also exists across generations in immaterial ways, in customs and traditions. In most Western societies, people greet each other by shaking hands. In some societies in Asia, it is much more common for people to greet each other by placing the palms of their hands together in front of their chins. Neither of these customs was invented by any living individual, but individuals have adopted the ways of those before them.

Patterns of thinking, as well as objects and forms of behavior, are inherited. In some places, people regard qualities such as independence and achievement highly. In other places, cooperation and modesty tend to be praised more. It may be that people everywhere want to distinguish themselves by their achievements and also admire those who interact smoothly with others. The relative importance given to different qualities does vary from one group to another, though, indicating that highly valued personal characteristics are passed within groups over time.

The use of objects, ways of behaving, and trends in thinking are passed over time because they are passed from person to person and are therefore shared by groups of people. Thus, there are social traits held by groups of people who are connected to each other over time and over space. Contrary to Prime Minister Thatcher's remark, then, societies do exist apart from individuals, and societies shape individuals. These societies, moreover, are essential to the lives of all those who are part of them. These words are typed on a computer built through the organized efforts of many people. They are put onto a printed page, bound, and marketed to the public by the efforts of many more. Individuals are shaped by the societies in which they live, and all individual actions are necessarily social.

The social nature of human beings does not mean that people act only as products of societies, however. People also influence their societies. Each person lives in a world constructed over history by group activities. Each of us conforms to the expectations of others. At the same time, though, each person contributes to the actions and expectations of the group; society exists in the connections among individuals. These connections persist, but they also change gradually.

Sociologists study social life. This means that they concern themselves with the social groups that exist apart from the individuals within them, into which people are born and out of which they die. Sociologists look at how people are influenced by their cultures, by the beliefs, values, and ways of acting that they receive from other members of their groups. These social scientists consider how groups transmit cultural traits to individuals through socialization. Sociologists study how the ways in which people work together or compete with one another lead to varying consequences for individuals in different social positions. Sociologists examine institutions, established ways of meeting fundamental human needs through social interaction. Family life, economies, and political systems are all institutions that enable people to perform their basic shared tasks. Those who study sociology investigate how individuals involve themselves in the social world through interaction with others and through interpretation of the actions of others.

Many of the ideas and techniques of sociology overlap with those of other behavioral sciences, including psychology, economics, political science, geography, and history. Psychology is concerned with mental processes and mechanisms in individuals. At least one field of psychology, social psychology, shares a great deal of territory with sociology because social psychology deals with how individual mental processes and mechanisms are related to interactions among people. Economics also shares much of its area of study with certain branches of sociology. Economics treats the creation, use, transfer, and exchange of valued objects and materials. Many of the interactions among people revolve around their connections to the objects they own or use, so there are few economic issues that are not also, in some sense, sociological issues.

Political science is concerned with the nature, organization, and administration of power in groups of people. Political sociology, discussed in one of the entries included in this book, deals with how social life is organized in terms of power and control. Geography deals with social life as the product of the physical environment. Sociologists will often consider the effects of environment on social institutions and forms of behavior. Historians attempt to reconstruct, analyze, and explain events in the past. Since all societies are products of historical change, this, too, is an area of interest to sociologists. However, while sociology overlaps substantially with all of these other behavioral disciplines, it is unique in its focus. In sociology, social relations lie at the center. The psychological, economic, political, geographic, and historical aspects of life are seen as different aspects of social relations.

Theory and Research: The Two Parts of Sociology. To say that sociologists study social life is to say that they attempt to collect information about life in human groups, to devise explanations for the information that they have, and to test their explanations. Carefully constructed explanations are theories. Observing human social life and posing theories about it are ancient human practices. The ancient Greek philosopher Plato, for example, developed theories about the nature and working of societies based on his observations of life in his time. Attempts to collect information and to test theories systematically only began with the modern social sciences, such as sociology and political science.

The type of social research that is closest to that of the physical sciences is quantitative research. This type of social scientific investigation is discussed in detail in this set in an essay by Bryan C. Auday. It involves collecting statistical information. Statistics can offer useful insights into many aspects of our social lives. Do Americans enjoy more luxurious standards of living today than Americans did a generation ago? We can answer this question by compiling statistics on changes in average house sizes, expenditures on automobiles, and so forth. If contemporary Americans do live in more abundant material circumstances than their parents did, is it because people today are really wealthier or because expectations have increased? We could argue that middle-aged and younger Americans grew up in relatively comfortable economic circumstances and therefore expect more than their parents did, even if real incomes have decreased since the 1970's. We could test this theory about attitudes and spending habits by looking at statistical data from polls on expectations, incomes, and expenditures.

To understand more about the expectations of American consumers, we need to do more than gather numerical evidence regarding spending habits and changing attitudes. We need to be able to understand how consumers view their activities and to describe spending money as a socially meaningful activity. Qualitative research, discussed in the essay by Bruce H. Wade, has the goal of understanding what social circumstances mean for those involved in them.

Information, whether gathered by quantitative or qualitative methods, means little by itself. Data compiled from research both lead to theories and are used to test theories. Explanations, though, do not automatically emerge from pieces of information. The theoretical explanations offered by sociologists are shaped by the questions sociologists ask. Some of the most fundamental questions about human society are: What holds people together in groups and enables them to live and work together? Why do some people enjoy greater benefits from our society than others do? How do individuals create a shared understanding of the world through communication? Sociologists who are concerned with maintaining social order and stability tend to ask the first question. Those who are concerned with issues of social justice and inequality tend to concentrate on the second question. Others are interested in examining how social life forms and is formed by human experience. These sociologists concentrate on issues connected to the third question.

Many of the major theoretical perspectives of sociology described in this set stem from these or related questions. Functionalist perspectives focus on the maintenance of order and cooperation in social groups. Conflict perspectives, including Marxism, concentrate on inequality and competition among individuals and groups. Symbolic interaction, ethnomethodology, and other perspectives described in these volumes investigate the realm of meaning in human society.

Theories, then, depend on the kinds of questions people ask. Research enables people to formulate those questions and to attempt to answer them. Just as the theories will vary according to the questions of interest, research will vary according to theoretical perspectives. The complexity of human social life yields a broad scope of theories and a means of investigating those theories.

Uses of Sociology. Why study sociology? When I ask undergraduate students this question, they frequently tell me, "because it's a requirement" or "because I needed a class that meets at this time." While these may be legitimate personal reasons, they can hardly serve as justifications for the existence of the discipline. If one asks professional sociologists, they are likely to respond, "because it is interesting." This is also a legitimate answer, but it should not be the only one. If we are to argue that sociology should interest other people, we must be able to point out its uses.

Perhaps the most fundamental use of sociology is its capacity to help us understand ourselves. We all live in a world composed of other people. Our images of ourselves are formed by comparison with others. Our thoughts and opinions depend heavily upon the positions we occupy in our society. By systematically studying our society, we are attempting to learn more about our own lives and identities. The pursuit of self-knowledge is a central goal of a liberal arts education, so sociology should be regarded as an important part of any program of higher education.

Sociology also has more immediately practical applications than advancing self-understanding. Since sociology is concerned with relations between persons, it has become a subject of study for social workers, personnel managers, and salespeople. Work and training in these fields often draw on ideas and terms derived from sociology.

Police officers and others who are involved with the enforcement of laws or regulations have been heavily influenced by sociological concepts, sometimes without realizing it. The modern tendency to see lawbreakers and delinquents in terms of social contexts such as peer reference groups, family influences, and economic situations is deeply sociological in character. Much of the field of criminology emerged from the work of sociologists.

Sociology has become an unavoidable part of attempts to influence public opinion through political campaigns or marketing. Focus groups, small groups of representative people who discuss their responses to products or candidates, are now commonly used both in sales of products and in elections. These groups were initially developed by sociologists at about the time of World War II. Many of the other research techniques that sociology shares with economics and psychology are used to determine and attempt to shape public opinion.

Policymakers routinely use sociological data and arguments in setting public policy. For example, the federal government and federal courts used sociological evidence about segregated education to make racial integration a major educational goal in the United States. Discussions of policies to remedy social problems frequently recognize that these problems are indeed social in nature, not simply results of moral failure or material hardship. Community policing, for example, is a public policy designed to reduce crime by recognizing the social role of the police. The idea behind this program is that the police will be more effective if they establish cooperative ties with members of the communities they guard. Poverty programs now frequently recognize that poverty is not simply a lack of material resources. It is a social situation; therefore, the poverty of the working poor may be quite different from the poverty of the chronically unemployed. It is notable that even the welfare reform movement of the 1990's, which aimed to reduce government support for the poor, based its claims on sociological arguments. Supporters of welfare reform generally maintained that poverty was a problem of social structure, not simply a result of individual differences in ability or industry. They advanced the sociological argument that public assistance had resulted in the creation of communities that were dependent on the government. Whether one agrees with this argument, it indicates the degree to which discussions of public policy are now carried on in sociological terms, and not simply in legal or moral terms.

A Handy Reference for Sociology. Sociology, then, has become an important and influential field of study during its short lifetime of less than two centuries. The purpose of this reference set is to provide a handy guide to the key ideas in the discipline of sociology. It seeks to present material in a clear, readable, and accessible manner, avoiding specialized language and technical jargon. The topics covered here have been identified as the essential topics that should be addressed in an introductory course of sociology. Although there is some overlap because some entries necessarily deal with closely related matters, these entries should offer fairly comprehensive coverage with a minimum of repetition.

The essays included here have been written by qualified authorities in the field. Since this is a reference work to be used by those who want information or clarification on specific subjects in sociology, the topics have been arranged alphabetically. Each entry provides an identification of the type of sociology and the fields of study relevant to the topic of the entry.

Lists of principal terms accompanying the entries facilitate comprehension. For the sake of clarity and easy understanding, each entry has an overview of the topic and a discussion of the topic's applications. Topics are place in the context of sociology and social issues. Short bibliographies enable readers to pursue subjects of interest in greater depth.

Intended Readers. Sociology is relevant to a wide range of readers, but this set will be of particular use to students in high schools, community colleges, and undergraduate divisions of colleges and universities. Many sociology instructors may wish to include these volumes in their syllabi. Further, they can be helpful to all of those who require comprehensible, reliable information on sociological ideas and terms. Teachers, social workers, counselors, public officials, police officers, community activists, and others will be able to find clarification of concepts that they come across in their professional training or reading. General readers will be able to look up unfamiliar terms such as "ethnomethodology" and "functionalism."

This concise but comprehensive reference book should be a useful addition to all public and academic libraries. Its relative brevity can also make it appealing to many readers for their personal collections. Librarians, instructors, students, and general readers alike will find that this collection makes a valuable contribution to their knowledge of the field of sociology.

Carl L. Bankston III

ANOMIE AND DEVIANCE

Type of sociology: Deviance and social control
Fields of study: Social implications of deviance; Theories of deviance

Robert K. Merton's theory of anomie is a popular and influential sociological perspective on the origins of deviance. Merton's theory helps explain how a society's social structures create and influence the forms of deviant behavior in social groups.

Principal terms

ANOMIE: state of normlessness in society stemming from social change and a society's inability to control the behavior of its individual members
CULTURAL UNIVERSALS: beliefs, values, and norms held in common by all members of a society
NORMATIVE SYSTEMS: society's collection of norms
NORMS: rules generated by society that specify acceptable and unacceptable behavior
SOCIAL STRUCTURE: relatively stable patterns of social relationships organized around statuses and roles
SOCIALIZATION: process through which individuals learn to become members of a social group by assimilating the group's norms, values, and beliefs

Overview

In *Social Theory and Social Structure* (1949), sociologist Robert K. Merton examines the role that social structures play in promoting deviant behavior. Merton criticizes traditional psychological and sociological theories that attribute deviance to conflicts between humankind's biological drives and the need for social order, arguing instead that variations in the amounts of deviance experienced by human societies are a consequence of differences in social structures.

Merton argues that two essential components of all social structural systems are culturally defined goals that specify objectives to which individuals should aspire and culturally defined means that regulate how those goals are to be attained. The culturally defined means of attaining goals reflect the values of a given society. Consequently, culturally prescribed means of attaining goals are not always technically efficient. For example, while control of population growth might be efficiently achieved by legally limiting family size, public sentiment and the value structure of a given group might prohibit such action. Additionally, a society may place differential emphasis on the goals for which its members should strive and the means by which they achieve them.

Culturally prescribed goals and culturally prescribed means of attaining goals are part of a society's normative system. Norms are rules, sometimes codified as laws, that regulate conduct. Anomie, or normlessness, occurs when the norms governing a particular aspect of behavior become weak and fail to regulate human conduct. A state of anomie reduces social order and increases opportunities for the occurrence of previously prohibited behavior.

Merton believes that deviance is likely to occur when a society places great emphasis on its culturally defined goals and places less emphasis on (and provides unequal access to) the culturally defined means to achieve them.

Merton illustrates his theory of anomie by applying it to American society. Merton argues that contemporary American society places great emphasis on the acquisition of material wealth (a culturally prescribed success goal). Merton claims, however, that the culturally prescribed means of attaining wealth are not as strongly emphasized and are not equally available to all members of society. Merton believes that individuals respond in one of five ways to the resulting state of anomie: conformity, innovation, ritualism, retreatism, and rebellion.

Individuals are most likely to conform when a society places equal emphasis on its culturally prescribed goals and means and provides all members equal access to the legal means of achieving success goals. For example, if material wealth is a culturally prescribed goal, conformity occurs when legitimate avenues for achieving wealth are emphasized and all members of the group have equal opportunities to receive an education, to work, or to own a business, and so on. Consequently, Merton argues, conformity is most common in the middle and upper classes of American society, where individuals have realistic opportunities to achieve wealth by conventional means.

Innovation involves the use of illegitimate means (crime) to achieve society's success goals. Innovation is most likely to occur when individuals have internalized the success goals of society but are denied equal access to the institutionalized means of achieving them because of their position in the class structure. Innovation, Merton holds, is most common in the American lower class, because members of the lower class have limited opportunities to achieve wealth by conventional means and have not completely assimilated society's value of conformity to the law.

Ritualists conform to social dictates but have accepted the belief they will never achieve society's success goals. Ritualists reduce the status anxiety produced by the competitive nature of modern society by lowering their aspirations and engaging in routinized behavior. Ritualism is most likely to occur in the American lower middle class where conformity is stressed but opportunities to succeed are limited.

Merton views retreatism as the least common mode of adaptation to anomie. Retreatists (such as alcoholics, drug abusers, hermits, and the mentally ill) have assimilated the success goals of society and the socially prescribed means of attaining them but have been unable to achieve success. Because of their failure to succeed, retreatists eventually withdraw from society. Rebels seek to create a new social structure. They regard the current normative system as arbitrary and seek to establish a new system of norms. Merton believes that rebellion is likely to occur when individuals believe the current social structure is a barrier to positive social change and when allegiance to the current social order is transferred to groups that possess "new myths." These new myths are ideologies that blame the present social structure for societal ills and propose alternative social orders that offer hope of constructive change.

Merton believes that the family plays a critical role in the creation of deviance. Merton notes that the family, through socialization, instills in children the value system of society. Additionally, parents frequently project their own ambitions onto their children. The pressure exerted on children by the family and the limited opportunities for reaching goals, create the foundation for deviance.

While Merton's theory of anomie has been influential, it has not been without its critics. Some sociologists question Merton's claim that all members of society share the same success goals (cultural universality). For example, many Americans who are capable of material success place a higher value on helping others and enter occupations that are less well paid, becoming religious leaders, social workers, or teachers, for example.

Other critics note that Merton's theory does not address the problem of white-collar crime. Merton implies that crime is primarily located in the lower classes, yet white-collar criminals cost American taxpayers billions of dollars each year. Similarly, Merton's theory is unable to explain violent crime, except in cases in which violence is used as a means to achieve financial gain. Other critics have noted that a substantial amount of juvenile delinquency involves nonutilitarian acts (petty vandalism, for example) that have no financial motivation. Further, some types of retreatism may best be explained by genetic factors that predispose individuals to engage in certain behaviors.

Finally, Merton's theory is unable to predict precisely which individuals are likely to engage in deviant behavior. Many individuals who have internalized the success goal of wealth and who are denied equal access to the legitimate means of achieving wealth conform. Some individuals who have internalized the success goal of wealth and who have access to the legitimate means of achieving wealth break the law anyway. Because it is unable to differentiate satisfactorily between potential deviants and potential conformists, Merton's theory has limited predictive and explanatory value.

Applications

Richard A. Cloward and Lloyd E. Ohlin modified Merton's theory of anomie and used it to explain the formation of delinquent gangs. Cloward and Ohlin argue that gangs form when a disjunction exists between culturally based aspirations for achievement (wealth) and the availability of legitimate means to realize them. Cloward and Ohlin claim that cultural and structural barriers deny some individuals the opportunity to achieve wealth by conventional means. Gangs subsequently form as a mode of adaptation to anomie. Unlike Merton, Cloward and Ohlin argue that innovation is likely to occur only when individuals have access to illegitimate opportunities to achieve financial gain. Specifically, they argue that opportunities must exist to learn, practice, and perform acts of innovation before innovation can occur.

Cloward and Ohlin distinguish among three types of delinquent gangs: criminal, conflict, and retreatist. Criminal gangs form when a criminal subculture exists that provides criminal role models and role preparation by age-level integration. Cloward and Ohlin argue that successful criminal activity involves learned skills that are passed on from one generation to the next. In addition, opportunities must exist for the inexperienced innovator to learn these skills by exposure to criminal role models and by practical application. Criminal gangs indoctrinate younger members into the group by providing them with opportunities to learn criminal skills. They exert control over their members and actively discourage nonutilitarian acts of violence. Like other economic enterprises, gangs seek to maintain social order and stability internally and within the community in which they operate. Social disorganization and nonconforming members are bad for business, and they represent potential threats to the normal operations of the gang. Consequently, gangs pressure members to conform to the norms of the gang and punish divergent behavior.

Conflict gangs occur when individuals have limited access to conventional and unconventional (criminal) opportunities to achieve wealth, no access to criminal role models, and no opportunity for age-level integration into criminal subcultures. In the absence of social control exerted by the larger community and by criminal subcultures, and because of limited opportunities to achieve culturally based success goals, individuals engage in violence as a means of status attainment. Cloward and Ohlin believe that conflict gangs disappear when opportunities for achieving wealth by conventional or unconventional means become available to their members.

Retreatist gangs use drugs as a way of escaping the realities of everyday life. Retreatist gangs emerge when individuals have internalized both the success goals of society and societal prohibitions against using illegal means to achieve them or when individuals have attempted to achieve success but have failed. In a sense, retreatist gangs act as a psychological defense mechanism to reduce status anxiety and guilt resulting from feelings of personal failure.

In another study of gangs, Martin Sanchez Jankowski found that urban street gangs exhibit an "entrepreneurial spirit" similar to that found in the American business community. Jankowski notes that gang members are competitive, believe in their ability to achieve success through personal effort, and possess a desire to accumulate material wealth to improve the quality of their daily lives. Additionally, gang members seek social status and share material possessions to gain prestige and power within the group. Gang members also develop extensive plans for the future and are willing to take calculated risks to achieve a desired end.

Jankowski argues that the entrepreneurial spirit of gangs stems from four primary sources. First, Jankowski believes gang members are individualists who distrust others and believe that "only the strongest survive." The individualism of gang members promotes competitiveness and risk-taking behavior that form the basis of the entrepreneurial spirit. Second, Jankowski notes there is a disjunction between the lifestyle of mainstream American culture and the resources available to gang members in low-income neighborhoods to achieve a similar lifestyle. Gang members believe material goods are a key to success and happiness, yet have limited legitimate means of earning money. The desire for money encourages creativity, strategic planning, and calculated risk taking to achieve financial gain.

Third, gang members believe that they are "one good idea" away from success. For the gang member, lack of a good idea, not individual liabilities and deficiencies, accounts for failure. This attitude promotes strategic planning and the cultivation of personal relationships. As in any business enterprise, contacts enable the gang member to put his or her plan into action by providing logistic and financial support.

Finally, Jankowski argues, the entrepreneurial spirit of the gang stems from its members' desire to avoid failure and poverty. Gang members typically believe that their parents have resigned themselves to a life of economic deprivation. Gang members reject these self-defeating attitudes and seek to maintain a belief that success is possible through individual effort and achievement.

In general, Jankowski's study supports many of Merton's claims concerning American culture. Jankowski suggests that gang members have assimilated the success goal of wealth yet are denied access to the legitimate means of achieving wealth. Gang members innovate to achieve goals unattainable through conventional means. Despite differences in the techniques used to realize their ends, gangs and conventional businesses share a similar set of core values. Like business organizations, gangs believe competition leads to economic success, and they mobilize resources to attain these ends. Gangs also act as a psychological buffer, protecting individual self-esteem and maintaining goal aspirations in the face of adversity.

Context

Merton's theory of anomie is an outgrowth of functionalism, a dominant theoretical perspective in modern sociology. Functionalism can be traced to the writings of Auguste Comte, Herbert Spencer, and Émile Durkheim and is a reaction to the social turmoil of late eighteenth century Europe.

The French Revolution and the Industrial Revolution produced massive social change and instability in Western Europe. Comte, a French intellectual, sought to examine the question of social order and identify the underpinnings of social organization through scientific investigation. Comte viewed society as a collective organism whose parts work toward common ends through action and reaction among its constituent parts and its environment. Comte believed that social progress consists of increased specialization that promotes harmony of structure and function and greater integration in society. Increased specialization, however, can result in social disorganization if society's sense of unity and identity is lost. Consequently, Comte believed that government must regulate specialization to promote social unity.

Herbert Spencer, the English social philosopher, argued that social systems become more differentiated as they increase in size. Spencer believed that the increasing complexity of modern society produces mutual interdependence and social integration. More important, Spencer noted that societies must fulfill certain needs (such as the production and distribution of goods and services and the maintenance of social control) if they are to survive. Spencer believed that the institutions that make up society function to fulfill these needs and enable a society to adapt to its environment.

French sociologist Émile Durkheim focused on the problem of how societies create and sustain social integration. Durkheim believed that crime is beneficial to society because punishing rule breakers reinforces a society's normative system and thus reaffirms group identity. According to Durkheim, norms function to create and maintain social order. A society without a properly functioning normative system runs the risk of social disorganization.

Other theorists have expanded Durkheim's theory. For example, Kai Erikson argues that social groups increase their enforcement of norms when their identity is threatened. Punishing deviants reaffirms a society's values and serves to reinforce group integration and identity. In a similar vein, Philip Jenkins argues that British perceptions of rampant increases in crime are a reaction to social change in British society. Specifically, Jenkins believes that rapid social change in Britain in the 1980's threatened group identity. Subsequent public reaction to perceived social problems served to reaffirm social identity and reinforce order.

Merton's theory of anomie is firmly grounded in the functionalist tradition. For example, he assumes that norms form the basis for social order and examines how disruptions in a society's normative system produce social deviance. Merton locates the origins of deviance in the social structure of society and suggests that it is a poorly functioning normative system, not the individual per se, that creates that foundation for deviant behavior. Deviance occurs because norms fail to regulate behavior and social institutions fail to meet the needs of society and its members.

Bibliography

Cloward, Richard A., and Lloyd E. Ohlin. *Delinquency and Opportunity: A Theory of Delinquent Gangs*. New York: Free Press, 1960. Claims that gang formation is a response to anomie. Presents the view that gangs innovate when gang members have the opportunity to learn, practice, and perform criminal acts. Stresses the role of social inequality in creating delinquent subcultures.

Durkheim, Émile. *The Rules of Sociological Method*. Translated by Sarah A. Solovay and John H. Mueller, edited by George Catlin. 8th ed. New York: Free Press, 1938. Outlines Durkheim's views on the science of sociology and his theory that crime serves to reinforce a society's belief system, thereby preserving social order and identity.

Erikson, Kai T. *Wayward Puritans: A Study in the Sociology of Deviance*. New York: Macmillan, 1986. Uses Durkheim's theory of crime to examine anomie in the seventeenth century Massachusetts Puritan colony. Argues that increased identification and persecution of deviants is related to social stress and perceived threats to group identity.

Jankowski, Martin Sanchez. *Islands in the Street: Gangs and American Urban Society*. Berkeley: University of California Press, 1991. Outlines Jankowski's theory of gang formation. Argues that gangs are economic organizations that innovate to achieve financial gain and that they hold values that are similar to those found in the corporate world.

Jenkins, Philip. *Intimate Enemies: Moral Panics in Contemporary Great Britain*. New York: Aldine de Gruyter, 1992. Argues that British exaggerated beliefs (moral panics) in the existence of rampant crime are a consequence of changes in British society. Suggests that moral panics serve to reintegrate society and promote social organization and identity.

Merton, Robert K. *Social Theory and Social Structure*. Rev. ed. New York: Free Press, 1968. Originally published in 1949 and expanded in 1968, this work contains the original statement of Merton's theory of anomie. Expanded version presents review of relevant writings and research on anomie by others. Extremely readable.

Sikes, Gini. *8 Ball Chicks: A Year in the Violent World of Girl Gangs.* New York: Anchor
    Books, 1997.
Ulmer, Jeffrey T. *Sociology of Crime, Law, and Deviance.* Stamford, Conn.: JAI Press, 1998.

Charles Vincent Smedley

Cross-References

Cultural Norms and Sanctions; Cultural Transmission Theory of Deviance; Deviance:
Analysis and Overview; Deviance: Functions and Dysfunctions; Social Stratification:
Analysis and Overview; Structural-Strain Theory of Deviance; Suicide; Values and Value
Systems.

BUREAUCRACIES

Type of sociology: Social structure
Field of study: Key social structures

Evolved to enhance the authority and operational effectiveness of modern organizations—governments, businesses, trade unions, and political parties—bureaucracies have become a worldwide phenomenon. Their defenders perceive them as efficient, essential, and flexible; their critics see them as disinterested, impersonal, and self-serving manufacturers of paperwork and red tape.

Principal terms

AD-HOCRACY: temporary work group of skilled persons designed to solve specific, non-routine problems

AUTHORITY: power accepted as legitimate by the people over whom it is exercised

BUREAUCRATIC PERSONALITY: tendency for bureaucrats to adhere strictly and impersonally to regulations beyond the point at which these regulations cease to serve organizational objectives

IDEAL TYPE: logical, exaggerated model used as a methodological tool for the study of specific phenomena

INFORMAL SYSTEM: organization within supposedly rational and impersonal bureaucracies which is composed of personal and closely knit social groups

OLIGARCHY: small group of people who control an organization's or system's power

PARKINSON'S LAW: observation that the work of bureaucracies expands to fill the time required for its completion; in other words, self-serving bureaucracies "make work"

PETER PRINCIPLE: explains the incompetence of bureaucrats by suggesting that in a hierarchy every employee tends to rise to his or her own level of incompetence

RATIONAL-LEGAL AUTHORITY: legitimization of power by law, rules, and regulations rather than by tradition or personality

Overview

Bureaucracies have developed throughout societies in which complex tasks must be placed under centralized control and administered efficiently. Millennia ago, Egyptian dynasties established bureaucracies to collect taxes, facilitate irrigation, and carry through massive dynastic works, such as tomb and pyramid construction. Similarly, beginning roughly two thousand years ago in order to collect taxes over a vast area, to control rivers, to maintain armies, and to assist in canal building, China created a sophisticated bureaucracy that was staffed and controlled by mandarins, a scholarly elite. It is the bureaucracies that have evolved since the 1780's within modern industrial and postindustrial societies, however, that have captured the attention of sociologists and other social scientists.

In eighteenth century France, for example, during an era when the absolutist monarchy was not only engaged in international wars but also attempting to regulate the national economy more closely, the word "bureaucracy" first appeared as the collective designation for groups of administrative officials. In Prussia soon thereafter, bureaucracy meant government by officials, while in 1860 in Great Britain, political economist John Stuart Mill defined the essence of bureaucracy as the placement of government work in the hands of "governors by profession."

These casual definitions were given scholarly substance by the German sociologist and political economist Max Weber (1864-1920). Weber recognized that modern society had become increasingly rational, so much so that humans were being caught in an "iron cage." Moreover, no aspect of modern society more completely embodied this rationality than did bureaucracies. Because of the importance of this phenomenon, Weber formulated an abstract, logical, ideal type of bureaucracy in comparison with which further study of real bureaucracies could proceed. Although they were subsequently refined and embellished, Weber's criteria of what constitutes bureaucracies have remained valid and continue to be employed by sociologists.

Bureaucracies, therefore, are understood to be organizations displaying at least a half-dozen common characteristics. Labor is divided among members of bureaucracies according to written prescriptions of responsibilities and functions. Authority, flowing from the top down, is allocated among their memberships according to well-defined rank order. Detailed, written rules and regulations subsequently determine the rights and duties applicable to every position. Likewise, specified procedures and regulations govern the handling of tasks. As is the case in the large, impersonal (*Gesellschaft*) societies that bureaucracies serve, impersonality or neutral attitudes mark relationships among bureaucrats and between bureaucrats and their clients. Finally, the selection, recruitment, and employment of bureaucrats, as well as their promotions within their bureaus, are based on demonstrable competence—usually measured by formal examinations—and expertise.

Weber's theoretical or ideal type of bureaucracy is a formal organization designed to achieve definite goals with maximal efficiency, but the authority under which it operates is described by sociologists as rational-legal authority. That is, the legitimization of bureaucracies stems from the law and a social system's basic rules rather than from the influences of personality, charisma, idiosyncratic decision making, or tradition.

Weber's abstraction, although a classic one, is only one of several. In 1911, Robert Michels supplemented Weber's work by including not only governments but also political parties in his concept of bureaucracy. Bureaucracies in Michels's study derived from the administrative necessities confronting all modern organizations; not least, he argued, they strengthened the oligarchic power of a handful of party leaders. Almost at the same time, and in a similar vein, Gaetano Mosca insisted that bureaucracies were fundamental to the governance of all major political systems. Moreover, those societies in which bureaucracies had not developed, he declared, could be classified as feudal.

As the twentieth century progressed, such theories allowed sociologists increasingly to study the ways in which bureaucracies functioned in reality. The yields of these studies have sharpened definitions of bureaucracy just as they have tended to divide sociologists and other social scientists over the efficiency as well as the effects of bureaucratization.

By the 1950's, for example, many sociologists were demonstrating that in reality bureaucracies were far from the efficient, goal-oriented organizations that classic models had proposed. Empirical study instead shows that in many cases bureaucratic operations were quite inefficient and even counterproductive. Conclusions from these studies, which examined governmental, private corporate, and political organizations, tended to confirm the idea prevalent in nearly all developed countries that bureaucracies had introduced vexatious, sometimes nightmarish, burdens into people's daily lives.

To begin with, while bureaucrats often handle routine tasks capably, they frequently appear to be paralyzed by unusual or nonroutine tasks as well as by unexpected changes (war, natural disasters, and so forth)—to the chagrin of their clients and at considerable cost to everyone. Like Max Weber (who was the subject of one of Bendix's studies), Reinhard Bendix worried about a world filled with people who clung to little jobs and struggled like careerists toward bigger ones.

Other sociologists described the formation of a "bureaucratic personality": the bureaucrat's inclination to follow rules beyond the point at which their organizational goals ceased to be served. Having noted that bureaucracies continuously sought bigger budgets and larger workforces, C. Northcote Parkinson posited a "law" that bureaucratic work seemed to expand with the time available for its completion, while Laurence Peter's famed "Peter principle" suggested that in every hierarchy each employee is likely to rise to the level of his or her own incompetence. To these impressions still other sociologists have added details on the inner world of forms, memos, studies, and regulations that characterize bureaucracies.

There are sociologists, however, who address the question of why, despite their unpopularity, rigid routines, and red tape, bureaucracies persist as a major institutional characteristic of modern society. A number of studies have supplied partial answers by noting what appear to be bureaucratic virtues. For example, although red tape and elaborate procedures anger some citizens, they can be shown to protect the rights of others. Similarly, bureaucratic impersonality and neutrality sometimes play positive roles. Thus, students seeking government-subsidized grants or loans and private builders seeking government contracts often prefer that personal or political influence—indeed, any type of discrimination—be excluded from decisions concerning their applications.

Other studies suggest that some bureaucracies may be less mechanical in their operations and bureaucrats often may be less hidebound in their reactions than is commonly assumed. Sociologist Melvin Kohn, for example, indicates that bureaucracies can and do encourage open-mindedness, imagination, and creativity among their employees. Moreover, according to test results, bureaucrats demonstrate high levels of intellectual performance. They likewise place heavy demands on themselves, value self-direction and nonconformity, and are more likely to favor change than are nonbureaucrats.

Applications

One hallmark of modernity is the pervasiveness of bureaucracies. In developed nations, they have grown steadily in size and number both in the public and private spheres since the late nineteenth century. In the 1990's, despite continuing complaints about their inefficiencies, their erosive effects on individualism, and their inhumanity, they remain expansive and wield enormous authority. Small wonder that German sociologist Henry Jacoby was able to title one of his major works *The Bureaucratization of the World* (1973). Small wonder, too, that like Jacoby and Weber, sociologists Hans Gerth, C. Wright Mills, Michel Crozier, and Robert Merton, among many others, asked what forces might be found to control "this monstrous system" and how liberal democracy might be preserved in the face of it.

Undoubtedly, there is a close fit between the operations of bureaucracies and Weber's ideal model of them. When the evolution of bureaucracies and their mature functions have been studied closely and comparatively by social scientists, however, these key institutions have been found to display their own unique characteristics.

These distinctions frequently appear within the bureaucracies of specific nations. For example, over long periods, the bureaucratic organization of American Telephone and Telegraph (AT&T), International Business Machines (IBM), Eastman Kodak, and Minnesota Mining and Manufacturing (3M Company)—all at one time models of effectiveness—have differed significantly from those of American steel, railroad, and automotive companies.

In addition, such distinctions also differentiate the bureaucracies of one nation from those of another. Comparatively, for example, America's federal bureaucracies are readily distinguishable from China's collectivist state bureaucracies, just as American corporate bureaucracies often reveal unique characteristics when compared with many corporate organizations in Japan. More specifically, China's collectivist models emphasize greater ideological commitment and higher technical competence among an organization's members than is true in the United States. They likewise strive for egalitarianism, minimize the range of rewards, and entrust authority to the collectivity as a whole. To motivate workers, the Chinese stress comradeship, personal appeals, and the diffusion of skills. In addition, they deemphasize the division of labor and tend to favor ad hoc decision making by formal groups.

By comparison, American corporate bureaucracies frequently reveal salient features that are quite different from those of Japan's corporate bureaucracies. Unlike many American corporations, in which managers are expected to show results quickly and thus concentrate on short-term rather than on long-term goals, risking their jobs if they fail, the opposite tends to be true in Japan. In fact, until Japan's lengthiest and deepest economic recession (which entered its third year in 1994) raised questions about prevalent practices, Japanese managers and workers could count on lifetime employment with their organizations.

Sociological studies have also proposed other comparisons, such as those advanced by Stephen Skowronek in 1982 and Bernard S. Silberman in 1993. Both specialists have examined the development of America's federal bureaucracy as well as the development of its major political parties. Silberman, in particular, has compared the evolution, structure, and functions of the U.S. bureaucracy and political parties by applying his focus to related developments in France, Japan, and Great Britain. To generalize, what has been learned is that distinct cultures produce their own unique brands of bureaucracy. To be sure, features of the ideal type proposed by Weber and by other classic sociological studies are in varying degrees detectable in the structuring and goal setting of all bureaucracies. Differences between their organization, functioning, and objectives in relation to their cultural contexts, however, frequently appear to be as significant as their similarities.

America's federal and state bureaucracies, for example, historically seemed to be assembled in defiance of rationality when contrasted with Weber's ideal bureaucratic model. Satisfying demands for patronage upon which political parties relied for much of their strength during most of the nineteenth century took precedence over administrative efficiency and effectiveness. Recruitment to administrative posts was not selective, based on technical or professional competence, or intended to place administrators and bureaucrats beyond the reach of political influence. On the contrary, selections were based on favoritism, pull, and bureaucrats' willingness to heed the wishes of the politicians and party that chose them.

Federal enactment of the Pendleton Act in 1883 and subsequent civil service acts (shortly followed by similar state laws) gradually eroded patronage but failed to depoliticize America's governmental bureaucracies. In fact, control over the federal bureaucracy during the twentieth century shifted from the executive branch of government to the Congress, and Congress has tightened and formalized bureaucratic recruitment, rank orders, technical competence, and its bureaucrats' rewards. Nevertheless, bureaucratic autonomy and depoliticization have not occurred. Thus, in the 1980's, federal bureaucracies paid nearly five hundred full-time lobbyists to plead their cases—most of which were related to budget and personnel—with the Congress. In this and many other respects, government bureaucracies in the United States contrast sharply with those of Great Britain, France, and Germany.

Context

Auguste Comte (1798-1857), a founder of sociology, in common with other of sociology's early pioneers, used the term "organization" in referring to bureaucracies. Not only did those scholars consider bureaucracies to be essential organizations, their references to them also were usually positive ones. Later in the nineteenth century, however, when industrialization was in full swing and the power of Western governments was rapidly expanding, the perspectives of sociologists changed. They continued to view bureaucratic organizations in the abstract as essential components of rational, modern societies, but bureaucracy nevertheless posed a dilemma for them. Although no one could suggest a substitute for these apparently indispensable organizations, the cold, mechanical, inhumane, often inefficient, and inflexible character of public and private bureaucracies in action were worrisome.

Weber's classic depiction of an ideal type of bureaucracy manifested this ambivalence. From a purely technical view, bureaucracies, he believed, represented the most rational of all organizations and therefore were capable of bringing the greatest efficiency and precision to bear in pursuit of their objectives—and of doing so cheaply. It was the effects of bureaucratization and the consequences of the modern passion for rationality which the process reflected that drove Weber to despair. Without knowing what to do about such problems (Alvin Toffler's concept of "ad-hocracies" lay half a century in the future), Weber feared the dehumanization of bureaucrats and their clients alike, as well as a general loss of individual freedom. Just how much Weber's negative perceptions of bureaucracy stemmed from his own bitter conflicts with his bureaucrat father remains conjectural. What is certain, however, is that hundreds of additional sociological studies of bureaucratic organizations have not dissipated anxieties and fears such as Weber's.

Weber died in 1920, but those sociologists who have pursued his interests in bureaucracies have sharpened their definitions of these organizations and directed their analytical focus toward the major institutional changes and problems of their times. Because professional sociology was largely a Western European and an American enterprise, sociologists have concentrated their attention, insofar as bureaucracies are concerned, on the structure and operations of important new institutions as well as on significant changes in older ones.

One of these new institutions of transcendent importance is the private business corporation, the activities of which since the end of the nineteenth century have played vital roles in the social and economic lives of Americans and Europeans. The older institution is government, which during the twentieth century has not only taken on novel forms but also has assumed vastly more intricate and expanded authority. Both new and changed organizations function by virtue of their bureaucracies.

Taking different tacks from those of earlier twentieth century sociologists such as Mosca and Crozier, for example, Jerald Hage and Wolf Heydebrand have studied the adaptations of bureaucracies to technical change, stressing their inner working, their informal groups, and their flexibility. Peter Blau and Marshall Meyer similarly have examined adjustments between bureaucracies and modern society with more sanguine results than Weber's, while Alvin Toffler concentrated on the efficacy of ad-hocracies, which he viewed as replacements for bureaucracy. Fresh analyses of the expansion of American administrative capacities, meantime, appear in the work of Herbert Simon, Gordon Tullock, Bernard Silberman, Reinhard Bendix, Paul DiMaggio, and Robert Skowronek, while organizational and bureaucratic elites have been analyzed by Robert Presthus, C. Wright Mills, Robert Dahl, Charles Lindblom, and Paul Goldman.

Bibliography

Crozier, Michel. *The Bureaucratic Phenomenon*. Chicago: University of Chicago Press, 1964. Precise and jargon-free survey of the subject by a French sociologist. Crozier's view is that modern bureaucracies are distinguished by their inability to correct their errors and hence are detrimental organizations.

Jacoby, Henry. *The Bureaucratization of the World*. Translated by Eveline L. Kanes. Berkeley: University of California Press, 1973. Surveys the bureaucratic origins of modern governments, the advent of the administered world, and the rule of bureaucracy and its problems. A clear, reflective work intended for the nonspecialist.

Ritzer, George. *Sociological Theory*. 5th ed. New York: McGraw-Hill, 1999. Clear, effective book. The chapter discussing Weber's views on bureaucracy is essential. Ritzer explains theory without jargon. Includes photographs and biographical sketches of sociological theorists.

Silberman, Bernard S. *Cages of Reason.* Chicago: University of Chicago Press, 1993. Detailed survey of the rise of rational (bureaucratized) states in France, Japan, the United States, and Great Britain. Silberman convincingly adduces evidence to contradict Weber's pessimism about bureaucratization.

Weber, Max. *From Max Weber.* Edited and translated by H. H. Gerth and C. Wright Mills. New York: Oxford University Press, 1946. Contains well-chosen excerpts, with annotations, from Weber's influential sociological essays. Weber always makes exciting reading.

Clifton K. Yearley

Cross-References

Capitalism; Industrial and Postindustrial Economies; Legitimacy and Authority; Secularization in Western Society; Social Groups.

CAPITALISM

Type of sociology: Major social institutions
Field of study: The economy

Capitalism refers to an economic system in which the means of production are privately owned and production decisions are made by firms in response to market conditions in order to realize profits. This concept is used to understand labor markets, global inequalities, and the culture and class structure of contemporary societies.

Principal terms

CAPITAL: wealth used to produce further wealth or accumulated goods used to produce further goods

CORPORATE CAPITALISM: form of economy characterized by large firms

LABOR: productive activity; in capitalism, labor power is bought and sold as a commodity in a market

MARKET: self-regulating mechanism of economic production in which goods are produced and distributed in response to supply and demand

POLICY: purposive course of action undertaken to solve or cope with a social problem; public policy is undertaken by government

PRIVATE OWNERSHIP: system in which the means of production are held by individuals and firms and are freely disposable in a market

Overview

Capitalism is a type of economy that is based on private ownership of the means of production and on the market as the regulating mechanism of production and distribution. Decisions about what to produce and how much to produce are made by private firms in response to conditions of supply and demand in markets; the point of economic activity for firms is maximization of profit.

This definition of capitalism is associated with distinct social characteristics. First, capitalism is a system based on free labor: Workers are paid wages or salaries for their labor power in a contractually limited relationship that is entered into freely. In this respect, capitalism differs from slavery and serfdom, in which labor is coerced, and from "primitive" and "household" economies in which custom and kinship ties, along with necessity, induce people to engage in economic activities. In capitalism, labor power as a factor of production is available in a labor market as a commodity.

Second, capitalism is an expanding system, in both technological innovation and geographical horizons. Driven by competition and the search for profitable investments and markets, capitalist firms introduce new machinery and expand operations globally. Capitalism is characterized by accumulation, by expansion of investment, and by buildup of machinery and material culture. Investments can shift quickly, bringing about rapid social change. Third, in capitalist society, the political system is relatively autonomous from the economy, unlike under feudalism, in which the state is formed directly by the landed nobility itself. Although the ideology of laissez-faire (minimal government intervention in the economy) has been more an ideal than a reality, there is a considerable degree of separation between economy and government in most capitalist nations. In the twentieth century, these two institutions have drawn closer together, with governments taking steps to regulate the economy, integrate economic production with national priorities, and undertake "counter-cyclical measures" to reduce the magnitude of economic crises.

Fourth, capitalism is associated with distinct forms of culture and ideology. Capitalism has historically been associated with rational calculation, impersonal norms, and individualism. People see themselves as individuals "freed" from traditional ties and obligations. Advertising creates new wants and needs to make possible the realization of profit on new products; acquisition of commodities is a central value, and desire for material goods escalates.

Marxist and non-Marxist social scientists differ in their evaluation of capitalism as a system. The former tend to emphasize inherent inequalities and limitations, while the latter are more inclined to "take it for granted" or to point to positive features. For Marxist social scientists, capitalism contains a fundamental split between those who own the means of production and buy labor power (capitalists) and those who do not own the means of production and must therefore sell their labor power (the working class). For Marxists, these two groups form two classes with opposed interests. Workers depend on capitalists for employment, but in a larger perspective, the potential of workers as human beings cannot be realized within the capitalist system. Non-Marxist social scientists point to the fluidity of these class categories, since capitalist classes are not hereditary or castelike; they see the sale and purchase of labor power as an even exchange rather than as an exploitive mechanism by which surplus value is extracted from labor. They emphasize that liberal-democratic states associated with capitalism have been responsive to mass pressures for improved living standards and social services. They suggest that capitalism is a necessary (though not sufficient) condition for democracy.

Marxist and non-Marxist social scientists differ in their view of the origins of capitalism. They agree that capitalism emerged as land, labor, and capital became commodities in Western Europe in the period between 1500 and 1800. Prior to that period, commerce and markets had existed, and money had circulated as a medium of exchange. Land, however, could be obtained only through inheritance or feudal obligations. Labor was coerced (as slavery and serfdom) or embedded in kinship relations; money did not circulate in a capital market, nor was it viewed as the basis of investment. Capitalism in its modern form emerged with several institutional changes. Modern systems of banking and credit were established; money relations replaced serfdom, and monetary land rents sped development of commercial agriculture. National and international markets in raw materials, land, and finished products expanded, and factory production using wage labor replaced guild manufactures and cottage industries.

Marxists explain the decline of feudalism in terms of class conflict between landholders and other social forces (such as peasants and merchants) or emphasize structural problems in the feudal economy. Marxists also examine the role of European expansion and point to wealth produced by African and American Indian slaves as an accelerant of capital accumulation in Europe. Non-Marxist historical sociologists put more emphasis on changes in values, especially the role of the Protestant Reformation in creating preconditions for "the spirit of capitalism." The German sociologist Max Weber theorized that Protestant values such as frugality and a strong work ethic accelerated practices associated with the accumulation of capital. The differences between Marxist and non-Marxist sociologists have been exaggerated and oversimplified; Marxists do not deny the role of ideas and values in history, and Weber did not neglect changes in class structure and the economy as elements in the advent of capitalism.

Marxists and non-Marxists differ in their view of the centrality of capitalism in "modern" society. For Marxists, capitalism defines "modern" society. Capitalist relations of production shape and limit all other practices in the society. Non-Marxists see a looser connection between economic, political, and social institutions and often give theoretical priority to political, cultural, or technological practices. For example, non-Marxists point to "technological imperatives" that come with the introduction of computers; machinery itself, they say, induces certain kinds of behavior regardless of its social context. Marxists emphasize that computers are introduced by capitalists in order to reduce labor costs, increase output, beat the competition, and widen profit margins; the capitalist socioeconomic context limits how machinery is used.

Marxists and non-Marxists also differ in their views of the trajectory of capitalism. Non-Marxists see no internal contradictions in the system that might lead to a final economic collapse or to political crisis. While they acknowledge that capitalism is associated with poverty in underdeveloped regions and inequality even in the most developed countries, they believe that these conditions can be alleviated by a variety of policies pursued within the framework of capitalism. Marxists identify "contradictions" within capitalism that revolve around the tension between capitalism's enormous productive potential and the limited and alienated condition that it imposes on human beings in terms of poverty, exploited labor, unemployment and underutilization of human talent, and the hollowness of consumer culture. Impending crisis is signaled by rising unemployment and falling rates of profit. Poverty and regional wars in the capitalist periphery are warning signs of the system's lack of viability: "Socialism or barbarism," say Marxists.

While Marxists see capitalism as a revolutionary and positive step forward from feudalism, they do not see it as a desirable end result. Non-Marxist sociologists are less inclined to think that capitalism should or will be replaced by another type of society and economy.

Applications
The most important application of the concept "capitalism" is to draw attention to the systemic nature and economic determinants of social behavior and social problems. Using this concept is a way of indicating that certain problems or issues are unlikely to be resolved unless a major political and economic change takes place. For many non-Marxist social

scientists, this change involves a more active relationship between the state and the capitalist economy. In their view, when the source of problems is an institution as large and pervasive as the capitalist economy, only government is a sufficiently powerful institution to represent the interests of those who do not own capital and to implement policies designed to solve or reduce social problems. For Marxists, the problems can only be solved by a global transition to socialism. Most Marxists support public policy to improve conditions in the short run, but they believe that as long as capital operates globally, national public policy is limited in its effectiveness. Some sociologists favor less government intervention, asserting that freer markets lead to better functioning societies on both a national and a global scale.

One major issue of capitalist societies is the class structure, whether conceived as sharply polarized or more minutely stratified. As long as capitalism generates class inequality, it is likely that many social problems will persist, especially in the view of Marxist sociologists. For example, poverty and street crime are direct results of these inequalities. A related problem is the social effect of unemployment, which is both a systemic feature of capitalism and a result of shifts in investments. Sociologists point to individual effects of unemployment, such as suicide and domestic violence, and to the effects of high rates of unemployment on communities and ethnic groups (such as African Americans).

Marxist and non-Marxist sociologists tend to agree that a full-employment economy would reduce inequality and associated problems. Many sociologists call for strategies of government intervention in the capitalist economy, such as job training, tax credits for employers who expand jobs, and stimuli for the economy as a whole, to reduce its tendency to function with high levels of unemployment. A higher minimum wage, access to health care, and better education are seen as supportive measures. Government can intervene directly in labor markets by policies such as affirmative action to reduce high levels of unemployment among minorities. Keynesian "countercyclical" measures are seen as a way of reducing cyclical unemployment and inflation characteristic of capitalist economies.

Sociologists use the concept of capitalism to study changes in developing nations, sometimes said to be on the "periphery of capitalism." Replacement of traditional economies by the global capitalist economy has produced new inequalities, disruption of village life, and the formation of urban shantytowns of the underemployed. Sociologists try to understand what public policies and/or grassroots movements can do to make this transition less traumatic; for example, they look at conditions that facilitate producer cooperatives, community organizations, and labor unions. Sociologists study how peasant populations enter industrial wage work in "newly industrializing nations." Since the paid labor force is increasingly female, sociologists also look at connections between the changing nature of work in the capitalist economy and traditional gender systems.

The changing nature of capitalism has stimulated new perspectives in sociology, notably in the 1970's and 1980's. The "stagflation" of the 1970's gave way to restructuring in the 1980's. Corporate mergers increased, unions became weaker, government involvement was cut back, layoffs included managers as well as production workers, a service economy replaced manufacturing, and the middle class came under economic pressure. Non-Marxist as well as Marxist sociologists gave renewed attention to labor markets. They demonstrated that there was not a single labor market; rather, there were "segmented" markets, differentiated by ethnicity and gender. They also looked at the social impact of rising unemployment. Some studies focused on how African Americans and other urban populations were affected by deindustrialization and by a loss of manufacturing jobs in central cities as investment shifted to other locations and activities. Sociologists also studied the impact of labor force participation on women, families, and the gender system.

The globalization of capitalism has also stimulated sociological analysis. Capitalism has been a global and transnational system from the start, but these tendencies accelerated in the late twentieth century with several trends: the rise of multinational corporations; the establishment of integrated regional economies such as the European Community; and the movement of industries into "underdeveloped" regions that offer lower labor costs. Sociologists study how work, culture, ethnic relations, and everyday life are affected by the mobility of capital and labor.

Sociologists study the internal workings of corporations, giving attention to bureaucratic decision making; work satisfaction; the roles of gender and ethnicity; and the process of technological innovation. Capitalist technological innovation also changes behavior and culture. For example, sociologists look at the impact of computerization and "video culture." They are exploring the relationship between postmodern culture and trends in capitalism such as globalization, media monopolies, and the service economy.

Context

Since the middle of the nineteenth century, when capitalism became discernible as the prevailing form of economy, sociologists have directed their attention to explaining it and understanding its social effects. All four of the great classical sociological theorists—Karl Marx, Émile Durkheim, Max Weber, and Georg Simmel—used capitalism as a central concept. Marx devoted his life to an analysis of capitalism. Durkheim was interested in how capitalism affected social integration. He believed that it weakened traditional types of solidarity, only partially replacing these bonds with an "organic solidarity" based on a complex division of labor and economic interdependence.

Max Weber examined preconditions of capitalism in religious thought, specifically the Protestant Reformation. He explored the relationship between capitalism and rational calculation characteristic of modern societies. Unlike Marx, Weber did not see much hope for socialism as an alternative to capitalism; he believed that all modern societies tend toward bureaucratic organization and impersonal rationality. Simmel looked at capitalism in terms of social forms and types of individuals created by a money economy. The metropolis is the site of the money economy and is characterized by a fast pace of activity, impersonal and objectified treatment of human beings, diversity in fashion and lifestyle, and social types that are defined by money, such as the miser, the spendthrift, and the prostitute.

In the period from World War I to the 1950's, interest waned in capitalism as a leading concept in non-Marxist sociology, especially in the United States. Exceptions were Robert S. Lynd and Helen Lynd's *Middletown: A Study in Contemporary American Culture* (1930) and *Middletown in Transition: A Study in Cultural Conflicts* (1937), examinations of life in a Midwestern city that emphasized the economic context of social behavior and identified socioeconomic class as a major force in everyday life. By the 1950's, C. Wright Mills reawakened the interest of sociologists in the capitalist economy with his concept of the power elite, which included the top ranks of large corporations and the "military-industrial complex." In *White Collar: The American Middle Classes* (1951), Mills looked at how the shift from small-scale business to corporate capitalism was transforming the American middle class; he noted that all types of white-collar work, from sales to intellectual production, were increasingly carried out within corporations. William H. Whyte reached similar conclusions in *The Organization Man* (1956), a study of corporate employees and their emerging suburban lifestyles. Because the 1950's was a period when labor unions became bureaucratized, sociologists explored conditions under which unions retained internal democracy, rank-and-file participation, and militancy.

With the changes in capitalism that occurred in the 1970's and 1980's, capitalism has remained a central sociological concept for non-Marxist as well as Marxist researchers and theorists. As long as most of the globe is involved in a capitalist economy, capitalism will persist as a topic of the social sciences; since capitalism itself is a dynamic and changing system, it is likely to stimulate new research and theory continuously.

Bibliography

Braverman, Harry. *Labor and Monopoly Capital*. New York: Monthly Review Press, 1974. Marxist analysis of the de-skilling of workers in capitalist firms. An influential and controversial contribution to the sociology of work, organizations, and technology.

Eitzen, D. Stanley, and Maxine Baca Zinn. *Social Problems*. 8th ed. Boston: Allyn & Bacon, 2000. A textbook that uses capitalism as an explanatory concept and presents a clear introductory overview. Excellent, balanced bibliographies.

Giddens, Anthony. *Capitalism and Modern Social Theory*. Cambridge, England: Cambridge University Press, 1971. A leading non-Marxist sociologist discusses the importance of the concept "capitalism" to the foundation of modern sociology. A clearly written guide to the work of Marx, Durkheim, and Weber; scholarly but not narrowly technical.

Heilbroner, Robert. *The Making of Economic Society*. 8th ed. Englewood Cliffs, N.J.: Prentice-Hall, 1989. Clear, comprehensible textbook that introduces economic concepts and issues; treatment of the material is historical and sociological. Includes helpful chapter glossaries and study questions. A good beginning for understanding market economies.

Hobsbawm, Eric. *The Age of Revolution, 1789-1848*. London: Weidenfeld & Nicolson, 1962.

_____. *The Age of Capital, 1848-1875*. London: Weidenfeld & Nicolson, 1975.

_____. *The Age of Empire, 1875-1914*. London: Weidenfeld & Nicolson, 1987. Three-volume social history of the growth of capitalism, including excellent coverage of cultural and political changes. Illustrated.

Marx, Karl. *Selected Writings*. Edited by David McLellan. Oxford, England: Oxford University Press, 1977. Definitive one-volume collection. Part I of the *Communist*

Manifesto remains an excellent overview of the dynamics of capitalism from a Marxist perspective.

Polanyi, Karl. *The Great Transformation*. Boston: Beacon Press, 1957. Classic work of social history that analyzes the onset and impact of the market economy in England and Western Europe; difficult reading but influential in social thought.

Wilson, William J. *The Truly Disadvantaged: The Inner City, the Underclass, and Public Policy*. Chicago: University of Chicago Press, 1987. Pioneering study of poverty among African Americans. Wilson proposes full employment policies to reduce class and racial inequality in the United States.

Roberta T. Garner

Cross-References

Industrial and Postindustrial Economies; Marxism; Social Stratification: Functionalist Perspectives; Social Stratification: Marxist Perspectives.

CASTE SYSTEMS

Type of sociology: Social stratification
Field of study: Systems of social stratification

A caste system is a hierarchy of social categories in which movement from one category to another is highly restricted by custom and law. Caste systems represent a particularly rigid example of how social stratification can be based on the status that one obtains at birth.

Principal terms

APARTHEID: the type of segregation that developed in South Africa; separateness was the principle guiding contacts between whites, blacks, and "Coloureds"

BURAKUMIN: social group in Japan that is discriminated against because its ancestry can be traced to outcastes in feudal Japan

ENDOGAMY: marriage between members of the same social category

OUTCASTE: lowest social category in a caste system

POLLUTION: Indian ideology that the higher castes can be polluted if coming into contact with the outcaste

REINCARNATION: Hindu religious belief that human souls are reborn after death

SEGREGATION: a principle of separation that guides contact between the higher castes and lower castes in a caste system

UNTOUCHABILITY: Indian concept according to which the lower caste and outcaste are regarded as impure and untouchable; contacts with them lead to pollution and should be avoided

Overview

The word "caste" has a Portuguese origin. In Portuguese, *casta* means breed, race, or kind. The present meaning of caste, according to John Henry Hutton, did not begin until the sixteenth century.

Modern definitions of caste contain many layers of meanings. Herbert Hope Risley, a scholar of Indian tribes and castes, defines it as

> a collection of families or groups of families bearing a common name; claiming a common descent from a mythical ancestor, human or divine; professing to follow the same hereditary calling; and regarded by those who are competent to give an opinion as forming a single homogeneous community.

Sociologist W. Lloyd Warner adds other aspects to this definition. Caste exists "where marriage between two or more groups is not sanctioned and where there is no opportunity for members of the lower groups to rise into the upper groups or of members of the upper to fall into the lower ones."

In a caste system, the castes are interdependent social phenomena. A caste system, first of all, is entirely based on ascribed status—the status that one obtains at birth. Just as one is born a male or a female, one is born into a certain caste (or into the outcaste) in a caste society. Rigid ranking exists among the different castes.

Discussion of the Indian caste system presents the problem of whether to consider it a historical or ongoing phenomenon. When India drafted its democratic constitution in 1948, discrimination against the lower castes was made illegal. Moreover, a type of affirmative action program reserved a significant number of government jobs for people from the lower castes. In that sense, the system is historical and may be discussed as such. Regardless of official policy, however, the system is deeply ingrained and still permeates Indian life and culture. Each person knows the caste into which he or she is born, and caste still limits social advancement and affects job opportunities and marriage choices.

There are four main castes in the Indian caste system. The highest caste is that of Brahmans, followed by the Kshatriyas, Vaishyas, and Shudras. Beyond these four castes are the lowest of the low—the outcastes. In this system, once a person was born into a certain caste (or the outcaste), he or she would remain in that caste (or the outcaste) for life.

Caste identification can be based on perceived physical differences, most often on skin color, but that is not always the case. In India, physical differences do not play an important part in distinguishing among castes. Social descent forms the most important and most prominent criterion for distinction. The difference between castes is largely a difference of social status.

Segregation was the rule that governed contact between a higher caste and a lower caste or outcaste. The Shudras and outcaste people in Indian society, for example, were often considered "untouchable." Traditionally, a member of a higher caste could be polluted by the slightest physical contact with a member of the Shudras or outcaste. In some extreme cases, a mere glance from an untouchable at a cooking pot could defile the food and make it uneatable. In certain regions, even the shadows cast by untouchables represented a potential danger to others; untouchables were therefore not allowed to walk in the villages during early morning or late afternoon.

Two important features of the Indian caste system helped sustain the ranking system. The first feature was the association of the castes with occupations. The Brahmans were either priests or scholars; the Kshatriyas, nobles or warriors; and the Vaishyas, merchants or skilled artisans. The lowest caste, the Shudras, were common laborers. The second feature was the enforcement of endogamy. In a caste society, a person is not allowed to marry outside his or her caste. A Brahman had to marry another Brahman, a Shudra another Shudra. The purity of the hereditary line was thus maintained, and the possibility of moving up in social status by way of marriage or occupation was ruled out.

A caste system must be supported by social institutions. Segregation between the higher castes and the lower castes, enforcement of endogamy, and association of occupation with caste cannot be achieved without the backing of social institutions. A caste system is also perpetuated by wide acceptance on the people's part. In India, the Hindu religion provided a necessary justification for enforcement of caste duties and obligations.

The Hindu religion maintains a belief in reincarnation; according to Hinduism, the soul will be reborn after death. Traditionally, if a person had sinned seriously in a previous life, he or she would be reborn as an untouchable. This belief in reincarnation carries two implications. On the one hand, it suggests that the caste into which a person is born is a reflection of the deeds he or she has done in a previous life. On the other hand, a person is given the hope that he or she can move up in the caste system at rebirth. Whether one will move upward or downward in the caste system at rebirth depends on how well one respects one's caste duties and obligations.

Caste systems are similar to class systems in that both are systems of stratification. Just as the class system is characterized by unequal access to resources in the society, the caste system is characterized by unequal access to prestige, privilege, and higher social status. The basic difference between the class and caste systems lies in the fact that the former is based at least partly on achieved status, whereas the latter is based solely on ascribed status. In this sense, a class system is an open system, while a caste system is a closed one.

Applications

The caste system is not limited to India, and it is not a phenomenon only of ancient times. In the postindustrial society of Japan, for example, the influence of the caste system can still be observed.

From the early seventeenth century to the late nineteenth century, during what is called the Tokugawa period in Japan, Japanese rulers established a very rigid system of closed caste ranks. At the top of the caste structure were warriors, the samurai (the military elite), and the higher aristocracy. This top caste was followed by peasants and artisans, with merchants at the bottom. The outcastes in Japan's caste system were called "*eta*," meaning "abundant filth."

The *eta* faced discrimination in every aspect of their lives. Laws were passed to stipulate their inferior status, and they were restricted to occupations such as butchers, executioners, and grave tenders, commonly regarded to be the dirtiest, most defiling, and least desirable tasks. Although their legal status as outcastes was eliminated in 1871, the stigma of having been *eta* continues for their descendants.

Today it is estimated that there are about one to three million Japanese having *eta* lineage. Commonly referred to as "*burakumin*," they have met extensive discrimination in modern Japanese society. *Burakumin* are physically indistinguishable from other Japanese, so one must look very hard to find that a person has this background; however, people do look very hard. It is common practice to undertake exhaustive investigations to check the background of a person for *burakumin* ancestors before agreeing to marriage or even offering jobs. Sociologist Mikiso Hane points out that this is a primary reason that the rate of intramarriage for *burakumin* is still as high as 90 percent. According to the Japanese sociologist Hiroshi Wagatsuma, the *burakumin* continue to be viewed by most Japanese as "mentally inferior, incapable of high moral behavior, aggressive, impulsive, and lacking any notion of sanitation or manners." They are often the "last hired and first fired."

Apartheid, the rigid system of racial segregation that existed in South Africa between the late 1940's and the mid-1990's, provides another modern example of a caste system. This system did not originate until the National Party of South Africa won a political victory in the 1948 elections. Apartheid (which literally means "apartness") had four major castes: whites, Coloureds (the South African spelling), Indians, and Africans. "Coloureds" were people of mixed ancestry. "Indians" referred to the Asian population in South Africa. Since Coloureds and Indians, like Africans, were both people of color, this caste system could be seen as a dichotomy, with whites over nonwhites.

Sociologist Pierre L. Van den Berghe distinguishes between "microsegregation" and "macrosegregation" under apartheid. "Microsegregation" refers to the dozens of laws and mandates passed between the early 1950's and the mid-1980's to maintain ethnic separation. In accordance with this legislation, restaurants, hotels, means of transportation, restrooms, hospitals, theaters, parks, schools, and many other places in which ethnic contact might be possible were segregated. The separate public facilities were invariably unequal in quality and quantity. "Macrosegregation" refers to the intention and practice on the part of South African authorities to assign geographical areas to different ethnic groups. Africans were not allowed to leave the assigned areas unless permitted by the white authorities. This policy was by nature one of exclusion.

Mere segregation or exclusion, however, does not sufficiently assure white supremacy. Since Africans were needed as a workforce in South Africa, discrimination against them in the workplace was also deemed necessary. Laws stipulated that blacks and whites should receive different wages, and they guaranteed that whites would get the higher-ranking jobs. In fact, no blacks could be promoted to a position higher than a white in the same occupational area.

Some social scientists argue that a variety of caste system exists in the United States; those who say this are generally referring to black and white relations. African Americans today still suffer from racism and racial discrimination. Segregation is characteristic of the residential patterns of African Americans and white people. Interracial marriages between African Americans and whites are rare occurrences, and African Americans as a whole are still a subordinate social group. Based on these facts, social anthropologist Gerald D. Berreman suggests that the American class system is complicated by caste features in the form of racial differentiation, segregation, endogamy, and hierarchy and that therefore the United States should be viewed as both a class and a caste society. This view is supported by sociologists W. Lloyd Warner, Charles Vert Willie, and many others. While acknowledging the emergence of a class structure among African Americans, they point out that a "caste line" exists between whites and African Americans in the United States. As Warner has put it: "Although [a person] is at the top of the Negro class hierarchy, he is constantly butting his head against the caste line."

Context

Caste systems, especially that of India, have been the object of considerable study by anthropologists and sociologists. The earliest study of the caste system, however, was done by some European "Orientalist" scholars. They brought to the attention of the Western intellectual world the key features of the caste system: the hierarchical ordering of castes, the importance of pollution and untouchability, the practice of endogamy, and the occupational feature of castes. The early Orientalists believed that the religious power enjoyed by the Brahmans was also a political power, and they explained the origins of the caste system as a process of evolution of occupations. It was not until 1908 that the French sociologist Celestin Bougle distinguished the two kinds of power. Bougle also noted that although caste occupations are important, the hierarchy of castes is not so much a hierarchy of skills as a hierarchy of pollution.

Western views of caste systems present differing perspectives. On the one hand, the inequities and injustices of caste systems are emphasized. In his *Population of India and Pakistan* (1951), the American sociologist Kingsley Davis refers to the caste system as "the most thoroughgoing attempt known in human history to introduce absolute inequality as the guiding principle in social relations." Berreman also speaks out against the "life sentence" that birth hands out to the member of a caste. On the other hand, the caste system is seen as performing social functions. Hutton suggests that the caste system is particularly suited to continuing culture patterns and helping to integrate different social groups while making it possible for them to retain their own distinctive character and separate individual life. Similarly, the French social anthropologist Louis Dumont contends that although all castes are not equally rewarded, all are integrated into the system. According to Hindu ideals, all are cared for; the system exists for the benefit of all.

As it is a product of the preindustrial period, scholars disagree as to whether the caste system is an obstacle to modernization. In *Hinduismus und Buddhismus* (1921; *The Religion of India: The Sociology of Hinduism and Buddhism*, 1958), the influential German sociologist Max Weber argued that the caste system, supported by Hindu beliefs in rebirth and rewards for virtuous or sinful behavior, serves as an obstacle to modern capitalism and industry. His opinion was shared by the Swedish economist Gunnar Myrdal. In contrast, the anthropologist Milton Singer and the historical sociologist Barrington Moore, Jr., have argued that the caste system is flexible and adaptive.

So far, available evidence seems to point to the breaking down of the traditional caste system, marked by specialized occupation, with modernization. It is difficult, however, to predict when the caste system will thoroughly disappear, if indeed it will. In the final analysis, it is unlikely that a social system that has had a history of more than a thousand years could be totally expunged within a few decades. The dying out of a caste system, whether in India, Japan, South Africa, or (as some social scientists would argue) the United States, is likely to be a slow and gradual process.

Bibliography

Berreman, Gerald D. *Caste and Other Inequities*. Meerut, India: Folklore Institute, 1979.
    Contains a series of essays that cover twenty years of research and thinking by Berreman about social inequality and social justice both in India and cross-culturally. Although many are reprints from articles first appearing in sociology and anthropology journals, they are readable for college students.
Cox, Oliver Cromwell. *Caste, Class, and Race: A Study in Social Dynamics*. New York:

Monthly Review Press, 1959. Discusses a large variety of subjects relating to caste, class, and race; each discussion is given a subheading that can be found in the table of contents.

Davis, Allison, Burleigh B. Gardner, and Mary R. Gardner. *Deep South: A Social Anthropological Study of Caste and Class*. Chicago: University of Chicago Press, 1941. Written before the Civil Rights movement of the 1950's and 1960's, this book gives a thorough account of the life of blacks and whites as well as a view of the class and caste structures in a community in the American "deep South."

De Vos, George, and Hiroshi Wagatsuma. *Japan's Invisible Race: Caste in Culture and Personality*. Berkeley: University of California Press, 1966. One of the few books written in English about the outcaste in Japan. The authors have taken historical, psychological, and comparative perspectives in their study of the burakumin. Includes pictures of Japan's outcastes and their living conditions.

Dumont, Louis. *Homo Hierarchicus: The Caste System and Its Implications*. Translated by Mark Sainsbury, Louis Dumont, and Basia Gulati. Rev. English ed. Chicago: University of Chicago Press, 1980. Important work on the caste system, and the translation is fairly readable for the general public.

Hutton, John Henry. *Caste in India: Its Nature, Function, and Origins*. 4th ed. London: Oxford University Press, 1963. Examines the caste system at various places in India—its structures, its sanctions, its functions, and the theories and factors in the emergence of caste. Recommended for students with a special interest in the caste system in India.

Marger, Martin N. "South Africa." In *Race and Ethnic Relations: American and Global Perspectives*. 5th ed. Belmont, Calif.: Wadsworth, 2000. In this chapter, Marger discusses the development of ethnic inequality, the emergence of apartheid, and the forces of stability and change in South Africa. Highly readable and well documented.

Smaje, Chris. *Natural Hierarchies: The Historical Sociology of Race and Caste*. Malden, Mass.: Blackwell Publishers, 2000.

Willie, Charles Vert. *The Caste and Class Controversy*. 2d ed. Dix Hills, N.Y.: General Hall, 1989. Addresses one of the most controversial issues of the late 1970's: Is the significance of race increasing or decreasing? The collection of essays included in the book will help students understand why some social scientists claim that a caste system exists in the United States.

Shengming Tang

Cross-References

Class Consciousness and Class Conflict; Conflict Theory; Cultural and Structural Assimilation; Ethnicity and Ethnic Groups; Prejudice and Discrimination: Merton's Paradigm; Racial and Ethnic Stratification; Social Stratification: Analysis and Overview.

CAUSAL RELATIONSHIPS

Type of sociology: Sociological research
Fields of study: Basic research concepts; Data collection and analysis

Determination of cause and effect relationships requires controlled experimentation. Since this is rarely possible when studying large-scale human interactions, the findings of most sociological studies are subject to more than one interpretation.

Principal terms

ALPHA ERROR: error that occurs when a researcher seems to have found a causal relationship but has actually observed a statistical fluke or artifact (also called a type 1 error)

BETA ERROR: error that occurs when a true causal relationship is not identified, either because of a statistical fluke or because it is masked (also called a type 2 error)

CONFOUND: uncontrolled variable in research which causes either an alpha error (artifact) or a beta error (masking effect), leading to misinterpretation of the study results

CORRELATIONAL RESEARCH: observational studies which seek statistical patterns among variables but which cannot determine whether those patterns are attributable to cause and effect relationships

DEPENDENT VARIABLE: variable which is observed in an experiment because it is thought to be dependent upon (an effect of) changes in another variable

ECOLOGICAL FALLACY: error in logic that occurs when a researcher tries to apply a conclusion drawn from one level of analysis (such as social systems) to another level (such as individuals)

EXPERIMENTAL RESEARCH: studies which manipulate an independent variable, observe its effects on a dependent variable, and control confounds, thus allowing the discovery of cause and effect relationships

INDEPENDENT VARIABLE: variable which is manipulated in an experiment because it is thought to cause change in another (dependent) variable

PANEL CORRELATION: special type of long-term correlational study which produces the only type of correlation that can be used to sort out cause and effect relationships

PATH ANALYSIS: complex mathematical model of the possible cause and effect relationships between multiple interacting variables

Overview

Although philosophers continue to debate the meanings of "cause" and "effect," most people, including sociologists, have fairly straightforward conceptions of these terms. Causes are events or phenomena that occur at a certain point in time (or develop over a certain period of time) and that have a direct consequence or result; that is, they lead to a change in something else. That consequence or result is called the "effect." Causal events, therefore, always precede their effects, so to be able to demonstrate that one phenomenon causes another, it must be shown that the event thought to be the cause preceded the event thought to be the effect.

Causal relationships are not necessarily one-to-one. Some causes can have many effects; for example, smoking can lead to lung disease, throat cancer, and heart disease. Likewise, some effects can result from more than one cause: Lung disease can be an effect of smoking, exposure to radon, or genetic inheritance. Causal relationships can also occur in chains, like a series of dominoes, each of which, in the act of falling, leads to the fall of its neighbor. When such a cascade occurs, the immediately preceding causal event is called the "proximate cause," and the original causal event is called the "ultimate cause."

Because causal relationships can be so complicated, it is difficult to draw conclusions about causality only by looking at the temporal or statistical relationship between two events; simply knowing that one event commonly precedes another is not enough to know whether the first event actually causes the second. To be sure that an event causes another event, all other possible causes must be ruled out; in order to do this, it is necessary to run a controlled experiment.

In a controlled experiment, the experimenter allows only one event or process to change at a time. This change is the "independent variable"; it is what the experimenter suspects might be a cause of something else. The experimenter looks for an effect by observing the "dependent variable"—whatever the researcher thinks will be changed as a result of the change in the independent variable. Presumably, if the dependent variable changes, then it must have changed because of the change in the independent variable; that is, the independent variable must have caused the change in the dependent variable.

This logic will work, however, only if the experimenter can be sure that nothing else was changing at the same time as the independent variable; if there was something else changing at the same time, then it might have been the cause of the change in the dependent variable. Such uncontrolled events are called "confounds," and whenever there is a confound in a research study there will be more than one possible interpretation of that study's results. If the dependent variable changed because of the confound rather than because of the independent variable, scientists say that the change in the dependent variable was "spurious." If the experimenter does not notice the confound and mistakenly believes that the independent variable caused the change in the dependent variable, the experimenter has made an "alpha error" or "type 1 error." On the other hand, if the independent variable really did have an effect on the dependent variable, but the confound had the opposite effect, so that there was no overall change in the dependent variable, scientists say that a "masking effect" has occurred. In this situation, if the experimenter does not notice the confound and mistakenly believes that the independent variable had no effect on the dependent variable, he or she has made a "beta error" or "type 2 error."

There are basically two ways to control possible confounds. First, the experimenter can ensure that a possible confound literally does not vary through the course of the experiment; in an educational setting, say, the researcher would want to ensure that the subjects (students) do not get a new teacher halfway through the study. Many confounds cannot be truly controlled, however; for example, all students will get older as a study goes on. To be able to differentiate the effects of the independent variable from the effects of aging, the experimenter must have a "control group" of students who go through the experiment in exactly the same way as the experimental group, except that the independent variable is not changed for them. The experimental group will experience the effects of the independent variable and of aging, while the control group will experience only the effects of aging. The two groups can then be compared to isolate the effect of the independent variable. Subjects must be assigned to the control group and to the experimental group at random; otherwise, the groups might be different to start with, and these existing differences would be a confound.

In sociological research, for both practical and ethical reasons, it is often impossible to control confounding variables or to randomize subjects to experimental and control groups. Most sociological data come not from experiments but from large-scale correlational studies—that is, surveys and other kinds of observational research in which statistical patterns are observed but no variables have been manipulated or controlled. Thus, the results of most sociological studies have more than one possible cause-effect interpretation. The goal of a good researcher, therefore, is to design a study which minimizes the number of possible confounds and thus minimizes the number of possible interpretations of the results.

Applications

One important area of sociological (and psychological) research is the search for causes of violence. Since violent behavior has been increasing in the United States for several decades, it is likely that some other change that also began a few decades ago is causing this increase. One possible candidate is the spread of television viewing and the subsequent exposure of children to televised violence.

To test whether exposure to televised violence causes violent behavior, it is possible to design an experiment in which some children see a violent television show and other children see a nonviolent show; subsequent behavior of the children could then be compared between groups. Any such experiment, however, could only assess the effect of short-term television exposure on immediate behavior, when what researchers really want to know is whether long-term television exposure has any long-term effects.

Since it is neither practical nor ethical to assign children randomly to high versus low levels of television violence over a long period, one could do a correlational study looking for statistical relationships between television viewing and patterns of violence. (Such studies have found that children who watch a considerable amount of television are more violent than children who watch little television.) There are, however, two problems with such studies. One is that, since both behaviors are observed at the same time, it is not possible to show that one preceded the other; thus, it is impossible to know whether one caused the other. The second problem is that since children are not randomly assigned to be frequent viewers versus infrequent viewers, there may be uncontrolled factors that cause some children to watch much television and be violent and others to avoid television and be nonviolent. For example, children with violent parents may become violent themselves and may also watch much television because they do not get quality parenting, whereas children with nonviolent parents may not become violent and may also watch less television because their parents provide more alternative activities. Simple correlational studies always have confounds, making it impossible to know which variables are causes and which are effects.

One kind of correlational study, however, a "panel correlation," allows researchers to make educated guesses about causal relationships. In a panel correlation, the researcher measures both the presumed causal variable (in this case, amount of television viewing) and the presumed effect (in this case, violent behavior), twice—once at an early age (say, six) and once at a later age (say, thirteen). Then it can be discovered whether television viewing at age six is related to violent behavior at age thirteen and whether violent behavior at age six is related to television viewing at age thirteen. Since causes must precede effects, if the first relationship is much stronger than the second relationship, the researcher can safely guess that the television viewing was the cause of the violent behavior, rather than vice versa. (This is indeed what such studies have found.) A panel correlation cannot rule out other possible causal interpretations, since it is not a controlled experiment, but it is better than a simple correlation of two variables measured only once at the same time.

Another area in which it is difficult to sort out causal relationships is the study of social stratification. An example is trying to determine the causes of the patterns of differential wages for men versus women and for whites versus minorities. Do women make less money than men do because they have different interests and seek different jobs (which happen to be lower-paying), or are women discriminated against when they apply for higher-paying jobs? Alternatively, could it be that once women break into a field that has been traditionally male-dominated, wages in that field start to drop? Since it is impossible to do controlled experiments to sort out the cause and effect relationships in this area, how can researchers deduce causal interpretations from analysis of statistical (correlational) patterns?

There are ways to make educated guesses about cause and effect relationships, even when there are a multitude of variables involved in a complex interaction. In such "multivariate" situations, a technique called "path analysis" can be used to try to diagram visually and mathematically the cause and effect relationships interconnecting a set of related phenomena. To begin, the researcher must have a good initial guess (model) about which variables come first, which come later, which are causes, and which are effects. The model is fed into a computer, along with actual statistical data on all the relevant variables; the result is a set of numbers describing the relative strength of each of the "paths" (causal relationships) between each pair of variables in the set. The researcher can run as many path analyses as desired, each time giving the computer the same data but a different model. When all the possible models have been run, the researcher can compare the results to find which model had the best fit to the data. Models with a good fit are more likely to have correctly specified the true cause and effect relationships than models with a poor fit. Although path analyses are better than simple correlations, they are not controlled experiments, so researchers still cannot be sure that they have made the correct interpretation. It is always possible that the researcher missed some important variables that were never included in the model-testing process.

Context

As computer modeling techniques become more complex and more advanced, it is likely that the findings of sociologists will be given more weight and will be increasingly incorporated into the political decision-making process. Still, the application of sociological research will always be controversial because the inability to be certain about cause and effect relationships means that there will always be the potential for mistakes in the interpretation of research. Making mistakes in socially sensitive areas can have severe consequences. If research suggests that exposure to televised violence, for example, is a cause of later violence in viewers, is it therefore a good idea for government to regulate television viewing or television content? Is it acceptable for government to restrict individual choices in order to effect social change? One problem is that even if television viewing increases violence in general, that does not mean that every person who watches considerable television will become violent. Moreover, it could be that the relationship really is not causal after all. No matter how much sociologists can refine their methods to sort out cause and effect relationships, how their conclusions are applied to public policy will continue to require ethical, as well as scientific, discussion.

Sociologists must also be able to integrate their findings and interpretations with those of scientists in related fields such as management, psychology, history, political science, and anthropology. It is tempting to draw causal conclusions at one level (for example, individuals or families) based on research findings at another level (communities or countries), but such conclusions are often in error. Just because there is a statistical relationship, say, between parenting practices and rates of violent behavior in families across different societies, that does not mean that the same relationship would necessarily exist across families in a single society. This is a common error of logic (called the "ecological fallacy"), and the only way to prevent it is to ensure ongoing cross-disciplinary discussion.

Finally, some people criticize sociology (and the other social sciences) as being "soft" science (as opposed to the "hard" science of physics, chemistry, and biology). Yet even though sociologists are less able than other scientists to do controlled experiments on their subject matter, there are many methods available to sociologists that are not available to others. Chemists, after all, cannot interview the subjects of their study. Sociologists utilize a variety of methods and then draw conclusions from the convergence of evidence derived from these methods. In this way, sociology is like any other science: It uses observation, statistics, and logic to arrive at ever better educated guesses about causal relationships in the world.

Bibliography

Cole, Stephen. *The Sociological Method.* 3d ed. Boston: Houghton Mifflin, 1980. Covers the kinds of questions sociologists ask, how they answer them, and how they use their results; includes a very simple introduction to complex (multivariate) causal relationships. Full of fun, interesting examples and very basic statistics, which can easily be skipped if so desired.

Cook, Thomas D., and Donald T. Campbell. *Quasi-Experimentation: Design and Analysis*

Issues for Field Settings. Chicago: Rand McNally, 1979. Classic text for graduate students in the social sciences. Chapter 1, however, "Causal Inference and the Language of Experimentation," provides an excellent background on various philosophical approaches to the analysis of cause-and-effect relationships, including summaries of the positions of John Stuart Mill and Karl Popper.

Homans, George C. *The Nature of Social Science*. New York: Harcourt, Brace & World, 1967. Written at about the same time as the Platt article mentioned below, this book has the same basic message but was written for lay readers.

Huck, Schuyler W., and Howard M. Sandler. *Rival Hypotheses: Alternative Interpretations of Data Based Conclusions*. New York: Harper & Row, 1979. Brief summaries of 100 flawed research studies. It is up to the reader to figure out the logical flaw in each. Answers are provided at the end, along with an appendix summarizing the most common types of logical errors in interpretation of cause and effect.

Platt, John R. "Strong Inference." *Science* 146 (October 16, 1964): 347-353. This classic article discusses "scientific falsification," the process whereby different causal hypotheses are ruled out one by one, leaving the strongest, presumably best hypothesis, as the sole survivor of rigorous attempts at disproof. Platt believes that the social sciences will remain unacceptably "soft" until this approach is used more regularly.

Smelser, Neil J. *Essays in Sociological Explanation*. Englewood Cliffs, N.J.: Prentice-Hall, 1968. The first essay in this book, "Sociology and the Other Social Sciences" (42 pages), does a wonderful job of describing the kinds of variables and relationships that sociologists study and the methods they use to do so. Compares sociology with economics, political science, anthropology, history, and psychology.

Trapper, Richard. *The Interpretation of Data: An Introduction to Statistics for the Behavioral Sciences*. Pacific Grove, Calif.: Brooks/Cole, 1998.

Linda Mealey

Cross-References

Hypotheses and Hypothesis Testing; Quantitative Research; Surveys; Validity and Reliability in Measurement.

CHURCHES, DENOMINATIONS, AND SECTS

Type of sociology: Major social institutions
Field of study: Religion

Churches, denominations, and sects are types of religious organizations. The distinction between them makes it possible to analyze various church bodies and to comprehend their varying relationships to society and to one another.

Principal terms

CHURCH: religious body, usually related to the state, occupying a position of privilege and generally devoid of tension with the society in which it exists

DENOMINATION: religious body generally at peace with its environment that serves the middle and upper strata of society

ECCLESIA: another name for a church that is closely tied to the state

ESTABLISHED SECT: sect that has survived for several generations without changing into a denomination

SECT: religious body at tension with its environment, rarely cooperating with other religious groups, and serving mostly the blue-collar working class

Overview

Sociologists consider religion a major social institution; nearly all societies have some form of religion, and it has been studied by sociologists since the nineteenth century. Religious organizations have been categorized according to a number of factors, including their size, their relationship to the state, and the tension that exists between the group and the larger society. The categories most often used are churches, denominations, sects, and cults. Churches are the largest of the groups, and they are frequently tied to the state in some way. Denominations are generally considered to be less centrally placed in society than churches are; they are also sometimes considered to be smaller in size. Sects and cults are smaller and less inclusive, and they usually exist in a state of tension (be it great or small) with the larger society.

The essential defining characteristics of a church are that it is relatively large and it exists in an influential and central position in society. Some countries have official state churches (Norway and Sweden have state-established churches), others have churches closely allied with the state (as in Iceland or Spain), and others have one church that, although not officially sanctioned, is strongly dominant or occupies a privileged position (as in England). Rarely is a church in a state of tension with the secular world. A church is an umbrella-like organization that seeks to serve the religious needs of all people within its geographical territory. Members are often "born into" the church in that their parents are members;

children are socialized into the church at a young age and join when they are old enough. Churches have a hierarchy of authority, but the way this is organized varies from church to church. Serving in the clergy is usually a full-time occupation and involves specialized education and formal religious training.

The United States, founded by people with a belief in religious freedom and the separation of church and state, does not have a state or national church. Nevertheless, Christianity is the overwhelmingly dominant religion in the country. In one common typology, Christianity in the United States is divided into two major churches, Roman Catholic and Protestant, with Protestants being divided into denominations such as Presbyterian, Methodist, Lutheran, and Baptist.

Denominations are generally considered to be religious organizations that are not affiliated with the state and that are relatively equal in their place in a society. The United States has been called a "denominational society" in that a large number of religious organizations, from huge ones to tiny ones, are able to coexist. In this sense of "denomination," both Roman Catholicism and Judaism could be considered denominations in the United States, but in practice, the term usually refers to Protestant religious groups. (Judaism, in fact, has its own divisions—Conservative, Orthodox, Reform, and Reconstructionist—that are in some ways akin to denominations but are not usually considered as such.) Some sociologists have simply made membership in the National Council of Churches a criterion for being considered a denomination. This distinction seems objective and has much to recommend it; however, others point out that some non-National Council of Churches groups (such as the Lutheran church—Missouri Synod) may exhibit more of the characteristics of a denomination than of a sect.

Many denominations began their activities as sects; these include the United Methodists and the American (northern) Baptists. Others did not have a sectlike origin but, rather, are transplanted European state churches. Examples include the Episcopal and Lutheran churches. A denomination has made its peace with society. It cooperates with other denominations, often through an overarching organization like the National Council of Churches. Worship services in denominational congregations are usually formal and are not spontaneous. Clergy typically have had four years of undergraduate college education and three or four years of theological school. Many eventually do additional graduate work and earn advanced degrees. The members come from the middle, upper-middle, and upper classes.

The line that divides churches and denominations from sects is somewhat more clearly distinguishable. Sects are smaller than churches and are not as integrated into society at large as either churches or denominations are. Sects often begin when a group breaks away from a larger, established religious organization. The founders frequently are attempting to return to the principles of the church's original founders, believing that the church as it exists has strayed from those principles or beliefs. As a sect progresses, its early history often becomes mythologized, a process that can make it more difficult to maintain adherence to the earlier principles. In their worship services, sects are usually more informal than churches, and the clergy of a sect often serve only part time and have less formal education and training than the clergy of a church or denomination. A sect expresses tension with the dominant society by warning its members against the "sins of the world," which are usually reflections of the lifestyle of the dominant society and may include such activities as drinking alcohol, wearing makeup, and dancing. Although members usually have low-paying jobs, a large number of them tithe (pay an automatic percentage of their incomes to the sect) to provide the group with sufficient funds. For many, the sect is the locus of social as well as religious life. Attending two or three services a week is common. Some sects remain stable in size, whereas others grow and eventually evolve into denominations or churches themselves. Examples of sects in the United States include the Amish, the Mennonites, and such holiness and Pentecostal groups as the Church of God and Church of God of Triumph.

An established sect is one that has existed for some generations without becoming a denomination even though it has gained acceptance in the community. Established sects include the Assemblies of God, Jehovah's Witnesses, and the several Churches of Christ. Some scholars include the Amish, Latter-day Saints (Mormons), and Jewish Hasidim in this category.

Applications

A look at the fastest-growing church body in the United States is instructive in understanding the nature of sects and established sects. The Assemblies of God was founded in 1914 at Hot Springs, Arkansas. In the beginning, it attempted to be nondoctrinal, allowing freedom of belief. When, however, it appeared that there were great doctrinal differences, especially that one large group was unitarian rather than trinitarian in its beliefs about God, about one-fourth of the original membership seceded. The remaining group has grown to more than two million members in ten thousand churches with twenty-two thousand ministers in the United States. Worldwide membership stands at fifteen million.

The Assemblies of God emphasizes emotion and charismatic healing. It distrusts science and stresses personal experience. These are considered more important than theological teaching. Typically the Assemblies of God rejects denominations as proclaimers of the rational, evangelical God of the intellect. It emphasizes a God one can feel, respond to, and love—one who cares about people's present and their future. Seventy-nine percent of the members are in church every Sunday, and another 11 percent miss only once a month. Church governance is local and is said to rely on divine guidance.

An example of a denomination is the Presbyterian church (USA), a transplanted national church. Presbyterianism traces its roots to French-born John Calvin, who converted to Protestantism in 1533 or 1534. He became the spiritual and political leader in Geneva, Switzerland, where he was pastor of St. Peter's Church. It was a Scot, however, John Knox, who eventually returned to his native land from Europe to become the father of the Scots' reformation.

The largest group of Presbyterians to come to the United States were Scotch-Irish immigrants from Northern Ireland, who settled along the mid-Atlantic. In the United States, this ecclesia became a denomination marked by typical denominational characteristics. It serves the middle, upper-middle, and upper strata of society, conducts formal services, insists upon a highly educated clergy, cooperates with other denominations and sects, and generally expresses little tension with its environment, although it has taken a moral and social stance in a number of matters. Doctrinally, it accepts the Bible as written by persons who were inspired by God. Emphasis is on the teachings shared with most Christians. Thus Presbyterianism clearly serves as a model for the religious organizations called denominations.

There are no state religions in North America. Therefore it is instructive to consider a small but typical state church, the Evangelical-Lutheran National Church of Iceland. Norwegians settled Iceland late in the ninth century; at the instigation of the Norwegian king, the Icelandic parliament adopted Christianity in the year 1000. Many farmers owned the churches built on their land and paid the salaries of the priests. At the time of the Protestant reformation in the sixteenth century, Iceland became Lutheran by royal fiat of the king of Denmark (of which kingdom Iceland had become a part). The church exchanged its farms for salaries of priests in perpetuity, allowing it to claim that it is a national, rather than a state, church. The titular head of the church, formerly the king of Denmark, has been, since independence, the president of Iceland; the functional head is the bishop, who is elected chiefly by the clergy.

As is typical of national churches, clergy are highly educated. Salaries of priests are paid by the state, and their homes are furnished either by the state (in small towns and in the countryside) or by the congregations (in the cities). Services are conducted with great dignity, observing ancient liturgical niceties, paraments, vestments, and ceremonies. Sermons are in the form of literary essays. The liturgy is chanted by priests whose performance shows their professional training. Hymns and liturgical responses are sung by choirs with a high level of musical ability. Ninety-four percent of the population belongs to the national church, and another 3 percent belongs to a Lutheran Free Church, whose only difference from the national church is that congregations pay their pastors' salaries and are free to dismiss them.

Other religions are permitted in Iceland, and there are a few Roman Catholic, Seventh-day Adventist, and Salvation Army congregations as well as a Pentecostal sect called Filadelfia. The national church practices no exclusivity toward the dissenters: They are included by the office of the bishop in such things as the Sunday morning national radio broadcast. The state-church bishop personally ordains priests who are called by Lutheran Free Churches and is frequently called upon to settle differences or arbitrate in their congregational matters. Clergy move freely between the national church and the Lutheran Free Church. Thus inclusivity is a distinct mark of this national church, which seeks to be an umbrella serving all in its territory. Yet it remains confessionally Lutheran in teaching and practice. Despite its attempts to serve all in its territory, the leadership seems to gravitate to members of the upper classes (this in a country which claims to have no social classes). There is clearly no tension between the church and the state, and a number of priests have served as members of the parliament, one also becoming his country's representative to the United Nations. Although the bishop is not a cabinet officer of the Icelandic government, he is consulted regularly on religious, moral, and other questions. Citizens of Iceland support the national church through their taxes; if they wish, however, they may divert their tax money to another recognized religious group or to the University of Iceland.

Sociologists have long spoken of the tendency of sects to turn into denominations despite the fact that they originally opposed them. In order to visualize how such movement takes place, one might imagine a continuum—a line with the number 1 at the far left and 7 at the far right. Along this continuum, sects would be placed at 1, established sects at 3, denominations at 5, and churches at 7. As sects move toward becoming denominations, their sociological characteristics change. For example, one could rank characteristics such as "tension with society" at 1, and "no tension with society" at 7. "Uneducated membership and clergy" might be placed at 1, and an educated membership at 7; a very informal service of worship could be placed at 1, and a formalized, liturgical service at 7. As a sect moves toward denominationalism, its characteristics gradually change to move closer to the higher numbers along the continuum.

Context

It was German theologian Ernst Troeltsch who, in 1912, first alerted the theological and sociological world to the great dichotomy between what he called churches and sects. His work was not translated into English until 1931, and was then entitled *The Social Teaching of the Christian Churches*. Subsequently, other scholars have enlarged his scheme to differentiate between sects and established sects and between denominations and churches. Notable among these are J. Milton Yinger, Howard Becker, Richard Niebuhr, and Colin Clark.

It was Yinger's contention that Troeltsch did not provide as many categories as were needed to describe the various religious bodies. His categories included the universal church, the ecclesia (which is a universal church that has become "settled in"), the class church or denomination, the established sect, the sect, and the cult. Richard Niebuhr used the relationship of religious bodies to their culture to differentiate among them. He identified groups marked by Christ against culture, Christ of culture, Christ above culture, and Christ and culture in paradox. Colin Clark analyzed sects and found seven types: pessimistic (or adventist) sects, perfectionist (or subjectivist) sects, charismatic (or Pentecostal) sects, communistic sects, legalistic (or objectivist) sects, egocentric (or new thought) sects, and esoteric (or mystical) sects.

The tension between sects and denominations in the United States is clearly seen in sociologists Roger Finke and Rodney Stark's 1992 book *The Churching of America, 1776-1990: Winners and Losers in Our Religious Economy*. They contend that mainline denominations in early New England, namely the Presbyterian and Congregational churches, crumbled badly in the face of (then sectarian) aggressive Methodist and Baptist activity in the period from 1776 to 1850. (Their chapter for that time period is called "The Upstart Sects Win America.") In their concluding chapter, "Why 'Mainline' Denominations Decline," they summarize their conclusions, noting that established religious bodies gradually become more worldly until their religious rewards are few; at that point, people begin to switch to other groups. Some join very high tension movements, while others move to "the newest and least secularized" denominations.

Bibliography

Finke, Roger, and Rodney Stark. *The Churching of America, 1776-1990: Winners and Losers in Our Religious Economy*. New Brunswick, N.J.: Rutgers University Press, 1992. Highly readable, well-documented approach to the history of religion in the United States by two noted sociologists of religion. It takes a market approach to religious bodies and also shows the many errors in early religious statistics.

McGuire, Meredith B. *Religion: The Social Context*. 4th ed. Belmont, Calif.: Wadsworth, 1997. In a chapter on the dynamics of religious collectivities, the author examines the transformation of sects and cults into other types.

Moberg, David O. *The Church as a Social Institution: The Sociology of American Religion*. 2d ed. Grand Rapids, Mich.: Baker Book House, 1984. Chapter 4 is an excellent, thorough discussion entitled "Church—Sect and Other Typologies." Especially valuable is the author's evaluation of the various typologies. Discusses Clark's seven types of sects. Although the volume has gone out of print, many university libraries have a copy.

Petursson, Petur. *Church and Social Change: A Study of the Secularization Process in Iceland 1830-1930*. Helsingborg, Sweden: Plus Ultra, 1983. Written by the son of the former bishop of Iceland is as valuable for a history of religion in that country from 860 to 1830 as it is for the century it purports to cover.

Poloma, Margaret M. *The Assemblies of God at the Crossroads: Charisma and Institutional Dilemmas*. Knoxville: University of Tennessee Press, 1989. Emphasizes the fact that the Assemblies of God's growth is related to its emphasis on emotion and charismatic healing. Since it has not made its "peace with the world," it remains a sect, although it is an established one.

Theissen, Gerd. *The Sociology of Early Palestinian Christianity*. Translated by John Bowden. Philadelphia: Fortress, 1978. Since many sects try to return to the earliest Christian practices, it is useful and instructive to see how a sociologist reconstructs those times.

Troeltsch, Ernst. *The Social Teaching of the Christian Churches*. Translated by Olive Wyon. Reprint. Louisville, Ky.: Westminster/John Knox Press, 1992. Landmark book, first published in German in 1912, examining differences among churches and sects; all subsequent work is in its debt.

Winter, J. Alan. *Continuities in the Sociology of Religion: Creed, Congregation, and Community*. New York: Harper & Row, 1977. Once-popular text especially useful for the fifth chapter, which traces the rise of sects and discusses clearly the Niebuhr-Pope hypothesis of sects turning into churches.

Donald R. Ortner

Cross-References

Religion; Religion: Functionalist Analyses; Religion: Marxist and Conflict Theory Views; Secularization in Western Society; Socialization: Religion.

CIVIL RELIGION AND POLITICS

Type of sociology: Major social institutions
Field of study: Religion

All societies develop ideological systems that bind them together, creating unity and social cohesion through a sense of national identity. The study of civil religion analyzes these belief systems in ways equivalent to other religions; this approach provides insight into the nature of American politics and religious life.

Principal terms

CIVIL RELIGION: religious system that concentrates on the nation or the society, serving to create social cohesion through building a national identity

LEGITIMATION: ideological and material process of supporting a specific worldview and the institutional powers that derive from it

NATIONAL IDENTITY: sense of who a nation is, involving symbolic and ideological notions of history, nature, and purpose, to be propagated and believed by the populace in order to support the society as a whole

RELIGION: system of symbols and institutions that embody values and worldviews, addressing ultimate questions of human existence and cosmic reality

RITUAL: an activity that expresses certain religious or ideological beliefs, living out a certain worldview through individual and corporate symbolic action

SOCIAL COHESION: forces that bind a society together, in ideological, social, and material aspects, to produce unity and harmony

Overview

Religion refers to complex patterns of beliefs, actions, and institutions that construct a sense of meaning for humans. As such, religion can take a wide variety of forms, all of which serve to provide meaning for individual people as well as for social groups. Religion's specific focus is on the questions of ultimate meaning, and thus classic religious questions include inquiries into the existence and nature of God as well as the purpose for human existence, the reasons for death and suffering, and the nature of good and evil. Some sociological theorists argue that all human groupings are religious, in the sense that all human groups deal with such basic issues of meaning, at least at a covert level of group assumptions.

At times, the political sphere forms a realm for these religious answers to such questions of ultimate human concern. In other words, the nation (or state or government) becomes part of the answer to the questions of meaning. Some political ideologies, for example, assert that service to the state is the reason for human existence or that the nation is the proper arena in which to conduct actions of goodness and morality. Such notions represent civil religions, in which there is a strong connection between the forms of political organization and the religious beliefs about ultimate reality.

From a functionalist perspective, civil religions serve to provide social cohesion. They offer a coherent system of beliefs about reality that bind together a political community into a group within common goals, orientations, beliefs, values, norms, and assumptions. As such, civil religions tend to legitimate the social order and its systems of power and advantage. As a belief system, the civil religion explains why the people in power should be in power and why obedience to the government is a moral issue akin to obedience to God. Civil religions function to construct a rationale for the existence of the state, and thus they address the common social problem of legitimation. By asking and answering such basic questions as "What is the identity and direction of America?" the civil religion assumes the existence of the nation and then proves the value of its purpose. It constructs identity and legitimates goals and values.

Civil religions, as other religions, are rarely monolithic. Different positions exist within the belief system. Martin Marty has made a distinction between "priestly" and "prophetic" versions of civil religion. The priestly form emphasizes the nation's greatness and rightness, celebrating the past history of successes and predicting the same for the future. The prophetic form, on the other hand, concentrates on the propagation of the ideal values of the community and calls the community to accountability for the injustices and inequalities still in its midst. These two types of civil religion are closely related, but they do operate distinctly from each other.

In the United States, a further distinction exists between "conservative" and "liberal" civil religions. The conservative form emphasizes loyalty to the nation as it is, connecting God's favor with the privilege systems currently in place. Conservative civil religion tends to be more static than its liberal counterpart. The liberal form of civil religion identifies an agenda of social change, involving issues such as the avoidance of nuclear war and the desire to allow all Americans to avoid poverty and violence. In many ways, these conservative and liberal distinctions parallel the priestly and prophetic forms, but there are important differences.

Civil religion thus not only provides a commonality of assumption that creates bondedness in lived experience but also provides a set of symbols and structures for the growth of difference and the expression of dissent. It serves as a rhetorical system of symbols in which individuals can experience commitment to the social organization or can distance themselves from its functioning through commitment to idealized social values. Both responses are experiences of the civil religion.

Applications

In the United States, the American civil religion has formed a coherent belief system of surprising power and endurance. Beginning with the belief that God has chosen the United States for a specific purpose, the civil religion explains why the nation should do what it does, why the history of the nation features the events that it does, and why the nation should progress in certain directions favored by those now in power. The belief system bases itself in the notion that the United States is a place of liberty, especially religious and economic freedoms. The mythology of American civil religion also emphasizes the idea that God's favor upon the American people manifests itself in the military and economic power of the nation as well as in the prestige and affluence of individual Americans. The civil religion supports the notion that there is a particularly American way of life that involves a high level of consumption that is both a national right and a display of individual worth.

Civil religions are like all other religions in the existence of myths, doctrines, rituals, ethics, and experiences as vital analytical categories. Again, the American experience serves as a good example, but other nations' civil religions develop in much the same sort of process. A civil religion bases itself in a myth, usually a story that describes the nation's founding period. In the American example, the myth involves the stories of the "Founding Fathers," such as George Washington and Thomas Jefferson. The myth continues to explain how later generations came into being, and so the religion traces the development of the present through other prominent figures, such as Abraham Lincoln, Franklin D. Roosevelt, and John F. Kennedy. These personages function in much the same way that saints operate in other religions; they are symbols of the life that one should lead according to the religion's values, and they are important parts of the history that is perceived to have produced a "national character."

This national character exhibits the presence of certain doctrines or beliefs that underlie the civil religion. For example, the United States values notions such as equality, liberty, and justice. These values find expression in the civil religion's "sacred texts" (the Declaration of Independence, the Constitution, the Bill of Rights, the Gettysburg Address, and so forth) and are held to be common values throughout the society, despite the varying ways in which they are interpreted and lived. These doctrines parallel a set of ethics, which are norms for behavior, including the striving for financial independence and affluence, plus the ability to afford goods such as health care, a single-family house, automobiles, education, and entertainment.

The celebration of the civil religion involves both holidays and monuments. Americans celebrate days such as Independence Day, Memorial Day, Thanksgiving, and Presidents' Day as reminders of the national history and opportunities for the propagation of the shared values of the national civil religion. Likewise, a series of "shrines" or holy places symbolizes history and values. The system of national parks offers several places, but more specifically there are monuments in Washington, D.C., such as those for Presidents Washington, Jefferson, and Lincoln, as well as various war memorials. Elsewhere in the nation, there are locations such as Mount Rushmore, dedicated to the memory of the national past. Pilgrimages to these shrines make tourism a major industry, and many Americans desire to see these places at least once in a lifetime.

These elements of the national civil religion certainly operate within the priestly notion. Other priestly aspects in American history include the doctrine of Manifest Destiny, which held that God desired the American nineteenth century expansion from the eastern location of the original colonies until the nation would reach "from sea to shining sea." National imagery compared the entire continent to the Old Testament idea of a Promised Land, which God had given to the chosen people if only they would lead moral lives and would expend the energy needed to conquer the territory and drive out its former occupants. This priestly version of the civil religion asserted the rightness of God's chosen Americans and insisted upon the lesser value of other peoples.

The civil religion's prophetic side has also found expression at many points throughout the history of the nation. Two examples will suffice. During his lifetime awnd before his admission into the pantheon of civil religion, Abraham Lincoln developed doctrines of national unity that reflected the priestly notions of protecting the status quo, but he also expressed certain prophetic ideas. Lincoln rewrote the history of the nation to emphasize the Founders' desire for freedom for all persons. Ignoring the fact that many of the nation's first generations of leaders were slave owners, Lincoln favored the abolition of slavery and defended the notion through appeals to the civil religion, including such master-

French philosopher Jean-Jacques Rousseau was the first political philosopher to articulate the concept of a "social contract" between government and the people it governs. *(Library of Congress)*

ful rhetorical pieces as the Gettysburg Address. In the 1960's, Martin Luther King, Jr., functioned as one of the national civil religion's most important prophets through his use of civil religious language to champion civil rights for African Americans. His use of metaphors drawn from the civil religion, such as "dreams" and "covenants," marked the prophetic nature of his speech, as he called the nation to renew its commitment to the "higher values" of its civil religion, such as liberty, equality, and freedom, and to change the national system of privileges to reflect better the commitments of the prophetic civil religion. The success of King's rhetoric derived in large part from the effective use of images from the civil religion.

Context

Eighteenth century French philosopher Jean-Jacques Rousseau, in his *Du contrat social* (1762; *A Treatise on the Social Contract*, 1764), emphasized the need for a widespread ideology to support a government and its social contract with the people. Such an ideology would be a civil religion—that is, a belief in the ultimate power of the society rather than in some otherworldly divine being who might at times question and challenge the political realities of the day. A civil religion would assert a beneficent deity whose interests and actions provide helpful guidance for the community. It would also be necessary to believe in some sort of life after death in order to provide proper reasoning for individuals to live in harmony with the state on this earth. Finally, such a civil religion would need to affirm the sanctity and rightness of the social order. These views were widely reflected in the movement of Deism, with strong roots in the founding philosophies of the United States.

Much later, sociologist Émile Durkheim returned to the notion of civil religion and emphasized the idea that religion, by definition, expresses social cohesion. Any society's representation of itself as a social unit is therefore a "religious" depiction and embodies itself in ritual observances such as holidays and in symbols such as flags. According to Durkheim, religion is the realization of the presence of a real and external force upon individuals' lives, and that force is society itself. Thus, every society has a civil religion, and all civil religions serve to promote social cohesion. Even though Durkheim's critics have rightly charged that there is also the potential for conflict and social opposition present in religion, including civil religion, Durkheim's connection of cohesion and religion has proved to be an insight of powerful explanatory potential.

Over the past century, scholars of religion have been less willing to recognize the influence of civil religion, but in recent years many theologians, especially among the more conservative elements of Christianity, have embraced civil religions as an analytical device. Usually these Christian scholars emphasize the differences between "correct" Christian belief and the doctrinal elements of the civil religion. This direction is likely to continue. At the same time, sociologists are also realizing the problems with overly facile equations of civil religion and standard Christian theological symbols; they are concentrating more on the civil religion's transformation of Christian symbols than on its appropriation of them. This distinction will allow the study of civil religion to recognize the increasing plurality of American religion and American political metaphor, occurring as individuals of non-Christian religions assume increasing numbers of leadership positions. As scholars in the 1950's began to recognize distinctions between Protestant, Catholic, and Jewish versions of the civil religion, so Islamic, Buddhist, and perhaps even New Age notions will make themselves felt increasingly in the future.

Bibliography

Bellah, Robert N. *The Broken Covenant: American Civil Religion in a Time of Trial*. New York: Seabury Press, 1975. Classic study of civil religion establishes the historical roots of this phenomenon and then analyzes the problems in American national self-identity created by the dissolution of this unifying concept.

Chidester, David. *Patterns of Power: Religion and Politics in American Culture*. Englewood Cliffs, N.J.: Prentice-Hall, 1988. Analyzes issues such as religion and the exercise of democracy, the conflict between different minority understandings of religion, and the connections between religion and the American legal system. Provides helpful insight into the way that the rest of culture reacts and responds to religious phenomena.

Durkheim, Émile. *The Elementary Forms of the Religious Life*. Translated by Joseph Ward Swain. New York: Free Press, 1965. Focuses on the religious practices of "primitive" societies. He concludes that religion symbolizes the society itself. He understands this view of religion to apply equally to modern societies, and thus he defines religion as the (ideological) forces of social cohesion.

McGuire, Meredith B. *Religion: The Social Context*. 4th ed. Belmont, Calif.: Wadsworth, 1997. Basic introduction to issues in sociology of religion, allowing the placement of civil religion within its setting of other human religious experience. The author provides a helpful summary of Durkheim's theoretical development of civil religion as social cohesion.

Pierard, Richard V., and Robert D. Linder. *Civil Religion and the Presidency*. Grand Rapids, Mich.: Academie, 1988. Documents changes in civil religion as supported by United States presidents, especially those of the late twentieth century. There is insightful and skeptical attention to the presidents' rhetorical use of civil religion for political ends, with a call for Christians to delineate between the cultural phenomenon of civil religion and the transcendent claims of "true faith."

Nederveen Pieterse, Jan P., ed. *Christianity and Hegemony: Religion and Politics on the Frontiers of Social Change*. New York: Berg, 1992. This anthology offers a series of analyses of civil religion and other types of religious influence on politics in the United States and internationally, including chapters on Iraq, Israel, the Philippines, Poland, South Africa, Western Europe, and Zimbabwe.

Rouner, Leroy S., ed. *Civil Religion and Political Theology*. Notre Dame, Ind.: University of Notre Dame Press, 1986. Essays on issues of civil religion's influence on American politics and, more explicitly, religious and theological attempts to influence political life. Several of the articles develop the view that civil religion is a corruption of Christianity that endangers both true religion and political freedom.

Wuthnow, Robert. *The Restructuring of American Religion: Society and Faith Since World War II*. Princeton, N.J.: Princeton University Press, 1988. Wuthnow is a premier interpreter of religion as an American social phenomenon. Here he traces the development of society's religious involvement during the second half of the twentieth century. Despite an emphasis on the institutional and denominational aspects of American religion, he includes a specific chapter on civil religion, with a strong comparison of conservative and liberal forms of civil religion.

_____. *The Struggle for America's Soul: Evangelicals, Liberals, and Secularism*. Grand Rapids, Mich.: W. B. Eerdmans, 1989. Readable account of the issues that have arisen between factions in American Christianity, with special attention to the way each group uses civil religion in its arguments and appeals.

Jon L. Berquist

Cross-References

Legitimacy and Authority; Religion; Secularization in Western Society; Socialization: Religion.

CLASS CONSCIOUSNESS AND CLASS CONFLICT

Type of sociology: Major social institutions
Field of study: The economy

Class consciousness refers to the ways in which members of particular classes view their common cultural, political, and economic interests as distinctly opposed to the interests of members of other classes. Class consciousness and class struggle have been studied to understand society's changing political, economic, and cultural configurations.

Principal terms

CAPITALISM: economic system generally defined as private ownership of the means of production (raw materials, buildings, and machinery); sociological meaning also includes the social system that encompasses capitalist social relations

CLASS: group of people with shared political, economic, and cultural experiences who identify their interests as different from those of other classes

CULTURE: values, norms, and material goods created by members of a particular group

DEMOGRAPHY: study of human population that investigates the size, age, and sex composition of a population in addition to its mobility patterns

IDEOLOGY: an array of ideas actively expressing the way a group views the appropriate functioning of society's political, economic, and cultural institutions and activities

INSTITUTIONS: relatively stable arrangements designed to promote efficiency in meeting a society's goals

MODE OF PRODUCTION: combination of the social relations of production and the sources of production; capitalism is one example of a mode of production

STRATIFICATION: a system by which categories of people in a society are ranked in a hierarchy

Overview

At a superficial level, class consciousness simply refers to a recognition that a number of classes exist in one's society and that one belongs to a certain class and not to others. This suggests an acknowledgment of differences in cultural, political, and economic characteristics of members of other classes. There are, however, degrees of consciousness. Sociologist Anthony Giddens has identified three distinct levels of class consciousness: conception of class identity, conception of class conflict, and revolutionary consciousness. A conception of class identity is the least developed of the three levels of class consciousness; all it requires is some recognition of class differentiation. This minimal level of consciousness can be further distinguished by the absence of a conflict orientation, which requires not only acknowledgment of class differentiation but also recognition of oppositional interests.

Conflict consciousness emerges with the unveiling of class structure—that is, through the identification of those qualities of capitalism that make levels of class inequality obvious. Historically this has meant the "homogenization" of the effects of industrialization on workers forced into large factory settings. While this concentration of labor was advantageous for capitalists, it had the unintended consequence of providing workers (now sharing common experiences and interests) with the ability to identify levels of inequality inherent in the production process. The product of conflict consciousness has been the emergence of unions and political parties, as well as other organizations and agencies, to promote the interests of the working class.

Conflict consciousness, however, carries working class interests only so far. A class which has attained a level of revolutionary consciousness not only identifies layers of class-based inequality but also, through heightened experiential and theoretical awareness, views the existing socioeconomic structure as illegitimate. A class attaining revolutionary consciousness proposes an alternative to the existing cultural, political, and economic order and identifies possible actions necessary to advance it. Many sociologists contend that the primary objectives of class struggle and class conflict are worker control over industry (centering primarily on creativity and the organization of production) and society; material and moral fulfillment; economic self-sufficiency; and freedom of self-expression. Consciousness alone will not produce a revolution. Sociological analysis suggests that revolutions are the product of both revolutionary ideology (consciousness) and institutional breakdown.

There are many institutional, associational, and demographic factors that mediate the transmission of class consciousness. Among those most readily identifiable are family, school, religion, media, peer groups, work associations, gender, and ethnicity. One goal of sociological research on class consciousness and class struggle is to unveil the apparent equality inherent in relations between capitalists and workers to show that these social relations are, in actuality, unequal. By studying the many ways in which class struggle manifests itself in structural, symbolic, and ideological confrontation, sociologists have been able not only to understand the objective experiences of the working class with respect to the socioeconomic constraints of capitalism but also to identify counterideology expressed through revolutionary consciousness.

Applications

Theories of class consciousness and class struggle have been used to explain, among other things, the de-skilling of workers and the investments that industries and corporations have made in technology.

Sociologist Harry Braverman published a book in 1974 entitled *Labor and Monopoly Capital* that has been widely influential among sociologists who study the organization of work and its effects on workers. Braverman emphasized the struggle taking place at the point of production over control of the productive process. He focused on identification and politicization of the division of labor as it manifested itself under the influence of scientific management.

Scientific management had been offered earlier in the twentieth century as a potential panacea for managers and owners attempting to resolve their "labor problems." More specifically, since workers at the beginning of the twentieth century were still in command of the primary skills and knowledge of how to produce specific products, attempts to increase production, reduce worker pay, or change work methods were frequently met with hostility, often disrupting production entirely. The labor problem, as Frederick W. Taylor (scientific management's major proponent) identified it, was how to get workers to produce in the most efficient manner possible without driving them to rebel or to withhold their effort.

The answer for Taylor, and other scientific managers, was a detailed division of labor. Since workers possessed the knowledge and skill needed for production, Taylor reasoned, management needed to formulate a method for separating the worker from as much "thought work" as possible. Successful application of the "separation of conception from execution," as Braverman referred to it, would begin to de-skill workers to the point where their knowledge of production would be limited solely to their own narrowly defined (by management) activity.

Taylorism consists of a process characterized by three fundamental principles. First, managers must assume the responsibility of gathering all the traditional knowledge formerly held by working men and women and reducing this knowledge to rules, laws, and formulae. No longer would managers be dependent on the craft knowledge of workers; they could rely instead on the planning of management. The second principle, related to the first, suggests that all brainwork should be removed from the shop floor and relocated in departments of planning or layout. This is what Braverman referred to as the separation of conception from execution. In the name of efficiency, it was Taylor's mission to see that the process of conceiving and implementing an idea would never again occur under the power of workers. The third principle of scientific management was to use management's new monopoly over knowledge "to control each step of the labor process and its mode of execution." This was to be accomplished through a detailed description of each job, including how to do the work, the time that should be required to complete it, and product specifications.

The direct effects of scientific management on workers were immediate and severe. The cheapening of the workforce that developed as a consequence of de-skilling not only reduced the price of labor (the wage workers could command) but also enhanced their interchangeability. Workers could no longer summon the attention of employers as effectively as they formerly had based on their ability to withhold productive effort. This made them more vulnerable to threats of dismissal and more likely to accommodate a dehumanizing work environment. The ideological significance of scientific management was its appeal to rational concerns over efficient production. Taylor's appeal to "science" masked the underlying class struggle implicit in employers' and managers' efforts to eliminate worker control over production. Braverman's contribution to the sociology of work was to expose the class struggle taking place at the point of production and to identify the efforts of managers to appropriate productive control through the implementation of scientific management. His insight into the de-skilling of workers continues to inform research on contemporary labor market characteristics.

In a compelling application of class theory, historian David Noble identifies the consequences of class struggle for the implementation of technology in the workplace. In two
well-documented works, Noble applies the conceptual strengths of the concepts of class and
class struggle to a historical account of the growth of industrial automation.

Noble begins by identifying the coordination of interests among the military, corporations, universities, and science establishments in the United States following the conclusion
of World War II. The primary purposes, according to Noble, were to form a political and
economic force capable of containing the Soviet Union abroad and controlling labor at
home. Labor union strength had grown rapidly during the war, climbing from nine to fifteen
million members between 1940 and 1945. The War Labor Board, however, assumed control
over arbitration. Wages were frozen at 15 percent above 1941 levels and labor was forced
to adhere to no-strike pledges. This occurred while prices increased 45 percent and profits
increased 250 percent. Despite no-strike pledges, the war years saw 14,471 strikes involving
more than seven million workers. According to Noble, the most frequent cause of strike
activity was a grievance over discipline (such as harassment). Wages and working conditions
constituted the remaining reasons as workers "endured speed-ups, long hours, and a
hazardous environment." He cites data suggesting that between 1940 and 1945, eighty
thousand workers were killed and more than eleven million were injured as a result of
industrial accidents.

According to historian Neil Chamberlain, "the end of World War Two marked the
beginning of the greatest industrial crisis in American history." Class struggle in the United
States during the period of 1945 to 1955 led to the greatest confrontation between capital
and labor in the history of a capitalist country. Noble cites more than forty-three thousand
strikes involving some twenty-seven million workers. Union demands moved beyond
instrumental concerns over wages to include control over working conditions, shorter hours,
health and welfare funds, and the pace of production.

Faced with continued work stoppages and dependence on workers in unionized firms for
most decisions concerning personnel, hours, and pay, management went on the offensive.
Two crucial events served to weaken the labor movement in the 1950's: returning veterans
(whose presence in firms formerly homogenized by a strong union made the labor force
more heterogeneous and hence more difficult to organize), and the anticommunist "red
scare." Renewed interest in de-skilling and control led employers to pursue innovative ways
to redesign the work process, avoiding the use of skilled craft workers as much as possible.

Efforts to utilize technology in increasingly sophisticated ways, thereby reducing the
need for skilled workers, were widely referred to in the 1950's and early 1960's as
"automation." Noble notes that among the forces encouraging factory owners to automate
was the desire to "weaken the power of unions, and otherwise adjust a recalcitrant work
force to the realities of lower pay, tighter discipline, and frequent layoffs." In other words,
the strength of labor, as it struggled for control of production and higher wages, was among
the forces that drove the combined interests of corporations, universities, the military, and
scientific communities to invest in the redesign of the workplace.

Central to automation was a technological development known as the numerical control device, a predecessor of the digital computer. Engineers gathered detailed information and specifications about the operation of machinery, then coded the information in such a way that the numerical control device could control the machines. Work that formerly required ten skilled workers could now be accomplished by machines, with only one semiskilled worker needed to monitor the equipment.

Context

To many scholars, the study of class, class consciousness, and class struggle is synonymous with sociology. Initiated in the works of Karl Marx and Friedrich Engels, and later transformed by German sociologist Max Weber, theoretical analyses of class consciousness and class struggle have continued to be a source of great sociological debate.

Marx identified the emergence of class consciousness as a product of shared experiences brought on by the increasing homogenization of labor. Workers' objective experiences with capitalist production, he wrote, would lead inevitably to a revolutionary class consciousness. Later Marx clarified his earlier propositions by arguing that it was the combination of objective experiences and class struggle, producing a unity of interest, that would transform that working class from "a class *in* itself" to "a class *for* itself" (a revolutionary class). Class struggle, according to Marx, exposes the true interests of capitalists and, in the words of sociologist M. Levin, reveals "the horrific extent to which a ruling class will go to preserve its interests."

Vladimir Ilich Lenin, like Marx, believed that class-based exploitation may not be readily apparent—it must be uncovered. Lenin proposed that consciousness can only be brought to workers from without. Only activists (intellectuals) having the ability to see through the veil of ideology could generate and lead a truly revolutionary movement. Workers, after all, had only a "working-class" consciousness. What was needed was a revolutionary consciousness.

Sociologist Jean Cohen suggests that class analyses since the 1940's have generally been of four basic types: theories seeking a revolutionary subject that is not a class to substitute for or spark the proletariat; "new working-class theories"; structuralist Marxist class analyses; and theories of the "new intellectual class." Those theories seeking a revolutionary subject argue that it is impossible for the working class to be the force for revolutionary change since the harshness of capitalism has been mediated by the welfare state. This has resulted in some theorists, among them sociologist Herbert Marcuse, searching for other populations experiencing the severity of capitalist exploitation as the source for revolutionary change. (Among those populations studied have been the underclass, blacks, students, and women.) New working-class theorists such as sociologists Serge Mallet and Andre Gorz argue that technological transformations in the mode of production within Western capitalist countries have placed workers once again at the forefront of class struggle and revolutionary consciousness. Technological homogenization places workers in positions of power and makes them crucial links in the productive process.

Structural Marxists such as Nicos Poulantzas and Eric O. Wright are considered the forerunners in the contemporary "boundary debate." That is, they have taken up Marx's efforts to identify clearly how many classes there are and who belongs in which ones.

Finally, sociologists Ivan Szelenyi, Alvin Gouldner, Barbara Ehrenreich, and John Ehren-reich, among others, are associated with identification and theorization of the new intellectual class. The theoretical crux of this approach is identifying the extent to which intellectuals have replaced workers as having revolutionary potential.

Bibliography

Braverman, Harry. *Labor and Monopoly Capital.* 25th ed. Introduction by John Bellamy Foster. New York: Monthly Review Press, 1998. Refocuses attention on the class struggle that occurs at the point of production. His primary endeavor was to identify the de-skilling process and discuss its ramifications for workers.

Cohen, Jean. *Class and Civil Society.* Amherst: University of Massachusetts Press, 1982. Valuable critique of traditional Marxist, neo-Marxist, and Weberian conceptualizations of class. She then attempts to salvage the strengths of Marx's class theory to provide a more stimulating critique of stratification.

Giddens, Anthony. *The Class Structure of the Advanced Societies.* 2d ed. London: Huchinson, 1981. Rearticulates class theory. He enters a debate with both Marx and Weber, offering valuable critique and theoretical insight.

Giddens, Anthony, and David Held. *Classes, Power, and Conflict: Classical and Contemporary Debates.* Berkeley: University of California Press, 1982. Offers an invaluable look at the classical and contemporary theoretical approaches to class, state, ideology, and conflict.

Marx, Karl. *Capital: A Critique of Political Economy.* Vol. 3. New York: Penguin Books, 1990. In the last chapter of volume 3 of his classic work, Marx begins to systematize his analysis of class and class consciousness. Available in a number of editions and translations.

_____. *The Eighteenth Brumaire of Louis Bonaparte.* New York: International, 1981. Here Marx designates the three historically relevant classes according to Marxist theory: capitalists, proletarians, and landowners.

Noble, David. *Forces of Production.* New York: Oxford University Press, 1986. Detailed account of the development and implementation of technology in industry. While focusing primarily on the development of numerical control, Noble's identification of class struggle, implicit throughout this work, serves to invigorate the "active" or subjective side of history.

Steinberg, Marc W. *Fighting Words: Working-Class Formation, Collective Action, and Discourse in Early Nineteenth-Century England.* Ithaca, N.Y.: Cornell University Press, 1999.

Thompson, E. P. *The Making of the English Working Class.* New York: Vintage Books, 1963. Masterpiece of historical and sociological insight documenting the emergence of English working-class consciousness. This book is essential reading for all students of class consciousness and struggle.

Willis, Paul. *Learning to Labor.* New York: Columbia University Press, 1981. Classic ethnography of the impact of political, economic, and cultural experiences on the reproduction of class stratification. Widely credited for its cogent observation of working class "counterideology."

Wright, E. O. *Class, Crisis, and the State*. London: NLB, 1978. Expands on the work of structuralist Marxists Althusser and Poulantzas to add new layers of class structuration. By doing so, Wright was able to identify what he called "contradictory class locations" held by individuals within society who did not seem to fit the orthodox Marxist class scheme.

Robert C. Schehr

Cross-References

Capitalism; Conflict Theory; Marxism; Social Stratification: Analysis and Overview; Social Stratification: Marxist Perspectives; Workplace Socialization.

COLLECTIVE BEHAVIOR

Type of sociology: Collective behavior and social movements
Field of study: Sociological perspectives and principles

Studies of collective behavior are dedicated to explaining the presence of emerging structures in any social system, including society. Scholars of collective behavior study many subjects, including gossip, rumors and urban legends, physical and technological disasters, panic, mass hysteria, and crowd behavior.

Principal terms

COLLECTIVE BEHAVIOR: coordinated behavior between two or more persons that emerges from traditional culture

CROWD: large temporary gathering of people in a face-to-face situation

DISASTERS: physical events that have an impact on a community, causing considerable social disruption

EMERGING BEHAVIOR: coordinated behavior between two or more persons that is new, untried, and responsive to stimuli external to the group

GOSSIP: hearsay and unverifiable statements about people with whom one is closely tied in a small group

MASS HYSTERIA: temporary delusional beliefs held by a large and scattered population of persons

PANIC: uncontrolled flight based on intense personal fear and emotional shock

RUMORS: hearsay and unverifiable statements about persons or events in society

TRADITIONAL CULTURE: established and understood social patterns that are the sources for collective behavior

URBAN LEGENDS: narrative stories that are hearsay and unverifiable that deal with contemporary urban life

Overview

Collective behavior deals with the description and explanation of emerging social structures in society. Until recent years, collective behavior scholars have also included in their studies the analyses of social movements. The study of social movements, however, has moved away from collective behavior research on emerging structures by taking an organizational approach to the subject.

Scholars of collective behavior have investigated three categories of emerging behavior. First are those activities that involve primarily talk that is hearsay and unverifiable about events or persons. This includes mass hysteria, gossip, rumors, and urban legends. Mass hysteria involves talk about events between people who are not in face-to-face contact. For example, the widespread sightings of unidentified flying objects (UFOs) are examples of mass hysteria.

Gossip occurs among intimates—people who know one another well. Rumors and urban legends differ in their complexity. Rumors are simply statements about persons or events that are passed from one person to the next in face-to-face situations; they generally do not involve people that one knows well. In contrast, urban legends are hearsay and unverifiable stories that have a narrative structure about urban life that is repeated in the same way each time the legend is told. In that they capture the essence of urban life, there is an element of truth to these legends. For example, sightings of Elvis Presley are examples of rumors, whereas reports of alligators in the sewers illustrate urban legends. The latter illustrate anxieties and fears people have of city life.

The second topic studied by collective behavior scholars is associated with panic or the sudden impact of physical disasters such as hurricanes, earthquakes, and tornadoes that involve immediate individual and organizational response. Most of the important research on social responses to disaster in the United States has been conducted by the Disaster Research Center, formerly at the Ohio State University and now at the University of Delaware. The two cofounders of the center, Enrico Quarantelli and Russell Dynes, have made significant contributions to the literature on the social impact of disasters. Quarantelli, in a series of studies, has found that there is little panic in disaster. Dynes, while researching the impact of disasters on communities, found that four types of organizations emerged to deal with the disaster. They range from organizations that change very little to those that change considerably because of emergent responses to the disaster. The first type of organization is called "established" and changes very little as a result of the disaster. For example, police and fire departments are established organizations that carry out normal emergency tasks. The second type is "expanding"; it carries out normal functions but is often called on to do emergency activities. It can perform these with little difficulty. Gas and electric utility companies are examples of expanding organizations. The third type is "extending." These are organizations that normally do not do emergency tasks because they are unfamiliar with them. They do, however, have the resources for emergency response. Local construction companies are examples of extending organizations. Finally, there are "emerging" organizations that do unfamiliar emergency tasks. An example of this type of group would be local neighborhood rescue and cleanup crews. Researchers have also examined the impact of technological disaster such as explosions in the chemical industry.

The third area of inquiry is research on crowd behavior. The central concern of most collective behavior research, both theoretically and empirically, is crowd behavior. Crowd researchers have studied a variety of subjects, including the behavior of people in ethnic, racial, and protest crowds as well as behavior at sports and music events. In addition, the long-term consequences of police violence on crowd members have been the subject of scholarly inquiry.

Applications

The core of inquiry into crowds has been directed toward emerging structures. The term "emerging structures" refers to the notion that people in groups respond in new ways to situations for which they are unprepared. These new ways become, for a short time, guidelines for behavior that results in new social forms. These emerging forms have a complex social structure and culture. Crowd behavior is a prime example of these new social structures.

In the late 1800's Gustave Le Bon, a French journalist, looked at rioters in Paris and concluded that crowds are crazy and have a "law of mental unity." Practitioners and researchers dealing with gatherings have had to reevaluate and challenge this conclusion. They have done this by looking at a crowd's complex social structure and culture. One area that has been closely examined is the roles of people in a crowd. Crowds are organized into various roles, and different behavior is associated with each role. In addition, these roles are spatially distributed. For the sociologist, a role is a set of expected behaviors carried out in a given context. A norm is a general set of guidelines that a person follows when dealing with others in their roles. For example, a police officer plays a role and follows certain norms as he or she gives instructions to automobile drivers at an intersection in a large city.

The basic structure of most crowds can be divided into three roles: the active core, the cheerleaders, and the observers. The core does different things than do the cheerleaders or the observers. The core carries out the action of the crowd; it is the crowd protagonist. The cheerleaders act in verbal support of the active core. They applaud and support the core's actions. Finally, any crowd has a set of observers who follow the actions of the active core and the cheerleaders but do not take part in core or cheerleader activities.

Crowds can come about any time and any place. They may emerge on the street, for example, created by such events as an automobile accident or a street entertainer's act. They also form in looting or celebrating situations. One can see these crowd structures when watching protesting crowds in which looting is also occurring or observing crowds in which fans are celebrating their team's championship victory.

The active core is closest to the focal point. The cheerleaders are nearby with the observers, watching the event happen and creating the arena in which it is carried out. For example, extensive rioting took place in Los Angeles in 1992 after white police officers were acquitted of all charges in the beating of a black motorist named Rodney King. The beating had been videotaped and was widely shown on television. After the acquittal, rioting broke out and many deaths occurred. Looting of stores was widespread in the riot area. In a riot situation in which looting takes place, the active core takes commodities from stores. Cheerleaders are close to stores but not as close as the active core. Their focus is on the actions of the looters. They verbally ratify the actions of the core. Lastly, the observers simply watch the proceedings and show their approval by staying or disapproval by leaving. All this happened during the 1992 riots in Los Angeles.

At celebrating riots after championship sporting events, the active core celebrates their team's victory by vandalizing stores, signs, and other items in public areas of large cities. The cheerleaders follow the core's action closely and support the active core with cheers and chants. The observers support the core and the cheerleaders by watching and creating an arena for the activities of the core.

The notion that crowds have a role structure and culture allows one to challenge two myths about crowds. The first myth is that crowds are crazy and irrational. There is no doubt that crowds commit antisocial acts. One need look no further than the 1985 Heysel stadium soccer riot in Belgium (in which thirty-nine people died) to confirm this truth. This does not prove, however, that crowds are crazy or out of touch with reality. Most people in crowds can recall what happened and why it happened although they may not have liked what happened. Assuming that crowds are crazy leads one to the conclusion that studying a crowd is impossible because the behavior is random and unpredictable and therefore not amenable to scientific investigation. Collective behavior scholars reject this position. When it is assumed that crowds have social structures with their own cultures, then it follows that they can be studied scientifically.

The second myth is that crowds are highly suggestible. This myth derives from the "crowds are irrational" perspective, and it is widely held by the press. If crowds were as suggestible as newspapers often say they are, then crowd management would be very easy. All police would have to do is "suggest" that the crowd leave, go home, or go have a drink and unwind at the local bar. The police's problems would be solved for the day. If crowds have social structures with cultures, however, then one would not expect them to be highly suggestible. Any proposal would likely be dealt with by discussion with friends or peers. Any proposal or suggestion would be filtered through the person's relationships to others in the crowd. In other words, crowds should be seen as information-processing entities rather than as emotional relay systems.

Context

Collective behavior, and particularly its approach to crowds, is a uniquely American specialty of sociology. While there have been a few European influences, notably the work of Le Bon, empirical work has come from American sociologists and has focused on problems related to the United States.

There are two theoretical approaches to crowds widely found in the scientific literature and usually presented in introductory sociology texts. The structural-functional position, with its stress on equilibrium and norms, is represented in collective behavior theory by the work of Neil J. Smelser in the early 1960's. Smelser was a student of and a collaborator with sociologist Talcott Parsons. The other theory comes from the interactionist tradition that stresses the analysis of face-to-face behavior. This theory was presented in the work of Ralph Turner and Lewis Killian (1987). The ideas of Clark McPhail (1991) build on Turner and Killian. Each theory can be illustrated with rock concert crowds.

Smelser's model is presented in his book *Theory of Collective Behavior* (1963). It is divided into six determinants, each with a set of subdeterminants. The determinants are structural conduciveness, structural strain, growth of a generalized belief, precipitating event, mobilization for action, and social control.

Structural conduciveness refers to conditions of social structure that describe social possibilities for an incident of collective behavior to happen. Structural conduciveness sets the parameters and constraints for the other components of the model, particularly structural strain. The conduciveness for rock concert violence is found in the bringing together in a small space excited people determined to have a good time in an emotionally charged environment.

Structural strain occurs within the parameters of conduciveness. The sociological researcher looks for strain in terms of uncertainty. At rock concerts the uncertainness is generally associated with the ability to reach a location in the auditorium or area that provides most enjoyment for the concert. For many rock concert fans, this is near the rock stars at the front of the hall. Smelser's model instructs the researcher to look for beliefs that guide action. Beliefs are rooted in uncertainty. Regarding rock concerts, these beliefs become shared in terms of uncertainty about access to desirable locations in the concert hall.

Regarding mobilization for action, the Smelser model encourages the investigator to look at the initial and derived phases of a crowd action. Most incidents of collective behavior change during the flow of events. Rock concerts are no exception. The Smelser model refers to this as the process of moving from the initial and derived phases. In looking at social control, the model directs one to investigate several dimensions that shape a rock concert and keep it from getting out of control. The investigator looks at issues of formal control from traditional sources, such as the police and ushers, as well as informal social control such as the rock artists themselves or the peer group.

Clark McPhail, in his book *The Myth of the Madding Crowd* (1991), has developed seven basic categories of crowd behavior including collective orientation, vocalization, verbalization, gesticulation, vertical locomotion, horizontal locomotion, and manipulation. Collective orientation usually describes where people are looking. One type of collective orientation is arcing/ringing, which refers to the process whereby small groups of people create an arc or a ring around a focal point. The arcing/ringing process at a rock concert occurs near the stage as young people attempt to get closer to the musicians. Collective vocalization is the process in which two or more persons engage in common vocal sounds. Booing and cheering are two subcategories.

Collective verbalization describes two or more people engaging in coordinated speech including singing; at rock concerts, audiences often sing along with the artists as they perform. Collective gesticulation occurs when two or more persons coordinate their physical gestures. This is often done with collective vocalization and verbalization. The categories of behavior that one often sees at rock concerts are praise or victory gestures. Fans raise their arms in these gestures while swaying back and forth to the music. This is often combined with chanting and singing.

Collective vertical locomotion refers to coordinated vertical behavior involving two or more crowd members. One type is jumping. Rock concerts begin with fans sitting. Once the music begins, fans seldom remain seated, moving into standing and jumping patterns, often combined with collective gesticulation, vocalization, and verbalization. Collective horizontal locomotion takes place when two or more people coordinate their movements in space. One example found at rock concerts is surging, which can be horizontal (side to side) or vertical (back to front). It is one major source of danger at rock concerts. Collective manipulation refers to the process of two or more people coordinating their hand activities, including synchronized clapping at rock concerts. It is coordinated with the music and dance of the performers.

Bibliography

Collective Violence: Harmful Behavior in Groups and Governments. Edited by Craig Summers and Eric Markusen. Lanham, Md.: Rowman and Littlefield, 1999.

Le Bon, Gustave. *The Crowd.* Introduction by Robert A. Nye. New Brunswick, N.J.: Transaction, 1995. First study of crowd behavior, first published in French in 1895. While many sociologists disagree with Le Bon's conclusions, it is an important book because of its core idea that crowds can be studied systematically. Le Bon's "law of mental unity" remains a popular notion in the general press.

Lewis, Jerry M. "A Value-Added Analysis of the Heysel Stadium Soccer Riot." *Current Psychology: Research and Reviews* 8 (Spring, 1989): 15-29. The most detailed use of the Smelser model in the sports riot literature. It is a study of the Heysel stadium soccer riot in Brussels, Belgium, in 1985 that caused the death of thirty-nine fans and the injury of four hundred more.

McPhail, Clark. *The Myth of the Madding Crowd.* New York: Aldine de Gruyter, 1991. Definitive presentation on categories of gathering behavior. McPhail reviews all previous theories of crowd behavior except Smelser's, showing each model's weaknesses. He argues that students of crowds must carefully describe the behavior of crowd members before efforts are undertaken to explain it. He proposes his categories as a way to classify the actions of crowd members.

Miller, David L. *Introduction to Collective Behavior.* Belmont, Calif.: Wadsworth, 1985. Presents Russell Dynes's typology of established, expanding, extending, and emerging organizations, developed by field researchers to classify organizational responses to disasters. It is based on the type of task carried by organization in the wake of a natural or technological disaster.

Posner, Eric A. *Law and Social Norms.* Cambridge, Mass.: Harvard University Press, 2000.

Smelser, Neil J. *Theory of Collective Behavior.* New York: Free Press, 1963. Presents the Smelser model in detail. It shows its roots in structural-functionalist social theory of Talcott Parsons. The data that are used to illustrate Smelser's ideas are taken from secondary sources.

Turner, Ralph, and Lewis Killian. *Collective Behavior.* 3d ed. Englewood Cliffs, N.J.: Prentice-Hall, 1987. Most influential textbook on collective behavior. It bases its theory of the crowd on symbolic interactionism of George Herbert Mead and Herbert Blumer.

Jerry M. Lewis

Cross-References

History of Sociology; Sociology Defined; Symbolic Interaction; Urbanization.

CONFLICT THEORY

Type of sociology: Origins and definitions of sociology
Field of study: Sociological perspectives and principles

Conflict theory is the sociological perspective that focuses on tension, competition, and division in society. It assumes that no society is devoid of conflicts of interest and that in the process of struggling for scarce and valuable resources groups develop strategies to maximize their rewards and minimize their losses.

Principal terms

CONFLICT: tension, hostility, or competitiveness that exists among groups in society as they struggle to obtain social resources and improve their positions in the social system

ELITES: those groups in society that manage to control the largest amount of social resources and obtain a privileged position in relation to other groups

NORMS: sets of shared patterns of conduct that provide a group with the guidelines for acceptable and nonacceptable behavior

SOCIAL CHANGE: ongoing process of societal transformation, caused by the constant struggle among groups for scarce resources or rewards

SOCIAL RESOURCES: desirable or valuable cultural items (such as power, prestige, and property) that empower their holders to achieve an elite status within the social system

SOCIAL STRATIFICATION: hierarchical ranking of groups and individuals in society, determined in accordance with the amount of resources they hold within the social system

Overview

The discipline of sociology contains a number of major theoretical frameworks within which sociologists examine social processes and institutions. Three perspectives that are generally considered of central importance are functionalism, conflict theory, and interactionism. Functionalism places an emphasis on the operation of a society in meeting the needs of its members; it therefore emphasizes the factors that are necessary for society to operate—or function—effectively.

Conflict theory, on the other hand, focuses on the tension, hostility, competition, and division in society. This perspective assumes that all valuable social resources or rewards—such as power, prestige, and property—are scarce in human groups. This scarcity generates conflict, since several groups must vie for control of the resources and for the privileged positions in the social system. Given that no society has managed to achieve an equal distribution of resources among all its members, it seems safe to assume that no society is devoid of conflicts of interests and that, in the process of struggling for scarce and valuable resources, groups develop strategies to maximize their rewards and minimize their losses.

To conflict theorists, the struggle for social resources never happens under equal or fair conditions. Some groups begin the race with additional opportunities, privileges, and advantages. Depending on which social resource one is studying, certain groups and individuals always seem to have an edge on the competition—an edge that may be the result of merit, skills, and hard work, or a consequence of shrewdness, opportunism, timing, trickery, and whatever other methods may be devised to gain an advantage over the competition. Those groups and individuals who manage to gain control over a large amount of social resources obtain a privileged status within the social system; they are the elite groups of the society.

Elite groups are not necessarily defined as only the wealthy in a given society; they may be any group in control of advantages in a field of scarce resources. They can be groups of famous artists, athletes, intellectuals, or scientists; they may be powerful generals, politicians, or business leaders. They may be at the top of the social hierarchy according to one measure of social stratification (education, income, class, or occupation) but not necessarily according to all measures. For the sake of a more precise analysis, however, some conflict theorists prefer to define elite groups more narrowly as those few at the top of the social stratification system who seem to benefit most from the status quo in society.

Conflict theorists document how elite groups manage to take control of scarce resources in society and maintain that control at the expense of all other groups. Their assumption is that in the process of becoming elites, certain groups fashion the social institutions, laws, and norms of a society for the purpose of maintaining their own privileged positions. Since the elite groups have more resources, they also have greater coercive power: They have the ability to use the system to push the rest of the population into compliance and conformity with their vision of the status quo. A good example of that ability is a society's laws governing the inheritance of wealth or property, according to which the affluent are able to transmit the scarce resources they have amassed to their offspring. Another example is the structure of higher education. Prestigious private universities, in catering to the children of the powerful, help them transfer their privileged position to their offspring by guaranteeing better social opportunities for their graduates.

According to conflict theorists, elite groups not only control the social system but also develop an ideology of domination that justifies their privilege. To maintain order, elite groups must convince other social groups that their subordination either is temporary or is in the best interests of the society as a whole. The ideology that the elite groups create in order to accomplish this must either give other groups the impression that the system is open (and that it is therefore possible to improve one's position) or give other groups the impression that subordination is necessary because of their lack of ability or because of the "natural" order of things. To the extent that other groups accept the elites' ideology, the stability of the system is guaranteed, and its patterns of domination and subordination remain unchallenged.

The work of three European scholars—Karl Marx, Max Weber, and Georg Simmel—provided a basis for the development of conflict theory. Karl Marx provided conflict theorists with the most critical evaluation of Western society. He believed that social systems distribute scarce resources unequally and that certain groups in society appropriate greater amounts of resources at the expense of all others, thus contributing to conflict among classes.

To Marx, the end of class conflict could only come with a reorganization of the social system under which egalitarian patterns of resource distribution would be put in place.

Weber added to Marx's insights by insisting that class alone is not sufficient for identifying the privileged in society. Although wealth and ownership of the means of production are important signs of privilege, status is also derived from prestige, breeding, and other social categories. Weber believed that the stratification of privilege in modern societies is more complex than Marx had presented in his model. Weber also pointed out more clearly the connection between ideology and distribution of resources.

Simmel further enriched the theoretical base of conflict theory by suggesting that conflict serves as a source of both integration and dissention. Intragroup conflict, for example, helps integrate society by serving as a safety valve for built-up hostility; if workers are fighting one another, they will not organize and unify to challenge their employers. Another good example of the power of conflict to promote societal integration is the fact that conflict with outside groups may lead to increased levels of social solidarity within the group being attacked—thus, in a country at war, dominant and subordinate groups might suspend their hostility for the sake of fighting a common enemy.

American sociologists C. Wright Mills and Lewis A. Coser each made significant contributions to conflict theory. Drawing on the insights of the classical theorists, Mills was one of the early conflict theorists in American sociology. He laid considerable groundwork for the perspective in two controversial books. In *White Collar* (1951), he identified a privileged occupational category and delivered a highly critical analysis of its dominance in American society. In *The Power Elite* (1956), Mills expanded the notion of a privileged group to encompass the business leaders, politicians, and military leaders who, in his opinion, personified the unified, all-powerful group that controls the United States. Mills's work was characterized by his effort to show that conflict is not an occasional or accidental aspect of society but rather an integral part of it.

Coser provided conflict theory with its next important contribution. In his book *The Functions of Social Conflict* (1956), Coser documented how conflict plays a role in preserving society as much as consensus does. For example, he shows how, in large, modern societies, the practice of democracy creates cross-conflicts by bringing together under the umbrella of large parties a variety of ethnic, economic, political, and regional groups who otherwise might be divided by basic, irreconcilable differences. Coser shows how conflict may serve also to bring some isolated individuals into active roles for change and may clarify the positions and boundaries of antagonistic groups so that they become better aware of their relative strengths and of possible means to create peaceful accommodation.

Applications

Conflict theory provides a means of understanding the dynamics of power and privilege in society. By identifying the groups who benefit from present social arrangements and studying the process by which they reached their present conditions, one can understand not only their privileged position but also the strategies they used to reach their goal and the ideology that has been employed to sustain the status quo. One application of the perspective comes in the area of gender stratification. Here, an ascribed trait or status (gender) is used to limit the access of one segment of society to available social resources. Studies of inequality of power, prestige, and property between the sexes show that the patterns of domination and subordination existing between men and women in the United States cannot be totally explained by either the merits of males or the inability of females.

For example, using insights from conflict theory, one can show that as late as 1991 very few women held powerful positions in American politics (two senators, four governors, and about 6 percent of members of Congress), which limited women's future ability to gain power or to create policy that would correct the situation. Furthermore, the lack of political power may have more to do with what might be termed the rules of the game (the regulations controlling elections, the funding of successful campaigns, and the willingness of voters to deem women reliable and competent leaders) than with an absence of capable women to run for office. The distribution of prestige and property seems no different from the distribution of power. In the early 1990's, the gender wage gap in the American marketplace (on average, full-time working women earn between 65 and 72 cents for every dollar earned by full-time working men) and the sex segregation of occupations (men-dominated occupations draw higher pay scales than women-dominated occupations) had more to do with the barriers and regulations created by the dominant group than with the amount of training, experience, or competence of female workers.

According to the Bureau of the Census, whereas women accounted for 45 percent of the labor force in 1988, they represented only 7 percent of engineers, 9 percent of dentists, 20 percent of physicians, and 20 percent of lawyers and judges. In a comparison of median annual earnings for full-time employment, the Bureau of the Census found that in 1987, female executives were making an average of $21,874 a year, compared with $36,055 for their male counterparts; accountants made $22,960 (females), compared with $34,867 (males); engineers made $32,506 (females), versus $40,309 (males). The principle seems to hold true for most professions. Furthermore, studies of gender stratification show how sexism has been used as an ideology of domination to justify the level of privilege enjoyed by males in American society.

Another area that has benefited from conflict theory's insights is the study of race relations. Although prejudice may be considered a result of individual bigotry, stereotyping, and false and incomplete information related to minority groups, discrimination is the process by which social structures are set in place by a dominant group to treat people of different racial background unequally and inequitably. In doing so, discrimination helps sustain the privileged conditions of the dominant group.

The resistance to changing segregation laws in the United States during the 1950's is well documented and was responsible for the growth of one of the largest mass movements in modern American history—the Civil Rights movement. Under legal segregation, an ascribed trait (perceived racial identity) was used to keep a distinct segment of the population from having access to social resources. Through segregated schools, housing, and job opportunities, the dominant majority managed to impose living conditions on the minority that benefited the status quo at the expense of the minority's well-being.

To this day, the effects of such discrimination are still felt nationwide. Race discrimination studies show that, even taking into account education, experience, training, and all other variables that represent merit, African Americans are barred from valuable resources in society because of norms that sustain the barriers against members of their ethnic group. In 1989, 25.9 percent of African American households had an annual income of less than $10,000, compared with 7.7 percent of white American households. At the other end of the spectrum, 13.8 percent of African American households earned an annual income of $50,000 or more, compared with 23.9 percent of white households. In 1987, about one African American in three lived below the poverty line, compared with one in ten white Americans. Unemployment rates for young African American men were three times higher than for young white men. Two of every three white households owned their own homes, compared with fewer than half of all African American households. Studies of race stratification have indicated that the dominant group supports its control through promulgating an ideology of racism to justify or explain the status quo.

Context

Conflict theory emerged in mainstream American sociology as a reaction to, and criticism of, functionalism. Functionalism was the leading theoretical approach in American sociology for a large part of the 1940's and 1950's. Led by Talcott Parsons, functionalists adopted an organic conception of society, one which placed a premium on social consensus, stability, and order. Using the metaphor of society as an organism, functionalists dissected society into its constituent parts, studying and explaining each part in terms of its contribution to the existence, operation, and survival of the larger whole. Every element of society was seen as functional in the stability of the whole, with society being held together by the harmony and cohesion that stemmed from the shared values, norms, and beliefs of its members.

To conflict theorists, society is anything but a balanced, harmonious organism. Many of the early theorists were frustrated with functionalism's inability to explain the tensions, hostilities, and cleavages they perceived in the social system. Assuming that the study of harmony and consensus explained only part of social reality, they began to emphasize the need for a study of tension and disagreement. Drawing on the work of European scholars Marx, Weber, and Simmel, American conflict theorists such as Mills and Coser produced a more critical appraisal of society when they highlighted the struggles and dissensions witnessed in the interaction of social groups with unequal access to resources.

Building on the work of Mills, Coser, and others, American sociologists continued to refine conflict theory. In *Conflict Sociology* (1975), Randall Collins summarized the contributions of conflict theory to American sociology. Drawing on the works of his predecessors, Collins defines conflict theory, explains its major premises, and explores how it helps sociologists to understand and study racial and ethnic cleavages, gender inequality, age inequality, religious dissension, and political antagonisms in modern society. Collins makes explicit the notion that social resources are scarce and valuable and that therefore their distribution creates the conflict of interests that leads to a hierarchy of privilege and power in modern society.

Jonathan Turner, in his book *The Structure of Sociological Theory* (1982), provides another treatment of conflict theory. Defining conflict as a process of events that leads to varying degrees of violence between parties, Turner outlines the outbreak of violence in nine steps. According to him, conflict takes place when social groups who do not receive a proportionate share of resources in a society begin to question the legitimacy of the system. As those groups become more aware that it is in their interest to challenge the system of resource allocation, they may rise to confront the status quo. Becoming better organized as hostility grows in intensity, they struggle until there is an outbreak of violence which ultimately defines the resolution (whether favorable or unfavorable to their cause) of the situation.

Bibliography

Bradley, Harriet. *Men's Work, Women's Work*. Minneapolis: University of Minnesota Press, 1989. Overview of the social processes through which occupations become segregated by sex and opportunities to obtain social resources are divided across gender lines.

Carmichael, Stokely, and Charles V. Hamilton. *Black Power: The Politics of Liberation in America*. New York: Random House, 1967. Provides an incisive application of conflict theory's most basic insights. Written during the time of the urban riots in the United States, it provides an incisive analysis of group dominance and the importance of its ideology of domination.

Collins, Randall. *Conflict Sociology*. New York: Academic Press, 1975. Outstanding presentation of conflict theory as a sociological perspective. In it one finds not only a discussion of previous works in the field but also an effort to present a synthesis—a unified description of the field that may aid in the understanding of different social cleavages in society.

Coser, Lewis A. *The Functions of Social Conflict*. Glencoe, Ill.: Free Press, 1956. Following Simmel, provides the reader with the most thorough exploration of how conflict can be a source of integration in society.

Mills, C. Wright. *The Power Elite*. Afterword by Alan Wolfe. New York: Oxford University Press, 1999. Expands the concept of privileged group to identify the members of a unified American power elite. According to him, the power elite represents the interests of three major sectors in society: business groups, political leaders, and military leaders.

_____. *White Collar*. New York: Oxford University Press, 1951. Critical analysis of white-collar workers as a privileged occupational group in American society. The book discusses the creation and maintenance of the white-collar occupation as a class and the justification for its position in the system.

Morris-Hale, Walter. *Conflict and Harmony in Multi-Ethnic Societies*. New York: P. Lang, 1997.

H. B. Cavalcanti

Cross-References

Education: Conflict Theory Views; Family: Functionalist Versus Conflict Theory Views; Functionalism: Analysis and Overview; History of Sociology; Religion: Marxist and Conflict Theory Views; Social Stratification: Marxist Perspectives; Sociology Defined.

CULTURAL AND STRUCTURAL ASSIMILATION

Type of sociology: Racial and ethnic relations
Field of study: Theories of prejudice and discrimination

Sociologist Milton Gordon made a major contribution to assimilationist theory by clearly distinguishing two types of assimilation: cultural assimilation, sometimes referred to as acculturation, and structural assimilation, which refers to the integration of minority groups into all aspects of social life.

Principal terms

ACCULTURATION: the process whereby a minority group takes on the values, language, and behavior of the dominant cultural group; also the process by which culturally distinct groups understand, adapt to, and influence each other's culture

ETHNIC GROUP: group that is united by a common and distinctive cultural heritage, language, and history

RACE: group that is socially defined on the basis of real or perceived physical characteristics, nationality, and ethnicity

RACIAL DISCRIMINATION: individual and institutional behavior, practices, and policies that result in harm, whether intended or not, to individuals on the basis of race

RACIAL PREJUDICE: dislike and fear of others based on real or perceived physical differences

SOCIAL INSTITUTIONS: social arrangements and interactions that order familial relations, religious beliefs and practices, governance, economic relationships, education, and culture in society

SOCIAL STRUCTURE: relations among individuals and groups to social institutions such as the economy, the government, educational systems, families, religion

Overview

According to Milton Gordon in *Assimilation in American Life* (1964), the study of how groups are incorporated into American society has been plagued by two major problems. First, the American legal system does not distinguish groups on the basis of race, religion, or nationality. Instead, all individuals are simply considered Americans. In contrast, Gordon says, the social reality is that there are distinct subgroups in American society, organized and identified on the basis of race, religion, and nationality. Since the legal system ignores this, the reality is hidden.

The second problem that Gordon defined lies in the manner in which the social sciences have dealt with the reality of diversity in American life. Gordon claims that social scientists prior to him focused primarily on the cultural behavior of individuals and groups and on studying the extent to which various ethnic racial groups had adopted the values and behavior of the dominant group in society—Anglo-Americans. They also focused on studying the attitudes of the dominant group, examining the extent and basis of racial prejudice. This is problematic, according to Gordon, because it ignores the issue of how so many diverse groups are incorporated into the social structure. Furthermore, neither social scientists nor policy makers have made clear what the goals of assimilation are—whether the United States would like to see total assimilation into one culture (a "melting pot" composed of a blend of cultures) or whether groups should maintain distinct cultures (a view sometimes referred to as cultural pluralism). To Gordon, the major question is: What is the impact of racial, religious, and national diversity on social relations and social institutions in a democratic industrial society such as the United States? To answer this question, Gordon argued, sociologists must clearly define assimilation and the various types of outcomes that might emerge from intergroup contact. Consideration of both cultural issues and the social structure must be included.

Gordon was the first to distinguish assimilation from acculturation and to propose two distinct types of assimilation: cultural assimilation (or acculturation) and structural assimilation. Generally, acculturation requires a change of culture on the part of the "out-group" in order to adapt to the dominant group. Structural assimilation requires that the out-group enter into the clubs, groups, and social institutions of the core group, thereby establishing primary relationships with individuals in the core. Ultimately, total assimilation implies that there are no cultural differences and that out-groups can no longer be distinguished from anyone else.

Gordon defines total assimilation as a process that may require seven steps toward its ultimate conclusion, the blended society. Step one is acculturation, in which an ethnic group changes its cultural patterns to those of the core group (in the United States this process is often referred to as Anglo-conformity). Step two is structural assimilation, in which the out-group establishes primary relations with the core group and enters the social structure of the core. The third step is marital assimilation, in which the out-group intermarries with members of the core and produces children. Step four is identificational assimilation, in which ethnic groups stop identifying with their ancestral ethnic group and identify with the core. The fifth step is attitudinal reception, in which the core is no longer prejudiced against members of the out-group. Step six is behavioral assimilation, in which the core stops discriminating against members of the out-group, and step seven is civic assimilation, in which the out-group has no value conflicts with the core group over governance.

According to Gordon, although acculturation is likely to be the first step, it may take place without leading to the other steps toward total assimilation. A group may acculturate itself to the norms of the dominant group without that acculturation being followed by any further acceptance or integration for a prolonged period of time. In other words, a group's successful acculturation neither guarantees its entry into the subsociety of the core nor guarantees that the core group will stop being prejudiced toward them or discriminating against them. Thus, the process of total assimilation requires cooperation from both sides: The entering group must adapt itself to the core group, and the core group must come to accept the entering group and treat its members on the basis of their individual merit rather than on the basis of their ethnic, religious, or national heritage.

Although Gordon did not believe that acculturation would ensure other forms of integration into the core's society, he did think that structural assimilation was the key to the remaining stages in the process toward total assimilation. For example, once the out-group has entered into close, or primary, relationships with the core group by entering their cliques, clubs, and institutions, Gordon believed that it followed "naturally" that individuals would form close relationships, fall in love, and marry outside their group. It would be "inevitable," following the formation of close ties with the core, that members of an out-group would begin to identify with the core subsociety, because they would lose their own ethnic identity. By this time, they would have taken on the appearance, dress, and behavior of the core group, so there would be no basis for prejudice against them. Once prejudice declines, it follows—for Gordon—that negative discriminatory behavior will cease. Since the formerly distinct group would now be completely accepted into the subsociety of the core, and would be identified with it, the group's members would experience no value conflicts with the core group in civic affairs.

Applications

Gordon applied his seven-stage theory of assimilation to an analysis of several diverse ethnic, religious, and racial groups in American society to examine variations in the assimilation process. Generally, he believed that the mode of acculturation in the United States is one of Anglo-conformity. In other words, if groups are to be considered acculturated, they must conform to the behavioral patterns and norms of those whose ancestors migrated from England. In fact, he believed that Anglo-conformity had largely been achieved in terms of acculturation. Gordon said that acculturation was very successful with the children of immigrants because of their immediate contact with public schools and the mass media. In cases in which acculturation was weak, as in the case of American Indians and African Americans, he claimed that factors existed which retarded the process of acculturation for these groups. In other words, he claimed that acculturation was still happening, but at a slower pace. In the case of American Indians, their ongoing ethnic identification with ancestral tradition, coupled with their isolation on reservations and special status as sovereign nations, mitigated against acculturation. Gordon said that, for blacks in the rural South, slavery and the long years of exploitation and discrimination which followed had led to the development of a subculture whose behaviors and values were so distant from Anglo culture that prejudice and discrimination remained intense. For those blacks who migrated to urban industrial centers, acculturation was also retarded because of prejudice and discrimination.

Generally, however, despite the failures of some groups to move speedily through the assimilation process, Gordon maintained the belief that assimilation would eventually occur. To the extent that he saw the development of a black middle class, he saw barriers breaking down, providing evidence that discrimination would have only a delaying effect on assimilation.

Contemporary applications of Gordon's theory have diverged, in part, from the earlier ideological concepts that called for Anglo-conformity. This can be seen particularly in the area of education. Curriculum reform has been directed toward multicultural education, with its goal of appreciating diversity. Many educators argue that when individuals come to appreciate the contributions various ethnic, racial, and religious groups have made to American society, they will come to appreciate and identify with one another. This is seen as an important step toward ending prejudice and discrimination. At the same time, however, many educators stress that it is important for immigrant children to learn English—an important step, Gordon acknowledged, toward acculturation on the basis of Anglo-conformity.

School desegregation programs also can be interpreted as applications of Gordon's concepts of acculturation and structural assimilation. Many—not all—social scientists argue that when children of different racial and ethnic backgrounds can go to school together, play sports together, and know one another intimately, they will grow up without prejudice and discrimination. Furthermore, school desegregation programs are expected to break down the isolation of groups. Residence has remained distinctly organized around race (in particular) and ethnicity. School busing programs, many of which were instituted in the 1970's and 1980's, promoted desegregation and structural assimilation by forcing children across the boundaries of their racial or ethnic communities. In many cases, these programs have operated without the support or cooperation of the core subsociety—Anglo-Americans.

Generally, scholars find that white ethnic groups have been more likely to be assimilated than have groups of other races. For example, in a study that Stephen Steinberg cites in his text, *The Ethnic Myth* (1981), Richard Alba found that rates of intermarriage had increased among six different European ethnic groups. Steinberg claims this as evidence for the occurrence of amalgamation, but only among European ethnic groups.

Context

Sociologists prior to Gordon, following the tradition of Robert Park, tended to define assimilation in terms of acculturation, amalgamation, or both. Generally, they defined acculturation as a process through which ethnic groups come to share a common culture and individuals are regarded on the basis of merit, without encountering prejudice. Amalgamation refers to a biological process, implying intermarriage between individuals of diverse backgrounds that leads to a biological blending through the offspring of those relations. Gordon claims, however, that sociologists did not clearly indicate whether acculturation should or does imply a reciprocal process whereby various ethnic groups take on attributes of one another's culture, resulting in a melting pot. It might imply a process in which groups are expected to conform to the values and behaviors of the dominant ethnic group, which he refers to as the host or core ethnic group (Anglo-Americans are the core group in American society). Furthermore, Gordon claims that acculturation may not be complete; one outcome might be cultural pluralism, under which groups remain distinct yet share in the social structure.

Gordon is considered one of the more sophisticated assimilationist theorists, and assimilationist theory was the forerunner of more recent sociological theories of race and ethnicity. Gordon has been criticized, however, for holding the same assumptions as other assimilationists. A major criticism evolved around the notion of "delayed" assimilation, or what some scholars refer to as a "lag" in full assimilation. Generally, this notion is applied to racial groups, who remain furthest behind in total assimilation. Scholars such as David Wellman, in his 1977 book *Portraits of White Racism*, argue that prejudice by whites is not predicated upon the cultural differences of racial minorities. Rather, Wellman argues, white racism—which embodies discrimination—is a rational defense of the privileges that have been accorded to whites and denied to people of color. He also argues, as does Robert Blauner in *Racial Oppression in America* (1972), that assimilationist scholars fail to distinguish between ethnic and racial groups, expecting that both kinds of groups can be (and are desired to be) fully accepted into the society dominated by Anglo-Americans. Wellman and Blauner also question the assumption of assimilationist scholars that all groups are willing to drop their own cultures and take on that of the core. More important, they separate prejudice from discrimination, so that prejudice is not viewed as a cause of discrimination. As evidence, they point to polls which indicate that prejudiced attitudes are declining among whites, even while racial minorities continue to have significantly less income, wealth, and political power than whites. Contemporary sociologists are more prone to focus on the relations between ethnic and racial groups and the larger social structure than to maintain the focus on explaining prejudice that was dominant in earlier decades. This trend has been spurred by the notion that American society is not, in reality, open to all, nor is it a meritocracy in which individuals are rewarded on the basis of merit rather than on the basis of race, ethnicity, religion, or national origin. In the early 1990's, prominent attention was given to works such as Andrew Hacker's *Two Nations: Black and White, Separate, Hostile, Unequal* (1972), which argue that American society is a dual society divided by race. Such works place emphasis on the notion—implied by Gordon's distinction between cultural and social structure—that regardless of whether individuals change their culture or maintain it, they may not be accepted in American society, particularly if they are people of color. The notion that race, not ethnicity, is the most significant factor emerges strongly in Michael Omi and Howard Winant's *Racial Formation in the U.S.* (1986). Omi and Winant argue that race is a central and persistent feature in American social structure. These types of arguments tend to mitigate against an ongoing commitment to the assimilationist thesis in sociological thought.

Bibliography

Blauner, Robert. *Racial Oppression in America*. New York: Harper & Row, 1972. Influential book criticizing predominant trends in the sociology of race relations, particularly assimilationist theories, and counters their focus on race prejudice with an analysis of racial privilege as embedded in a system of internal colonialism.

Feagin, Joe R., and Clairece Booher Feagin. *Racial and Ethnic Relations*. 6th ed. Upper Saddle River, N.J.: Prentice-Hall, 1999. Introductory text on the sociology of race relations examining sociological theories against the background of extensive case histories of various ethnic and racial groups in the United States. Bibliographies for each group can be found at the end of each chapter.

Gordon, Milton. *Assimilation in American Life*. New York: Oxford University Press, 1964. Assesses previous theories of assimilation and explains his own seven-stage theory of assimilation, distinguishing between cultural and structural assimilation as well as giving three models of assimilation outcomes: Anglo-conformity, the melting pot, and cultural pluralism.

Steinberg, Stephen. *The Ethnic Myth*. New York: Atheneum, 1981. Introductory text on race and ethnic relations. Ethnicity and the contemporary interest in ethnicity are reexamined in terms of the social structure, with a focus on economic institutions. Theories of race relations are presented and reviewed in the light of specific historical cases of racial and ethnic groups.

Wellman, David. *Portraits of White Racism*. New York: Cambridge University Press, 1977. Presents an excellent critique of assimilationist perspectives on race relations, offering his own theory of white racism to counter the notion that prejudice is responsible for discrimination. He then presents case studies based on interviews with white individuals of varied ages and backgrounds to explain the dynamics of white racism.

Sharon Elise

Cross-References

Ethnicity and Ethnic Groups; Immigration and Emigration; Race and Racial Groups; Race Relations: The Race-Class Debate; Racial and Ethnic Stratification; Social Stratification: Analysis and Overview.

CULTURAL NORMS AND SANCTIONS

Type of sociology: Culture
Field of study: Components of culture

Cultural norms are rules or expectations regarding how people should behave; sanctions are rewards or punishments for behaving or not behaving appropriately according to the norms. A variety of sanctions are used by individuals, organizations, and institutions to encourage compliance with their norms. While some sanctions are more effective than others, they generally act to sustain cultural values.

Principal terms

CULTURE: shared knowledge, values, beliefs, norms, and sanctions of a particular group of people

DEVIANCE: violation of cultural norms

INTERNALIZATION OF NORMS: process of making compliance with cultural norms an automatic part of one's personality

LAWS: norms that have been formally included in a written legal code

MULTICULTURAL EDUCATION: educational programs recognizing and showing respect for the cultural diversity within a society

SOCIAL CONTROL: methods used to ensure conformity to cultural norms; these usually include the application of positive and negative sanctions

SOCIALIZATION: social learning process through which people develop their personalities and internalize cultural values and norms

SUBCULTURE: group that shares some values and norms of the dominant culture but that also has its own distinctive values and norms

Overview

When people share cultural norms, they not only have guidelines for their own behavior but also have some ability to predict the behavior of others. Formal norms, usually written rules, and informal norms, or unwritten rules, often are derived from the shared values and beliefs of a society. Sociologists recognize that societies have a large variety of formal sanctions (such as report cards and pay raises) and informal sanctions (such as frowns and praise) to encourage compliance with their norms. A positive sanction is a reward for compliance, while a negative sanction is a punishment for noncompliance.

To understand many of the social controversies within a culturally diverse society such as the United States, it is important to be aware of its different cultures and subcultures as well as of their sometimes conflicting components. Contrary norms exist not only between different cultures but within each culture. Most societies have one dominant culture.

Sociologist Robin M. Williams noted in 1970 that the dominant culture of the United States has between fifteen and twenty core or central values. Other sociologists have pointed out that the core values and related norms in the United States change over time. Interpretations of values also can change.

To see how norms often are derived from a culture's values, four values identified by Williams may be considered: success, progress, freedom, and patriotism. Related norms include the ideas that one should strive to do well in school to become successful later; that the government should support scientific research to help society progress; that citizens should exercise their freedom to vote; and that it is a patriotic duty to rally around the president if the country is threatened with war. An example of a change in the interpretation of a core value is that, in the early years of the United States, freedom to vote included only white men who owned property, so the norm was that only these people were expected to vote.

The most reliable method of ensuring compliance with cultural norms involves the internalization of norms. In other words, people must be taught or socialized in such a way that they automatically want to comply with cultural norms. For example, the norm that students should study hard may be internalized. Initially, the reason a child may study hard could be the expectation of parental praise. Eventually, the child may feel enough self-esteem (an internal sanction) for studying hard that an external sanction, such as parental praise, is no longer necessary to encourage compliance with the norm. If the child occasionally does not comply with the now internalized cultural norm, he or she may feel guilty. Such an unpleasant feeling can be a negative sanction that reinforces the internalized norm. In other words, it could make the child's desire to study hard stronger in the future.

Social groups, organizations, and institutions seek to socialize people into internalizing norms. For example, some people willingly donate money to charity; some people do not cheat when paying taxes. In these cases, charity organizations and the government, respectively, may have successfully convinced them that such uses of their money will make them feel good about themselves.

Such socialization of people is an easier and more reliable method of ensuring norm compliance than either having to provide an external positive sanction each time norm compliance has occurred or applying external negative sanctions after people have violated norms. (It would be extremely difficult for the government to reward people each time they obeyed a law.) Moreover, research has shown that prison sentences (an external negative sanction) often do not convert criminals into law-abiding citizens upon their release from prison. Nevertheless, often people believe, correctly or incorrectly, that external sanctions must be used to force compliance with certain norms. Usually these are norms that are considered especially important to supporting a group's interests, cultural values, and sense of social order.

Norms that are believed to have moral significance to individuals or society, such as "One should not cheat on one's spouse" and "One should not steal," are called mores by social scientists. Sometimes, such mores and other norms considered especially important to a society are codified into laws. The seriousness of the negative sanction or punishment imposed following the violation of a more or a law suggests how important the underlying norm is to the culture. Violating a law resulting in a twenty dollar fine signifies a less significant form of cultural deviance than a crime resulting in a twenty-year prison sentence.

Another type of norm is a folkway. Sociologist William Graham Sumner coined the term "folkway" in his book *Folkways* (1907). Folkways refer to those norms of a cultural group that have little or no moral significance (for example, that one should wear proper clothes to a wedding). Rules of etiquette concerning eating are other examples of folkways. In the United States, for example, it is commonly expected that people place one hand under the table while eating, whereas the folkway in German culture entails placing both hands on the table. Even though parents might consider it very important that children internalize a culture's rules regarding "proper" eating and other "good manners," for most people violations of these and other folkways do not represent an important form of cultural deviance. If external sanctions are imposed at all, they generally will be mild; people might frown if someone wears shorts to a formal wedding, but they would not impose a fine or jail sentence.

Applications

Sociologists have observed how highly authoritarian forms of government ensure compliance with their cultural norms concerning social order: They often apply strong negative sanctions to punish people who violate mores and laws. When Chinese soldiers brutally attacked university students demonstrating in Tiananmen Square in 1989, much of the world was horrified to learn how far the Chinese government would go to reinforce its norms. Killing protestors was the government's approach to preventing others from challenging government rules and regulations.

Sanctioning of cultural norms by more democratic governments can also be severe, as when the National Guard attacked protesting university students at Kent State University in Ohio in 1970. In that case, an agency of the federal government was reacting against those who did not believe that the United States should be fighting a war in Vietnam. Cultural norms embodied in most governmental policies and programs in the United States are promoted through milder sanctions, yet even these can be quite effective in promoting the cultural norms of those in power. Since these norms sometimes clash significantly with the values and norms shared by members of some subcultures in culturally diverse American society, some critics have referred to the government's attempts to enforce compliance with its policies as "social engineering."

For example, educational policies of public schools sometimes become quite controversial because members of an ethnic, political, or religious subculture do not share the cultural norms being promoted by state, federal, or school board policies. While a state policy may require teachers to educate children about sex, some parents believe that sex education should be solely a family responsibility. Other controversies have involved whether students should be required to pledge allegiance to the flag, to learn another language, to have a "moment of silence," to learn evolution, to learn creationism, to celebrate religious holidays, to learn about the history of ethnic groups other than their own, to read certain books, or to be bused to distant schools for the purpose of desegregation.

Governments and school boards have used a variety of negative and positive sanctions in order to force compliance with their policies. If a policy is only a recommendation (say, to raise student awareness about the dangers of drugs), then schools may not experience any negative sanctions for not complying with that policy. Violations of stricter governmental policies, however, have resulted in strong negative sanctions. Examples include cases in which lawsuits were filed against school districts or in which federal troops were called in to force desegregation. On the other hand, positive sanctions come into play when teachers and administrators who comply with cultural norms embodied in state or federal policies are rewarded. For example, schools may receive extra funding for offering drug awareness programs that the government recommends.

Efforts to increase multicultural education in higher education and to increase cultural diversity among university faculty have been resisted by some professors and others in higher education. University or government policies that seek to introduce new norms regarding what should be taught in the classroom or which people should be hired and promoted conflict with some professors' traditional subcultural norms. Generally, professors value academic freedom and independence highly. These values have become embodied in norms such as "We should be able to hire and promote whomever we believe is most qualified to become a professor," and "We should be able to teach whatever we believe is important." Proposed policies calling into question traditional hiring and teaching practices are often seen as outside interference and can be strongly resisted by these professors.

Controversies over traditional versus new cultural norms have resulted in numerous negative sanctions being applied by opposing sides within universities. On some campuses, budget cutbacks have served as a justification for cutting the funding of relatively new multicultural education programs that often employ minority group members. Some professors also have supported "reverse discrimination" lawsuits in instances when they felt forced to hire an affirmative action candidate that the administration selected instead of a white male whom they believed was better qualified. When such negative sanctions are effective in punishing people (or programs) seeking to introduce new cultural values and norms, these sanctions support the traditional norms regarding hiring, promotions, and curricular content. Students are also affected by such actions. They may have fewer opportunities to take multicultural courses, and there may be fewer requirements that they take them.

On the other hand, strong opposition to the norms of the traditionalists also has arisen. For example, negative sanctions have been used against professors resisting change—they may be shunned by some students and colleagues, and letters criticizing them and their views may appear in the press. When powerful administrators of a university have strongly supported new multicultural norms, they have applied positive sanctions to support multicultural programs and personnel. These have included special funding for professors engaged in research promoting multicultural education.

Context

Research about norms and sanctions has been important to analyses of societies ever since sociology became a discipline. Anthropologists and sociologists have long used functionalist theoretical perspectives to analyze how norms, sanctions, and other parts of a culture affect a cultural system and function to meet the needs of the society. Anthropologist Marvin Harris, for example, noted that a seemingly irrational religious norm in India, the taboo against eating beef, actually serves India's impoverished economy well. Cows can more efficiently be used to produce milk and butter, oxen for plows, and manure for fertilizer, fuel, and flooring material than to provide beef to the masses. From this perspective, it would be dysfunctional for India to sanction the eating of beef.

In the 1950's and early 1960's, functionalist approaches dominated sociological analyses of society in the United States. Talcott Parsons, the most prominent American functionalist, explained how major American values and norms function: They maintain the country's social order while serving the needs of the people. For example, when people share the traditional belief that mothers ought to be the main providers of emotional support to family members, then society has an established method of providing emotional support in times of crises.

The views of C. Wright Mills and other conflict theorists who opposed functionalism began to be voiced more widely among sociologists in the United States beginning in the late 1960's. Social scientists and the general public were becoming increasingly aware of ways that the country's relatively powerless people, such as its ethnic and political minorities, were being harmed when values and norms benefiting only those in power were sanctioned by societal institutions such as the government, the economy, the media, and the educational system. Acts of civil disobedience and inner city riots brought attention to the racism built into the country's laws and economic practices. Instead of focusing on how society is held together by common values and norms, conflict theorists pointed to the many conflicting interests and values of people within it. Functionalists, they complained, focused only on the values and norms of the dominant culture.

They also criticized functionalism for being a politically conservative perspective in that it suggested that people who protest against or even criticize the culture of the powerful and its unjust norms are engaging in behavior that is dysfunctional for society. Functionalists were also seen as supporting negative sanctions, such as jail sentences, being used to punish people who violate unjust laws and other norms.

Today, most sociologists in the United States accept certain of the insights of functionalism, such as its recognition of the effects of cultural values, norms, and sanctions on the rest of society. Yet they also recognize the inherent conflicts that exist within a multicultural society and do not assume that positively sanctioning all the values and norms of the dominant culture is functional for the entire society.

Bibliography

Banks, James A. *Multiethnic Education*. 3d ed. Boston: Allyn & Bacon, 1994. Clearly outlines what educators can do to encourage students' appreciation of cultural diversity. For example, the author suggests specific programs that promote respect for the values and norms of students coming from diverse ethnic groups.

Gove, Walter R., ed. *The Labelling of Deviance*. Beverly Hills, Calif.: Sage Publications,

1980. The labeling perspective suggests that violations of cultural norms result in a deviant label mostly for relatively powerless people. Nine articles examine different social reactions for violations of criminal and noncriminal norms.

Lappe, Frances Moore. *Rediscovering America's Values*. New York: Ballantine Books, 1989. Raises probing questions regarding certain American norms derived from such cultural values as choice, opportunity, and responsibility. Especially interesting is the question of how seriously Americans take these values in the light of poverty, illiteracy, hunger, homelessness, and other social problems.

Moffat, Michael. *Coming of Age in New Jersey*. New Brunswick, Conn.: Rutgers University Press, 1989. Highly readable ethnographic study of the subculture of students at a state university. It includes students' own accounts of their values, norms, and sanctions regarding topics of interest to them, including friendships, racism, and sex.

Nuckolls, Charles William. *Culture: A Problem that Cannot Be Solved*. Madison: University of Wisconsin Press, 1998.

Sumner, William Graham. *Folkways*. New York: New American Library, 1960. Sociological classic introducing the concepts of folkways and mores and providing numerous examples of cultural differences. Topics include cannibalism, sexual mores, blood revenge, and primitive justice. Other examples of cultural variation involve norms concerning marriage, sports, drama, and education.

Grace M. Marvin

Cross-References

Culture: Material and Expressive Culture; Culture and Language; Deviance: Analysis and Overview; Deviance: Functions and Dysfunctions; Subcultures and Countercultures; Values and Value Systems.

CULTURAL TRANSMISSION THEORY OF DEVIANCE

Type of sociology: Deviance and social control
Field of study: Theories of deviance

Cultural transmission theory postulates that deviance is sociologically transmitted from one generation to the next when communities or neighborhoods develop cultural traditions and values that tolerate or encourage deviant conduct and rule breaking. This theory offers explanations of why some communities persist in having high rates of deviance, such as crime and delinquency.

Principal terms

CULTURE: total way of life, consisting of values, beliefs, norms, and modes of conduct

NORMS: social rules of a society or group; they include both formal laws and informal customs

SOCIAL CONTROL: formal and informal techniques used by society and groups to regulate conduct

SOCIAL DISORGANIZATION: breakdown in the social control system that regulates behavior

SOCIALIZATION: process by which a person is molded into a social being through learning the values and norms of society

SUBCULTURAL THEORIES OF DEVIANCE: a group of theories that use subcultures as a medium for explaining deviance; for example, delinquent gangs or drug subcultures

SUBCULTURE: group that holds different values, beliefs, norms, and behavior from those of the dominant culture; for example, ethnic, age, or social class groups, drug subcultures, and delinquent gangs

Overview

Cultural transmission theory, which is an outgrowth of studies of urban crime and delinquency, is given its most systematic statement by sociologists Clifford R. Shaw and Henry D. McKay. The central tenet of cultural transmission theory is that deviance can be passed down from generation to generation because of community traditions and values that are either permissive toward or supportive of violating conventional rules of conduct, including criminal laws.

According to cultural transmission theory, in communities in which traditions that are permissive toward deviance have become relatively fixed over time, children are socialized into deviance by learning values and beliefs that tolerate or condone violating conventional rules. Even though the residential population in the community may change over time, deviant behavior patterns persist, to the extent that these subcultural traditions and values remain. Thus, cultural transmission asserts that deviance not only can be sociologically inherited from one generation to the next but also persists in a community after the succession of new residents.

Some communities or neighborhoods are more likely than others to develop subcultural traditions that tolerate deviance and law breaking. This is especially true of inner-city districts, which are often transition areas for ethnic groups and immigrants. Rapid changes in residential composition can lead to community difficulties in adjusting to the diversity of cultural backgrounds. An influx of new businesses and industry can also introduce disruptive elements by bringing in new workers and by radically altering the social and physical environment of a community. These changes can create value conflicts and otherwise weaken informal, as well as formal, social controls. Thus, if a community is unable to accommodate these changes, social controls break down. This process is called social disorganization. When a community does not function effectively as a medium of social control, deviance becomes tolerated, if not accepted, and community residents become more susceptible to deviant behavior patterns.

The rationale of cultural transmission theory is best illustrated by Shaw and McKay, who investigated variations in crime and delinquency rates over a fifty-year period in metropolitan Chicago. In their books *Social Factors in Juvenile Delinquency* (1931) and *Juvenile Delinquency and Urban Areas* (1942), Shaw and McKay observed that delinquency rates vary widely by neighborhood. The highest rates tend to be nearest the central business and industrial districts, decreasing as one moves from the city center to the edge of the city. Although the racial and ethnic composition in high delinquency areas changed almost completely over a period of several decades, delinquency rates remained virtually unchanged. These "delinquency areas" tend to be characterized by physical deterioration, economic insecurity, family disintegration, conflicting cultural standards, and little concerted action by the community residents to solve common problems. Shaw and McKay interpreted these phenomena as symptoms of social disorganization.

Shaw and McKay also observed that when communities went into decline, more prosperous families would relocate as soon as it was feasible to other neighborhoods or suburban areas. This had the effect of intensifying social disorganization, since the remaining ethnic groups were often slow to integrate into the community. Because family socialization patterns are also undermined by social disorganization, which promotes family disharmony and frustration, the play and peer groups of juveniles take on new social meaning by offering order to their daily lives. This process creates social circumstances that give rise to delinquent gangs. When these gang subcultures become rooted in the community, successive generations of children are socialized to norms that encourage delinquent behavior.

In his books *The Jack-roller: A Delinquent Boy's Own Story* (1930), *The Natural History of a Delinquent Career* (1931), and *Brothers in Crime* (1938), Shaw examined three case studies of juvenile delinquents that trace how delinquency is socially transmitted and how youngsters are socialized into deviant conduct. Differential association theory, proposed by sociologist and criminologist Edwin H. Sutherland, offers a more precise statement of this socialization process by specifying how criminal, delinquent, or deviant behaviors are learned. In this respect, cultural transmission and differential association are closely related.

A variation of cultural transmission can also be seen in subcultural theories—a group of theories that emerged beginning in the 1950's. Subcultural theories of deviance, most of which focus on explaining crime and delinquency, are based on the assumption that people are socialized into the values and norms of the groups to which they belong. If the immediate values and norms are at odds with the dominant culture, the resulting behaviors may be deviant, even illegal. Thus, subcultures are the medium for transmitting deviant values and beliefs. Subcultural theories have been developed to explain violence, sexual deviance, drug addiction, and other forms of deviance.

Applications

Cultural transmission theory, together with related subcultural theories of deviance, has had a major impact on both scholarly and lay thinking about the causes of crime, delinquency, and other forms of deviance. In a general sense, cultural transmission theory has helped to sensitize the public, community leaders, and policy makers to the social problems that come from neighborhoods that fall into decline. The works of Shaw and McKay point to reasons that the quality of community life must be protected and enhanced by carefully planned and implemented social policies and programs.

Informed by the concepts of cultural transmission and the results of his research studies, Shaw took an active part in shaping programs in slum neighborhoods that could restore natural social controls within the community and that could reduce crime and delinquency. In 1932 he began the Chicago Area Project, which established twenty-two neighborhood centers in six areas of Chicago. Shaw used committees of local residents instead of an outside or centralized staff to control community center activities. Members of the neighborhood were employed as staff. His project was a pioneering effort in using theory and research to inform the design and implementation of community-based programs in which local residents themselves play active, often leading roles in protecting their welfare and in enhancing the quality of neighborhood life. Tenant organizations in public housing projects that confront the classic ills of slum neighborhoods, such as crime, delinquency, narcotics trafficking, and prostitution, are extensions of the concepts of community involvement and democratic decision-making that Shaw advocated and implemented in the Chicago Area Project. In addition to reducing community problems, participation in these activities rejuvenates interest among residents in safeguarding the welfare of their community. Shaw and McKay's work can be seen as contributing to an American tradition of empowering people to solve their own problems as well as an example of tapping the knowledge and insights of local residents to develop policies and programs for themselves and their communities.

The logic of cultural transmission and its corollary, subcultural theories, is also connected to delinquency prevention programs. For example, if local cultural traditions and delinquent subcultures function to socialize youngsters to delinquent values and to encourage deviant conduct, then programs that neutralize or disrupt this socialization process are potentially useful as preventive measures. Historically, this rationale has been popular in many government and community prevention programs. Such programs have tried to redirect delinquent gang behaviors into constructive activities. This approach, extensively utilized in Chicago, Boston, New York, and Los Angeles, uses well-trained street workers who establish relationships with gang leaders and organize their members into clubs; they provide opportunities for recreation and access to jobs and education.

A similar rationale can also be seen in the numerous government-funded and privately funded drug education programs. By educating children (particularly those growing up in communities with a firmly established drug subculture) to the social and personal consequences of drug use, programs can help to neutralize the subcultural forces that attract young people to drugs in peer group settings.

Implications of Shaw and McKay's cultural transmission theory and of their analyses of crime and delinquency in communities suggest that the stability of neighborhoods, especially those in transition, can be fragile. Shaw and McKay recognized that the expansion of industry and business disrupts the social stability of surrounding neighborhoods as well as the social controls that promote conformity among residents. Although their Chicago Area Project focused on curbing delinquency, rather than on empowering the community to protect itself from invasions by business and industry, their work pointed to the importance of designing sound local government and zoning policies to safeguard the quality of residential life.

Sociologist Clifford R. Shaw believed that crime and delinquency in slum neighborhoods could be reduced by introducing programs that would restore natural social controls within the community. *(Library of Congress)*

Context

Cultural transmission theory is closely tied to a school of sociological thought and to an approach to the study of social life that began in 1914 at the University of Chicago's Department of Sociology. Often called the Chicago school by sociologists, it was led by Robert Park, who had previously been a Chicago newspaper reporter and had investigated social conditions in the city for twenty-five years. Park borrowed ideas from the field of ecology, a branch of biology in which animals and plants are studied in relation to one another and to their natural habitat. Park reasoned that there is also an ecology to the organization of human communities. Using concepts such as "symbiosis," which refers to how organisms of different species can live together to their mutual benefit, he formed a theory of human ecology.

This theory became a dominant intellectual influence that shaped the scholarly thinking and research conducted by University of Chicago sociologists for the next fifty years. In 1928, Ernest W. Burgess, guided by Park's concepts of human ecology, pointed out that there are patterns of ecological growth in cities. Cities, he noted, not only grow around their edges but also have a tendency to expand radially from the center in concentric circles. This pattern can be likened to the circles created by a rock that is tossed into a still pond. Each circle gradually expands outward. Burgess observed that social life and activities differed in each concentric zone or circle. Zone 1, for example, was the central business district; zone 2, an area of transition with typically poor families and ever-changing by expanding businesses from zone 1. Zone 3 was typically working-class neighborhoods and was followed by residential and commuter zones. This viewpoint of city growth clearly influenced Shaw and McKay, who in 1945 advanced a different concentric-zone model of the city.

At the time Shaw began his work in the 1920's, the United States was engulfed in a crime wave because of resistance to the Eighteenth Amendment (Prohibition), which outlawed the manufacture and distribution of alcoholic beverages. Crime and delinquency problems were particularly severe in Chicago. Shaw, who worked as a probation and parole officer, believed that the delinquency problem was attributable to juveniles' detachment from conventional groups. After his appointment to the Institute for Juvenile Research in Chicago, Shaw developed a plan to study delinquency, using Park's human ecology theory to guide his work. Later joined by McKay, his research used court records to pinpoint the residences of delinquents. Using "zone maps," the two were able to identify problem neighborhoods and to compare prevalence of delinquency by zones. Because not all youths in problem neighborhoods were in court records, Shaw also compiled extensive life histories from juvenile delinquents to ascertain influences from their social environments.

Other theories, such as differential association and subcultural theories of crime and deviance, utilize frameworks and concepts that are related to cultural transmission theory. Nevertheless, Shaw and McKay's work can be set apart from most theories of deviance in that their ideas and research findings served in part as a blueprint for a specific community program—the Chicago Area Project.

Bibliography

Cohen, Albert K. *Delinquent Boys: The Culture of the Gang*. New York: Free Press, 1955. Classic theory of delinquent gangs and subculture that links the theories of Émile Durkheim and Robert K. Merton to elements of the work of Shaw, McKay, and Sutherland. This book is relatively easy reading for those with an elementary background in sociology or criminology.

Jack-roller, the, Jon Snodgrass, et al. *Jack-roller at Seventy*. Lexington, Mass.: Lexington Books, 1982. Written shortly before the Jack-roller's death and long after Shaw's death in 1957, this book completes the story begun in Shaw's 1930 book *The Jack-roller*. It also contains additional sections on related issues written by James Short, Gilbert Geis, and Solomon Kobrin.

Shaw, Clifford R. *The Jack-roller: A Delinquent Boy's Own Story*. Introduced by Howard S. Becker. Reprint. Chicago: University of Chicago Press, 1966. First published in 1930, this is a case study of a jack-roller—a thief or "mugger" who commits personal robbery—that has come to be a classic in sociology. Shaw traces the subject's life history so that readers can see the influences shaping his life and his delinquent career. The study provides evidence presumed to support cultural transmission theory.

Shaw, Clifford R., and Henry D. McKay. *Juvenile Delinquency and Urban Areas*. Rev. ed. Chicago: University of Chicago Press, 1969. Revised edition of Shaw and McKay's original 1942 book reporting findings from their study of crime and delinquency in Chicago. The authors identify variations in delinquency rates by city districts, using zone maps of the city to plot data. The book contains an excellent introduction by James Short that addresses the significance and impact of Shaw and McKay's work. Contains a useful bibliography.

Symposium on Juvenile Delinquency, University of Chicago, 1972. *Delinquency, Crime, and Society*. Edited by James F. Short, Jr. Chicago: University of Chicago Press, 1976. Essays summarizing and discussing the contributions of Shaw and McKay, with special emphasis on their delinquency area studies, the Chicago Area Project, and cultural transmission theory. This book also discusses Shaw and McKay's importance within the University of Chicago research tradition. Recommended for those with at least a moderate background in sociology. Contains a useful bibliography.

Vold, George B., and Thomas J. Bernard. *Theoretical Criminology*. 4th ed. New York: Oxford University Press, 1998. Chapter 10, "The Ecology of Crime," includes a discussion of Shaw and McKay's research work and cultural transmission theory; also see chapter 11, "Strain Theories," for summaries of subcultural theories. Recommended for students. Contains a good bibliography.

Gerald R. Garrett

Cross-References

Anomie and Deviance; Deviance: Analysis and Overview; Deviance: Functions and Dysfunctions; Structural-Strain Theory of Deviance.

CULTURE
Material and Expressive Culture

Type of sociology: Culture
Field of study: Components of culture

The material and expressive products of culture are valuable resources for sociologists interested in different social groups and in the processes of social and cultural definitions. Material culture is the physical manifestation of a society; it includes, among other things, works of art, the ways people produce and process food, and ritual objects of various sorts.

Principal terms

AESTHETICS: the critical study of the creation, appreciation, and philosophy of the beautiful

CULTURAL MATERIALISM: a controversial anthropological explanation of human behavior developed by Marvin Harris

CULTURAL STUDIES/CRITICISM: theoretical and methodological perspective which treats all cultural products as symbolic "texts"

CULTURE: socially transmitted rules for human behavior involving both physical and mental processes

EXPRESSIVE CULTURE: cultural products which are created to communicate emotion, transmit social information, or satisfy some physical need; usually given meaning in some public context within different taste cultures

MATERIAL CULTURE: tangible, usually everyday, objects whose production, variation, use, and forms may be investigated across time and space

Overview

The terms "material culture" and "expressive culture" are rather cumbersome phrases for elements of society and culture which are produced by human hands and illustrate the powerful connection between physical objects and human behavior. Other collective nouns often used for such products are "objects," "things," and "artifacts." "Artifact," however, often contains an unspoken assumption of artistic value or merit. Visual and decorative arts, architecture, literature, and film are all examples of artistic expressions which have traditionally been the interest of aestheticians and scholars of the humanities. The modern Western idea of art—sometimes called "art with a capital 'A' "—is essentially a bourgeois concept, derived from a strong emphasis on individualism. It emphasizes the expression and reception of pleasure in ways that often illustrate hierarchical social relationships. As a result, much of the study of expressive culture has depended on, or reflected, specific classification systems and power structures rather than examining the values that artifacts and objects have for individuals or groups in society.

The study of art from a social science perspective demands concepts and methods that are value-neutral. Therefore, the definitions of the terms "expressive culture" and "material culture" may be more flexible and broad, and less bound by artificial distinctions, than one might originally expect. Particularly in the social sciences, the term "material culture" is often used as an umbrella term—as a general term for the products (material and expressive) of culture and society that illustrate the process by which form is given to conceptual thought.

Careful and informed study leads to consideration of the complicated interactions that take place among creators, audiences, and their cultures. Artifacts and things reveal social and creative processes which illustrate continuities and differences both among people and their societies and among cultures across time and space. Material and expressive culture can be studied as records that provide valuable information about people's lives, ideas, attitudes, and behaviors.

Objects reflect and influence the mental constructs intrinsic to culture. No things exist in vacuums; all are parts of systems. Therefore, the creation and exploitation of artifacts leave a kind of cultural "fingerprint" which a researcher can use to organize a comprehensive picture of social life and meaning. Each member of society makes or uses objects of different sorts. Through these activities, human beings surround themselves with objects which conform to individual and social identities, requirements, and desires. Individuals use accessible resources and technologies and adapt them as circumstance and custom dictate. Investigation of how people define their aesthetics and display their artistic efforts, how they organize the world around them, and how they develop and manifest their attitudes and beliefs about their environment, both natural and social, allows researchers to both record behaviors and infer their meanings.

The cultural worlds in which people live are both individually and socially constructed. People are socialized to the rules and requirements of their environments, but they also repeatedly revisit and rediscover the world on their own. Expressive artifacts—including art, architecture, crafts, clothing, and foods—act as records and symbols of the tangible and intangible relationships of cultural life. The most significant quality of things is their physicality, their concreteness. People tend to associate objects with certain time periods and experiences, particular social groups and situations, and specific locations and landscapes. Material and expressive cultures, then, reveal the connection between the mind and behavior, between goods and social and political life, and between individuals and society.

As elements of social systems, things are accessories to group memories and affiliations; they make the connections between people tangible and external. Artifacts can give the past a physical reality in the present, embodying events, people, and values central to the social group. Things can function as social bonds; gifts, for example, indebt the receiver to the giver.

Things also embody ideologies. Physical and expressive cultural artifacts can convince or convert. Artifacts give ideas, attitudes, and social experiences compelling and tangible presences in people's lives. Things help people place themselves in a broad spectrum of social, ideological, and economic categories. Things can symbolize an individual's sense of place in the world by embodying status, taste, and attitudes. In important and significant ways, people are what they make, own, use, and see.

Applications

The study of material culture combines the insights of several disciplines, including art, architectural, and decorative arts history; cultural anthropology; archaeology; folk life studies; cultural geography; and social and cultural history. Ethnography and archaeology are both sociological subdisciplines which, perhaps because of their connections to the humanities, have traditionally dealt with material cultural processes and products.

Material culture needs to be understood both in its "natural" context and in relationship to its makers and users. Material and expressive cultural objects are more than artifacts, they are conduits to the connections between human existence and expression. Things inform the study of people and their constructed realities. Thus, researchers in material culture look for universals; at the same time, they note patterns and preferences peculiar to an individual or group.

Generally, material culture study emphasizes group commonalities such as ethnicity, race, religion, region, and occupation. People generally use objects in planned ways that express group identities situationally. The researcher in material culture collects and interprets objects and artifacts peculiar to a group in order to examine the durability and vigor of particular groups. Folklife studies often include racial and ethnic material culture. For example, Robert Thomas Teske's "Living Room Furnishings, Ethnic Identities, and Acculturation Among Greek-Philadelphians" (1979) surveyed living room and parlor furniture and accessories as indicators of assimilation into mainstream American life. In another example, Mihalyi Csikszentmihalyi and Eugene Rochberg-Halton, behavioral scientists at the University of Chicago, developed a survey, interviewed people about their furnishings and special mementos, and collected their findings in an important book, *The Meaning of Things: Domestic Symbols and Self* (1981).

Material culture related to one's job, age, or sex has been given less attention than that of folk, ethnic, or racial groups. One important and suggestive work in this area is Lizabeth A. Cohen's article "Embellishing a Life of Labor: An Interpretation of the Material Culture of American Working-Class Homes, 1885-1915" (1980). Cohen is a historian interested in the everyday social (rather than political or occupational) lives of working-class Americans. This article uses domestic settings and the objects in them to document the lives of a group who left little in the way of standard historical documents. Cohen's conclusions are an elegant melding of sociological theories, social historical perspectives, and material culture studies methodology.

Understanding and investigating artifacts and objects as part of a society's culture has had significant impact on scholars of the sociology of art as well as on students of material culture. Vera L. Zolberg, in *Constructing a Sociology of the Arts* (1990), illustrates the primary importance of contextualizing art in terms of time and space, both in a general sense and in a specific way, so that training, rewards, institutional norms, and support systems are taken into account. Her argument enlarges the meaning and importance of expressive and material culture objects by keeping them at the theoretical center of a research problem while acknowledging that they are parts of larger sociocultural networks.

It is in this area that material culture study and sociological study of the institutions and artifacts of the arts offer their greatest contributions to students of the social sciences. Material and expressive culture objects can provide researchers with rich sources of information about social life, depending on the combination of purposes and perceptions that are brought to them. Objects may hold many meanings, depending on where they are, who uses them, and who looks at them. Objects represent meanings and ideas, processes and behaviors, and statements about culture and society.

Context

Because material and expressive artifacts are the result of human motives and activities, they are extremely useful in the study of human life and society. Particularly since the 1960's, scholars in a variety of disciplines have discovered the power of artifacts as subjects of and tools for research. Studying things enhances traditional areas of inquiry such as history; interest in physical and expressive artifacts has also given researchers new insights into the lives of ordinary people and nonliterate cultures, the subtle workings of the mind, and the social significance of materialism.

Individuals and groups whose experiences are not recorded through written records can be accessed through their material and expressive culture. For such groups as the working class, the poor, women, and people of color, artifacts, no matter how modest, are important resources for historians and scholars. In the 1960's, historiography underwent a significant change under the influence of what came to be called the "new social history," whose primary interest was including ordinary people in the historical record.

Structuralism and semiotics were also developed in the 1960's, as scholars in a variety of disciplines were influenced by new theories and methods in anthropology and linguistics. From these perspectives, artifacts can be investigated to gain insights into how the human mind works. As products of thought, artifacts can provide links between the internal structures of the mind and the external constructions of the world. Visual thinking, while most highly developed in artists, designers, and architects, is a modality common to all human beings. One of the best ways to understand it is through the study of the products of visual thought. Meaning resides not in things themselves but in the minds of the people who create them.

Things, in and of themselves, however, do shed light on materialism. In a materialistic society, things are an end in themselves. For example, in American society, goods have a heightened significance, and the American Dream is tied to a life filled with material abundance. Things are central to such a system, and the only way to understand its functionings and symbolism is through examination of its significant objects.

Yet sociologists have spent much less time and effort investigating material or expressive culture than they have on many other subfields of sociology. This may be largely attributable to a historic tension between sociology and the humanities, which have been seen as the "natural" custodian of art studies. There have been slow but steady developments in the sociology of the arts since the 1960's, probably as a result of the growth of interdisciplinary studies, theories, and methods since the end of World War II. While some of this change may be attributed to a realization that the arts must be understood and studied within a social context, this change in attitude may also reflect an increase in the status of the arts in American society.

Arguably one of the most important developments in the sociology of the arts was the publication of a collection of essays entitled *The Sociology of Art and Literature: A Reader* (1970). Although intended as a classroom text, the anthology also promoted an institutional approach. Each of the book's three editors contributed an important essay. Milton C. Albrecht introduced the reader to the idea of art as an institution, expanding the meanings of the term "art" to include visual, musical, and literary products. James H. Barnett reprinted his synthetic essay of 1958, "The Sociology of Art." Mason Griff, drawing on his empirical study of art students in Chicago, presented an important and creative article on the recruitment and socialization of artists.

Beginning in the 1970's, the sociology of art began to solidify its disciplinary base and to formalize its theories and methods. Increasing sociological interest in the mass media, popular culture and arts, and visual communication contributed to a period of growth and activity. The production of culture became an issue of concern to sociologists, and material and expressive objects became increasingly significant to sociological research. The meaning of things began to be reevaluated in such works as Marvin Harris's *Cultural Materialism: The Struggle for a Science of Culture* (1980), and the symbolic importance of artifacts began to be defined by their environments and the changing circumstances in which they played a part rather than by their physical properties alone.

There is no real consensus as to the "meaning" of art, and therefore there is no consistency to definitions of the sociology of art. Perhaps because the field is still open to influences and insights from various other disciplines, the social sciences have much to offer to the study and understanding of the material and expressive elements of culture. As the barriers between traditionally humanistic and social scientific methods and theories weaken and blend, the study of material and expressive culture will continue to be a rich resource for a variety of approaches, including the sociological.

Bibliography

Albrecht, Milton C., James H. Barnett, and Mason Griff, eds. *The Sociology of Art and Literature: A Reader*. New York: Praeger, 1970. Early but still significant resource. Divided into six subject sections: artists, distribution and reward systems, forms and styles, history and theory, methodology, and tastemakers and publics.

Becker, Howard S. *Art Worlds*. Berkeley: University of California Press, 1982. Seminal theoretical work on art as collective action.

Chilton, Elizabeth S., ed. *Material Meanings: Critical Approaches to the Interpretation of Material Culture*. Salt Lake City: University of Utah Press, 1999.

Cohen, Lizabeth A. "Embellishing a Life of Labor: An Interpretation of the Material Culture of American Working-Class Homes, 1885-1915." *Journal of American Culture* 3-4 (Winter, 1980): 752-775. A social history that uses material culture to discover patterns of sociability and social identity in the urban working class at the beginning of the twentieth century.

Csikszentmihalyi, Mihalyi, and Eugene Rochberg-Halton. *The Meaning of Things: Domestic Symbols and Self*. New York: Cambridge University Press, 1981. Unusual and interesting look at material objects in the home and their meanings for their users from a behavioral point of view.

Foster, Arnold W., and Judith R. Blau, eds. *Art and Society: Readings in the Sociology of the Arts*. Albany: State University of New York Press, 1989. Well-executed collection of essays showing the range of subjects and approaches in the field.

Gowans, Alan. *Reading the Visible Past: Social Function in the Arts*. Ann Arbor: UMI Research Press, 1990. Entertaining, informative examination of social contexts in the visual arts and architecture by an iconoclastic art historian and scholar.

Harris, Marvin. *Cultural Materialism: The Struggle for a Science of Culture*. New York: Vintage Books, 1980. Provocative and controversial work of cultural anthropology which applies Darwin's biological theories to cultural evolution in combination with Marx's ideas about a cultural dialectic, materialism, and social evolution.

Schlereth, Thomas J., ed. *Material Culture Studies in America*. Nashville, Tenn.: American Association for State and Local History, 1982. Excellent introductory text, with a fine essay on the history of material culture studies in the United States and essays by practitioners arranged as statements about theory, method, and practice.

Teske, Robert T. "Living Room Furnishings, Ethnic Identity, and Acculturation Among Greek-Philadelphians." *New York Folklore* 5, nos. 1-2 (1979): 21-31. An ethnic material study that demonstrates the positive results the method can offer to careful practitioners.

Zolberg, Vera L. *Constructing a Sociology of the Arts*. New York: Cambridge University Press, 1990. Unusual methodology and a cogent statement of theory enliven this study of patrons, patronage, and avant-garde art forms.

Jackie R. Donath

Cross-References

Cultural Norms and Sanctions; Culture and Language; Socialization: The Mass Media; Subcultures and Countercultures; Values and Value Systems.

CULTURE AND LANGUAGE

Type of sociology: Culture
Field of study: Components of culture

Culture and the language that expresses it are intertwined to such a degree that no one has yet been able to determine which has more influence over the other. The debate continues regarding whether a culture's perception and ordering of the world is determined by its language or whether a culture's language is solely a result of the way the society orders its world.

Principal terms

CULTURE: human traditions and customs that are transmitted through learning between generations; the learned and shared beliefs of a society

DIALECT: variety or subset of a language used by a group of speakers set off socially or geographically from the main or original body of the speakers of that language; a dialect may or may not be intelligible to other speakers of the parent language

ETHNOLINGUISTICS: the study of the relationship between a language and the cultural behavior of the speakers of that language

HONORIFICS: linguistic markers that signal respect toward the addressee

JARGON: specialized vocabulary or means of speech specific to a particular group or activity

LANGUAGE: in this work, verbal symbolic communication including a vocabulary and system for its use; language is symbolic in that the sound representing an item or idea is not necessarily related to that item or idea

LINGUISTICS: the study of human speech, including the units of which the language is made as well as its grammatical structure and history

NATIVE LANGUAGE: that language acquired by a person during the early years of development, which is that person's first language of thought and communication

SOCIETY: organized life in groups, especially among humans; members of a society generally share the same cultural characteristics

Overview

Language and culture are expressions of the world that are found in all societies. The nature of their interrelationship and influence on each other is not easily grasped. For the social scientist, the study of language within a culture is a means of looking at that culture's social structure and interpersonal relationships, since it is language that expresses the various aspects of culture, such as labeling, kinship, actions, and beliefs.

The terms "language" and "dialect" are often used interchangeably, although such usage is inaccurate. A language is a communication system that may include a number of variations, known as dialects. In this work, the term "language" will be used to indicate the spoken communication of a cultural group.

Language is the means by which most human thought is communicated. Also, much of social and cultural behavior is expressed by the means of the spoken word. Language is a cultural universal: It appears in all cultures throughout the world. Within each language are universals: greetings, farewells, formal language, and politeness. Language is an oral expression of concrete forms that also carries symbolic meaning; what one says may not be what one means. Thus, in addition to naming the world, language expresses relationships among things. This means that although a word such as "tomorrow" may be translatable from one language to another, it may not have the same meaning in both languages. In one, "tomorrow" may mean "the next day," while in another "tomorrow" may mean "some time in the future."

Culture is the overt and covert expression of the behavior and beliefs of a group of people. It is expressed in the traditions and customs of that people. It includes but is not limited to knowledge of the physical world, beliefs and rituals, moral direction, law, and artistic expression, including graphic arts, dance, music, and so forth. One of the most important aspects of culture is that it gives order to the world in which its participants live. Colors, actions, kinship, and familial relationships are all a part of culture. These relationships are expressed by language, although they may be expressed differently in each cultural setting. In one setting, cats and snakes may be grouped together, since both have similar eye types, large mouths with fangs, and slithery bodies, and both make hissing sounds. In another setting, there may be no relationship between the two creatures.

Language, as a means of communication, has a twofold role in a society. Language is a source of information about a culture and a society (it shows how a group of people label the world), and it is a means by which members of a society socialize or interact. Linguist Irving M. Copi discusses the three basic functions of language within a culture as being, first, to communicate information; second, to express emotion (to communicate feelings); and third, to give commands or requests. He states that these three groups of expression are not necessarily mutually exclusive. The interaction that is facilitated by language use enables individuals in a society to work together more effectively and eases social pressure.

The nature of the relationship between language and culture is not entirely understood. Ronald Wardhaugh has suggested at least four possible correlations of language and culture: (1) social structure may influence linguistic structure (for example, there may be gender-based differences in speech); (2) linguistic structure may determine social structure (it is the language itself, not the speakers of the language, that is gender-biased); (3) language and societal influences are bidirectional—that is, they may influence each other; (4) there is no relationship between language and culture. Most ethnolinguistic studies have eliminated the possibility that the last relationship is valid. They hold that there must be some relationship between language and culture. The remaining correlations are fuel for debate among ethnolinguists. Preceding Wardhaugh, Benjamin Whorf (1897-1941), an insurance adjuster turned linguist, pursued the idea that language had the greater effect on culture. He proposed that the world is experienced differently by different language communities and that these differences are caused by different cognitive associations as expressed by the language.

During the 1960's and 1970's, British sociologist Basil Bernstein suggested that although the relationship of language and culture is reciprocal, culture has the greater influence on language. According to this theory, it would be the speakers of the language, not the language, who were gender-biased.

The study of the relationship between language and culture is valuable in leading to an understanding of the cognitive processes of various societies. Since each language is the medium by which its speakers express their organization of the world, each language system must be equally valid. One language is not "better" than another. Each language is valid because it expresses complex relationships in the world of its speakers. The "simple, primitive" language does not exist.

Applications

Language has many functions within each culture. It is the primary means of the retrieval of sociocultural knowledge for each group. Language is also the agent of socialization within a culture, teaching each member his or her place within that society. In addition, language is used as an agent of power, distinguishing social rank, which is slightly different from simply socialization. Finally, as world communication develops and languages become less isolated, language planning is coming into prominence as a means of adaptation to increasing lingual and cultural encounters.

A child in any society usually grasps the main aspects of the primary language before the age of five years. The babbling of infants includes the sounds of many human languages, some of which do not occur in the language of the child's family or society. Positive reinforcement encourages the child to continue certain sounds and delete others from the babbling repertoire. Later learning extends to grammar, meaning, and symbolism. All this is achieved without formal instruction.

Language, however, is not culturally bound. A person is not born with a genetic tendency to speak a language. A person of Yakima Indian ancestry does not "naturally" speak the Sahaptin language. If he or she has learned English as a primary language, his or her genetic structure does not make the learning of Sahaptin any easier.

The sociocultural knowledge of a group includes not only daily instructional activities but also the more subtle communication of humor, slang, figures of speech, proverbs, and so forth. An American child who is not fully enculturated into English-speaking society may not understand figures of speech. A child relating a made-up story to an adult while sitting on the adult's lap may be told, "You're pulling my leg." The child may reply, "No, I'm not. I'm sitting on your lap." The same difficulty exists with proverbs. Although a Westerner might understand the Arabic proverb "one bird in the hand is better than ten on a tree," he or she might find it more difficult to understand the proverb "he does not know the difference between an 'alif' and a minaret."

In addition to rules of grammar, a child learns the appropriate social use of language, including his or her place in society. Often this relationship is indicated by "honorifics." Honorifics include terms of address to others that vary by gender, age, and family position, and terms that indicate social distance to those persons outside one's family. In English, social distance is indicated, for example, by the use of Mr., Mrs., and Ms. in combination with the surname of the addressee. A person addressing a close acquaintance would generally use a given name or nickname to identify the person. Social distance may be maintained by persons of differing age groups, social status, duration of acquaintance, or kinship. In Spanish and other languages, other formal terms of address are used in addition to a formal or informal version of the language. A person of high social status may speak to a person of lower social status in the familiar form of address (for example, *tu* in Spanish), while the person of lower status must speak to a superior in the formal form (*usted* in Spanish). As one increases in age and/or social status, one's linguistic patterns change in accordance with the culture's standards.

While power as expressed in verbal communication in society may be related to social distance and rank, it also has a broader application. Language as a means of social power occurs in groups that use "jargon," or a specialized vocabulary or way of speaking. Black English is sometimes included in such a category; persons outside the "in" group may not be able to understand what is being said. Even more frequent are those terms used by particular academic or business groups. Many computer-illiterate people have walked into a computer store and been overwhelmed by the "bits," "bytes," and other technical terms that are used with ease by the computer professional. Other professional groups with specialized vocabularies include physicians, lawyers, academics in various fields, and religious professionals. A visit to a physician, attorney, or cleric can be particularly intimidating, since these individuals not only use language specific to their training but also have power by virtue of their positions.

As a result of increasing world communication and the demise of language isolation, language planning is becoming a concern in many societies. Language planning is not a new idea. The inception of the "dictionary" was an early attempt at planning that resulted in some degree of standardization of spelling and pronunciation. As modern technology becomes widespread, the sharing of words between societies introduces ideas that are foreign to the adopting culture. For example, ethnolinguist George Herzog has noted terms used to describe a car among the Pima Indians of Arizona before 1941. The automobile is described with a Pima term meaning "moves by itself." The pistons are "arms," the wheels are "legs," and the tires are "shoes." As new technological vocabularies were introduced from the West to Japan, Western theories and technologies were included. Philosophies and relationships alien to the Japanese culture were included in these vocabularies—ideas that could not be expressed within the Japanese language. In order to communicate, the Japanese language had to be changed to include words and expressions that were able to incorporate the new technologies.

As language and culture interact, it is possible to see language as a means of ordering culture in the areas of knowledge acquisition, societal roles, and power. Language also functions adaptively as a means of assimilating new ideas and technologies.

Context

The question of the interrelatedness of language and culture has been debated since at least the eighteenth century. During the late 1700's, two German scholars considered this problem. Johann Gottfried von Herder declared that the origin of language is in human nature and that knowledge is possible only through language. Wilhelm von Humboldt stated that the character and structure of a language expresses culture and individuality, and that people perceive the world through language.

During the late nineteenth century, the Swiss linguist Ferdinand de Saussure asserted that language was a product of culture and that the individual was a passive participant in an established language system. Saussure maintained that language was immutable and not subject to change. The next great sociolinguist was Edward Sapir, who is considered to be the founder of the field of ethnolinguistics. He was influenced in his thinking by both Wilhelm von Humboldt and the noted anthropologist Franz Boas. Sapir proposed that human perception of the world occurs mainly through language. This explains the diverse behavior among people of different cultural backgrounds. Sapir's most noted student was Benjamin Whorf, a fire-prevention inspector for an insurance company. Whorf's experiences in "habitual thought," or word patterns that lead people to act in a certain fashion, caused him to question these word patterns. He proposed that humans see and hear and experience the world in a given way because the language habits of the community predispose certain choices of interpretation.

Concurrently, but separately from Sapir and Whorf, the Soviet linguist V. N. Volosinov developed very similar views about the interconnectedness of language and culture.

Following Sapir and Whorf, Noam Chomsky asserted that language is a universal innate facility. He produced some seminal works in the field of ethnolinguistics (*Reflections on Language*, 1975). More recently, British sociologist Basil Bernstein has been interested in the role of language in the socialization process. He examines the ways in which members of various social groups develop language dialects as a means of communicating with one another. He suggests that it is culture that has the greater effect on language.

Ethnolinguistics seems to be moving toward a concern for language planning and political correctness as they affect the identity of citizens and society. The trend toward linguistic and cultural pluralism can be seen in the demise of the Soviet Union and Czechoslovakia and the rise of ethnic (and linguistic) states. Issues of bilingual education—the adoption of English as the official language in the United States, the use of French in Quebec, the acknowledgment of formerly low-status languages in Africa—are coming to the fore as studies in ethnolinguistics. Such issues as these affect the view that each individual in the societies involved has of himself or herself, and they may direct the focus of ethnolinguistics.

Bibliography

Anderson, Wallace L., and Norman C. Stageberg. *Introductory Readings on Language.* New York: Holt, Rinehart and Winston, 1966. Essays including a reprint of Edward Sapir's 1921 article "The Nature of Language." It is a good overview of the field of ethnolinguistics (sociolinguistics).

Baugh, John, and Joel Sherzer, eds. *Language in Use: Readings in Sociolinguistics.* Englewood Cliffs, N.J.: Prentice-Hall, 1984. Classic papers in sociolinguistics from the 1970's and 1980's. Included are "Linguistic Diversity of Social and Cultural Context," "Language in Social Interaction," "Language and Speech in Ethnographic Perspective," and "Social Bases of Language Change."

Bonvillain, Nancy. *Language, Culture, and Communication*. 3d ed. Upper Saddle River, N.J.: Prentice-Hall, 2000. A comprehensive text on the subject of sociolinguistics. This book discusses not only the relationship between language and culture but also means of communication between individuals, communities, and nations.

Chomsky, Noam. *Reflections on Language*. New York: Pantheon Books, 1975. Compilation of lectures and essays from Chomsky's wide-ranging career. It is a general and nontechnical summary of some of the basic questions regarding language and human activity.

Saussure, Ferdinand de. *Course in General Linguistics*, edited by Charles Bally and Albert Sechehaye. Translated by Wade Baskin. New York: Philosophical Library, 1959. Only existing collection of the work of Ferdinand de Saussure. Based on lectures given to students in Geneva, it was published after Saussure's death by his students Bally and Sechehaye. This work is considered by many to mark the beginning of twentieth century linguistics.

Spier, Leslie A., Irving Hallowell, and Stanley S. Newman. *Language, Culture, and Personality: Essays in Memory of Edward Sapir*. Menasha, Wis.: Sapir Memorial Publication Fund, 1941. Essays considered classics in the field of ethnolinguistics. This book is a good example of the status of the field at the time of its publication.

Wardaugh, Ronald. *An Introduction to Sociolinguistics*. New York: Blackwell, 1986. Introductory text covering most of the topics discussed in a sociolinguistics course. It requires little previous knowledge and includes questions for discussion.

Weinstein, Brian, ed. *Language Policy and Political Development*. Norwood, N.J.: Ablex, 1990. Papers on language policy by fourteen political scientists and linguists from Europe, North America, and India who met to discuss language policy and language planning. It contains good examples of language policy and planning from throughout the world.

Susan Ellis-Lopez

Cross-References

Cultural Norms and Sanctions; Culture: Material and Expressive Culture; Knowledge; Symbolic Interaction.

CULTURE OF POVERTY

Type of sociology: Social stratification
Field of study: Poverty

The term "culture of poverty" has been used to describe the values, principles, and lifestyles associated with people living at the lowest economic levels of society. Whether there actually is a distinctive "culture" of poverty has been debated, but the concept has at the very least proved useful in the study of how customs and traditions among the poor are handed down from parents to children.

Principal terms

CULTURE: way of life of a people, based on their shared values and beliefs
NONMATERIAL POVERTY: sense of inferiority that develops among the poor, along with a sense of frustration and resentment resulting from economic inequality
POVERTY: economic inequality based on an inability to work or by working for low wages
SOCIAL POVERTY: poverty resulting from economic inequality; the lack of means to provide a minimally acceptable standard of living
VOLUNTARY POVERTY: conscious renouncing of wealth and possessions, most often in order to pursue religion, philosophy, or art

Overview

"Culture of poverty" is a term that refers to the pattern of life, the set of beliefs, and the typical behavior found among people who live in an environment dominated by economic deprivation. The word "culture" can be defined as the way in which people live their lives and includes all the habits learned by an individual from other members of the community. In its broadest sense, a culture contains the essential information one needs to live in a given environment. Since the environment found in impoverished communities is built upon deprivation, isolation, discrimination, poor education, lack of jobs, crime, drugs, alcohol abuse, and welfare, the attitudes, expectations, and behavior of residents are shaped by these negative forces.

Oscar Lewis, an American anthropologist famous for his description of the effects of poverty on human lives in *La Vida: A Puerto Rican Family in the Culture of Poverty—San Juan and New York* (1966), believed that the values children learn from their parents about how to survive in such desperate circumstances make them less able to move out of poverty. Lewis suggested that only a violent revolution overturning capitalist society would enable the poor to find dignity and equality. Working within the system would not solve any problems, because the values poor people learn include hatred for education (which rarely helps to get a person out of the slums), self-indulgence (since alcohol and drugs offer a quick way out of misery), and unwillingness to save or sacrifice for the future well-being of one's self or family (since the future offers little hope for improving one's economic circumstances). None of these values leads to educational or occupational advancement. The culture learned by the poor works against their ever getting out of poverty. For things to change, according to Lewis, the environmental conditions need to change.

Culture, then, in this context, refers to the lifestyles of the poor. "Poverty," though, is difficult to define, being relative to time and place. Incomes that define persons as poor in industrialized societies would provide a moderately decent standard of living in many nations of Africa, Asia, and Latin America. Poverty has three different meanings: social poverty, which is defined as economic inequality, or the lack of means to provide a minimally adequate standard of living; pauperism, a word that signifies an inability of individuals to take care of themselves; and voluntary poverty, which includes those who for religious and philosophical reasons give up material possessions to pursue prayer, meditation, or art. In the United States, most of the poor fall into the first two categories and include the unskilled, the uneducated, and a large number of children. As of 1993, the government defined as poor nonfarm families of four with incomes under $12,500, about half the income of an average American family of four. Farm families qualify as poor with slightly less income.

Race itself is not a cause of poverty; however, the American tradition of racial segregation and discrimination has guaranteed that large numbers of African Americans—almost two out of every five—live under the poverty line. The major causes of poverty in the United States are chronic unemployment resulting from low levels of education and lack of skills; low wages in unskilled entry-level occupations as well as in agricultural labor; old age (though the number of elderly Americans under the poverty line declined dramatically with the introduction of Medicare in 1965); catastrophes such as floods, fires, or large medical bills; and inadequate welfare payments in almost every state.

According to government figures, in 1992 about 32 million Americans, or 13 percent of the population, lived under the poverty level. That figure represented an increase of almost 4 million people since 1984, the largest proportion reported by the U.S. Bureau of the Census since the 1950's, when 22.4 percent of the nation lived in officially declared poverty. In 1988, the bureau issued a report on the American poor that showed that 10 percent of whites, 31.6 percent of blacks, and 26.8 percent of Hispanics were impoverished; 20 percent of American children lived in poverty. More than half the families labeled poor were headed by single mothers, and those numbers were growing. Many of the poor, almost 45 percent, worked full time but in jobs that required few skills, offered no opportunities for advancement, and generally had no benefits such as health insurance. For the "working poor," jobs themselves seemed to offer no opportunity for moving up the economic ladder. Working hard for forty hours a week or longer did not guarantee success.

Low-wage jobs keep people in the cycle of poverty and help to reaffirm beliefs associated with the culture of poverty. Working hard does not pay off in terms of material success; working people still live in bad housing, send their children to ineffective schools, and suffer the humiliations of inferior status. The material deprivations associated with poverty are many, but so are the nonmaterial deprivations. Poverty is seen by many as a sign of wickedness and moral degeneracy: People are poor because they are lazy and corrupt. These attitudes must be faced and absorbed into one's consciousness every day, and they only increase a sense of frustration and hopelessness. As poverty in the United States increased in the 1980's, the poor had no spokesperson or party representing their point of view. Their political interests were not represented, since one value stressed by the culture of poverty is that political participation is not important. (The lower one goes down the economic scale, the smaller the percentage of people who vote.)

Applications
Knowledge of the effects of the culture of poverty makes it possible to understand the difficulty of fighting and eliminating poverty. According to the culture of poverty thesis, ending employment discrimination, raising wages, and increasing employment opportunities through job training programs would all help to reduce poverty, but the attitudes of the poor would change only very slowly, since a whole way of life would need to be transformed. Education is the key to changing attitudes, especially by reducing the sense of despair frequently associated with poor people. Yet dropout rates approach 45 percent in high schools in slum districts, and a majority of impoverished adults are functionally illiterate; a major change in educational outcomes thus would be required before schools could be accepted as a way out of poverty. It is true that many mothers who receive welfare benefits place great value on education as a key to their children's success; however, statistics showing that children in slum school districts do not read as well or compute as well as students in middle- or upper-income districts provide little support for the hopes of these parents. The children who need education the most—to promote a feeling of control over a very hostile environment—receive the worst. Even highly motivated students seldom find success in such circumstances.

In American society, more than 71 percent of the African American poor live in large cities or surrounding suburbs, while most poor whites (almost 68 percent) are found in small towns, suburbs, and rural areas. In his book *The Truly Disadvantaged: The Inner City, the Underclass, and Public Policy* (1987), University of Chicago sociologist William J. Wilson observes that many African Americans live in neighborhoods with high concentrations of people in similarly desperate economic circumstances, with average incomes of less than $5,000 a year. Poor black people, especially, tend to live in areas surrounded by other poor blacks and thus have little opportunity to meet or learn from individuals with more secure economic futures. In the worst areas, two out of every three children live in single-parent households with incomes well below the poverty level. These are the truly disadvantaged members of American society, the people who feel most cut off from the American mainstream, and the people most influenced by the culture of poverty. They make up the underclass in the American economy.

In the environment of the slum, cultural patterns emerge that promote survival in the midst of dangerous and violent conditions. Crime rates, murder rates, and levels of drug addiction, alcoholism, mental illness, hypertension, and other measures of social disintegration, including divorce, child abuse, and spouse abuse, are far higher in inner cities than in any other parts of the United States. Survival in these circumstances requires a toughness of spirit and a distrust of others. Since slum residents usually do not get adequate city services such as garbage collection and police protection, distrust of government grows, leading to increased levels of hopelessness and helplessness. Not even the schools, historically the institutions most used by immigrant and minority groups as the path to success, typically offer the type of skills and training necessary to make it out of the ghetto. Most ghetto high schools are so bad that about as many students drop out as are graduated. The dream of college seems very distant to people without enough money to buy food.

The goals of the poor may be similar to those of the more well-to-do in terms of better jobs, improved educational opportunities, and a more pleasant future for their children, but the experience of the poor does not provide evidence that such dreams will ever come true. In many impoverished and racially segregated neighborhoods, crime, usually involving drug sales, offers a far quicker route to material success. Welfare payments, whether through Aid to Families with Dependent Children (AFDC), general assistance, or other aid programs, are another source of survival for the truly poor. Yet receiving such help, inadequate as it usually is, increases dependency and tends to reduce self-respect, as it is considered a sign of personal weakness to receive welfare. In a society that exalts the work ethic such as the United States, not to work, even if no jobs are available or one lacks the necessary training and skills required for a better job, becomes a sign of individual worthlessness and insignificance. This attitude represents one of the most devastating nonmaterial effects of being poor.

Context

The idea of a separate and distinct culture based on economic circumstances dates back at least to the early 1800's, when economists and historians talked about "working-class culture" or the "culture of the poor." In his famous history of human society *Das Kapital* (1867; *Capital: A Critique of Political Economy*, 1886), Karl Marx referred to the differing values and worldviews of capitalists and workers. Marxists were quite clear in their view that human thought and culture reflected the environmental conditions in which a person was born and reared. Socialist parties taught that only the abolition of poverty would lead to improved living conditions for the poor and that economic inequality would only be eliminated by the overthrow of capitalist ideas and values. Liberals, on the other hand, stressed economic expansion as the key to the ultimate victory over poverty and despair. With a constantly expanding economy, liberal theorists speculated, the poor would gradually be absorbed into the economic mainstream, and most poverty would disappear. Those people who could not succeed on such terms—chiefly those with physical or mental disabilities, widows, and orphans—would be taken care of by charity groups. When terrible economic depressions, especially in the 1890's and 1930's, showed that free-market capitalism had not solved all economic problems, liberal economists and many frightened conservatives pushed for social-welfare programs principally to prevent violent revolts. If the poor were given some stake in society in the form of pensions, housing, or medical care, it was thought, they would be less likely to follow revolutionary parties seeking to overthrow the whole capitalist system. The problem with "welfare" programs, however, was that they cost enormous amounts of money and required ever-higher levels of taxes to support and maintain. Though poverty was no longer believed to be a necessary part of the capitalist system and most economists believed that it could be abolished, there still was a major debate over how that could be accomplished.

The social welfare programs instituted in the 1930's, mainly Social Security payments, public-housing programs, and unemployment insurance, helped to reduce levels of poverty in the United States. Yet even in the generally prosperous 1950's, as many as 40 million people (22.5 percent of the population) were poor. It was at this point that students of poverty such as Michael Harrington in *The Other America: Poverty in the United States* (1962), Oscar Lewis in *La Vida*, and psychologist Kenneth Clark in *Dark Ghetto: Dilemmas of Social Power* (1965) began reporting on the long-term psychological and social damages caused by living in economically deprived communities. Most of these observers advocated a total change in the economic system, either through establishing a socialist economy (Harrington) or through violent revolution (Lewis). Liberal critics countered that such far-reaching changes were not necessary and that problems could be solved simply by ending job discrimination, improving educational opportunities, and promoting economic growth. The War on Poverty (1965-1967) was based on these ideas, though some recognition (especially through the Head Start program) was given to the notion that cultural attitudes would also have to be changed if the noneconomic effects of poverty were to be challenged.

Poverty in the United States did go down in the late 1960's and throughout the 1970's; by the end of the 1970's, the poverty level stood at 11.4 percent of the population (24.5 million people), the lowest level in history. Then, however, the numbers began increasing, as money for social programs was reduced by the Reagan administration. By 1988, the number of poor people in the United States had risen to 15 percent of the population (32.5 million people). This increase resulted from the antiwelfare philosophy of the Reagan administration, a position supported by books such as Charles Murray's *Losing Ground: American Social Policy, 1950-1980* (1984).

Murray supported the idea that a distinct culture had developed among the American poor, but he found that the attitudes and values expressed by people in poverty resulted from their acceptance of welfare rather than from discrimination, bad education, and long periods of economic deprivation. If welfare caused the attitudinal problem by making people dependent on government handouts rather than encouraging them to find jobs, Murray reasoned, then welfare had to go. Even mothers with four or more children would be better off working in low-paying, unskilled jobs than staying home taking care of their families, Murray suggested. With such attitudes finding favor with policy makers, the numbers of poor and homeless increased dramatically in the 1980's.

Bibliography

Ellwood, David T. *Poor Support: Poverty in the American Family.* New York: Basic Books, 1988. Detailed and informative review of welfare policy in the United States. Contains a brief but thoughtful analysis of the debate over the culture of poverty issue. Finds that the poor do have different attitudes and customs than do others.

Hacker, Andrew. *Two Nations: Black and White, Separate, Hostile, Unequal*. Expanded and updated ed. New York: Ballantine Books, 1995. Thorough analysis of racial issues in the United States, with many statistics affirming the existence of a separate culture of poverty.

Jaynes, Gerald D., and Robin M. Williams, eds. *A Common Destiny: Blacks and American Society*. Washington, D.C.: National Academy Press, 1988. Much evidence and several chapters devoted to refuting the idea of a distinct culture of poverty. Sees discrimination and racism as the only impediments to full equality.

Murray, Charles. *Losing Ground: American Social Policy, 1950-1980*. 2d ed. New York: Basic Books, 1994. Sees a culture of poverty developing from American welfare programs. Calls for eliminating welfare and increasing incentives to work. The key text of antiwelfare conservatives.

Pfeffer, Rachel. *Surviving the Streets: Girls Living on Their Own*. New York: Garland, 1997.

Robertson, James. *Beyond the Dependency Culture*. Westport, Conn.: Praeger, 1998.

Wilson, William J. *The Truly Disadvantaged: The Inner City, the Underclass, and Public Policy*. Chicago: University of Chicago Press, 1987. Shows the devastating impact of poverty and the culture of poverty on millions of Americans. Details the complex relationship between culture and economics.

Leslie V. Tischauser

Cross-References

Gender Inequality: Analysis and Overview; Industrial and Postindustrial Economies; Poverty: Analysis and Overview; Race Relations: The Race-Class Debate; Racial and Ethnic Stratification.

DEMOCRACY

Type of sociology: Major social institutions
Field of study: Politics and the state

Democracy is a political system characterized by direct or indirect rule by the people. There are different models of democratic government, but the liberal conception as found in Western Europe and North America has emerged as the dominant view of democracy since the end of the Cold War era.

Principal terms

DEMOCRATIC CONSOLIDATION: process of institutionalizing newly democratic regimes
DEMOCRATIZATION: process of moving from an authoritarian to a democratic system
DIRECT DEMOCRACY: form of government based on popular participation, majority rule, and political equality
ELITISM: belief that in any society a small number of people—an "elite"—rule the rest
PEOPLE'S DEMOCRACY: Marxist-Leninist model of democracy in which the communist party governs in the interest of the working class
PLURALISM: theory of democracy that believes in multiple, competing elites determining public policy through bargaining and compromise
REPRESENTATIVE DEMOCRACY: system of representative government based on free elections and limits on state activity
SINGLE-PARTY DEMOCRACY: model of democracy found in the Third World in which the ruling party acts in the interest of the entire population and opposition parties are constitutionally banned

Overview

Democracy is a set of ideals and a form of government in which the people rule directly or indirectly. The term "democracy" is derived from the ancient Greek words *demos* (people) and *kratos* (rule), which combined simply mean rule or government of the people. Until the late eighteenth and nineteenth centuries, however, democracy did not achieve prominence, and only in the twentieth century did it become a value with considerable legitimacy. In the twentieth century, democracy became popular because of the growing faith in the abilities of the common man and woman. Unlike ideologies such as communism and fascism, however, democracy lacks conceptual precision. The meaning and inherent features of democracy continue to be the subject of debate.

Democracy is a dynamic entity that has been given many different definitions. It has become one of the most elastic political concepts in use since World War II. Because democracy is a principle of legitimacy, political regimes of all kinds have claimed to be democracies. A wide range of political systems inspired by diverse ideological orienta-tions—socialist, communist, and one-party states—have claimed to be democratic. Nondemocratic political systems have often used the term by adding adjectives such as "people's," "soviet," "guided," "basic," and "one-party" to the word "democracy." As a result, there are a number of definitions and competing theories or models of democracy.

The classical meaning of democracy, based on the use of the term in ancient Greek city-states, especially Athens, is the rule by the majority (who were poor) through direct democratic participation or by the rotation of governing offices among the citizens. Democracy was conceived as a system of government by the people themselves in which the citizens met periodically to elect state officials by lot and to enact laws. Though Athenian democracy excluded a vast majority of the population from political life—slaves, women, and foreigners—it conceived of the concept in terms of direct popular government, popular sovereignty, popular power, and popular participation. From the ancient Greeks to eighteenth century philosophers such as Jean-Jacques Rousseau, democratic government has been identified with direct popular participation. Since popular participation was understood in terms of unrestrained mob rule, democracy was considered an undesirable form of government.

In the twentieth century, however, democracy has become a positive term that is synonymous with some kind of representative system. Since modern nation-states are much larger entities than were the small Greek city-states (Athens had an estimated population of fifty thousand), direct democracy is considered an impractical form of government. Contemporary political analysts seem to agree about the procedural and normative worth of democracy as a way of organizing political relations.

The most commonly used definition of democracy is that of Joseph Schumpeter in *Capitalism, Socialism, and Democracy* (1950): "The democratic method is that institutional arrangement for arriving at political decisions in which individuals acquire the power to decide by means of a comparative struggle for people's vote." This definition of democracy is rather narrow because it focuses on the procedure and mechanism for choosing political leaders at election time and nothing more. While accepting certain aspects of Schumpeter's definition, Larry Diamond, Juan Linz, and Seymour Martin Lipset have defined political democracy more broadly in *Democracy in Developing Countries: Asia* (1988) as

A system of government that meets three essential conditions: meaningful and *extensive* competition among individual and organized groups (especially political parties) for all effective positions of government power, at regular intervals and excluding the use of force; a highly inclusive level of *political participation* in the selection of leaders and policies, at least through regular and fair elections, such that no major (adult) social group is excluded; and a level of civil and *political liberties*—freedom of expression, freedom of press, freedom to form organizations—sufficient to ensure the integrity of political competition and participation.

Since the mid-1970's, there has been a genuine move from authoritarian government to a full or partial form of democratic government in many parts of the world, and the end of the Cold War in 1989 gave further impetus to the process of democratization. At the end of

1991, about half of the world's independent states (eighty-nine) were democratic—twice the number of twenty years earlier—and the number of democratic and semidemocratic governments (such as Russia, Malaysia, and Thailand) has since been growing. Two years later, there were more than 110 states (out of a total of about 180 sovereign independent states) committed to certain basic democratic principles, such as open, multiparty, secret-ballot elections with universal franchise.

Applications

Democracy as an ideal and a method of governance has been applied in three competing political systems: liberal democracy in the industrialized West, "people's democracy" in the communist political systems, and one-party democracy in most of the Third World. While there are important differences between them, each claims its model of democracy to be superior, or at least appropriate to its own historical and socioeconomic conditions.

The history of the development of democratic theory and its practice in the West is intertwined with that of liberal ideology (as put forth in the writings of philosophers such as Thomas Hobbes, John Locke, Rousseau, James Madison, and Thomas Jefferson) and its economic expression—capitalism (articulated in the works of Adam Smith, especially The Wealth of Nations [1776], and utilitarian philosophers such as John Stuart Mill, Jeremy Bentham, and T. H. Green). At the core of liberal democracy lie the four cardinal principles developed by Locke: equality; individual rights and freedoms, including the right to own property; government based upon consent of the governed; and limitations on the state.

When applied to a system of government, liberal democracy emphasizes the following principles: political equality—that all adult citizens have the same opportunity, at least in theory, to participate in the political decision-making process; popular sovereignty—that the ultimate power to make political decisions is vested in all the people rather than in some of them (as in the case of an oligarchy), or one of them (as in case of a monarchy or dictatorship); political consultation—that through some institutional machinery the public officials must learn and act upon the public policy preference of the people; and majority rule and minority rights—that decisions should ultimately be made by popular majorities but that the rights of minorities must be respected.

The idea of citizen involvement in political decision making through elected representatives is the most fundamental characteristic of liberal democracy and distinguishes it from other types of democracies. Until the nineteenth century, severe restrictions on citizenship had been imposed based on criteria such as age, sex, literacy, property, social status, race, and religion. In contemporary liberal democratic states, all native-born or naturalized adults enjoy citizenship and legal equality. The groups that had earlier been excluded—the working class, women, and racial and religious minorities—have now been enfranchised and given political equality.

Two distinct approaches to citizen involvement in a democracy have been taken by social scientists: pluralism and elitism. The pluralist theorists—Robert Dahl, Arthur Bentley, and David Truman—believe that individuals exert influence not as voters but as members of organized interest groups such as business or trade associations, trade unions, professional associations, and community groups. These interest groups dominate modern democratic societies, in which government acts essentially as a broker to facilitate compromise among them. Democracy, in this view, is premised on diversity of interests and the dispersion of power.

The theorists of democratic elitism (Robert Michels, Giovanni Sartori, and C. Wright Mills), however, believe that elites, not masses, govern in all societies, including liberal democratic societies. Taking their cue from Italian political sociologists Vilfredo Pareto and Gaetano Mosca, elitist theorists reject the pluralist view and argue that the ability of all interest groups to exert influence is not the same in a liberal democracy. Since financial, professional, and economic resources are distributed unequally in any society, a relatively small group ends up actually controlling the government as well as industry, the professions, and major interest groups. In this view, democracy allows competition among rival elites. Schumpeter, for example, argued that in a democracy people actually choose which elite will rule them.

The concept of "people's democracy" was the prevailing version of the democratic ideal followed by the communist countries until the late 1980's. It differs radically from liberal democracy because, following the Marxian notion of class and class oppression in a capitalist society, the communists advocate the establishment of a genuine, or "social," democracy by overthrowing the bourgeois democratic state, which they view as an instrument of the oppression of the working class (proletariat), or common people. This view is similar to the Greek democratic idea of rule by and in the interest of the common people. The emphasis of the communists, however, is on economic, not political, equality. Their version of democracy is based on the Marxist-Leninist principles that were practiced in the former Soviet Union and Eastern European states until the late 1980's and that still provide the ideological basis for the governments in China, Cuba, North Korea, and Vietnam.

In a people's democracy, the communist party enjoys a monopoly of power and guides both government and society. According to Vladimir Ilich Lenin, the communist party is the vanguard of the proletariat and conforms to the principle of democratic centralism—freedom of discussion, with centralized control and responsibility. In practice, however, freedom of discussion has been denied by most communist leaders—notably, Joseph Stalin in the Soviet Union, Mao Zedong in China, and Fidel Castro in Cuba. The communist regimes have invariably turned into authoritarian states. After the collapse of communism in the former Soviet Union and Eastern Europe and the adoption of an open competitive political system, however, the concept of people's democracy has been discredited. Yet the most populous country in the world—China—remains committed to the Leninist principle of communist party dictatorship. China's Communist Party maintained control over government and society by violently suppressing the democracy movement at Tiananmen Square in Beijing in June, 1989. The Chinese communist leaders, especially their paramount leader Deng Xiaoping, find Western liberal democratic ideas to be unacceptable and they insist on the need for China to continue with a "people's democratic dictatorship."

A third conception of democracy, different from both liberal and people's democracy, has been formulated by developing nations. In the wake of decolonization in Asia and Africa in the 1950's and 1960's, the newly independent states experimented with some form of liberal democratic (mostly parliamentary) government, but the new democracies in the Third World did not last very long, and they gave way to one-party government or military dictatorship. Many Third World leaders quickly recognized that neither the liberal model, which puts emphasis on political competition and open discussion, nor people's democracy, which works in the interest of the proletariat, was appropriate for them. Since most Third World societies emphasize cooperation and social harmony, they conceived of democracy in terms of a one-party system based on their own culture and tradition. In this conception of democracy, government would work for the overriding common purpose of the society—Rousseau's "general will"—through modernization and national economic development instead of serving certain interest groups and associations.

The experience of single-party democracy, however, suggests that the governments in those countries became highly corrupt and authoritarian mainly because of the absence of an open competitive political system. Instead of serving the people, one-party states often served the interest of the rulers and a small number of individuals in power. The people, therefore, demanded an end to the one-party rule and establishment of an open and competitive political system. In sub-Saharan Africa, for example, the masses have demanded a "second independence," this time from indigenous repressive rulers; they are convinced that their material improvement will come only when they gain power through political participation. Liberal democratic ideas thus have gained ground in the Third World, especially since the end of the Cold War. In the 1990's, the single-party democracies have given way to multiparty systems, political freedom and openness, and popularly elected and constitutional civilian governments. Francis Fukuyama, in *The End of History and the Last Man* (1992), has declared that, because of these historical developments of the late 1980's and early 1990's, the worldwide triumph of liberal democracy is imminent.

Context

Prior to World War I, only four democracies had extended suffrage to women—Australia, Finland, New Zealand, and Norway—but there has been an unprecedented movement toward liberal democracy since then, especially since the mid-1970's. Samuel Huntington, in *The Third Wave: Democratization in the Late Twentieth Century* (1991), presents data on transitions to democracy in the "third wave" of democratization that began in 1974 and continued in the 1990's. He finds that thirty countries made transitions to democracy between 1974 and 1990, which brought the total of free and democratic countries to seventy-five by 1991 compared to twenty-nine during the "first wave" of democratization (1820's to 1926) and thirty-six in the "second wave" (1943 to 1962).

A third wave of democratization, which started in Southern Europe (Greece, Portugal, and Spain) in the mid-1970's and moved to Latin America (Argentina, Uruguay, Peru, Ecuador, Brazil, Paraguay, and Chile) and Central America (Honduras, El Salvador, Nicaragua, Guatemala, and Mexico) in the 1980's, reached Eastern Europe and the former Soviet Union by the late 1980's and early 1990's. In Asia, it includes countries such as Papua New

Guinea, Thailand, Pakistan, Bangladesh, the Philippines, South Korea, Taiwan, Mongolia, and Nepal. In Africa since 1989, there has been a general move from authoritarian rule to establishing a multiparty system and free elections. This is a significant development for sub-Saharan Africa, which had only four countries (Botswana, The Gambia, Mauritius, and Senegal) with a reasonable record of democratic rule between 1965 and 1987 and had experienced more than eighty successful and countless unsuccessful military coups during the same period.

Harriet Stanton Blatch, the daughter of famed suffragist Elizabeth Cady Stanton, exhorts a Wall Street crowd on the need to extend suffrage to women. *(Library of Congress)*

The transition from authoritarian to democratic rule in the ex-Second World and in many parts of the Third World is indeed historical. Huntington has identified five factors that contributed to the occurrence and timing of the third-wave transitions to democracy. First, the authoritarian regimes lacked legitimacy in a world where democratic values were widely accepted. Second, the middle class in many countries has expanded as a result of the unprecedented economic growth of the 1950's and 1960's. Sociologist Seymour Lipset has also argued that there is a strong empirical correlation between economic development and democracy. Third, the role of the Roman Catholic Church shifted, especially in Latin America, from defender of the status quo to opponent of authoritarianism. The church advocacy of the doctrine of liberation theology is strongly antiauthoritarian in nature. (Approximately three-quarters of the countries that became democratic between 1974 and 1989 were predominantly Catholic.) Fourth, the European Community, the United States, and the former Soviet Union all contributed to the democratic transition—for example, the *glasnost* and *perestroika* reforms of the late 1980's, initiated by the former Soviet leader Mikhail Gorbachev. Finally, the demonstration, or "herd," effect of transitions stimulated democratization in other countries.

A sixth factor could be added to Huntington's list: the communication revolution of the 1970's and 1980's, which has made the world a global village. In the age of satellite communication, fax machines, and the global reach of CNN and MTV, authoritarian rulers cannot conceal the comparative success of the open political systems and free market economies of the Western industrialized nations in meeting basic human needs. They also cannot control the thought processes of their citizens as they could a generation ago. Therefore, people's aspirations for freedom and democracy all over the world could no longer be suppressed, especially after the end of the Cold War in 1989.

The phenomenon of democratic consolidation—whether and how the new democratic regimes can become institutionalized—has received attention from social scientists in the wake of the global resurgence of democracy in the 1990's. In 1992-1993, events in Haiti, Peru, Nigeria, Venezuela, Guatemala, and the ex-Yugoslavia have indicated that Fukuyama's prediction of the imminence of global transition to liberal democracy is fallacious. Emerging democracies are facing various challenges to democratic consolidation.

First, the absence of a democratic political culture has complicated the process of democratic institution-building in many countries. Second, lack of experience in multiparty politics poses a threat to stability, as witnessed in the December, 1993, Russian parliamentary elections. Third, introduction of a free-market economy in new democracies, which has resulted in poverty for a large number of people and increased social inequality, poses a threat to democracy, especially in ex-communist countries where the victims of economic reform have begun to long for the economic security of the old system. Fourth, the military, which played a central role in Latin American and African politics, continues to occupy an important position within the political elite in those societies and threatens the stability of new democratic regimes.

In spite of these challenges, democracy has made great progress throughout the world in the 1980's and 1990's, and a reversal toward authoritarianism in newly democratic states seems less likely, though its possibility cannot be ruled out. Social scientists are divided on the future of democracy. While optimists such as Fukuyama predict that liberal democracy will triumph, pessimists like Huntington argue that the global democratic revolution will not last forever and that there might be a new surge of authoritarianism. The trend in the early 1990's nevertheless indicates that more countries will move in the direction of a free, open, competitive, and democratic political system, notwithstanding the difficulties experienced by countries such as Haiti, Nigeria, and Peru. Experts predict that even China will allow some degree of political competition when a younger generation assumes leadership following the death of Deng Xiaoping, and will gradually move toward democracy. The durability of new democracies, however, will depend to a large extent on their economic performances.

Bibliography

Diamond, Larry, and Marc F. Plattner, eds. *Capitalism, Socialism, and Democracy Revisited*. Baltimore: Johns Hopkins University Press, 1993. Reexamination of Joseph Schumpeter's classic study *Capitalism, Socialism, and Democracy* (first published in 1942) and its thesis regarding the relationship between political democracy and alternative economic systems.

_____. *The Global Resurgence of Democracy*. 2d ed. Baltimore: Johns Hopkins University Press, 1996. Contains more than two dozen essays by leading scholars. Part 1 deals with theoretical aspects of the global democratic resurgence after the mid-1970's; parts 2 and 3 deal with problems of democratic institutionalization and political corruption and democracy, respectively; and part 4 addresses the global democratic prospects. All essays are accessible to nonexperts.

Fukuyama, Francis. *The End of History and the Last Man*. New York: Free Press, 1992. Provocative argument that after the collapse of communism in the Soviet Union and Eastern Europe there is no viable alternative to Western-style liberal democracy. The author therefore predicts the end of history.

Held, David. *Models of Democracy*. 2d ed. Stanford, Calif.: Stanford University Press, 1996. Excellent analysis of the classical and contemporary models of democracy. It also examines central problems of democratic theory and practice.

Huntington, Samuel P. *The Third Wave: Democratization in the Late Twentieth Century*. Norman: University of Oklahoma Press, 1991. Theoretical and empirical study of the "third wave" of transitions of about thirty countries from authoritarian to democratic political systems between 1974 and 1990. (The first and second waves of democratic transitions took place in 1828-1926 and 1943-1962, respectively.) Huntington provides an explanation of the political, economic, social, and cultural roots of the democratic process.

Lipset, Seymour Martin. *Political Man: The Social Bases of Politics*. Baltimore: Johns Hopkins University Press, 1981. Through an analysis of an enormous amount of empirical data, this classic study explores the conditions necessary for democracy; the relationship between political participation and voting behavior; and the support for pro- and antidemocratic movements and values.

Mainwaring, Scott, Guillermo O'Donnell, and J. Samuel Valenzuela, eds. *Issues in Democratic Consolidation: The New South American Democracies in Comparative Perspective*. Notre Dame, Ind.: University of Notre Dame Press, 1992. Eight essays by leading scholars providing perceptive analyses of the complex processes related to the transitions from authoritarian to civil rule in Latin America.

O'Donnell, Guillermo, Philippe Schmitter, and Lawrence Whitehead, eds. *Transitions from Authoritarian Rule: Comparative Perspectives*. Baltimore: Johns Hopkins University Press, 1986. Essays treating transitions from authoritarian to democratic regime in Spain, Portugal, and several Latin American countries in the late 1970's and early 1980's.

Schumpeter, Joseph. *Capitalism, Socialism, and Democracy*. 3d ed. New York: Harper & Row, 1950. Classic study of the three political systems and the nature of political systems that mix parts of each.

Vanhanen, Tatu. *The Process of Democratization: A Comparative Study of 147 States, 1980-88*. New York: Crane Russak, 1990. Through an application of the Darwinian theory of natural selection to the study of political systems, this comparative study explains variations of political systems and democratization in 147 states.

Sunil K. Sahu

Cross-References

Bureaucracies; Civil Religion and Politics; Legitimacy and Authority; Political Sociology; Power Elite.

DEMOGRAPHIC FACTORS AND SOCIAL CHANGE

Type of sociology: Social change
Field of study: Sources of social change

Demographic factors refer both to a human population's static characteristics, such as age and sex compositions, and to its dynamic characteristic, such as birth, death, migration, and growth rates. These factors both contribute to and respond to various dimensions of social change.

Principal terms

CARRYING CAPACITY: the maximum population that a given society can support, given a set of resource and ecological conditions

COMPOSITION: proportion of a population composed of individuals possessing select characteristics; for example, a population's age composition indicates whether most of its members are old or young

DEMOGRAPHY: study of population

POPULATION: group of individuals or objects that share one or more common characteristics

RATE: number of events occurring in a time period divided by the population at risk of experiencing the event

SECULARIZATION: dispersal of an autonomous, individualistic outlook on life

SOCIOCULTURAL SYSTEM: term nearly synonymous with the term "human society," except that it emphasizes the interdependence of a society's components

SUBPOPULATION: term that refers to a subset of the total population that shares one or more distinguishing characteristics, such as age

Overview

Human sociocultural systems, or societies, consist of a number of interdependent components. A societal component both reflects the attributes of the other components of society and produces changes in them. One component is population, the group of people living within a society. The study of human populations is the domain of demography; accordingly, the characteristics of a population are often referred to as demographic factors. Demographic factors are sometimes divided into two groups: static factors and dynamic factors.

Static factors are the characteristics of a population that may be observed from a "snapshot" depicting a population at one particular moment. A population's composition, distribution, and size are among its static attributes. Population size, the most straightforward demographic factor, simply refers to the number of people living in the geographic area occupied or possessed by a given society. This basic factor performs a vital role in terms of social change; it has a major impact on a society's economic productivity, organizational complexity, and rate of technological innovation. For example, compared with their smaller counterparts, societies possessing relatively large populations are generally characterized by relatively high levels of productivity, complex governments and patterns of social interactions, and high rates of technological innovation.

Changes in other components of society also affect population size. Demographers contend that the biophysical environment in which a society is situated, together with that society's technological capabilities to extract, produce, and distribute subsistence resources defines an upper limit on the size of a society's population, a limit often referred to as the society's "carrying capacity." Thus, societies that are characterized by a more productive level of technology and a more egalitarian pattern of resource distribution generally are capable of supporting larger populations than are those societies with less productive technologies and more marked inequality.

The distribution and composition factors refer to the relative size of select segments of a given society's population. Like the overall population size, these factors both contribute to and reflect other social change. The factor of population distribution, for example, addresses the issue of the proportion of a population living in one geographic area as opposed to the proportion living in another. A common distribution metric is the proportion of a society's population that resides in urban areas. On the one hand, populations characterized by a heavily urban distribution reflect previous social changes, perhaps most notably the presence of an economic surplus that freed some members of the population from the land-intensive task of agricultural production and industrialization, a much less land-intensive mode of production. On the other hand, heavily urban populations often lead to a variety of social changes, including the development of large, complex public service organizations such as police and fire-fighting forces; health care facilities; transportation systems; and water, sewer, and power utilities.

Dynamic factors refer to the changes that occur in the static factors during a given time period. Thus, as the static factors pertain to a population's size, the dynamic factors pertain to changes in a population's size. Demographers specify three possible sources of this change: fertility, mortality, and migration. These factors make up the so-called demographic equation, wherein a change in the size of a population between two points in time is attributed to births minus deaths plus in-migrants minus out-migrants. Population growth occurs when this summation is a positive figure, and population decline is experienced when the sum of deaths and out-migrants is greater than the sum of births and in-migrants.

Demographic research on the so-called demographic transition provides several good examples of the interdependence of the dynamic factors with other societal components. The demographic transition refers to a basic pattern of dramatic reductions in mortality rates and fertility rates that have occurred in many of the wealthier societies of the world. Such social changes as improvements in living standards and advancements in medical technology appear to have led to the substantial reductions in mortality rates. Until matched by a decline in fertility rates, reductions of mortality rates sometimes yield population growth that approaches some societies' carrying capacities. Although demographers have not yet determined all the sources of the fertility decline that complete the demographic transition, they have identified a variety of social changes that appear to have contributed to the decline, notably industrialization, improvements in living conditions, and secularization. Changes in fertility rates also have been identified as stimuli for social change. Reductions in fertility rates have been attributed to postponements in the average age at first marriage, increased female participation in the labor force, and a reduction in gender inequality. Overall, a population is generally larger after the demographic transition than before it, and, as noted above, the larger size leads to a variety of social changes involving the level of societal complexity, the roles of a number of social institutions (including the family), and the population's age structure.

Applications

Several good examples of the relationships between demographic factors and social change surface in comparisons of the earliest type of human societies, hunting and gathering societies, with later types. Hunting and gathering societies were characterized by a very rudimentary mode of subsistence technology which generally limited their populations to fewer than fifty people. The small size of these societies was often associated with a low level of societal complexity and with the central role of the family in social organization. For example, there was very little occupational specialization in hunting and gathering societies; by and large, the men hunted and the women gathered. This lack of differentiation carried over into the political and economic spheres, as these societies were generally marked by very little inequality. Typically, the populations of these societies were fairly homogeneous, and most members were related to one another. Indeed kinship—that is, the family—formed the basis of and outlined the structure of social organization. Sociologists Gerhard Lenski, Jean Lenski, and Patrick Nolan, for example, point out that in most hunting and gathering societies, "kin groups perform[ed] many of the functions that are performed by schools, business firms, governmental agencies, and other specialized organizations in larger, more advanced and more differentiated societies."

Compared with hunting and gathering societies, horticultural, agrarian, and industrial societies possess much more productive subsistence technologies and, as a result, possess much larger populations, ranging from several hundred members to several million members. The greater population sizes give rise to more heterogeneous population compositions and, in turn, increase societal complexity and reduce the parallelism between the society and the family that is found in hunting and gathering societies. The larger populations also contribute to reductions in the roles and functions performed by the family. In many of these societies, for example, one finds well-developed political, religious, and economic institutions that transcend the bounds of a single family, as well as economic, occupational, and other social relationships that rival the family for primacy in terms of organizing social interaction and relationships.

It bears emphasizing that the previously noted differences in societal complexity, population composition, and the role and functions of the family are at least the partial result of differences in population size. One might consider as an analogy some of the differences between a small family dinner and a large family reunion. The population of a small family dinner may consist of parents and their children, and the conversation and other interactions would likely be relaxed and informal, with the relationships between members being apparent to all. In contrast, the populations of family reunions may consist of several hundred people who do not regularly interact. As a result, interactions between members are often less relaxed and more formal, requiring name tags, seating charts, scheduled activities, and sometimes even a hired, outside planner. In short, a larger population yields greater complexity and more formal interactions. In a similar manner, the growth of the populations of human societies also spawns considerable social change.

Perhaps a more immediate example of the relationship between demographic factors and social change involves changes in the age composition of the United States' population since the nineteenth century. The median age of this population increased from about sixteen years in 1800 to more than thirty-two years in 1989. Thus, this population has grown older. Population aging is a result of the reductions in both mortality and fertility rates that compose the demographic transition. Decreased mortality rates make a population's age composition older by extending life. Decreased fertility rates contribute to the aging of a population by reducing the number of young people born into it and thus reducing the proportion of the population that is young.

The American population's aging also entails a demographic phenomenon that has become known as "graying." Graying refers to an increase in the proportion of the population aged sixty-five years or greater. John Weeks, a demographer and sociologist at San Diego State University, reports that the number of Americans aged sixty-five years and over increased from about three million in 1900 to thirty-one million in 1990. This aspect of the changing age composition of the United States population has produced profound social changes. For example, the growing elderly population was a major impetus for the passage of the Social Security Act in 1935. By providing a means for retirement, this legislation was intended to remove the burgeoning elderly subpopulation from the competition for the all-too-scarce jobs of the Depression era.

The graying of America has also left its mark on the economic dimension of society. On the one hand, the growth of the elderly subpopulation may be viewed as an economic asset. It has led to the development or expansion of numerous thriving industries that cater to the needs and desires of the sizable elderly subpopulation, a significant proportion of which receives income from pensions. These industries include health care, residential assistance, travel, and social clubs, to name but a few. On the other hand, a number of possible economic detriments of the graying of the United States' population have surfaced. For example, as the average length of life continues to be extended and as the proportion of the population that is elderly and retired or semiretired continues to grow, the United States' pay-as-you-go system of Social Security may be placed in jeopardy. In any event, the social changes associated with the graying of the U.S. population are likely to continue and expand as the large baby boom cohort moves into retirement.

Context

The existence of a relationship between demographic factors and social change has been acknowledged for centuries, and the characteristics of the relationship have been the subject of debate for almost as long. One of the most famous perspectives on the relationship between demographic factors and other social characteristics was that espoused by Thomas Malthus in his 1798 work *An Essay on the Principle of Population*. Malthus, writing in response to utopian social philosophers who contended that continuing technological advance would be able to support an infinitely large human population, argued that populations had the capacity to grow more rapidly than the support of subsistence resources. Hence, Malthus contended that unchecked population growth inevitably resulted in poverty, and that poverty could only be avoided through reducing fertility and, as a result, slowing the growth of a population's demand for subsistence resources. Many of the fundamental tenets of Malthus's theory remain popular and are reflected in the work of neo-Malthusians such as Stanford University biologist Paul Ehrlich, who argues that much of the world's misery and poverty could be reduced by the widespread adoption of low-fertility practices. Indeed, in 1990, the poorest societies of the world were generally among those with the fastest growing populations.

Malthus's basic position has been and continues to be met with considerable opposition, however; among Malthus's most notable critics were nineteenth century social philosophers Karl Marx and Friedrich Engels. Marx and Engels argued that the poverty described by Malthus was not attributable to the existence of too many people relative to the supply of resources but rather to inefficient, unjust systems of resource production and distribution. Devotees of this position persist, but attempts to apply it have met with, at best, limited success. The fact that the Marx-inspired Chinese government had to implement a coercive policy allowing only one child per family, for example, suggests that even large-scale social reorganization is not sufficient to meet the consumptive demands of a population experiencing unlimited growth.

Another very important but less controversial sociological perspective on the relationship between demographic factors and social change was proposed by Émile Durkheim. In 1893, Durkheim undertook a comparative approach and argued that increased population size produces greater societal complexity, in particular greater occupational specialization—a greater division of labor. Durkheim contended that "the division of labor varies in direct ratio with the volume and density of societies, and, if it progresses in a continuous manner in the course of social development, it is because societies become regularly denser and more voluminous." Durkheim's classic position is generally accepted and has been widely applied to the study of such phenomena as the complexity of large business organizations.

Bibliography

Ehrlich, Paul, and Anne H. Ehrlich. *The Population Explosion*. New York: Simon & Schuster, 1990. Update of Ehrlich's popular 1968 book, *The Population Bomb*. Like its predecessor, addresses the problems that may arise from the continued growth of the human population in conjunction with environmental degradation. It also assesses changes due to rapid population growth experienced since the publication of the earlier work.

Haupt, Arthur, and Thomas T. Kane. *The Population Reference Bureau's Population Hand-*

book. 3d ed. Washington, D.C.: Population Reference Bureau, 1991. Invaluable resource for anyone interested in demography. It provides clear explanations and examples of demographic concepts and metrics, as well as information on various sources of demographic information.

Lenski, Gerhard, Jean Lenski, and Patrick Nolan. *Human Societies*. 8th ed. New York: McGraw-Hill, 1999. Clear overview of the relationships among population and other societal characteristics during the process of social evolution. Durkheim's proposed relationship between population size and societal complexity may easily be seen in the numerous examples.

Malthus, Thomas. *An Essay on the Principle of Population*. New York: Penguin Classics, 1985. Although written in 1798, this classic document is surprisingly easy and enjoyable to read. This publication includes the first edition of the Malthus essay, a summary of the essay penned by Malthus, and an enlightening introduction by Anthony Flew.

Preston, Samuel. "Children and the Elderly: Divergent Paths for America's Dependents." *Demography* 21 (November, 1982): 435-457. Preston's accessible, engaging essay discusses some of the implications of the graying of the American population. In particular, it focuses on the direct and indirect competition for public resources that occurs between the large and growing elderly subpopulation and the infant and child subpopulation.

Wattenberg, Ben. *The Birth Dearth*. New York: Pharos Books, 1987. Provocative and controversial treatise arguing that the low levels of fertility that have characterized the U.S. population since the 1970's may lead to numerous negative social changes. Included among these hypothesized changes are a decrease in personal happiness, increased turmoil within American society, and an overall decline in the international stature of the United States.

Weeks, John R. *Population: An Introduction to Concepts and Issues*. 5th ed. Belmont, Calif.: Wadsworth, 1992. Perhaps the most popular demography textbook, Weeks's work provides a well-rounded introduction to demography that is both detailed and accessible.

Arlen D. Carey

Cross-References

Demography; Immigration and Emigration; Social Change: Sources of Change; Technology and Social Change.

DEMOGRAPHY

Type of sociology: Population studies or demography
Field of study: Data collection and analysis

Demography is the study of the characteristics of human populations in relation to birth, death, and migration patterns; it encompasses both empirical data and causal relationships. The field also studies population characteristics such as age, sex, race, income, education, and religion.

Principal terms

AGE/SEX PYRAMID: a graphical construction of the age and sex distribution of a population at one time period

COHORT: a group of people who simultaneously share some common social events, with year of birth being one possible social characteristic

DEMOGRAPHIC TRANSITION: the concept that nations, as they move from underdeveloped to developed, go through three phases that ultimately stabilize the population at relatively low birth and death rates

DEPENDENCY RATIO: ratio of people of dependent ages (age zero to fourteen and age sixty-five and older) to people of economically active ages (ages fifteen to sixty-four)

EXPECTATION OF LIFE: average duration of life beyond any particular age (of persons who have attained that age), calculated from a life table

GROSS NATIONAL PRODUCT PER CAPITA: common measure of average income in a nation, calculated by dividing the total value of goods and services produced by the total population size

Overview

Demography is the scientific study of the characteristics of a human population, both static (stable) and dynamic (changing). In the study of a human population, it is necessary to be aware of the components of growth, which are related to fertility, mortality, and net migration patterns in a society. The fertility patterns of a society refer to the number of children born. In his book *Population: An Introduction to Concepts and Issues* (5th ed., 1992), John R. Weeks demonstrates that fertility may have both a biological and social component. The biological component includes the ability of women and men to conceive children, while the social component includes such factors as the timing of marriage (for example, child marriages in India versus marriage at a later age in Ireland) and restrictions on sexual behavior.

The mortality component of population growth is related to the expectation of life for individuals in a social order. This average expectation is related to the death rates for the younger and older members of a society. Nations may be described either as underdeveloped or developed in relation to their gross national product (GNP) per capita, with underdeveloped nations having a relatively low GNP (for example, $1,000) and developed nations having a relatively high GNP ($15,000). In underdeveloped nations there is a high death rate for both the very young and very old, whereas in developed nations the death rate is low for the very young, and then increases steadily with age. In underdeveloped nations people die from both communicable diseases (such as malaria) and chronic diseases (such as heart disease, cancer, and stroke), whereas in developed nations people are more likely to die from chronic illnesses.

With regard to migration, one may differentiate between internal and international migration. Internal population shifts are most often related to changes in economic conditions in different geographic areas; the human population is likely to move internally from areas of low economic growth to areas of higher economic growth. In the United States since World War II there has been a general westward migration related to increased economic opportunity in Western states. Roderic Beaujot's book *Population Change in Canada: The Challenges of Policy Adaptation* (1991) illustrates these influences at work in Canada, with British Columbia, with its growing economy on the Pacific Rim, experiencing the greatest rate of population growth. International economic factors are also very important in explaining migration trends among nations.

The shifts in population growth within societies over time may be explained by the process known as demographic transition. As nations begin the process of modernization, which involves a shift from an agrarian economy to an industrial economy, they experience high rates of both fertility and mortality. As they undergo economic transformation, however, they experience an initial fall in their mortality rates, with their fertility rates remaining high. This initial demographic shift causes a significant increase in population for these nations. In the case of European nations, international migration served as a safety valve for many nations when they underwent this process. Over time, industrializing nations experience a fall in their fertility rates because industrialization increases the economic costs of children while reducing their economic benefits. When the fertility and mortality rates are in balance, these nations experience stable population growth. Many underdeveloped nations of the world are undergoing the process of demographic transition. In his book Preparing for the Twenty-first Century (1993), Paul Kennedy demonstrates that these nations are in a disadvantaged economic position compared to the European nations that underwent this process earlier, so the transition will be more difficult for these nations.

There are a number of measures that can be employed to examine the changing components of a human population. One measure is a cohort—people who experience some common social event. All individuals are members of a birth cohort, but at times a generational cohort may be formed by certain historical events. One illustration of a generational cohort is all individuals who participated in the American Civil War.

Another useful tool for examining a human population is an age/sex pyramid, which gives a graphical representation of the number of people of a given age and sex in a society during a particular time period. The population pyramid conveys useful information about the demographic characteristics of a society. For example, underdeveloped nations have a pyramid with a large base, since they have a high rate of fertility. By contrast, the upper portion of the pyramid is larger in developed nations because of falling fertility and an increased expectation of life. If a society experiences a significant rise in fertility (as the United States did with the baby boom between 1945 and 1955) or mortality (as in the Soviet Union between 1941 and 1945), these demographic changes will influence its population pyramid.

Another useful population measure is the dependency ratio (DR), which determines the relative ratio of the dependent population (most often given as ages zero to fourteen and age sixty-five and older) to the economically active population fifteen to sixty-four. As developed nations undergo aging, they experience a rise in their aged DR; underdeveloped nations continue to have a high youth DR until they become modernized.

The scientific study of human population involves a determination of the factors that cause shifts in fertility, mortality, and net migration within a society. In his classic study *Principles of Demography* (1969), Donald J. Bogue illustrates how one can quantify the previous measures and employ them to examine the characteristics of human populations mathematically.

Applications

The knowledge obtained from demographic studies can be employed in a number of substantive areas. The first area is the field of aging. An understanding of demography allows gerontological researchers to study changes in the relative age composition of a human population and to determine the social consequences of these changes. A fall in fertility and mortality rates, as is occurring in developed nations, implies that there will be fewer younger people to provide care for the elderly and proportionally more older people in these societies. The process of demographic transition is also occurring in underdeveloped nations. For example, the significant fertility drop in China, the result of strict government policies, will have social implications for that country well into the twenty-first century. The increased aging of the human population in developed nations also means that the aged DR will increase, which will put more social pressure on public institutions, such as the United States' Social Security system.

A second area in which demographic principles may be applied is the strategic planning of business organizations. These economic organizations need to have demographic information on the sizes and locations of their markets. Market research techniques are employed to locate different socioeconomic groups within this market. Marketing work related to the beer brewing industry provides an example. Market researchers for this industry have determined that young males are their prime market, and the industry targets these individuals with extensive advertising on televised sporting events. A dynamic examination of demographic trends indicates a shrinking of this market (attributable partly to the aging of the American population), which has caused this industry to diversify and create new products such as nonalcoholic beer.

A third area in which demographic information is crucial involves governmental activities. In order to apportion elected officials in the House of Representatives, the United States government needs information on the changing geographical distribution of the American population. The federal government also needs demographic information to manage a series of entitlement programs, including Social Security and Medicare. For these entitlement programs it is necessary for the government to have information on the numeric size and longevity of the elderly population as well as on future population trends. Similarly, the Department of Veterans Affairs needs demographic information on veterans in the United States, especially the large World War II cohort.

Demographic information is also useful in the scientific study of deviant behavior. A number of studies have shown that younger males make up the group most likely to commit criminal acts. Robert A. Easterlin has developed a theory arguing that the relative size of a cohort will influence its members' propensity for deviant behavior. According to this theory, smaller age cohorts, such as the youth cohort in the 1940's and 1950's, had greater economic opportunities, were subject to fewer social pressures, and therefore were less likely to commit deviant acts. The opposite is true for large cohorts, such as the youth cohorts in the 1960's and 1970's, and members of these cohorts have a greater probability of becoming deviant.

Race and ethnic relations is another area in which demographic information is useful. In this area there is a need for information on the relative size of minority populations, their fertility and mortality patterns, and their geographic distribution within the nation in order to formulate government policy. It is also necessary to have information on their socioeconomic situations as well as on their health characteristics. Studies carried out by the U.S. Bureau of the Census indicate that nonwhites have approximately half the income of whites, they own approximately one-twelfth the property of whites, and their children have a significantly greater probability of being in poverty.

Demographic studies are important in the field of international relations. United Nations organizations collect information on the demographic characteristics of nations throughout the world, and they use this information to aid nations in family planning and the control of mortality within their population. Early studies of mortality in underdeveloped nations showed a high level of mortality among young people caused by infectious diseases, and the United Nations proceeded to develop programs to control these diseases (malaria control in southern India is one example).

Religious organizations and the mass media also use demographic information. Religious organizations require information on the relative number of their adherents, their geographic location, and the socioeconomic characteristics of this population. The mass media (television, radio, popular magazines, and newspapers) require information on the size of their potential market and the demographic characteristics of the population that consumes their products.

Context
Since ancient times, leaders and philosophers have been concerned with population issues. Usually these concerns involved the replacement of people lost through high mortality rates. Prior to the Middle Ages, societies encouraged high fertility levels among their populations.

During the Middle Ages, under the influence of Christian doctrines, there was an attempt to limit fertility, but this view changed with the Renaissance.

Prior to the 1700's, societies did not possess accurate information on the composition of their populations. The Roman Empire, for example, did conduct periodic census enumerations, but they had limited scientific value since they were taken only for administrative purposes and included only citizens and adult males. In 1749 Sweden began the first modern census, and it was soon followed by Norway, Denmark, and the United States. With the growth of statistical procedures in the nineteenth century to analyze the census information, this information began to be

English economist Thomas Malthus (1766-1834) is generally regarded as the founder of scientific demography. *(Library of Congress)*

useful to policy makers and social scientists. In addition to performing numerical counts, censuses began to ask questions about the age, occupation, literacy, and employment characteristics of the population being examined.

The first scientific examination of the social consequences of population changes may be found in Thomas Malthus's work *An Essay on the Principle of Population* (1798), which maintained that population growth was subject to a natural law. According to Malthus, population unchecked would grow at a geometric rate, while agricultural production would only grow at an arithmetic rate. In order to have social stability, he said, it was necessary to bring them into balance. He identified two types of checks that could do this. First, there were positive checks, which increased mortality; these included war, famine, and plague. Second, there were preventive checks, which limited human births; these included abortion and the delay of marriage.

In the nineteenth century, Marxian theory criticized the Malthusian perspective, arguing that, historically, each society develops a means of economic organization that determines both the level and consequences of population growth. Later in the nineteenth century, Émile Durkheim related population growth to societal specialization.

With the growth of more accurate quantitative data and more sophisticated statistical techniques in the twentieth century, demography developed as a scientific discipline. Better census data, as well as the introduction of survey data, allowed the further development of the field, with an ability to test scientific theories (such as the theory of demographic transition). The field was also able to provide precise information that could be employed in a number of other disciplines. The computer revolution, which began after World War II, has been instrumental in expanding knowledge in the field. Computers have allowed investigators to develop techniques to better understand the current population distribution in a society and make future projections concerning this population.

Bibliography

Beaujot, Roderic. *Population Change in Canada: The Challenges of Policy Adaptation.* Toronto, Ont.: McClelland & Stewart, 1991. Using Canadian society as its empirical base, this book presents an excellent discussion of basic demographic concepts and uses them to interpret population changes in Canada.

Bogue, Donald J. *Principles of Demography.* New York: John Wiley & Sons, 1969. Thorough and complete analysis of demographic principles, with a mathematical exposition of techniques for population projections. An outstanding and classic work in the field of demography.

Coale, Ansley J., and Edgar M. Hoover. *Population Growth and Economic Development in Low-Income Countries.* Princeton, N.J.: Princeton University Press, 1958. Classic discussion of the economic consequences of continued population growth for countries such as India and Mexico. The work demonstrates the need for family planning in underdeveloped nations.

Kennedy, Paul. *Preparing for the Twenty-first Century.* New York: Random House, 1993. Well-written essay from a Malthusian perspective on the social, economic, and political consequences of population changes in developed and underdeveloped nations.

Mason, William M., and Stephen E. Fienberg, eds. *Cohort Analysis in Social Research.* New York: Springer-Verlag, 1985. Essays by scholars defining and exploring issues related to cohort analysis in the social sciences. Contains excellent discussion of how scholars may de-aggregate age, period, and cohort effects when analyzing longitudinal data.

Menard, Scott W., and Elizabeth Moen. *Perspectives on Population: An Introduction to Concepts and Issues.* New York: Oxford University Press, 1987. Readings by population scholars that considers demographic issues in a number of disciplines.

Weeks, John R. *Population: An Introduction to Concepts and Issues.* 7th ed. Belmont, Calif.: Wadsworth, 1999. Good general introduction to demography, with broad discussion of the history of the discipline and the broad analytic elements in the field. Many illustrative figures are used, and each chapter emphasizes central demographic principles.

Zopf, Paul E., Jr. *Population: An Introduction to Social Demography.* Palo Alto, Calif.: Mayfield, 1984. Broad and illustrative introduction to the field of demography, with many useful illustrations of issues in the field (such as zero population growth). The book will be most useful for students who need to have an elementary understanding of basic demographic concepts.

Ira M. Wasserman

Cross-References

Demographic Factors and Social Change; Immigration and Emigration; Social Change: Sources of Change; Technology and Social Change.

DEVIANCE
Analysis and Overview

Type of sociology: Deviance and social control
Fields of study: Forms of deviance; Social implications of deviance; Theories of deviance

Deviance refers to behaviors that are defined by those in power as violations of societal norms. Some forms of deviance break codified law; other behaviors are defined as deviant because of the negative reactions of others. Deviance and its counterpart, social control, are present in all societies and are essential to the existence and smooth functioning of societies.

Principal terms

ELITE DEVIANCE: deviant behaviors with little risk to the perpetrator; some are specifically criminal, some are unethical, and some endanger public health, safety, or financial well-being

HEGEMONY: preponderance of influence and power held by a society's formal leadership; governments and major religions tend to be the most predominant hegemonic structures in societies

IDEOLOGY: system of beliefs and values; a dominant cultural ideology is assumed to exist and be reflected in laws and regulations; in actuality, many ideologies coexist in a society

LABELING: process of naming deviance and deviants; a label "sticks" when bestowed by those in power, often creating stigma and master status

MASTER STATUS: deviant label that, once applied, is very difficult to shed; the labels "convict" and "child molester" are two examples

MORAL ENTREPRENEURS: persons who attempt to define behavior as deviant; some have official power, but many do not

NORMS: behavioral expectations of a group or society, based on values held to be fundamental; some become codified into laws

POWER: ability of a person or group to force its will on others even in the face of explicit (or implicit) opposition

SECRET DEVIANCE: classification for acts such as gambling, prostitution, homosexual behaviors, and individual drug use; participation in such activities is said to be voluntary and consensual

SOCIAL CONTROL: attempts by the leaders of a society to regulate the behavior of citizens by specifying certain behaviors as deviant and establishing consequences for engaging in such behaviors

Overview

Most sociologists would probably agree on a basic description of deviance as behavior that violates basic values and norms of society. Differences quickly arise, however, when more probing questions are raised. One might ask, for example, whose basic values are being violated—and who defined certain values as "basic." Who defines what behaviors are violations of these basic values? Why is it that only some people who violate certain norms and values are labeled "deviant"?

A principal objective of all societies is survival, and all societies believe that to ensure survival, order must be maintained. The maintenance of order is accomplished through the passage of laws and regulations, the purpose of which is to control the behaviors of the population so that individuals do not succumb to individualistic behaviors which would be destructive to the collectivity. Thus, in a democracy, through the ideology supported by elected officials and other leaders, laws are passed "for the greater good" that prescribe and proscribe behaviors in which citizens may and may not engage.

In sociological terms, proscribed behaviors are known as "deviant" behaviors and are defined in relation to what people in power have defined as the society's basic values. Assisting the leaders of societies in their definition of deviant behaviors are what sociologists call "moral entrepreneurs"—people and groups who want particular behavior defined as deviant because the behavior violates their own norms and values. Over time, society labels numerous behaviors as deviant, even behaviors that do no harm to others—that have no "victims." For example, secret deviance (such as extramarital affairs and same-sex sexual relations) and victimless crimes (gambling, excessive drinking) are behaviors that are engaged in voluntarily and consensually.

Until fairly late in the twentieth century, most definitions of deviance were focused on what could be called "one-to-one" deviance—that is, acts committed by one person (or by a small group) against a single other person (a victim). In the mid-to late twentieth century, attention began to focus on what might be called "one-to-many" types of deviance: so-called elite deviance and white-collar crimes (such as violations of environmental laws, financial system scams and embezzlement, medical and health improprieties, and computer crimes) in which the action of an individual has wide-ranging effects.

The counterpart to deviance is social control, the purpose of which is to regulate the behaviors of people in a society in order to maintain the relatively tranquil survival of social systems. Social control may be seen as both necessary and functional. Yet in order for there to be a need for control, there must be behaviors in which people engage which have been defined by those in power as not under control (as deviant). This raises an interesting question: Which came first, the deviance or the social control? Perhaps it does not matter which came first; both deviance and social control exist in all societies, and both appear to be necessary and functional for the continuance of societies. Social control is needed for stability; deviance, as a catalyst for social change. Deviance and social control exist in a dialectic relationship with each other; that is, each acts on the other to produce yet another version of each.

A related phenomenon which must be considered when dealing with deviance and social control is the identification and labeling of perpetrators of the so-called deviant behaviors. Throughout the history of sociology and the development of various theories of deviance, the subjects of the studies on which theories of deviance have been based have, to a great extent, been those segments of the population without power. These subjects were most frequently from the lower classes; they were often people who were incarcerated, in therapy, or in hospitals—all representing some type of "captive" population. Moreover, a significant part of these populations has been male and/or African American. Thus, social control techniques would also seem to have been rather specifically directed at selected segments of the population: perpetrators who were primarily male, lower class, and often African American.

Applications

Numerous policies, practices, and jobs in societies derive from the various explanations of deviance and social control. For example, theories that describe deviance from biological or psychological perspectives place the locus, but not the responsibility, of deviance within the individual. From these explanations, numerous treatments and therapies were devised to correct the deviance (as opposed to practices intended to punish the deviant). These treatments and therapies removed, to an extent, the responsibility for the deviant behavior from the individual engaging in the deviant acts: The cause of the behavior was, by definition, often viewed as being beyond the control of the individual.

For example, some theories identify hormonal imbalance as the cause (or at least one cause) of deviance; thus, to exercise social control of the deviance, hormone therapies were developed to be administered in treatment programs in hospitals and prisons. Other types of treatments involve various psychoanalytical and group therapies (including groups such as Alcoholics Anonymous and Narcotics Anonymous), which some people exhibiting deviant behavior are required to attend as part of their rehabilitation, sentencing, and/or parole conditions. These requirements in turn produce a need for a large number of positions for psychologists, psychiatrists, counselors, and so on.

Later theories (cultural transmission, subcultural, delinquency and opportunity, differential association, anomie, and social control theories) moved away from biology, psychology, and medicine as explanations and began addressing deviance in terms of social norms and community activities. These theories began to question the relationship between so-called deviant cultures and communities and the dominant culture. Social control theory, for example, posits that all people are "bonded" and attached to society (the larger, dominant society) and that this bonding and attachment produces social control. Weakening of the bonds results in deviance. Studies have shown, for example, that the ties between delinquent adolescent boys and their parents are significantly less strong than the parent-offspring ties of other boys of the same age. A central aspect of control theory is that everyone has the urge to deviate occasionally and that it is the attachment to others that holds such urges in check.

Differential association theory, on the other hand, is a type of cultural transmission theory; conceived by Edwin H. Sutherland, it was intended to describe how delinquents and criminals learn the motives and skills involved in rule-violating behavior. Differential association theory is based on the idea that, in the socialization process, people learn "definitions" both favorable to obeying laws and favorable to disobeying laws. According to Sutherland's "principle of differential association," people engage in criminal behavior when they have more definitions that support violating the law than they have definitions that go against violating the law. The strength of these various definitions is influenced by how early in life one is exposed to them and how long one is exposed to them.

According to these theories of deviance, the ways to regain social control and reestablish the social order are to "fix," or realign, local communities or nondominant cultures so that their values more resemble the values of the dominant and hegemonic culture and to provide alternative opportunities—particularly to delinquent male youth—in order to dissuade them from activities in delinquent subcultures. These theories tend to view deviant communities as existing separate from and outside the dominant social system and consequently see a need to reintegrate them into the dominant, hegemonic culture.

Like biological and psychological perspectives, theories addressing deviant cultures, social norms, and communities have resulted in various social programs and occupations. Activities such as scouting, the Big Brother/Big Sister programs, YMCAs and YWCAs, youth bureaus, job training programs, support groups of various kinds, educational opportunities, and sports programs are designed to address and change the values and activities of individuals in "disorganized" communities—and sometimes the values of entire local communities themselves. The objective of such programs is to make the nondominant communities more resemble the dominant culture so that the individuals residing in the nondominant communities will be exposed to nondeviant activities, and thus to values that more resemble those of the established dominant culture. Through these activities, an attempt is made to reintegrate individuals residing in so-called deviant cultures and communities, or exhibiting deviant social norms, with the dominant culture (with its presumably prosocial norms) and thus to establish or regain social control. Society as a whole can thereby continue to function smoothly, using the assumed values of the hegemonic culture as the benchmark.

These explanations of deviance focus primarily on acts of "one-on-one" deviance (or, in some cases, secret deviance) and either on the individual or on the individual's community as the locus of the cause of deviance. Little or no attention is given to how the individual and the individual's community form a part of the larger society or to the fact that power differentials exist across various communities within the larger social structure. Yet such an awareness is essential to understanding the problematic nature of defining "deviance" and understanding the resulting differences in the consequences of such behaviors.

In terms of elite deviance, history suggests that there has been only a limited effort at exerting social control over perpetrators of corporate, governmental, and white-collar deviance. In everyday life, the response to individuals engaging in these forms of deviance has been quite mild in comparison with societal reactions to perpetrators of "one-on-one" deviance. One may note, for example, the mild types of sentences and places of incarceration meted out to people involved in governmental abuses (such as those that occurred during the Watergate and Iran-Contra scandals) or financial improprieties, even those involving billions of dollars and defrauding thousands, even millions, of people. Relatively meager fines are also levied against corporations violating environmental laws. These social control reactions may be compared with the sentences meted out to burglars, armed robbers, and, particularly, some drug users. The latter types of deviance tend to receive much more vigorous responses than the former, especially considering the difference in the numbers of individuals victimized. In other words, applications of the definitions of deviance and the mechanisms of social control vary widely according to many factors; among them seem to be the initial explanation of the cause of the deviance, who or what the victim of the deviance was, and the status of the perpetrator.

Context

The first clearly recognized development of the notion of deviance and its counterpart, social control, can be traced to a work by Émile Durkheim, "The Normal and the Pathological," found in *Les Règles de la méthode sociologique* (1895; *The Rules of Sociological Method*, 1938), as well as to his foundational work on deviance, *Le Suicide: Étude de sociologie* (1897; *Suicide: A Study in Sociology*, 1951). Durkheim, as one of the founders of sociology, was extremely influential in the development of theories about deviance and social control.

Immense growth in the development of the areas of deviance and social control occurred in the United States in the first half of the twentieth century. After an early focus on biological, psychological, and social psychological explanations of deviance, sociologists identified certain factors—massive immigration, urbanization, and industrialization—which some scholars claimed produced social disorganization in urban areas. They argued that these phenomena caused an erosion of the social norms of the dominant society, thereby giving rise to deviance). In terms of social control, the most prominent programs dealt with community development, urban renewal, employment, educational opportunities, and sports opportunities; some programs were also developed to address unequal distribution of wealth and power, although it is debatable whether these last types of programs have accomplished much.

The 1970's saw the development of theories of deviance which recognized power and class as significant social facts—social facts which caused some sociologists to rethink and reformulate earlier theories of deviance and social control. This decade saw not only the growth of so-called critical, radical, and conflict theories of deviance but also the beginnings of a focus on secret deviance, on victimless crimes, and on elite, corporate, and white-collar deviance. Analytically, deviance is important as a concept—a tool to help explain human behavior. Social control is important as a concept that helps to explain the maintenance of a fundamental societal goal: smoothly functioning systems of social institutions and people living together. Deviance and social control are both important components in the dynamics and existence of social systems.

Throughout the history of humankind, definitions of deviance and social control have established hierarchies of people. There are, for example, the official labelers of what and who is deviant; the recipients of the label "deviant"; the makers of policy and writers of society's rules, regulations, and laws; and the recipients of programs, policies, and practices (social control mechanisms) designed to address the labeled deviant acts and behaviors and thus to restore smooth social functioning. Occasionally, at various times, people who resist the label "deviant" also serve as catalysts for social change, for revisions in the dominant, hegemonic definitions of what is considered deviant.

Bibliography

Becker, Howard S. *Outsiders: Studies in the Sociology of Deviance*. New York: Free Press, 1963. Readable classic in the sociology of deviance. Becker raises critical issues and questions, such as whose rules determine what is defined as deviant, who does the labeling, and who gets labeled. Recognizes and discusses the issue of power vis-à-vis definition creation and label bestowing.

Conrad, Peter, and Joseph W. Schneider. *Deviance and Medicalization: From Badness to Sickness*. St. Louis: C. V. Mosby, 1980. Deals well with the history of deviance and classifications of deviance. Examines the sociocultural contexts in which deviance is defined and created, including the ways in which interested groups (moral entrepreneurs) affect definitions of deviance. The authors place special emphasis on the role of medicine in relation to deviance.

Durkheim, Émile. *Suicide: A Study in Sociology*. Edited by George Simpson. Translated by John A. Spaulding and George Simpson. New York: Free Press, 1966. First published in 1897, this classic on deviance has both methodological and historical importance. Details the ways in which an act, defined as deviant and seen as singular and personal, is explained by macro facts of social structure.

Hills, Stuart L. *Demystifying Social Deviance*. New York: McGraw-Hill, 1980. Short book with easy-to-follow but thought-provoking content. Offers selective topics within which to explore the notion of deviance and presents challenges to status quo definitions thereof.

Kelly, Delos H., comp. *Deviant Behavior: A Text-Reader in the Sociology of Deviance*. 5th ed. New York: St. Martin's Press, 1996. Good groupings of the classic theories of deviance. Includes a variety of readings, some dealing with subjects not generally considered in the layperson's conception of deviance. Treats both individual-level and macro-level deviance and discusses both perpetrators and control agents.

Little, Craig B. *Deviance and Control: Theory, Research, and Social Policy*. Itasca, Ill.: F. E. Peacock, 1989. Useful book with examples of specific types of deviance and their related social control mechanisms (social policies). One of the few books to deal with heterosexual sexual deviance; includes a good chapter on elite deviance. Very helpful charts.

Rubington, Earl, and Martin S. Weinberg, comps. *Deviance: The Interactionist Perspective*. 7th ed. Boston: Allyn and Bacon, 1999. Readings organized into four sections, each preceded by a brief introduction. This work has a single theoretical approach, that of interactionism (the idea that meanings are created by people in their exchanges with one another). If a balanced approach to the study of deviance is desired, other books must be consulted as well.

M. F. Stuck

Cross-References

Cultural Transmission Theory of Deviance; Deviance: Functions and Dysfunctions; Labeling and Deviance; Structural-Strain Theory of Deviance; Suicide.

DEVIANCE
Functions and Dysfunctions

Type of sociology: Deviance and social control
Field of study: Forms of deviance

No society exists without deviant behavior. Deviance is both dysfunctional and functional. It is dysfunctional in that it undermines and impairs society's capacity to provide for the well-being and safety of its members and to maintain their trust. It is functional because it facilitates the process of learning the meaning of laws and rules, acts as a warning signal, unites groups, and promotes solidarity.

Principal terms

CRIME: behavior that violates laws prohibiting such behavior and may be punished; often poses a threat to personal well-being and safety

DEVIANCE: behavior that violates widely accepted rules of social conduct

DYSFUNCTION: impairment or abnormality in normal functioning that has adverse effects upon social organization

FUNCTION: normal, characteristic, and proper actions of a social organization which promote the survival and well-being of the organization and its members

"HARD" DEVIANCE: deviant behavior that causes physical damage to the personal well-being, safety, and security of members of a society and their possessions; examples are violent crimes and suicide

"SOFT" DEVIANCE: deviant behavior that does not cause physical harm or damage to those affected; examples are mental disorders, prostitution, and illegal gambling

Overview

Deviance refers to behavior that violates widely accepted rules of social conduct and that has the potential to cause significant social disorganization. Such violations are viewed sufficiently negatively by society that formal sanctions and controls are directed at them. Such deviant behaviors include criminal acts and behaviors caused by mental disorders.

If a society is to survive, it must be able to guarantee the survival of its members and provide for stable and predictable economic relationships. Society and its citizens mutually recognize that economic and interpersonal relationships must be regulated. Deviant behavior undermines and impairs society's capacity to provide for its members' survival and stability. Additionally, the diversion of funds and resources necessary to deal with deviant behavior, as well as the personal tragedy and economic loss inflicted by this deviancy, only add to the potential social disorganization.

Albert K. Cohen (1966) discussed three other ways in which deviancy is dysfunctional and destructive of social organization. First, deviance can adversely affect the social system at vital points by depriving it of essential components and by impairing or destroying the functioning of the larger social unit. For example, Gilbert Geis argued that white-collar and corporate crime, by its insidious nature, destroys confidence, depletes the integrity of commercial life and has the potential to cause devastation. Imagine, says Geis, what would happen if nuclear regulatory rules were violated or if toxic wastes were dumped into a city's water supply.

Second, deviance has the potential to destroy the willingness of society's members to continue to contribute to the well-being of society. If "idlers," "fakers," "chiselers," "sneaks," "deadbeats," and others of this ilk are perceived as being disproportionately rewarded without undergoing the sacrifice and effort of honest, hardworking citizens, willingness to play by the rules of loyalty, self-discipline, and morality may be undermined.

Third, and most destructive according to Cohen, is that deviant behavior may undermine trust in the social system. Individuals make an investment in society's future by committing their resources and forgoing some alternatives on the assumption that if one conducts oneself according to society's rules, others will also behave appropriately. Distrust undermines motivation, leading people to view their efforts as pointless, wasted, and foolish, and the future as uncertain and hazardous. Trust is an indispensable prerequisite for any viable social enterprise.

Émile Durkheim argued in 1938 that deviancy is an inevitable part of any society, that it is impossible for any society to exist utterly free of it, and that therefore deviancy is a normal integral, useful, and necessary part of any healthy society. Deviancy may be regrettable ("pain has likewise nothing desirable about it"), but it does have a positive purpose. Similarly, Kai T. Erikson (1986) took exception to the view that one of the characteristics of an appropriately designed society is that it prevents the occurrence of deviant behavior.

According to Durkheim and Erikson, deviant individuals provide a needed service to society. By permitting members of society to understand what is deviant, they can also allow them to know what is not deviant and thereby help them to live according to appropriate shared standards. Deviance threatens the collective conscience and produces punishment, and punishment facilitates social solidarity and cohesion. Deviancy promotes respect for beliefs, traditions, and collective practices, and it increases society's capacity to adapt to changing conditions and new life situations. Deviancy is a critical mechanism for producing successful social changes and maintaining the vitality of the social system. Other sociologists have also advanced this theme. Cohen listed seven positive contributions made by deviant behaviors:

1. Identification with and concern for the well-being of a group may lead to the violation of rules. For example, a military unit needs supplies in excess of its normal quota, and the procurement officer violates rules to obtain those supplies.

2. Deviancy provides a safety valve that makes it possible to satisfy illegitimate desires that, if suppressed in enough people, might lead to an attack on rules or social institutions by the disaffected. Prostitution, for example, takes some strain off the legitimate order without threatening the integrity of the family.

3. Pushing the limits of rules and laws allows one to learn what those rules and laws

mean, thereby reducing ambiguity and allowing the group to reach a common understanding.

4. The deviant population can function as a built-in out-group that unites the
dominant in-group in emotional solidarity.

5. Deviance provides a contrast effect that makes conformity special and prized
behavior and a source of gratification. As Shakespeare stated, "a good deed shines
brightest in a naughty world."

6. Deviance may serve as a warning signal of defects in and discontent with the
social order that need to be identified, addressed, and corrected.

7. Deviance may unite the group and promote solidarity and the virtues of kindness
and patience in the form of working on behalf of the deviant, to reclaim or protect him
or her.

8. An eighth function of deviance can be added to this list. By definition, a deviant
is an outcast from the dominant, conforming society. By identifying with the world of
other and similar deviants, the individual becomes a member of an exclusive group.
Paul A. Inciardi has observed that the fraternity of professional thieves provides them
with friendship, understanding, sympathy, congeniality, security, recognition, and
respect that can be obtained nowhere else.

Applications

Violent crime is what Nachman Ben-Yehuda (1985) refers to as "hard" deviance (sexual
deviance, drug abuse, and mental illness are "soft" deviance). Examples of "hard" deviant
behavior are assault, homicide, suicide, organized crime, burglary, rape, and other crimes of
violence. Such behavior illustrates both the dysfunction and function of deviant behavior.
In violent crime, severe mayhem, injury, or loss is inflicted upon a person or property. Such
behavior poses a significant threat to the well-being, safety, and security of people and their
possessions; therefore, such behavior is labeled deviant. In this regard, violent crime is
clearly dysfunctional.

According to the Uniform Crime Reports, published by the Federal Bureau of Investigation, the rate of violent crime has increased nearly 20 percent from 1988 through 1992. For
example, gun deaths, including suicides, exceeded 37,000 in 1992. This is a homicide rate
of about 10 for every 100,000 Americans (versus five and less than one for Canada and
Japan, respectively).

Although this dysfunctional characteristic of violent crime indirectly or directly touches
all Americans, nowhere is it more apparent than in African American communities. Tom
Morgenthau has observed that in many African American communities, an "oppositional
culture" rules the streets and neighborhoods. Composed of "profoundly nihilistic" teenag-
ers, this culture condones and romanticizes violence and believes in the law of the streets,
the power of guns, bravado, and respect. One result of this situation has been a steady
escalation of black-on-black violence. In 1992, the rate per 1,000 people for victims of
violent crime was 50.4 for blacks and 29.9 for whites. For blacks under age twenty-four, the
homicide rate per 100,000 people increased from 84 in 1980 to 159 in 1991 (but also

decreased significantly for those age 25 and over). The homicide rates per 100,000 people vary from nearly six to nine times greater for blacks than for whites, depending on age group. According to Morgenthau, black "gangsta" teens "are terrorizing the inner city as ruthlessly as the KKK ever terrorized the South." The result of this violence has been that communities have been paralyzed by the fear of crime. Black children worry significantly more than white children do that a family member will become a victim of a violent crime, and feel significantly less safe than white children do from violent crime in their neighborhood after dark. According to Morgenthau, this "puerile and self-destructive" violence subverts the positive values that form the foundation of society: hope, work, love and civility, the belief in success through hard and honest work, and faith in a happy and productive future.

From dysfunction, however, comes function. The increase in violent crime has seemed to galvanize and unite disparate groups in America, joining them in a common effort to get tough on crime. An October, 1993, poll by the newspaper *USA Today* revealed that 80 percent of the sample favored hiring more police and paying higher taxes to pay for it; 82 percent favored making it more difficult to parole violent prisoners; 79 percent favored harsher prison sentences; 75 percent favored making it more difficult to post bail; and 64 percent favored stiffer gun control laws.

For many years, crime has been one of Washington's phoniest debates. Congress habitually expressed concern and dismay at the rise in violent crime but contributed only a paltry $750 million a year to communities to help fight crime (95 percent of violent crimes are the responsibility of state and local governments). Additionally, the National Rifle Association (NRA), one of the most powerful, wealthy, formidable, and well-connected lobbies has adamantly and effectively campaigned against any gun control or restriction laws.

Against this background of congressional inaction lie polls revealing that Americans are more frightened, frustrated, and outraged than ever about what they perceive as a rising tide of violence. Clearly, the compact between citizens and government in which citizens consent to be ruled in exchange for the provision of personal safety and well-being by the government is perceived by the citizenry as not being fulfilled. As a result of this concern, disparate groups have coalesced to exert pressure on Congress to do something, and this pressure seems to have been effective. On this issue, partisan divisions between Democrats and Republicans receded, and in late 1993, Congress passed a crime bill and a gun control bill that were departures from politics as usual.

Additionally, the African American community has come together and mobilized in an attempt to deal with black-on-black crime. For example, the Reverend Jesse Jackson organized a summit meeting in 1994 to discuss strategies for combating crime. Also, African Americans increasingly seem to agree that they must confront the moral and social problems of inner city crimes in order to save the vast majority of ghetto youth.

Whether congressional actions and the efforts of the African American community will prove fruitful is open to doubt. The dysfunctional nature of violent crime has served the function of uniting an entire society to begin to honestly address and develop adaptive solutions to violent crime and the threat it poses to society.

Context

Deviancy is an integral and normal part of any society, and it serves various useful functions. It is impossible for any society to be free of deviance altogether. Therefore, the important consideration is how much deviance a society can afford to tolerate so that the functional and dysfunctional aspects of deviance remain in balance and society can survive and continue to provide for the well-being, safety, and security of its members.

Daniel Patrick Moynihan has argued that deviant behavior (he discusses crime, mental disorders, and family breakdown) has reached epidemic proportions in the United States. There is more deviance than can be tolerated. Dysfunction has gained dominance over function. Presumably helpless to arrest this explosion of deviancy, society has attempted to restore deviance to a manageable level by "defining deviancy down." That is, deviance has been redefined so that what was formerly considered to be deviant is now normal. Deviancy, once redefined, becomes manageable and tolerable. For example, violent crimes that previously would have stirred the nation's sensibilities (for example, the St. Valentine's Day Massacre in 1929) now routinely occur. They are treated in a routine manner or played down, evoke only moderate responses, and rapidly are forgotten. There is considerable evidence that the disintegration of the two-parent family can produce intellectual, physical, and emotional damage, but divorce is now represented as part of a normal family life cycle. To many observers it is not deviant or tragic but is a basis for "individual renewal and new beginnings." Similarly, it is said that the main problem of the large population of street people, many of whom are former patients of mental hospitals, is that they lack affordable housing.

Charles Krauthammer argued that deviancy has also been defined "up." That is, behaviors that were formerly considered normal or at worst ill-mannered are now considered to be deviant and even criminal. Krauthammer views defining deviancy "down" and "up" as processes. The deviant is defined as normal, the normal is defined as deviant, a moral equivalence is achieved, and an ideological agenda is accomplished: "a bold new way to strip the life of the bourgeois West of its moral sheen." Additionally, defining deviancy "down" allows coping by denial, a pretense that deviancy has disappeared. Defining deviancy "up" is also denial, but through distraction. By being distracted from feelings of helplessness in coping with real deviancy, by focusing on innocuous behaviors, an illusion is created that deviancy is in fact being addressed.

Denial and illusion create more problems. First, they prevent identifying, confronting, and solving the real problem: the fact that the voluminous increase in real deviancy has tilted the balance between functional and dysfunctional aspects of deviance toward the latter. Second, denial and illusion desensitize society's sense of outrage. Moynihan cites Judge Edwin Torres's description of how violent crime has resulted in a relentless and unabated slaughter of innocent people—subway riders, cab drivers, babies, bodega owners—in virtually every kind of location. Torres says, "This numbness, this near narcoleptic state can diminish the human condition to the level of combat infantrymen, who, in protracted campaigns, can eat their battlefield rations seated on the bodies of the fallen, friend and foe alike. A society that loses its sense of outrage is doomed to extinction." It was noted earlier, however, that public outrage and concern have forced politicians to face and to begin to deal more honestly with crime. Perhaps this is a positive sign of a willingness to confront the real issues and to restore a healthy balance between the functional and dysfunctional aspects of deviance.

Bibliography

Alder, Patricia A., ed. *Constructions of Deviance: Social Power, Context and Interaction.* 3d ed. Belmont, Calif.: Wadsworth, 1999.

Ben-Yehuda, Nachman. *Deviance and Moral Boundaries.* Chicago: University of Chicago Press, 1985. Good introduction to the sociology of deviance and the seminal contributions of Émile Durkheim. Also discusses deviance within the context of a modern and complex society and discusses "offbeat" forms of deviance such as the occult, deviant science, and witchcraft.

Cohen, Albert K. *Deviance and Control.* Englewood Cliffs, N.J.: Prentice-Hall, 1966. Brief but well-written and incisive analysis of deviant behavior. The book has an interesting discussion of the functional and dysfunctional aspects of deviancy.

Durkheim, Émile. *The Rules of Sociological Method.* Translated by Sarah A. Solovay and John H. Mueller, edited by George Catlin. 8th ed. New York: Free Press, 1938. Seminal text forcefully and persuasively arguing that deviance is normal, that it is impossible for a society to exist without it, and that it serves useful functions. This theme is also discussed in Durkheim's *The Division of Labor in Society* (Free Press, 1964).

Erikson, Kai T. *Wayward Puritans: A Study in the Sociology of Deviance.* New York: Macmillan, 1986. Another classic text on the sociology of deviance. The book is a study of crime rates in the Massachusetts Bay Colony. Erikson found that the amount of deviance remains constant over time, suggesting that society does not seek to wipe out deviance but rather tries to keep it within reasonable bounds.

Krauthammer, Charles. "Defining Deviancy Up." *The New Republic* 209 (November 22, 1993): 20-25. This article provides the other half to Daniel Patrick Moynihan's argument that the epidemic of deviancy in American society has become so great that society deals with it by defining it away. Krauthammer argues that there is a complementary social phenomenon that has taken large areas of previously normal behavior and made them abnormal.

Moynihan, Daniel Patrick. "Defining Deviancy Down." *American Scholar* 62 (Winter, 1993): 17-30. Moynihan convincingly argues that deviant behavior in America has reached epidemic proportions. In order to avoid being overwhelmed and to comprehend the situation, Americans have "defined deviance down"—that is, redefined to be normal what was formerly considered to be deviant. Moynihan uses criminality, family breakdown, and mental disorders to state his case.

Laurence Miller

Cross-References

Cultural Transmission Theory of Deviance; Deviance: Analysis and Overview; Functionalism; Labeling and Deviance; Structural-Strain Theory of Deviance; Suicide.

Dramaturgy

Type of sociology: Socialization and social interaction
Field of study: Interactionist approach to social interaction

Dramaturgical analysis considers the individual engaged in social interaction to be an "actor" who can, and will, change his or her performance "roles" as situations demand. This social-psychological perspective is more a descriptive tool than a theoretical perspective. Dramaturgy's focus is on the examination and explanation of everyday life in relation to the creation and maintenance of the individual self.

Principal terms

DEFINITION OF THE SITUATION: individuals' definition of a social interaction by means of explicit or implicit agreement

EXPRESSIONS GIVEN: performance-centered verbal communication

EXPRESSIONS GIVEN OFF: audience-centered perceptions of nonverbal performance cues such as clothing and props

IMPRESSION MANAGEMENT: individuals' attempts to control the impressions that others have of them

OFFSTAGE/ONSTAGE: private/public elements of performances

PERFORMANCE: actions meant to influence others in some way

ROLES: performances that control both the impressions of and definitions of a particular interaction

Overview

The dramaturgic approach to social interactions is based on an overarching metaphoric framework that sees the world of human experience as a "theater" in which individuals "stage" a variety of "performances." From this perspective, everyday life is a kind of ongoing drama, complete with rehearsals, staging, costumes, roles, and an audience. This is not to say that life is "imitated" or copied by drama; instead, theater and ordinary experience share significant organizational and ritual elements, such as body language and an interest in spatial arrangements, and communicate meaning through similar symbolic and formal languages, such as speech, music, and dance.

Theater and ordinary life are also connected by parallels between dramatic performance and the ways in which social behavior creates and maintains social order. As a matter of fact, the degrees of ritual and "theatricality" of a social experience are directly related to the level of tradition and flexibility permitted by the structure in which it takes place. Matters of self-consciousness, awareness of conventions and rules of performance, and flexibility of rules help define the differences between theatrical and social experiences. Drama, as an art form, is more likely to allow for or, in the case of avant-garde theater, encourage radical manipulation of conventions, while social experiences and conventions tend to enforce more conservative perspectives and behaviors.

What defines dramaturgic analysis and separates it from other sociological approaches is its interest in a detailed recording of the experiences of subjects as they are being lived. Dramaturgy is a situation-based examination of interactions which focuses on social behaviors and social hierarchies as the products of encounters between people and groups rather than as the frameworks for such encounters. For dramaturgists, society is not a fixed construct that simply requires description to be understood. Instead, dramaturgy is built on a revolutionary sense of social realities; emphasizing their constructed nature opens up an infinite universe of pluralistic, and possibly contradictory, ways to meet the challenges of ordinary social life.

Dramaturgic sociologists generally assume that individuals are aware of their active parts in the creation and presentation of themselves to others. This should not be understood to imply, however, that these presentations are either self-consciously manipulative or exploitative. Social interactions should be seen as positive attempts to fit the self into individualized understandings of specific situations. The self and the mind are products of shared understandings and communication, reflecting the opinions of others.

George Herbert Mead conceptualized the self as having two interdependent parts: the "I," which is the subjective, nonreflective, spontaneous part of the self, and the "me," a reflective, evaluative, objectified aspect. In addition, Mead believed that an individual's self-concept was dependent on, and reflective of, the opinions of others. The bottom line for the "actor," then, is that if the "audience" recognizes and accepts the self that has been presented, then the "performance" is "good." Dramaturgical investigators are concerned with how this complex web of theatrical (dramatic) relationships and procedures sustains social interactions and creates and maintains social life.

Social interaction, then, becomes a performance within a set of prescriptive rules. Individuals are expected to present and preserve a consistent public "face" and to help other members of the group to do the same. One need not always do this alone; social performances may be put on by teams, or "casts," of players, such as spouses entertaining guests at home or military personnel working under a supervising sergeant. In this context, the social world may be divided into public (front) and private (back) staging areas. Life is like theater in that everyone tries, to some degree or another, to control the reality that others see. Success in this manipulation may enhance one's freedom, power, or status. Onstage, performers define and maintain their public roles and selves; offstage, in private, they can relax a bit, and if they care to, remove their performance "masks" when they are with other "insiders."

Successful realization of one's social roles incorporates both practical and expressive elements. Performances are essential to a lucid, consistent, and knowable social reality. In this way, social performances simultaneously create and control the world. Situations do not, however, simply define themselves; social interactions are shaped by symbolic communications, which may take on lives of their own, transcending the individuals who create them and live in them. For example, organizations are often symbolically represented by architecture and can exist without any of their current members, who are, for the most part, invisible and easily replaced. Therefore, the world is filled with things that exist only in people's minds, which must constantly be enacted and reenacted to maintain their presence. Society is, in very real and important ways, a theater, and performances in it—symbolic communications and rituals—are critical to its survival.

Applications

Dramaturgical analysis provides a framework of theatrical metaphors for looking at social relationships and in doing so focuses on the underlying, shared, and often unspoken assumptions that function in social life. The best-known and perhaps most influential practitioner of dramaturgy is Erving Goffman. His book *The Presentation of Self in Everyday Life* (1959) examines the ways in which individuals manage their roles and the various selves they present in them. With close observations of social interactions in everyday life, such as informal street encounters, and in a variety of social settings, such as restaurants, Goffman adopts the terminology of the theater and uses the metaphors of dramatic performance to describe and organize the ways in which people operate in society. In *Asylums: Essays on the Social Situation of Mental Patients and Other Inmates* (1961), Goffman was most interested in the "backstage" behaviors of patients, nurses, and doctors. His analyses illustrate many similarities between daily behaviors and the performances of actors on a stage, such as playing as a member of a team, "breaking role," and audience complicity.

Dramaturgical analysis argues that life is lived episodically and situationally, and examines the instruments and acts of communication that people use to construct and interpret social experience. Situations are reduced to their component elements, and then the symbolic nature of the communications is examined. For example, in *Frame Analysis: An Essay on the Organization of Experience* (1974), Goffman studied the impact of the situation on interpersonal behaviors. He used the concept of "frame analysis" to isolate and concentrate on the elements of any situation which affect its meaning. Situations may be changed by "keying" one's actions to situations that have different "frames"—different definitions of image, theme, script, or plot. Goffman identified several major "frames," including deception, fantasy, ritual, analysis, and rehearsal.

Goffman's work, and dramaturgical analysis in general, shows how people live in the world today. Successful use of this method depends on detailed and accurate observation in the field. Although it is basically a behavioristic approach, dramaturgy actually simply begins with behavior and then goes much further. Observation and description lead to interest in not only what people do but also how they live, what variables and variations affect behavior, and what similarities in behavior might be discovered in dissimilar situations. Dramaturgy's particular strength as a sociological method is its relationship to the observer's own experiences as a member of the social scene, as opposed to the researcher's application of some abstract, theoretical approach to his or her data.

Examining interrelated rings of experience in society, starting with the self, moving outward to others, and then to institutions and organizations, allows the dramaturgical sociologist to illuminate issues and questions that seem so familiar as to be taken for granted. For example, looking at the different ways in which people perform the same roles can indicate the parameters of behaviors which are legitimated by society and what level of self-disclosure people find comfortable. Similarly, observing face-to-face interactions reveals the ways in which deviance and labeling function in both individual and group experiences, and might lead to significant insights about the processes of social control. Finally, investigation of how individuals interact to create and re-create social institutions could lead to an improved understanding of their origins and effects on people's lives.

Context

Dramaturgy, as a sociological concept, is historically rooted in the development of the American philosophy of pragmatism in the 1920's and 1930's. John Dewey and George Herbert Mead, preeminent proponents of this movement, were committed to strengthening the connections between the life of thought and the practicalities of daily life. For these philosophers, action was the only way to prove the correctness of an idea. The philosophical system they constructed had connections to the social sphere. Both men believed that meaning was socially constructed and that even individual self-consciousness depended on group communication and understanding. For Mead, role-playing was not simply a means of socialization, it was a central interactive channel for the emergence of individuality and identity, essential to the development of both the individual and social selves. Mead's uses of the concept of role, and the vocabulary of analysis which is its logical extension, are at once dramatic and metaphoric. Beginning his analysis at the level of personality, Mead stressed the symbolic and human-centered nature of roles. The relationship between role and personality, however, adds a level of complexity to any use of dramaturgical analysis, because of the various approaches one may take to understanding their relationship.

A number of sociologists have built on Mead's understanding of personality as a synthesis of personal elements and social roles. For example, C. Wright Mills's important work in his and Hans Gerth's *Character and Social Structure* (1953) focused on the issue of multiple social roles and their relationship to the social structure.

Thomas Luckmann and Peter Berger went a step further in their use of role-playing as an analytical tool, fusing George Herbert Mead's role theory with the institutional theories of Émile Durkheim and Max Weber. Berger and Luckmann emphasize the dramaturgical nature of these connections. As indicated by their arguments in *The Social Construction of Reality* (1967), Berger and Luckmann understood social roles and institutions to be inextricably connected in two major ways. First, the performance of a specific role represents one's particular place in an institution. Second, the role performed may describe or symbolize an entire network of institutional behaviors.

The social scientist Erving Goffman is most often associated with the development and application of dramaturgical analysis as part of social interaction theory. In his first book, *The Presentation of Self in Everyday Life*, Goffman focused on situational conditions that seemed to affect interaction, such as settings, the performers, the audience, and explicit and implicit rules of performance. In particular, he was interested in the ways in which interactions were maintained or, if disrupted, restarted. Goffman's work has consistently been concerned with episodic and repeated interactions rather than with interactions as evolving, sustained dramas.

Dramaturgy is, in fact, a subarea and may be a descriptive tool for sociologists interested in social interactions. Both theoretically and methodologically, dramaturgical analysis is concerned with the process of interaction, and the linguistic and symbolic components of self-construction and definition. As a theory of social and personal roles, dramaturgy emphasizes overt role-playing and the observable relationship between expectation and performance. Dramaturgy is also related to other social-psychological areas of research, such as ethnomethodology. Ethnomethodology goes beyond dramaturgy in its minute analysis of the ways in which people construct everyday reality. A principal finding has been that although people behave as though reality is unambiguous, solid, and reliable, the social world is actually subjective, changeable, and contradictory. The potentially revolutionary implications of this viewpoint are that social structures exist only because people believe they exist and that individuals or groups with enough assurance or power can challenge these assumptions.

Dramaturgy's future may depend on its ability to extend these insights into testable observations. Expansion of the dramaturgical perspective into new spheres of investigation, such as anthropology and political science, also holds promise. Although description is an essential part of the sociological enterprise, observation is not enough to generate the scientific theories and empirical explanations that are central to the social sciences. Dramaturgy's ability to develop and organize complete and sympathetic portrayals of social experience, however, permits this perspective to contribute essential understandings about the complexities of everyday life.

Bibliography

Berger, Peter L., and Thomas Luckmann. The Social Construction of Reality. New York: Doubleday, 1967. Basic, important investigation of the social context of human experience and understanding.

Biesecker, Barbara A. *Addressing Postmodernity: Kenneth Burke, Rhetoric, and a Theory of Social Change.* Tuscaloosa: University of Alabama Press, 1997.

Brissett, Dennis, and Charles Edgley, eds. *Life as Theater: A Dramaturgical Sourcebook.* 2d ed. New York: Aldine de Gruyter, 1990. Well-conceived and well-executed compilation of essays that illuminate dramaturgical methods and interests.

Burke, Kenneth. *Dramatism and Development.* Barre, Mass.: Clark University Press, 1972. Useful introduction discussing the "dramatistic pentad" (act, scene, agent, agency, and purpose) in terms of motives and actions.

Goffman, Erving. *Asylums: Essays on the Social Situation of Mental Patients and Other Inmates.* Garden City, N.Y.: Anchor Books, 1961. Front- and backstage, labeling and deviance, and role performance are investigated in this examination of the drama and rituals of institutional life.

_____. *The Presentation of Self in Everyday Life.* 1959. Reprint. Woodstock, N.Y.: Overlook Press, 1973. Basic definition and applications of dramaturgical analysis are provided by the preeminent practitioner of the method.

Hare, A. Paul. *Social Interaction as Drama.* Newbury Park, Calif.: Sage Publications, 1985.

First half of this excellent volume includes insights from playwrights and actors as part of its discussion of the dramaturgical perspective. Second half uses these insights to analyze conflict and conflict resolutions.

Mead, George H. *Mind, Self, and Society from the Standpoint of a Social Behaviorist*. Edited by Charles W. Morris. Chicago: University of Chicago Press, 1934. Basic statement of Mead's central ideas and arguments about roles, planning, and action.

Mills, C. Wright, and Hans Gerth. *Character and Social Structure*. New York: Harcourt, Brace, 1953. Develops Mills's concept of social structure to refer to the integration of psychic and social roles.

Perinbanayagam, R. S. *Signifying Acts: Structure and Meaning in Everyday Life*. South Carbondale: Southern Illinois University Press, 1985. Elegant study of symbolic inter-actionism as an outgrowth of the work of George Herbert Mead's work that includes an excellent chapter on "Dramatic Acts."

Shechner, Richard, and Mady Shuman, eds. *Ritual, Play, and Performance: Readings in the Social Sciences/Theater*. New York: Seabury Press, 1976. Important and informative selection of readings focusing on philosophical, aesthetic, and methodological areas of convergence of aesthetics, sociology, and dramatism.

Jackie R. Donath

Cross-References

Cultural Norms and Sanctions; Microsociology; Role Conflict and Role Strain; Significant and Generalized Others; Statuses and Roles; Symbolic Interaction.

EDUCATION

Type of sociology: Major social institutions
Field of study: Education

The sociology of education is the study of the institution of education. Sociologists examine the functions education fills for a society and explore the role of education in preparing citizens for adult life. School life is a central focus; sociologists study how schools contribute to the socialization of children and how schools function as organizations. They also study the role of education in stratification.

Principal terms

EDUCATION: formal teaching of a culture's skills, knowledge, and values from one generation to the next

FORMAL ORGANIZATION: large collection of people whose activities are specifically designed for the attainment of explicitly stated goals

HIDDEN CURRICULUM: set of unwritten rules of behavior taught in school to prepare children for academic success and social relations outside school

SOCIAL INSTITUTION: patterned behaviors and social structures that fulfill societal needs

SOCIAL STRATIFICATION: social system in which groups are ranked hierarchically and have unequal rewards or resources

Overview

Sociologists who study the educational institution look at the roles of education in various societies. In preindustrial societies, children are educated by their family members through informal interaction and socialization. Children generally do not attend school, which is a more formal approach used in industrial societies. The educational institution meets several basic needs of societies. First, education helps to teach future citizens about the culture in which they live. They are taught their culture's values, beliefs, knowledge, and language. They are taught what it means to be a member of their society. Second, education helps to reinforce the socioeconomic power structure. In the United States, for example, educators prepare students for their places in the capitalist system. This system involves a relatively small number of people who control the resources and a larger number of people who work for those in power.

Third, schools help to select and allocate talent. Schools socialize children from different social classes differently in order to prepare them for their future places in the social structure. For example, educators commonly assign students to different tracks, such as the general track, the vocational track, and the college-preparatory track; in the process, they segregate students largely by social class. Although efforts have been made to provide greater equality of educational opportunity, students in the college-preparatory track still are more likely to come from middle- and upper-class family backgrounds than are students in the other tracks. Fourth, schools teach students self-discipline. Students are taught the rules they need to follow in order to fit into the larger society. This process is accomplished through the hidden curriculum, an informal set of processes and rules that reinforce the basic rules (such as the need to line up or to raise a hand to be recognized). Fifth, schools teach children the basic skills they need to survive as members of a society, such as reading, writing, thinking, and mathematics. Schools in the United States have been criticized for poor performance in this area, especially when American students are compared with those from other countries. For example, about one-third of U.S. young adults in the 1990's cannot read at even an eighth-grade level.

Sociologists also look at schools as formal organizations. Schools share many of the characteristics of other formal organizations, such as corporations, hospitals, and even prisons. Schools have a division of labor in which trained specialists perform specific jobs. The English teacher, for example, does not typically also teach physics. Schools have many rules and other standard operating procedures. There are dress rules, disciplinary rules, and rules on how much of the curriculum teachers must cover. Teacher Bel Kaufman provided a detailed account of such rules and their negative effects for students, teachers, and parents in one New York high school in her book *Up the Down Staircase* (1964). Schools also have a hierarchy of authority; a chain of command exists that details who is responsible to whom. At the local level, the school board is typically at the top of the hierarchy, followed by the superintendent, principals, teachers, and students. Sociologist David Rogers detailed the negative consequences of such a hierarchy in his book *110 Livingston Street: Politics and Bureaucracy in the New York City Schools* (1968).

Sociologists also look at the informal structure in schools. While the formal structure meets the needs of the organization, the informal structure meets the needs of the organization's members. For example, schools vary in their predominant social classes, a difference that affects the nature of informal interactions. Different schools often emphasize different values, such as athletics or academics. Students may form themselves into different cliques, or groupings, according to particular interests or social classes. A school's informal climate may also be affected by more formal structural arrangements such as class size, more "open" classrooms, and discipline standards.

Applications

Sociological research on education is applied in several ways to better understand schools and students and to provide possible solutions to problems in the educational system. Sociologists have studied high school dropouts, for example. Nearly one-third of ninth graders do not graduate from high school, and most major cities have dropout rates of 50 percent or higher. The high dropout rate has major implications for both individuals and society. The difference between the lifetime earnings of a typical dropout and a typical graduate exceeds $300,000. Reducing the dropout rate would increase personal incomes and revenues obtained through taxes, decrease the social costs of welfare and crime, and reduce the unemployment rate.

Sociologist Theodore Wagenaar summarized the research on high-school dropouts in

Research in the Sociology of Education and Socialization (1987). The reasons cited most often by dropouts for the decision to drop out pertain to school, particularly poor grades and a dislike for school. Additional reasons vary by gender; males note economic or work issues, and females note family issues. Having a job tends to matter to male dropouts, and marriage and pregnancy tend to matter to female dropouts. The dropout rates for females and males are similar. The rates for minorities are at least one-third greater than for whites, a statistic that may reflect class differences, since studies show higher dropout rates for lower-class students. Lower-class students do not have the same socialization experiences as middle- and upper-class students. For example, lower-class parents spend less time with their children, talk about school less often with their children, and hold lower expectations for their children. Minorities and lower-class students may also experience discrimination in the schools. For example, they are less likely to be placed in the college-preparatory track and generally receive a poorer-quality education.

Dropouts have significantly lower self-concepts and tend to believe that they have little control over their lives. Particularly critical is the fact that dropouts tend to select as friends other young people who are alienated from school. This peer culture supports the potential dropout in making such decisions as skipping school and doing less homework. As a result, potential dropouts experience increased difficulty with teachers and principals and are disproportionately punished, reinforcing the decision to drop out. Dropouts also tend to feel less socially integrated into the schools, as evidenced by their lower involvement in extracurricular activities.

School factors are also relevant. Smaller schools offer more personal attention to students and suffer fewer disorders. Students in small schools are more satisfied with their educational experiences and show greater involvement in the school and in the educational experience. Larger schools also tend to generate feelings among teachers of less control and less personal responsibility. An orderly school environment, a clear rewards system, and a drive for academic excellence also help to reduce dropout rates. Support services such as counseling are also important.

This research has implications for reducing dropout rates. The persistent effects of family background suggest that early intervention in school is needed to target potential dropouts and to provide appropriate school- and community-based action. Potential dropouts need intensive support—both academic and personal—in the early elementary grades. Communities, schools, and employers can work together to provide social structures and opportunities for social interaction in order to reduce the social isolation and normlessness that commonly characterize potential dropouts. Clear and fair rules, low student-to-teacher ratios, enhanced counseling services, training and work experience, teachers who accept personal responsibility for their students, teacher involvement in decision making, and strong parental involvement and support also help to reduce dropout rates. These factors underscore the central roles schools play in the socialization of youth.

Another application of sociological studies of education involves efforts to provide equality of educational opportunity to students from all social classes, races, and genders. Schools often function to reproduce the existing social class system, but societal values of

Before the Supreme Court's 1954 *Brown v. Board of Education* ruling forced the desegregation of public schools, most African American children in the South were educated in poorly equipped and supplied schools. *(Library of Congress)*

individualism and hard work as bases for moving up the social ladder mean that schools need to provide equal opportunities for doing so. The Supreme Court ruled in 1954 that segregated education was inherently unequal, and the Civil Rights Act of 1964 prompted greater desegregation of U.S. schools. The first nationwide study of school inequality was performed by sociologist James S. Coleman and published as *Equality of Educational Opportunity* (1966). Coleman found substantial differences between mostly black schools and mostly white schools in such things as funds spent per student, ages of school buildings, quality of library facilities, teacher characteristics, and class sizes. More surprising, he found that such school characteristics had little effect on learning. Most critical for school success was the student's social environment, which included the attitudes and behaviors fostered by family members and peers.

Coleman's report led the U.S. courts to determine that every student had the right to attend a school with a particular proportion of advantaged students. Since minority students were typically more disadvantaged than white students, the courts mandated the busing of students to achieve greater equality of minority composition in the schools. Busing was very successful in reducing school segregation, but it created considerable opposition from both blacks and whites, leading to the eventual abandonment of the practice in the 1980's. Some think that busing contributed to "white flight," causing white parents to remove their children from urban public schools by sending them to private schools or by moving to the suburbs. Coleman's report also led to compensatory "enrichment" programs designed to enable disadvantaged students to have some of the experiences of more privileged students.

Sociologists studying education also study gender socialization. Schools often promote gender stereotypes, oversimplified but strongly held ideas about the appropriate characteristics of females and males. The educational institution reflects and reinforces the beliefs and values of the larger society. For example, the illiteracy rate for females is much higher than the rate for males in most developing parts of the world. In elementary school, boys are encouraged to solve problems, while girls are more likely to be given answers. Teachers encourage boys to work independently but encourage dependency among girls. Junior-high-school teachers tend to use very different adjectives to describe boys and girls, such as "curious" for boys and "calm" for girls. Although girls' academic performance exceeds boys' into high school, it drops thereafter, as young women begin to conform to expectations for lower performance. Also, females tend to realize that males do not react positively to bright females. Females' occupational plans and values increasingly conform to societal expectations as they move through high school; their interest in science and mathematics drops considerably. Textbooks in both elementary and high school still show males and females performing traditionally expected roles. In college, females tend to talk less in class and to receive less encouragement from professors to contribute to class discussions.

Sociologists have identified strategies that may help to reduce schools' contributions to gender-role stereotyping. Some sociologists advocate changing the sex composition of the predominantly female elementary teaching force in order to provide early role models of both women and men. Others call for the use of gender-neutral instructional materials. Research shows, for example, that females perform higher on mathematics story problems when the figures in the story are female. A cooperative learning environment in which males and females work together has also been shown to help capture and maintain females' interest in science and mathematics. In their book *Failing at Fairness: How America's Schools Cheat Girls* (1994), researchers Myra and David Sadker suggest girls-only education as one approach to reducing the negative effects of girls' school experiences. Studies show that girls in single-sex schools achieve more, have higher self-esteem, and are more interested in mathematics and science than girls in co-ed schools are. Some co-ed schools have begun experimenting with single-sex classes in science and mathematics to bolster females' performance. These suggestions for reducing gender stereotypes address the social context in which children learn and show how important that context is.

Context

Sociological attention to education began around the end of the nineteenth century, shortly after the discipline itself emerged. In the late 1800's, Émile Durkheim was the first to suggest the importance of a sociological approach to education. Early sociological efforts in the United States focused on solving educational problems posed by massive immigration, rapid urbanization, and the development of a large educational system. The term "sociology of education" emerged in the 1920's as sociologists took a more scientific interest in education, gathering data and observing in schools to better understand how schools worked as social systems. With the publication of Willard Waller's *The Sociology of Teaching* (1932), the field became more widely recognized. Waller examined the different goals and orientations of teachers and students and suggested the development of extracurricular activities to enhance students' commitment to school. While the next few decades saw less sociological interest in education, the 1960's saw increasing interest, as sociologists focused both on the role of education in society and on the inner workings of schools. James S. Coleman, for example, studied the informal friendship groups that characterize high schools in his book *The Adolescent Society: The Social Life of the Teenager and Its Impact on Education* (1961).

Sociologists have taken several approaches to the study of education. Some have stressed looking at the bigger picture by studying how the educational institution helps to meet the basic needs of a society and fits in with the larger social structure. Some have noted how schools have become places where those in power wish to make sure that their views and values are taught. Still other sociologists have looked inside schools to study how they operate sociologically. These researchers study such things as how children play at school, how students cope with school demands, and how males and females react differently to the school experience.

Sociological attention to education has helped to broaden the understanding of schools and education by looking at the social context within which schools exist and by describing aspects of school life that were previously ignored. Sociologists have increasingly turned to cross-cultural studies of education to better understand the role of education in society. They continue to study how education contributes to social stratification; they also have devoted increased attention to the social contexts that schools create for students by looking at such issues as school reorganization (such as the creation of schools without grade levels). Moreover, sociologists increasingly focus on how school experiences differ by race and social class, and they make suggestions for improving the school experiences of minority and lower-class students. Sociologists also examine how the growth of technology alters the social structure of schools. Finally, sociologists consider the implications for schools of an increasingly global society.

Bibliography

Ballantine, Jeanne. *The Sociology of Education: A Systematic Analysis*. 4th ed. Upper Saddle River, N.J.: Prentice-Hall, 1997. Emphasizes a systems perspective, which should be particularly useful as sociologists increasingly examine schools in a global society. She describes the role of education in stratification and provides an excellent review of educational reform and change.

Freedman, Samuel G. *Small Victories: The Real World of a Teacher, Her Students, and Their High School*. New York: Harper & Row, 1990. Provides an insider's perspective on daily life in a school. Although not written by a sociologist, the book adds much to the knowledge of how the social contexts of schools affect the daily lives of teachers and students.

Kozol, Jonathan. *Savage Inequalities: Children in America's Schools.* New York: Harper-Perennial, 1992. Kozol acted as an observer in many schools throughout the United States. He delivers a sharp criticism of the inequalities students experience as a result of race and social class. He provides many specific examples.

Mulkey, Lynn. *Sociology of Education: Theoretical and Empirical Investigations.* Fort Worth, Tex.: Harcourt Brace Jovanovich, 1993. Provides an excellent overview of how sociologists study education. She outlines the various approaches to the field and reviews empirical studies.

Sadker, Myra, and David Sadker. *Failing at Fairness: How America's Schools Cheat Girls.* New York: Charles Scribner's Sons, 1994. Provides a detailed and insightful look into the inner workings of America's schools and focus on how schools work against girls' development. They propose several strategies for reducing the negative effect of schools, including single-sex schools.

Sizer, Theodore. *Horace's Compromise: The Dilemma of the American High School.* Boston: Houghton Mifflin, 1984. Sizer has spent many years working at various levels in the public school system. He examines what is wrong with American high schools and offers a detailed prescription for improving them.

Theodore C. Wagenaar

Cross-References

Compulsory and Mass Education; Education: Conflict Theory Views; Education: Functionalist Perspectives.

EDUCATION
Conflict Theory Views

Type of sociology: Major social institutions
Field of study: Education

Conflict theory, or radical, approaches to the sociology of education analyze the role that education plays in producing and reproducing society's political, economic, and cultural inequities. Conflict theorists argue that education is characterized by a "hidden curriculum" whose purpose is to reproduce the norms, values, and beliefs of society's dominant class.

Principal terms

CLASS: self-identification of a group of people who share political, economic, and cultural experiences as being different from and opposed to other groups

CULTURAL CAPITAL: linguistic and cultural sophistication inherited by individuals that is dependent on their particular class

CULTURE: values, norms, and material goods created by members of a particular group

IDEOLOGY: array of ideas actively expressing the way groups, both dominant and subordinate, view the appropriate functioning of society's political, economic, and cultural institutions and activities

INSTITUTIONS: relatively stable arrangements designed to promote efficiency in meeting societal goals

REPRODUCTION: theoretical proposition that institutions within the capitalist social system reproduce class, gender, and racial inequities to benefit those in positions of power

SUBJECTIVITIES: conscious and unconscious dimensions of experience that inform student behavior

Overview

Two major sociological viewpoints have served as a basis for extensive studies of the institution of education. The functionalist approach looks at the ways education prepares individuals for participation in society so that society can continue to function effectively. Sociologists who study education from the conflict perspective, on the other hand, emphasize the idea that different groups or classes are in competition (conflict) with one another for society's resources and that education is a part of that process. Conflict theorists are also known as radical sociologists, essentially because their views represent a radical departure from the functionalist perspective that was dominant when conflict theory first became a significant sociological movement. Radical educational sociologists stress the role of schools in the reproduction of cultural capital, work skills, and the ideology of society's elite. Sociologist Henry Giroux has identified three predominant theoretical models used by radical sociologists to critique liberal and conservative theories: the economic-reproductive model, the cultural-reproductive model, and the hegemonic-state reproductive model. Theorists applying these models to the study of education ask how schools function in society and how schools influence the ideologies, subjectivities, and needs of students. They also examine the role of education in reproducing capitalist social relations and the role of the state in encouraging or discouraging reproduction within schools.

Initially, the most influential conflict analysis of education was advanced via the economic-reproductive model. Drawing on the theoretical influence of Karl Marx, theorists such as Samuel Bowles and Herbert Gintis proposed a correspondence between the values, norms, and skills taught in the classroom and the reproduction of attitudes toward work. This theoretical proposition has been referred to as the hidden curriculum. This concept suggests that students learn to identify their roles within the social system, especially their roles in the workplace, through daily interaction with the temporal, spatial, and ideological characteristics of the schools. More specifically, Bowles and Gintis hypothesized that those social relations characteristic of working-class schools, with their emphasis on order, capitulation to the authority of the teacher, strict adherence to time, limited epistemological freedom, and architectural separation (separate rooms, offices, and recreational areas) are necessary for the continued reproduction of working-class students into working-class jobs. Thus, contrary to the liberal and conservative models of education, which stress individual growth and social mobility, the economic-reproductive model hypothesizes that students, depending on their class, race, and gender, are imbued with different skills, attitudes, and values primarily based on their experiences with the hidden curriculum. The product of these experiences is often leveled aspirations and the reproduction of social inequity rather than personal growth and social mobility.

The cultural-reproductive model attempts to identify the role and function of education and its association with culture, class, and domination. Most often associated with the work of sociologist Pierre Bourdieu and his colleague Jean-Claude Passeron, the cultural-reproductive model avoids attributing to education a purely functional role. That is, while Bourdieu and Passeron recognize the significance of education as an important institution in the reproduction of class, race, and gender inequality, they do not, as Bowles and Gintis did, suggest that schools are overtly determined by class relations. Their model of reproduction centers on the relatively autonomous way in which the school acts as a transmitter of dominant culture. The centerpiece of the cultural-reproduction model is the struggle over meaning within the realm of culture. Culture becomes, as Giroux says, "the mediating link between ruling-class interests and everyday life." Perhaps the most illuminating insight offered by the cultural-reproductive model concerns not how but what students learn or do not learn. Ruling class domination is reproduced by the school through the subtle transmission of ruling class culture.

To accomplish reproduction in this manner, the school is said to participate in the proliferation of cultural capital. By this term Bourdieu means linguistic styles and cultural competencies (such as style, taste, and wit) inherited by individuals as members of a specific class. Schools, it is argued, reproduce dominant cultural capital by legitimating certain forms of knowledge and styles of speech, art, and music—those characteristic of the class-based experiences of only some (dominant-class) students. The result is a simultaneous confirmation of the culture of the dominant class and disconfirmation of the cultures of other social classes. The act of neglecting or underrepresenting the culture and values of the working class and the poor marginalizes their social significance. Conversely, overrepresenting the interests of the dominant class through the dissemination of its cultural capital gives the appearance of inevitability and neutrality. That is, as the interest and values of the dominant class begin to define the dominant culture, they become culture.

Finally, Bourdieu suggests that students of different class origins are differentially socialized in ways that affect cognitive, physical, and emotional development. He attempts to identify the ways in which students participate in the reproduction of their own class position by internalizing cultural prescriptions for physical and emotional behavior (such as proper posture, manners, and voice tone).

The last of the three most prominent radical sociological analyses of education has been put forward by theorists who view the state (the nation-state) as an actor that is in part responsible for the continued reproduction of the social relations of production. That is, the state is, above all else, interested in the preservation of the capitalist mode of production. It is helpful, then, to identify the way the state exercises economic, ideological, and repressive control over schools to accomplish these ends. Through the use of state-established certification, the school curriculum has been weighted in favor of the natural sciences and has deemphasized "nonscientific" knowledge such as the arts or disciplines within the social sciences and humanities. Moreover, in keeping with the state's interest in preserving order, schools serve the function of keeping children and young adults off the streets. Finally, the state plays a crucial role in legitimating the separation of knowledge from power. By training and giving credentials to "academics," the state legitimates forms of knowledge (cultural capital) that prohibit the working classes from participating in decision making. In this scenario the state is participating in what sociologist Nicos Poulantzas has termed a mental-manual division.

Applications

Theoretical insights offered by conflict theory views of education have been applied to many prominent areas of sociological concern. They include, among others, the use of technical control, as embodied in teaching systems, and the perpetuation of racism.

One of the most creative and interesting applications of the reproductive theme in radical sociological analyses of education concerns the "de-skilling" of both teachers and students. Some conflict theory analysts contend that the correspondence between the interests of industry, the state, and schools (in the reproduction of capitalist social relations) has the effect of de-skilling the teaching profession. To be more specific, there are, as sociologist Michael Apple notes, industry-driven programs initiated in the school system to facilitate increased awareness of industry needs and interests. Sponsoring organizations, identified in name by their self-evident concerns, have such names as "Chairs of Free Enterprise," the "Ryerson Plan," and "The Institute for Constructive Capitalism."

The primary focus in the radical sociological literature is on how material is taught—the organization and presentation of curricular material. The most prominent way in which the message of industry is transmitted to teachers and students is through prepackaged course materials often referred to as "systems." Systems were originally marketed during the Cold War era of the 1950's and 1960's as a way to make teaching "teacher-proof." Today, systems continue to be marketed in mathematics, reading, social studies, and science. Systems include sets of standardized material stating the objectives of each lesson, all material needed for teaching the lesson, specified teacher actions, tests, and descriptions of appropriate student responses.

Some sociologists argue that such teaching systems represent a form of technical control. That is, through the use of packaged material, all planning, coordinating, and assessing of student learning is under the control of a person or group of people beyond the classroom. The ramifications for teachers are that, over time, skills once needed to perform the "thought work" of teaching and to foster interaction between students and teachers may atrophy. Students, expecting to pass from the first level of a system to the second, are under the control of a distant, centralized force. If students do not adhere to the appropriate responses as mandated in the packaged system's material, they are judged (graded) critically. Finally, teachers may be more isolated from one another. Since they have decreasing input in their own work, the argument goes, there is less need to interact. It may also be, as it is in other occupations in which de-skilling has been observed, that teachers using systems take less interest in their work.

How systems work ideologically to fashion individuals who will function "appropriately" within a capitalist society is a complex yet significant concern. The educational criterion that determines the "good" pupil is his or her ability to accumulate certain technical skills (cultural capital). These skills are said to be technical in that they are measured using tests and are acquired in logical progression. That is, mastery over one set of ideas leads to the discovery of the next, and so on. What is important about this process is that it is individualized: Facts are "consumed" by students in a manner similar to the consumption of goods sold on the market. Since systems allow no room for responses other than those specified, possibilities for discussion of alternative outcomes are rare. Students educated in this manner become adults with a "rules orientation"—that is, they internalize the rules and goals of the organization as their own. This leads to a homogenization of the labor force. Conflict is minimized, since employees have adopted the rationality of the firm and the firm's directives.

One compelling insight stemming from the work of educational sociologists has been articulation of the significance of language in the reproduction of dominant culture within the schools. Educators, acting as agents of dominant cultural capital, promote the cultural superiority of standard English. Language or dialect that strays from the dominant form is marginalized and devalued. Many African Americans and people of Afro-Caribbean descent, for example, speak different forms of English than standard English; these forms have been given a variety of names, among them patois, Creole, and Black English.

Traditionally viewed by educators as debased forms of standard English and as lacking in the formal properties which encourage organized thought and expression, these variants are generally considered inferior to standard English. The ramifications for students speaking them are potentially devastating. Numerous studies have identified teacher biases in their evaluations of students speaking patois or Black English. In general they are viewed as lazy, illiterate, unintelligent, and educationally subnormal. In many cases these students are offered programs for the "verbally deprived," "culturally disadvantaged," or "culturally deprived." There is no evidence, however, to support the dominant cultural belief that Black English is inferior to "proper" English. Research on this topic has demonstrated that Black English is a complex linguistic system with its own internal logic and coherence. When educators fail to recognize the cultural significance of this language form for African American students, they are acting in a racist fashion. The stigmatization too often leads to disfranchisement of students of color.

Context

Debate over the role of education in society has been ongoing since the 1850's. Initial focuses of education included aiding in the assimilation of immigrants into "American" culture and creating sturdy individuals who would be able to locate their places within the growing industrial economy. By specifying appropriate American values and morals and by facilitating the acquisition of skills and behaviors needed in industry, it was believed that schools would preserve a uniquely American sense of community. Early curriculum theorists included Franklin Bobbitt, W. W. Charters, Edward L. Thorndike, Ross L. Finney (a sociologist), Charles C. Peters, and David Snedden. Speaking primarily to the concerns of the middle class, these theorists made the notion of community synonymous with homogeneity and consensus.

Traditional analyses of education, located within what has been called the "achievement tradition," have difficulty formulating connections between education and its political, economic, and ideological context. To respond to these theoretical shortcomings, radical sociologists specializing in education initiated rigorous theoretical investigation. Beginning in the late 1960's and continuing through the 1970's and 1980's, two theoretical schools emerged: the status attainment school and the hidden curriculum school. Following the work of sociologists Eric O. Wright, and Samuel Bowles and Herbert Gintis, status attainment research seeks to determine the balance between achieved and ascribed characteristics in determining future educational and occupational success.

The 1960's and 1970's gave voice to a pivotal theoretical breakthrough with the publication of sociologist Michael F. Young's edited collection *Knowledge and Control: New Directions for the Sociology of Education* (1971). Young, along with sociologists Basil Bernstein and Pierre Bourdieu, argued that the organization of knowledge, its transmission, and its interpretation are crucial determinants to understanding the reproduction of dominant ideology and class position. Since the initial theoretical breakthrough, applications of this approach can be seen in the work of sociologists Jean Anyon, Joel Taxel, Landon Beyer, Michael Apple, Lois Weis, and Linda Valli, among others; such applications are typically classified as studies of the hidden curriculum.

Bibliography

Apple, Michael, ed. *Cultural and Economic Reproduction in Education*. London: Routledge & Kegan Paul, 1982. Collection of articles on topics related to applications of the radical sociological analysis of education. Topics include the arts, patriarchy, the state, and television.

_____. *Ideology and Curriculum*. 2d ed. New York: Routledge, 1990. Apple is considered to be among the theoretical forebears of the radical approach to the sociology of education. This book illustrates the intellectual strength and lucidity of quality sociological analysis. Examines the works of Marx, Bourdieu, Freire, Girioux, and others while presenting very abstract material in a clear and concise way.

Bourdieu, Pierre, and Jean-Claude Passeron. *Reproduction in Education, Society and Culture*. Translated by Richard Nice. London: Sage Publications, 1977. While challenging for novice readers, this book has been the cornerstone of the "cultural" approach to reproduction.

Bowles, Samuel, and Herbert Gintis. *Schooling in Capitalist America*. New York: Basic Books, 1976. Centerpiece in the literature on reproduction. This book serves as one of the first clearly articulated attacks against mainstream education from a Marxist theoretical perspective.

Fletcher, Scott. *Education and Emancipation*. New York: Teachers College Press, 2000.

Freire, Paulo. *The Politics of Education*. Translated by Donaldo Macedo. South Hadley, Mass.: Bergin & Garvey, 1985. Series of essays presenting Freire's views on power, especially that embedded in the process of education. Places equal emphasis on what is taught and how it is taught.

Giroux, Henry. "Theories of Reproduction and Resistance in the New Sociology of Education: A Critical Analysis." *Harvard Educational Review* 53 (August, 1983): 257-293. Giroux serves as a valuable source for sifting through the complex and abstract theoretical analyses that characterize much of the radical approach to the sociology of education.

_____. *Theory and Resistance in Education*. South Hadley, Mass.: Bergin & Garvey, 1983. The strength of Giroux's analysis lies in his insistence on the politicization of education. This book articulates his specific remedies for mainstream education informed by analyses of reproduction.

MacLeod, Jay. *Ain't No Makin' It*. Boulder, Colo.: Westview Press, 1987. Ethnography of two groups of young males, one mostly white and one mostly black, each living in the same subsidized housing unit. While not solely an analysis of education, the book discusses the ways in which class position is reproduced.

Walker, Stephen, and Len Barton, eds. *Gender, Class, and Education*. New York: International Publications Service, Falmer Press, 1983. Essays presenting a critical analysis of the differential treatment of women within the educational system. The essays are written for students, teachers, and administrators.

Robert C. Schehr

Cross-References

Conflict Theory; Education; Education: Functionalist Perspectives; Social Stratification: Analysis and Overview.

EDUCATION
Functionalist Perspectives

Type of sociology: Major social institutions
Field of study: Education

Functionalist perspectives on education focus on the school's responsibility in transmitting to youth beliefs, knowledge, skills, and values that are essential to adult participation in society. Functionalist theory helps clarify the role of schooling in enabling societies to maintain themselves culturally, economically, politically, and socially.

Principal terms

HIDDEN CURRICULUM: educational system's implicit means of aiding youth in internalizing social norms and values

HUMAN CAPITAL THEORY: assumption regarding interrelationships between schooling and working in which investment in the former results in higher paying or more prestigious jobs in the latter

MERITOCRACY: any society in which ability and effort are deemed more important than inherited privilege and status in the allocation of cultural, economic, political, and social position

REPRODUCTION: process that is said to occur during schooling in which existing cultural, economic, political, and social norms and structures are perpetuated

SOCIAL STRATIFICATION: a phenomenon on which people are differentially ranked in hierarchic fashion according to their social positions; schooling overtly emphasizes achieved social position based on ability and performance rather than ascribed social position based on natal circumstances

SOCIALIZATION: process of developing the knowledge, skills, and values essential to future adult role performance

STATUS ATTAINMENT: in education, a research tradition that seeks to clarify why students from different socioeconomic backgrounds differ in school achievement and in the duration of their investment in the schooling process

STRUCTURAL DIFFERENTIATION: concept that as societies become more complex, systems (for example, schooling, or the educational system) become more distinct and specialized in function

Overview

The institution of education in modern society has been given much attention by sociologists. Two major theoretical frameworks within which social institutions are examined are the functionalist approach and the conflict theory approach. In general terms, functionalism looks at society as a system of interrelated parts, the relatively harmonious operation (functioning) of which is necessary for the society's survival. Conflict theorists, on the other hand, emphasize the idea that different groups or classes are in competition (conflict) for society's resources. Education has been examined extensively from both these viewpoints.

Functionalist perspectives on education focus on understanding how the component subsystems of higher education and school systems effectively transmit the cultural, economic, political, and social values of a society to youth. The purpose of schools, according to Émile Durkheim (1858-1917), a French pioneer in applying a sociological approach to the study of educational systems, "is to arouse and to develop in the child a certain number of physical, intellectual, and moral states which are demanded of him by both the political society as a whole and the special milieu for which he is specifically destined."

Theoretical perspectives on education descended from Durkheim's work have been given a number of names, including functionalist-reproductionism, structural-functionalism, consensus theory, and equilibrium theory. They proceed from the premise that schools, colleges, and universities are interdependent parts of total social systems. The vitality of the total society, much like the health of the total human organism, depends on how effectively these parts—education, the family, and the economy, for example—contribute to the well-being of the entire system. An overarching social aim is to achieve an equilibrium of functioning. This condition implies that there is an interdependence among the system's components that is based on a consensus (a recognition of shared values).

Functionalist perspectives in education particularly emphasize how schools, colleges, and universities contribute to the socialization of individuals within a meritocratic society in which occupational and social roles are determined by ability and effort rather than inheritance. Moreover, functionalists view this meritocratic society as dependent on the production of highly trained people to fill these roles, roles largely shaped by new rational knowledge originating in the research activities of colleges, think tanks (the Rand Corporation, for example), and universities. Schools function to provide basic cognitive and highly specialized skills essential for participation in this expert society. Within functionalist perspectives on schooling, human capital theorists view education as an economic investment in which benefits (increased earnings) outweigh costs (a delayed entry into the workforce). Functionalists assume that the expansion of education's socialization function optimally occurs in a democratic society committed to the realization of human objectives. Schools, colleges, and universities become, in the functionalist paradigm, pivotal agencies for the socialization of youth into what a key contributor to functionalist theory, Talcott Parsons, termed "the commitments and capacities which are essential prerequisites of their future role performance." Among the essential characteristics of an educated citizenry, in the functionalist view, are a sense of social justice and a commitment to use that sense of justice to resolve issues important to the quality of life within the society.

Functionalist research in education has an intricate agenda: Functionalists study the structural parts of educational systems as cultural and social organizations. Sociologists within this theoretical tradition examine how the achievement of certain societal goals occurs through the functioning of educational subsystems—for example, elementary schools. Functionalists, following a Durkheimian tradition, examine schools, colleges, and universities as training grounds for occupational and social roles, places where discipline and morality, the requisites for an ordered society are learned. Functionalist perspectives in education, developed in the 1950's and 1960's by sociologists such as Burton Clark, Robert Dreeben, and Talcott Parsons, highlight the functioning of the educational system, assuming that it is aimed at developing broad-based skills essential for functioning in an increasingly technological world.

Applications

Among the functions attributed to the institution of education are socialization and the allocation of roles that individuals will continue to play when they leave school. Parsons performed pioneering research on structural differentiation processes in educational systems, and his work provoked numerous studies of education's role in a meritocracy. The school's dual role as an agency for occupational and social role allocation, together with its involvement in the reproduction of social norms, is highlighted in the application of functionalist assumptions to research on the "paracurriculum" and status attainment.

Robert Dreeben's *On What Is Learned in School* (1968) revealed how the explicit objectives of the school's formal curriculum contribute to learning the social norms ("specific standards for behavior") of achievement, independence, specificity, and universalism. Other functionalist studies have examined how what is taught outside the formal curriculum, yet in school, results in learning social norms. This informal teaching was termed the "hidden curriculum" by Benson R. Snyder in a 1971 book of the same title. It is frequently called the "lived curriculum"; in Britain it is sometimes called the "paracurriculum" at the suggestion of David Hargreaves, who has argued that "hidden" is a misnomer. This concept of an informal or unofficial curriculum refers to the implicit demands made on students to adapt to what Philip W. Jackson referred to as the three Rs of "rules, regulations, and routines."

Functionalists assume that the curriculum and the paracurriculum exist side by side in delicate balance. Success of the schooling endeavor depends on the forging of consensus, constructed in the assimilation of formal rules, regulations, and routines informally transmitted through the paracurriculum. In this consensus, cooperation and obedience are norms that are as important to the schooling process as achievement and performance are.

Although the concept of the hidden curriculum or paracurriculum is not unique to functionalist perspectives on education, functionalists consider how the informal curricular accent on assertiveness, competitiveness, and punctuality aids academic success and, subsequently, the attainment of high socioeconomic status. Moreover, from the functionalist perspective, students' relative degrees of adoption of this informal curriculum are very important to their future socioeconomic status. A central question is whether (as functionalists aver) what is learned in school affects students' educational and occupational expectations independently of the socioeconomic status of the students' families. Do the school's formal and informal curricula indeed occupy a pivotal point in the transition from home to work? Research in a sociological subfield known as status attainment has provided evidence for the functionalist view of a meritocratic society and has generally answered "yes" to these questions.

Status attainment research has clarified why the duration of students' involvement in formal education and their school achievement differ for students from different socioeconomic backgrounds. The most well-known study in this area is the "Wisconsin Social-Psychological Model of Status Attainment," a longitudinal study of Wisconsin students and their career paths after being graduated from high school. Performed by William H. Sewall and Robert M. Hauser, the study was inaugurated in 1957; the first results were published in 1976 in Sewall and Hauser's *Schooling and Achievement in American Society*; later findings were published in 1982. They concluded that the family's class position does have an effect on status attainment, but only insofar as it affects the type of personal influences that family members have on the student; parent and teacher encouragement during adolescence are also important. Beyond that, however, family background was viewed as inconsequential. The single most important factor in status attainment was the level of the person's schooling.

In that research on educational and status attainment has discovered large differences in educational attainment among individuals from differing social backgrounds, it supports an assumption implicit in functionalist perspectives on education: that ability (as measured by standardized intelligence tests), mitigated by the amount of support for educational achievement a student receives from friends, family, and teachers, is the best predictor of educational attainment and grades. Findings have suggested that teachers base their encouragement on student ability and student grades rather than on student social status. Schools operate, functionalists assert, in an essentially meritocratic fashion. These findings are not universally accepted, however; it should be noted that other studies have suggested a number of ways that students' socioeconomic status affects both their scores on tests and the ways the students are perceived and treated by teachers.

Status attainment research has two notable weaknesses. Because this research depends for its reliability on large samples, and because its conclusions are predicated on those samples, it is difficult to apply status attainment generalizations uniformly to smaller groups—to African American students, for example. The meritocratic model of student attainment does not explain the achievement of black students as satisfactorily as it does that of white students. Black students, scoring lower on standardized tests of ability than white students, have higher educational attainment than white students with similar test scores. What factors other than the influence of friends, parents, and teachers on black student aspirations explain this outcome? School-sanctioned discrimination against black students is not clearly evident as an explanatory factor. In addition, status attainment research only maps the effects of social status on ability and aspirations and, in turn, their effects on achievement and attainment. It does not explain why social status has the effects that it seems to.

Context

Prior to the pioneering work of Émile Durkheim on the functions of education (essentially, he saw it as contributing to the maintenance of the social order), few educational sociologists had researched relationships between school and society at large. They did not study the relationship between schools and social stratification, for example, a topic that has been the focus of contemporary sociologists operating within the functionalist framework. Durkheim's contemporary Max Weber suggested that a school's chief activity was teaching "status cultures" rooted in student power, prestige, and wealth, but few sociologists seriously explored the effects of societal domination by bureaucratic and rational ("modernizing") structures on schools.

Talcott Parsons's work in the 1950's on the school class as an agency of socialization in American society and Robert Dreeben's 1968 study of the school as an institution of socialization with the task of developing "capacities necessary for appropriate conduct in social settings that make different kinds of demands on them" were in the forefront of functionalist perspectives on education. The functionalist view of education has not been without its critics. Critics have found fault with the functionalist accent on the contribution of schooling to the consensually smooth operation of society as well as with the priority given in functionalist perspectives to the maintenance of social equilibrium and order in general.

Critics have made a number of interrelated observations regarding weaknesses in the functionalist perspective as applied to education. Jean Floud and A. H. Halsey noted in 1958 that functionalism accentuates a status quo orientation in industrial societies, which, Floud and Halsey argued, actually experience constant and rapid social change. Colin Greer's *The Great School Legend* (1973) and Joel Springs's *Education and the Rise of the Corporate State* (1972) assume that educational expansion has not resulted in greater equality of opportunity. Progress, they suggest, has collapsed because of (in Jeanne H. Ballantine's words) "the number of divergent interests, ideologies and conflicting interest groups in society." These conflicts and divergences are related to an increasing factionalism over what functions are important in education. This disagreement can be at least partly attributed to the frequent shifts in what David Tyack, Michael W. Kirst, and Elisabeth Hansot term the "issue-attention cycle" in education. This cycle tends to move public attention swiftly from one facet of educational systems to others—from, say, an examination of the core curricula required of everyone to programs for the gifted and talented.

The primary contrasts with functionalist perspectives on the role of education in society are conflict perspectives and interactionist perspectives. With roots in the writings of Karl Marx and Max Weber, conflict theorists argue that schools mirror tensions existing in the larger society between dominant and subordinate groups in their contest for power. Martin Carnoy's *Education as Cultural Imperialism* (1974) and Randall Collins's *Conflict Sociology* (1975) highlight conflict perspectives in education.

Interactionist perspectives in the sociology of education emphasize the need to study individuals as they interact with one another. A "microcosmic" approach, the interactionist perspective focuses on interactions between members of various groups: peer, teacher-principal, and teacher-student interactions, for example. This approach was central to the development in Britain and France in the early 1970's of a "new" sociology of education. Two of its chief proponents were Basil Bernstein and Pierre Bourdieu. Both conflict and interactionist modes for studying relationships between schooling and social stratification were stimulated by critiques of earlier perspectives.

Bibliography

Ballantine, Jeanne H., ed. *Schools and Society: A Reader in Education and Sociology*. Palo Alto, Calif.: Mayfield, 1985. Useful compendium of readings on the theoretical perspectives of functionalism. Helpful chapter introductions to basic writings on functionalist perspectives authored by Burton R. Clark, Randall Collins, Robert Dreeben, Émile Durkheim, Philip W. Jackson, Talcott Parsons, and Max Weber are accompanied by notes on specific questions raised by each primary source included.

_____. *The Sociology of Education: A Systematic Analysis*. 4th ed. Upper Saddle River, N.J.: Prentice-Hall, 1997. Readable introduction to the sociology of education with excellent discussions of functionalist perspectives toward the purposes of schooling and higher education, the "hidden curriculum," and social stratification. Contains helpful chapter summaries and footnotes but no separate bibliography.

Dreeben, Robert. *On What Is Learned in School*. Reading, Mass.: Addison-Wesley, 1968. Classic study of the school as an agency of socialization, arguing that schooling provides a vital functional linkage between children's kinship relations and adult public life. Includes useful end-of-chapter reference sections on functionalism and education.

Hurn, Christopher J. *The Limits and Possibilities of Schooling: An Introduction to the Sociology of Education*. 3d ed. Boston: Allyn & Bacon, 1993. Clearly written and readable text containing informative discussions on the functional paradigm of schooling, human capital theory, weaknesses of the functional paradigm, equality of opportunity and schooling expansion issues, meritocratic issues of educational achievement, status attainment research, and tracking or ability grouping in schools.

Pai, Young. *Cultural Foundations of Education*. 2d ed. Upper Saddle River, N.J.: Merrill, 1997. Contains an excellent and succinct treatment of functionalist/reproductive theory as well as opposing ideological views of the schooling process, conflict and interactionist/interpretivist theories in particular. Pai discusses the "hidden curriculum" or "paracurriculum" appropriately.

Malcolm B. Campbell

Cross-References

Education; Education: Conflict Theory Views; Functionalism.

ETHNICITY AND ETHNIC GROUPS

Type of sociology: Racial and ethnic relations
Field of study: Basic concepts

Ethnicity refers to a sense of belonging and identification with a particular cultural heritage. Ethnic groups are socially defined on the basis of their cultural characteristics. Members of ethnic groups consider themselves, and are considered by others to be, part of a distinct culture or subculture. These concepts help explain the cultural diversity which can occur in a given society.

Principal terms

ASSIMILATION: process by which members of subcultures and minorities acquire cultural characteristics of the dominant group

CULTURAL PLURALISM: a system where different ethnic and racial groups can coexist without losing their respective traits

CULTURE: beliefs, values, behavior, and material objects shared by a particular people

DISCRIMINATION: treating various groups of people unequally

ETHNIC GROUP: group that shares a cultural heritage and is viewed by itself and by others as distinctive

ETHNICITY: shared cultural heritage

MINORITY GROUP: group that occupies an inferior or subordinate position of power, prestige, and privilege

RACE: group that is socially defined on the basis of physical characteristics

RACISM: ideology contending that actual or alleged differences among different racial groups assert the superiority of one racial group

Overview

Despite the considerable amount of attention devoted to the subject, scholars have not reached a consensus on the precise meaning of ethnicity. Since ethnicity is such a complex concept, many scholars have chosen to identify ethnic groups as those groups characterized by some of the following fourteen features: common geographic origins; migratory status; race; language or dialect; religious faith or faiths; ties that transcend kinship, neighborhood, and community boundaries; shared traditions, values, and symbols; literature, folklore, and music; food preferences; settlement and employment patterns; special interests in regard to politics; institutions that specifically serve and maintain the group; an internal sense of distinctiveness; and an external perception of distinctiveness.

Sociologist Milton Yinger defines an ethnic group as one whose members are thought by themselves and others to have a common origin and who share a common culture which is transmitted through shared activities that reinforce the group's distinctiveness. The term ethnic group has been used by social scientists in two different ways. Some definitions of ethnic groups are broad and include both physical (racial) and cultural characteristics. Others are narrower and rely solely on cultural or nationality characteristics. Sociologist Joe R. Feagin emphasizes that ancestry, whether real or mythical, is a very important dimension of ethnic group identity.

Sociologist William Yancey and his associates argue that ethnic groups have been produced by structural conditions which are linked to the changing technology of production and transportation. Structural conditions including common occupational patterns, residential stability, concentration, and dependence on common institutions and services reinforce kinship and friendship networks. According to Yancey, common cultural heritage is not a prerequisite dimension of ethnicity. Ethnicity is a manifestation of the way populations are organized in terms of interaction patterns, institutions, values, attitudes, lifestyle, and consciousness of kind.

A new consciousness is emerging concerning the meaning of ethnicity. Ethnic groups are joining together into larger ethnic groupings. The adoption of a panethnic identity is common among Asians, American Indians, and Hispanics. Sociologist Felix Padilla writes about the development of a Latino collective identity among Mexican Americans and Puerto Ricans. Ethnicity and one's ethnic identity is becoming more of a matter of choice, especially for white Americans of European descent. Most people have multiple layers of ethnic identity because of generations of interethnic marriages; these layers can be added to or subtracted from one's current identity. Sociologists Richard Alba and Mary Waters acknowledge that people often know their ancestors are from a variety of ethnic groups but for one reason or another identify with only some of them (or none of them). Often people identify with those with whom they have the least connection.

Sociologist Robert Blauner, in his influential book *Black Lives, White Lives* (1989), addresses the confusion that is often produced in the American consciousness by the concepts of race and ethnicity. Blauner argues that the imagery of race tends to be more powerful than the imagery of ethnicity and therefore often overshadows it. The reason for this is that race—although generally viewed by scientists and social scientists as a social construct rather than a scientific reality—is associated with biological and scientific imagery, whereas ethnicity is associated with cultural imagery. Other important concepts, such as class and religion, are also overwhelmed by the powerful social meanings of race. The confounding of race and ethnicity is a daily occurrence in American society. Blauner holds that African Americans represent both a racial and an ethnic group and argues that when blacks assert their ethnicity, whites perceive it instead as an assertion of racial identity. He postulates that part of the American heritage of racism has been to deny the ethnicity or cultural heritage of African Americans.

Most theories used to explain ethnicity, ethnic behavior, and ethnic and racial relations have been concerned with the issues of migration, adaptation, exploitation, stratification, and conflict. These theories can be classified into two groups: order theories and power-conflict theories. Order theories emphasize the assimilation of ethnic groups in a society, whereas power-conflict theories address the issue of persisting inequality of power and resource distribution between majority and minority groups.

Sociologist Milton Gordon has described three images of assimilation: the melting pot, cultural pluralism, and Anglo-conformity. The most compelling of the three images, according to Gordon, is Anglo-conformity, according to which immigrant groups give up much of their cultural heritage for the dominant Anglo-Saxon core culture. This process has occurred for the majority of immigrant groups. Gordon's perspective fits well as an explanation for the majority of white Americans of European descent, but it does not fully explain the experiences of non-European immigrant groups such as Asians, Hispanics, and African Americans.

Power-conflict theories (caste, internal colonialism, Marxist, split labor market, and enclave theories) focus on involuntary immigration and/or colonial oppression. Power-conflict theorists have stressed the forced nature of cultural and economic adaptation, and they emphasize the role played by the processes of coercion, segregation, colonization, and institutionalized discrimination.

Applications

In his book *Ethnic America* (1981), economist Thomas Sowell argues that the experiences of white ethnic groups and racial minorities have been different in degree rather than in kind. Historian Ronald Takaki, however, in his book *From Different Shores* (1987), challenges Sowell's assumption. Takaki emphasizes the facts that only blacks were enslaved, only American Indians were placed on reservations, only Japanese Americans were placed in concentration camps, and only the Chinese were excluded from naturalized citizenship. To understand fully the experiences and histories of ethnic groups one must acknowledge the role of economic and governmental contexts within which particular ethnic groups have immigrated and adjusted. The time of immigration and the resources brought by the immigrants have affected not only their economic and political success but also their social class position in the United States.

In his book *Race and Ethnic Relations* (1994), sociologist Martin N. Marger describes the American ethnic hierarchy as consisting of three parts. The top third consists primarily of white Protestants from various ethnic backgrounds. The middle third consists of Catholics from various ethnic backgrounds, Jews, and many Asians. The bottom third consists of blacks, Hispanics, American Indians, and some Asians. The most important aspect of this ethnic hierarchy is the gap between those groups in the bottom third of the hierarchy and the other two segments.

The median income of African American families in 1990 was $21,423, which was 58 percent of that earned by white families ($36,915). Black families are three times more likely than white families to live in poverty. In 1990 one in four black families was in the middle class, and one in ten was affluent.

The median income of Asian (Chinese, Japanese, Filipino, Asian-Indian, Korean, Vietnamese, and others) families in 1990 was $42,240, while the national average was $33,500. Part of the explanation of why Asian Americans have a much higher median family income is that 39 percent of them have completed four or more years of college, whereas only 21.4 percent of the entire U.S. population has completed four or more years of college. The poverty rate among Japanese Americans is half that for the United States as a whole, but the poverty rate for Chinese Americans, especially in Chinatowns, is much higher than other groups in the inner city.

The median income of Hispanic (Mexican, Puerto Rican, Cuban, and others) families in 1990 was $23,431. The median income of Cuban Americans was well above that of other Hispanics at $31,439. Mexican Americans earned $23,240, while Puerto Ricans were well below the median income at $18,008. According to the U.S. Bureau of the Census, in 1990 25 percent of Mexican Americans, 37.5 percent of Puerto Ricans, and 13.8 percent of Cuban Americans were living in poverty. The number of Hispanic households with at least $50,000 in annual income more than tripled between 1972 and 1988.

By the 1970's Jews had attained the highest income levels of all European ethnic groups in the United States, closely followed by Irish, German, Italian, and Polish Catholics. Most white Anglo-Saxon Protestants trailed these white ethnics in income and educational levels. According to sociologist Andrew Greeley, Irish Catholics are one of the most prosperous of

Shortly after Japan's surprise attack on Pearl Harbor drew the United States into World War II, President Franklin D. Roosevelt issued an executive order that led to the forced relocation of virtually all persons of Japanese descent on the West Coast into internment camps. Meanwhile, many Americans were not hesitant to express their anti-Japanese feelings. *(National Archives)*

the white ethnic groups, while Irish Protestants tend to be one of the least prosperous groups. Sociologist Douglas Massey, of the University of Chicago, has shown that African Americans are more segregated within cities, less likely to move out of cities, and much more likely to move to segregated suburbs when they do leave cities than Hispanics and Asians. Asians are the least segregated and the most suburbanized of the three groups.

Context

Sociology became an accepted part of American academia during the end of the nineteenth century and at the beginning of the twentieth century primarily through the efforts of Sociologist Robert Park and his colleagues at the University of Chicago. Sociologists Ernest Burgess, Louis Wirth, Harvey Zorbaugh, Frederick Thrasher, and others produced now-classic studies of the urbanization process in Chicago. The study of community coincided with and included the study of ethnicity. Urban sociology began with studies of immigrants. Chicago was then (and still is) one of the United States' most ethnically diverse cities, and the intellectual tradition of urban community studies has continued with works such as Ruth Horowitz's *Honor and the American Dream: Culture and Identity in a Chicano Community* (1983) and Mitchell Duneier's *Slim's Table: Race, Respectability, and Masculinity* (1992).

Sociologist Scott Greer indicates that some of the early thinking about ethnicity in American sociology was stimulated by the National Origins Quota Act of 1924, which temporarily restricted the immigration of certain groups, primarily southern and eastern Europeans. This act was instituted because of a belief that groups of non-Anglo-Saxon background were much more prone to criminal activity; they were assumed to be genetically inferior. This act was repealed in 1931. Another watershed act that later contributed to a heightened interest in ethnicity was the Immigration Act of 1965. This legislation opened the doors of the United States to many groups, primarily Asians and Hispanics, who had been discriminated against by earlier immigration policies. Also, the civil rights legislation of the 1960's and the aftermath of government regulations and programs such as affirmative action provided opportunities for debate, research, and analysis concerning the state of ethnicity.

In his book *Ethnicity in the United States* (1974), Andrew Greeley concludes that no ethnic "revival" was occurring in the late 1960's or early 1970's; rather, white ethnic groups simply felt less inhibited in talking about themselves and their cultural heritage. Greeley indicates the attention given to black cultural diversity in the 1960's and 1970's legitimized other kinds of cultural diversity. Richard Alba, in his book *Ethnic Identity* (1990), describes the transformation of ethnicity which has taken place in the United States. Around the time of World War II and soon thereafter, the expectation was that ethnic Americans would assimilate and their sense of ethnicity would gradually disappear. This assumption was known as the melting pot theory. During the 1950's, 1960's, and 1970's, however, sociologist Nathan Glazer and political scientist Daniel Patrick Moynihan (among others) questioned the viability of the melting pot theory. Glazer, Moynihan, and others suggested that the United States was leaning more in the direction of cultural pluralism.

In the 1980's and early 1990's, the debate about the melting pot versus cultural pluralism, according to Alba, no longer dominated discussions of ethnicity, especially concerning white European ethnic groups. Alba argues that ethnicity is not less embedded in the structure of American society but rather that ethnic distinctions are undergoing change. He believes that ethnic distinctions based on European ancestry are dissolving, while a new ethnic group is forming based on ancestry from anywhere on the European continent.

Bibliography

Alba, Richard D. *Ethnic Identity*. New Haven, Conn.: Yale University Press, 1990. Argues that what the United States was experiencing in the 1970's and 1980's was not a revival of ethnicity but a rise in symbolic ethnicity. A new ethnic group called "European Americans" is emerging with its own myths, Alba suggests; he argues that ethnicity among non-Hispanic whites is in the midst of a fundamental transformation.

_____, ed. *Ethnicity and Race in the U.S.A.* Boston: Routledge & Kegan Paul, 1985. Studies by leading scholars of ethnicity and race presented at a conference on ethnicity and race in 1984. Many are based on 1980 census data. Chapters are devoted to blacks, American Indians, Hispanics, Asian Americans, white ethnics, and "unhyphenated" whites.

Feagin, Joe R., and Clairece Booher Feagin. *Racial and Ethnic Relations*. 6th ed. Upper Saddle River, N.J.: Prentice-Hall, 1999. Standard college textbook. Several introductory chapters discuss key racial concepts and theoretical models relating to ethnic relations. Chapters are devoted to discussing specific racial and ethnic groups: English Americans, Irish Americans, Italian Americans, Jewish Americans, American Indians, African Americans, Mexican Americans, Puerto Rican and Cuban Americans, Japanese Americans, and Chinese, Filipino, Korean, and Vietnamese Americans.

Glazer, Nathan. *Ethnic Dilemmas 1964-1982*. Cambridge, Mass.: Harvard University Press, 1983. Papers analyzing issues of racial and ethnic conflict such as cultural pluralism, bilingualism, and the affirmative action debate. Glazer argues that the fight against discrimination chose the wrong solution. An important source.

Glazer, Nathan, and Daniel P. Moynihan. *Beyond the Melting Pot*. 2d ed. Cambridge, Mass.: MIT Press, 1970. Classic, controversial, and often-cited book that focuses on five ethnic groups (blacks, Puerto Ricans, Jews, Italians, and Irish) in New York City during the early 1960's with an update for the 1970's.

Maldonado, Lionel, and Joan Moore. *Urban Ethnicity in the United States*. Beverly Hills, Calif.: Sage Publications, 1985. Contains ten articles discussing the "new immigrants" (Hispanics and Asians) divided into two sections. The first builds a context for the study of contemporary racial and ethnic issues in American cities, and the second investigates the reciprocal impact of new immigrants and institutions.

Padilla, Felix M. *Latino Ethnic Consciousness*. Notre Dame, Ind.: University of Notre Dame Press, 1985. Examines process of Latino/Hispanic ethnic group formation in Chicago. It identifies and explains the conditions that have enabled Mexican Americans and Puerto Ricans to adopt a new or collective Latino or Hispanic identity distinct and separate from the groups' individual ethnic identities. Highly recommended.

Takaki, Ronald, ed. *From Different Shores*. New York: Oxford University Press, 1987. Essays on race and ethnicity by well-known neoconservative, liberal, and leftist scholars. Sections of the book are devoted to articles on ethnic and racial patterns, culture, class, gender, and prospects for the future.

Thernstrom, Stephan, ed. *The Harvard Encyclopedia of American Ethnic Groups*. Cambridge, Mass.: The Belknap Press of Harvard University Press, 1980. Arguably the most important single source in print concerning ethnicity and ethnic groups. The encyclopedia contains 106 entries on specific ethnic groups from Acadians to Zoroastrians, twenty-nine thematic essays dealing with such issues as assimilation and pluralism, and eighty-seven maps. The specific group entries discuss origins, migration, arrival, settlement, economic life, social structure and organization, family, kinship, culture, religion, education, and politics. Highly recommended.

William L. Smith

Cross-References

Cultural and Structural Assimilation; Race and Racial Groups; Racial and Ethnic Stratification.

ETHNOGRAPHY

Type of sociology: Sociological research
Field of study: Data collection and analysis

An ethnography is a description of a culture, a subculture, or a group of people with a distinctive lifestyle. It describes the people, their customs, the events in which they partici-pate, and their conversations. It also describes the materials they use (food, clothing, shelter, and utensils) in everyday life and how they use them.

Principal terms

CULTURE: patterns for thinking, feeling, behaving, and interpreting experience used by a group of people to organize their way of life

ETHNOGRAPHY: descriptive study of a culture that includes information about what people of the culture do and say as well as about their values, beliefs, and customs

FIELD NOTES: written account of the social behavior observed by a field researcher while studying a culture

FIELD RESEARCH: research in which an observer goes to a culture and either records observations of that culture or participates to some extent in the culture and makes observations based on that participation

QUALITATIVE RESEARCH: collection and analysis of descriptive data, rather than numerical data, that depict the social behavior within a culture

SUBCULTURE: group with ways of thinking, feeling, and behaving that differ from those of the dominant culture in some essential respects

Overview

The term "ethnography" refers both to a type of research and to the specific studies that such research ultimately produces. Sociological research is often considered to be divided into four major types: experiments, surveys, observation, and historical or archival research. The terms "observation" and "ethnography" are sometimes used synonymously. In this sense, although ethnography originally referred to the study of ethnic groups, it may refer to the observational study of a number of different types of societal subgroups.

An ethnography is a descriptive study of a culture, a subculture, an institution, or a group of people. A study of the Yanomamo, a group of Indians who live in Brazil and Venezuela, would be the study of a culture. The study of the Amish, an American religious group that lives without modern conveniences, would be a study of an American subculture. The study of an elementary school would be the study of an institution. The study of a peer group of neighborhood children, residents of a retirement community, or a group of cocktail wait-resses would be an ethnography of a group of people.

An ethnography describes what people do. Depending on the nature of the group under study, it may include a wide range of human activities. It may include how people obtain food, clothing, shelter, and other basic necessities. For example, in the case of food, people might hunt animals, gather herbs and fruit, plant crops, or buy food from others. The study might also describe how a group distributes food once it is obtained. Other aspects of life that could be examined include kinship structure (how families are formed and how they interrelate), religious rituals and behavior, political systems and activities, and leisure activities. Many other aspects of daily life may be examined by an ethnography, including conversations and other social interactions and descriptions of objects used in everyday life. Finally, most ethnographic studies attempt to provide some interpretation of the meaning of the culture under study—the "whys" behind the behaviors observed.

One of the most famous and classic ethnographic books is Margaret Mead's *Coming of Age in Samoa* (1928). Mead described the life of Samoan adolescent females as they made the transition from childhood to being Samoan adults. She discussed how Samoan adolescent life for these females involved casual or free love experiences. By avoiding the sexual repression demanded of youth in many Western cultures, Mead reported, the Samoan females enjoyed easy, pleasant, and nontroubling adolescent years.

Ethnographies are usually intended to be as holistic as possible. In other words, they attempt to study as much of the culture or cultural group as is feasible rather than to focus on limited aspects of life. An ethnographic study of a community would focus, for example, on how the people make a living and on how their families operate, as well as on their religion, politics, and neighborhood groups—a full round of life.

The sociologists and anthropologists who undertake ethnographic studies are usually called "field-workers" because they go to where their subjects live and study them in their natural environment. Ethnographic research is distinct from the approach of researchers pursuing experimental or survey research. Ethnographic research is qualitative rather than quantitative—that is, it is concerned with describing and interpreting rather than with asking questions and counting and classifying answers. It is also subjective. The ethnographic researcher has more latitude than other researchers do when it comes to planning a study and has more flexibility regarding changes in the study once it is under way. What behaviors are observed, how they are observed and recorded, and which ones are selected as being especially significant are all decisions made by the researcher.

This subjectivity can be seen as both a strength and a weakness of ethnographic research. The ability of the ethnographer to adapt and modify a study once it is under way is a strength of the approach, but it requires that the researcher be constantly vigilant and open to new perceptions and ideas. Both survey researchers and experimenters, on the other hand, approach the study of human behavior with a predetermined plan of action—a set of questions or an experimental design—that they bring to the subjects of their studies. Whereas various rules and guidelines are specified in texts and guidebooks, field researchers may pick and choose from any number of different observational approaches. A drawback to this is that it becomes far more difficult to draw comparisons between different ethnographic studies than it is to compare experimental or survey results. Observations are usually recorded in the form of field notes. Researchers write down the things people do and say, and they record what objects people use; they record where things happened and exactly who was present. The field notes are later combined and organized to form the basis for writing the ethnography.

Applications

A number of steps are involved in producing an ethnography. The first step in studying a cultural group is the selection of the culture or group to be studied. This decision is usually based on a combination of the interests, background, and resources of the researcher. Although a researcher may be interested in studying a cultural group in an isolated part of the world, for example, such a study might not be possible because of the researcher's limited time, funds, or knowledge of the group's language. Another crucial factor is the willingness or unwillingness of the group itself to be studied.

A second step is to decide on the role that the researcher will take during the study—how involved he or she will be in the activities of the group under study. A researcher may act either as a participant observer (either overt or covert) or a nonparticipant observer. Most researchers choose to become a limited participant observer: They observe a group while participating in it in limited ways that would be appropriate for a visitor to the group. Fewer researchers choose covert participant observation—becoming involved in the group's activities without revealing that they are studying the group. The advantage of this approach is that it avoids the possibility that people's behavior will change because they know they are being observed. The serious disadvantage is that it raises ethical questions. Covert observation can be seen as invading the privacy of those under study and as dishonest in that the researcher usually must mislead or lie to members of the group to conceal his or her identity. A third approach is nonparticipant observation, in which a researcher observes the group without becoming involved in the group's lives or activities at all. The drawback to this method is that the researcher, by maintaining distance, may miss aspects of the group's culture that would be apparent upon closer (participant) examination.

One of the unique features of ethnography is the methods of observation and data collection that are used. Techniques in this research approach are much less standardized than those in experimentation or survey research. Each ethnographer must choose from an array of possible fieldwork techniques in order to record, interpret, and understand the group's actions. Researchers may take notes and photographs and may make audio or video recordings of activities. To clarify actions, individual or group interviews can be used. Napoleon A. Chagnon, in his ethnography *Yanomamo: The Fierce People* (1983), a study of kinship and village life among an Indian group in Brazil and Venezuela, used photographs effectively to help develop elaborate kinship charts to identify relatives living in different villages. Individual life histories can be obtained, and personal documents such as birth records, religious books and records, and personal belongings and papers can be used as sources of information.

Most ethnographers use one or more "informants" in their research. An informant is a member of the culture being studied who has considerable insider knowledge of that culture. Informants can be helpful in acquiring access to certain persons or events in the culture that would otherwise be off-limits or unattainable for the researcher by himself or herself. Informants can suggest things for the researcher to focus on or explain things about the culture from an insider's perspective that the ethnographer is having difficulty understanding. Informants can provide information to the researcher about events and ceremonies, for example, that the researcher as an outsider or member of the opposite gender would not be permitted to observe (such as the birth of a child or a puberty ritual).

Observations are almost always recorded by the researcher in the form of field notes. Important observations should be recorded as quickly as possible while they are still fresh in the mind. The notes can later be rewritten, modified, or expanded based on further developments in the ethnographic investigation. Computers are being used increasingly in the recording of field notes; they enable ease of additions, revisions, and reorganization. It is important that researchers record conversations as well as actions; moreover, a crucial aspect of conversation is how the hearers attribute meaning to what is said. Behaviors must be related to one another to form a larger picture of what is occurring. In American culture, for example, a number of behaviors, such as arguing, fighting, changing one's place of residence, and hiring lawyers, are part of a larger event known as divorce. Any meeting of two or more people must be viewed as a social interaction, and roles and relationships must also be examined.

Once data collection is completed, the ethnography itself can be written. Recurrent or important themes from the field notes are developed into an overall presentation about the group. The ethnographer usually recounts key experiences and describes the techniques used during the observation and writing of the study.

Context

Ethnographic research, or field research, is one of the four major approaches or methodologies for obtaining information on human behavior. The other three methods are experiments, surveys, and the use of available or existing data (often archival or historical data). Of these four methods, ethnographic studies produce results that are most directly related to real-life events and activities, because they occur in the natural environment of the people under study. Ethnography also lends itself to openness, flexibility, and new discoveries. Researchers can freely change course to pursue emerging interests or ideas and to abandon themes that become unproductive. It is weak on control, however, the strong point of experiments, because the researcher as an observer cannot (and should not) shape events in the real world as an experimenter can manipulate variables.

Before World War II, ethnographic research was the most common and most influential form of sociological research in the United States. In the early twentieth century, leading sociologists at the University of Chicago, under the guidance of Robert Park, conducted much ethnographic research based on communities and lifestyles in Chicago and around the country. Following World War II, many sociologists embraced survey research and its seemingly more scientific approach to examining human behavior. The widespread utilization of computers, beginning in the 1960's and increasing thereafter as computers became more sophisticated, furthered the trend toward survey research.

Other sociologists have remained firm in their commitment to ethnographic research, a qualitative rather than quantitative approach. They argue that the understanding of human behavior is most appropriately accomplished by observing people in their natural environments rather than by looking at behavior in a laboratory or by asking questions. They point out that the very nature of testing hypotheses or framing questions to be asked imposes the ideas and worldview of the people doing the testing or writing the questions. Computers have significantly affected sociologists' approach to survey research. Because they are able to analyze closed-end questions (questions with a limited number of precoded options as answers), they have made this type of survey very popular. Closed-end questions provide a restricted view of the respondents' opinions, however, because they make it impossible for them to elaborate on their answers or to go in different directions, as is possible with open-ended questions. Computers are also useful in ethnographic research, it should be noted, and their increasing use in this area may ultimately increase the popularity and prominence of ethnographic research in sociology.

Bibliography

Chagnon, Napoleon A. *Yanomamo: The Fierce People*. 3d ed. New York: Holt, Rinehart and Winston, 1983. Offers a thorough and entertaining explanation of how he conducted his ethnographic research among the Yanomamo, a large tribe of tropical forest Indians who live along the border between Brazil and Venezuela. He studied their kinship patterns, ways of making a living, and political alliances and warfare patterns.

Fetterman, David M. *Ethnography: Step by Step*. 2d ed. Thousand Oaks, Calif.: Sage, 1998. Explains how fieldwork is conducted. He covers cultural concepts and terms and discusses how to enter the culture or begin the study. Methods of observation, interviewing, note taking, and analysis of cultural data are presented in a step-by-step manner. Finally, suggestions on how to write the ethnography are detailed.

Hall, Larry, and Kimball Marshall. *Computing for Social Research*. Belmont, Calif.: Wadsworth, 1992. Chapters 7 and 8 of this book present ways of using computers to collect, analyze, and present ethnographic data. These chapters explain how to use computers to take field notes, how to organize and analyze field data with word processors and indexing programs, and how to use specialized field research programs.

Liebow, Elliott. *Tally's Corner*. Boston: Little, Brown, 1967. Presents an empathetic study of the lives of African American street people in Washington, D.C., in the 1960's. It explains how they see work and family relations with their wives, former wives, children, friends, and lovers.

Mead, Margaret. *Coming of Age in Samoa*. New York: W. Morrow, 1928. Classic ethnography describing the roles of adolescent girls in Samoan culture. The most famous and influential descriptions are those of the casual nature of free love and the lack of adolescent turmoil among the Samoan teenage girls.

Spradley, James P. *Participant Observation*. New York: Holt, Rinehart and Winston, 1980. Explains, in twelve steps, how to conduct ethnographic research. Spradley presents guidelines on how to select a cultural group to study, how to observe cultural events, how to take field notes, and how to analyze cultural data. Finally, guidelines are presented for writing the ethnography.

Spradley, James P., and Brenda J. Mann. *The Cocktail Waitress*. New York: John Wiley & Sons, 1975. Draws on ethnographic research methods to study the role of cocktail waitresses in a college bar setting. The emphasis in this ethnography is on the meaning of work from the perspective of women who are employed in a world predominantly populated and dominated by men.

Larry D. Hall

Cross-References

Ethnomethodology; Horticultural Economic Systems; Hunting and Gathering Economic Systems; Qualitative Research; Surveys.

ETHNOMETHODOLOGY

Type of sociology: Socialization and social interaction
Field of study: Interactionist approach to social interactions

Ethnomethodology investigates the methods of commonsensical reasoning that ordinary social actors use to recognize features of the social world and to produce and understand everyday social actions. This approach treats commonsensical reasoning as a fundamental topic of sociological analysis and challenges approaches to sociology that ignore the role of ordinary reason in social action.

Principal terms

ACCOUNTABILITY: commonsensical recognizability of objects, events, persons, and descriptions of these within the framework of a set of shared understandings

BACKGROUND KNOWLEDGE: body of shared but tacit and taken-for-granted knowledge of the social world that is employed in making sense of everyday events

DOCUMENTARY METHOD OF INTERPRETATION: description of commonsensical reasoning as a dynamic process in which the actors' grasp of a situation depends on the mutual elaboration of particular objects of perception and the contexts in which those objects occur

ETHNOMETHODS: commonsensical reasoning about the social world that actors use to produce and recognize courses of action in their everyday activities; also called "members' methods"

INDEXICALITY: property of objects, events, and descriptions through which their meaning is shaped by the context in which they occur

JUDGMENTAL DOPE: Harold Garfinkel's terms for models of social actors that treat their actions as the causal products of determinate rules

REFLEXIVITY: property of the recognition of objects, events, and descriptions through which that recognition shapes the context of a situation

Overview

According to ethnomethodology's founder, sociologist Harold Garfinkel, social order is located, in the first place, in shared understanding among ordinary social actors (an "actor" being anyone performing an action). Shared understanding or, to use Garfinkel's phrase, "knowledge held in common" is the primordial basis for an orderly, social world. To Garfinkel, knowledge held in common depends on a set of shared practices by which actors produce and recognize social reality as meaningful. All major social institutions and interactions—including, for example, socialization, exchange, and even warfare—depend on shared understanding. While ethnomethodology is similar to other sociological perspectives in emphasizing shared understanding as the foundation for social order, it is distinctive in treating shared understanding as a practical accomplishment.

Shared understanding is an *accomplishment* in that it depends on the everyday activities of society's members. Through their actions, members constitute the social world as the ordered, coherent, and reasonable place that it is typically understood to be. Moreover, as Garfinkel describes the situation, there are "no time-outs" from the achievement of social order; it is an "ongoing accomplishment."

The accomplishment of shared understanding is *practical* because it depends on a common set of procedures whereby social action is produced and recognized as meaningful. Because these practices are rarely the objects of social actors' conscious reflections, Garfinkel described them as "seen but unnoticed." Though unnoticed, this shared set of practices is not unimportant. Garfinkel insisted that the practices, as well as the background knowledge that informs them, constitute the primordial basis for social order. Focusing on the procedural character of commonsensical reasoning and practical action, Garfinkel showed how social actors produce and maintain their sense of an orderly and meaningful social world even when incongruous events challenge that understanding. Garfinkel referred to this orderly, but typically unacknowledged, set of practices as "ethnomethods" and sought to explain both their properties and their import for the constitution of ordinary social activities and situations.

A major constituent property of ethnomethods is the "documentary method of interpretation." Garfinkel derived the term from the work of sociologist Karl Mannheim and used it to refer to the process by which ordinary social actors make sense of situations. According to Garfinkel, actors understand individual objects of perception in terms of the context in which the objects appear, and, at the same time, they understand context on the basis of particular objects occurring within it. Thus, rather than being discrete entities, the meaning of an object and its context are mutually elaborative: Each informs the meaning of the other. The most basic implication of this insight is that neither particular objects nor contexts can be understood as fixed; both are actively constructed by social actors themselves.

Ethnomethodologists argue that every social action is reflexive and indexical, requiring the interpretive work of social actors to attribute meaning to it. On the basis of this interpretive work, social order is achieved as an "ongoing accomplishment." To exemplify this process, Garfinkel conducted an exercise in which subjects were told to ask yes/no questions of a person described to them as a psychological counselor. The counselor's "answers" were predetermined in a random pattern. Nevertheless, in the context of a "counseling session," subjects used their background knowledge to make sense of the counselor's responses as if they were answers to their questions.

Most of Garfinkel's studies focus on concrete, everyday actions and are designed to explore the ways in which they are produced and understood. Garfinkel used a series of "breaching experiments" in which the experimenters would disrupt the details of a commonplace situation to make it somehow incongruous with the subjects' commonsensical expectations.

For example, Garfinkel used the game of ticktacktoe. After allowing the subject to move first, the experimenter would intentionally make an invalid move, without acknowledging it. In response, subjects either "normalized" the situation—by treating the invalid move as a joke or by concluding that the game being played was something other than ticktack-toe—or they "demonized" the situation, usually by demanding that the experimenter acknowledge, correct, and sometimes even apologize for the invalid move. Garfinkel concluded that either sort of response depended on an intricate intertwining of cognitive and moral expectations that he termed "accountability."

Garfinkel found the breaching experiments useful because the incongruous situations forced attention on the mundane details of everyday activities (such as describing an experience or playing a simple game) that are normally taken-for-granted. Not all of his ethnomethodological investigations depended on instigated instances of incongruity. In some of his studies Garfinkel investigated naturally arising incongruities. Most famous, perhaps, is his study of "Agnes," who was reared as a boy but as an adult assumed the identity of a female. To "pass" as a woman, Agnes had to overcome her lack of appropriate female anatomy and biography. Based on her experiences, Agnes learned how commonsensical practices work to create the normally accepted understandings of gender as both moral and natural. As Garfinkel's study of Agnes demonstrated, ordinary beliefs about gender as something fixed once and for all rest upon an entire range of seen but unnoticed assumptions and actions based on those assumptions.

Ethnomethodology consistently stresses the procedural character of social action. On the basis of shared sets of practices, actors are able to construct their own lines of conduct as well as to interpret the actions of others. Thus, rather than being imposed externally, social order emerges as a product of actors' own courses of action.

Applications

Ethnomethodology contends that any social setting, from the everyday conversations of two friends to the work of astrophysicists in a laboratory, is appropriate subject matter for ethnomethodological study. Many ethnomethodological studies have influenced related research in fields such as anthropology, artificial intelligence, cognitive science, linguistics, and psychology. Within sociology, investigators have applied ethnomethodology to understand the use of organizationally produced statistics on deviance, the social organization of the natural sciences, and, in a branch of sociology known as "conversation analysis," the orderly properties of talk.

Statistics have played a central role in sociology at least since sociologist Émile Durkheim's *Le Suicide: Étude de sociologie* (1897; *Suicide: A Study in Sociology*, 1951). In this tradition, sociologists have used statistics, collected by official organizations and regarding the rates of social phenomena such as crime, joblessness, and suicide, to assess the incidence and significance of these phenomena and to advance explanations for them. Ethnomethodology challenges this way of working by questioning the relationship between statistics and the phenomena the statistics represent. In sociological works such as J. Maxwell Atkinson's *Discovering Suicide: Studies in the Social Organization of Sudden Death* (1978) and Aaron Cicourel's *The Social Organization of Juvenile Justice* (1976), ethnomethodology suggests that these organizationally generated statistics are themselves social accomplishments.

Both those studies introduced concerns about the definitions and procedures used by official institutions for identifying deviant acts. The studies call into question not only the reliability of the organizationally collected data but also, more fundamentally, the validity of the data. In showing that the definitions and procedures for identifying deviance are themselves social practices, embedded in bureaucratic organizations, ethnomethodology shows how rates of deviance themselves are constituted by the institutions created to measure them. Consequently, quantitative studies of social phenomena must take into account the social practices involved in collecting official statistics.

Ethnomethodology has also contributed to the sociological understanding of the methods of natural science. In research such as sociologist Michael Lynch's *Art and Artifact in Laboratory Science* (1985), ethnomethodology shows how social practices inform supposedly "objective" findings in scientific investigations. Lynch examined the social processes by which neuroscientists using electron microscopes discovered, recorded, and described the destruction and regrowth of axons in rats' brains. According to Lynch and other ethnomethodological studies of natural science, the scientists' social practices of investigation have as much influence on their findings as do the objects of their investigation. Thus, ethnomethodology informs sociology's understanding of the performance and findings of natural science.

Finally, the principles of ethnomethodology have contributed to the field of sociology known as "conversation analysis" (CA). The pioneering work of Harvey Sacks, in collaboration with fellow sociologists Emanuel Schegloff and Gail Jefferson, continues to be a major resource for sociologists as well as researchers in the fields of anthropology, applied linguistics, and social psychology. The naturally occurring details of talk in interaction constitute the data of conversation analysis. By investigating audiotaped and videotaped records of actual, naturally occurring interactions, conversation analysts have been able to describe the organizational principles of talk as a social phenomenon in its own right. The organizational principles thus described by conversation analysts are embodied in the participants' own actions and are observably displayed in their orientations to and interpretations of those actions.

Conversation analysis proceeds by analyzing turns to talk and how these turns are built into connected sequences of interaction. Talk is thus viewed as being at once interactionally and sequentially organized. Therefore, conversation analysts consistently ask: How is the talk under study being constructed by the participants? What is the talk responsive to? What is it being used to do? By posing such questions, practitioners of conversation analysis have succeeded in providing detailed analytic descriptions of the organization of conduct for a variety of social settings, ranging from everyday conversation to talk in institutional contexts such as courtrooms, television news interviews, and medical interactions. In each instance, conversation analysis exemplifies the fundamental ethnomethodological insight that social order is produced and recognized by the participants themselves in the course of locally situated actions.

Context

Ethnomethodology began in the 1950's as a result of Harold Garfinkel's discontent with conventional approaches to social action that treated social order as governed by rules. Garfinkel provided an exhaustive, yet appreciative, critique of his mentor, sociologist Talcott Parsons, and Parsons's theory as presented in *The Structure of Social Action* (1937). At the time Parsons was the dominant figure in American sociology, but Garfinkel's critique did much to dislodge Parsons from that position. Garfinkel's critique of Parsons was twofold.

First, Garfinkel objected to Parsons's treatment of social order as fundamentally an analytical problem. Parsons had provided a theoretical explanation of social order. In contrast, Garfinkel treated social order as a practical problem. Instead of creating a theory of social order, Garfinkel sought to show how people in their everyday lives "enacted the world" as orderly. Whereas Parsons's theoretical perspective emphasizes the knowledge of the social scientist as a theorist, Garfinkel's perspective recognizes the reasoning practices of the actors being studied.

Second, Garfinkel rejected Parsons's theoretical reliance on rules, or norms, as either the motivators of social action or the foundations of social order. In Parsons's theory, social order depends on a commonly shared set of norms, that, ideally, each member of society internalizes. Norms, in turn, define coherent sets of social roles and stable social institutions. According to Garfinkel, Parsons's treatment of norms turns social actors into "judgmental dopes," incapable of thinking reflectively about the situations of their actions or the rules that supposedly guide them. Thus, whereas Parsons treated norms as determinative of social action, Garfinkel treated norms as resources by which members recognize and make sense of social actions and the contexts in which they occur.

One important consequence of Garfinkel's shift in perspective is that he shunned Parsons's aim of creating a general theory that could provide causal explanations of social action. Garfinkel resisted organizing ethnomethodology's findings into a single, general theory, preferring instead to describe individual cases of social action as deserving of investigation in their own right.

In seeking to improve on Parsons's rule-based theory of social action, Garfinkel drew heavily on the work of sociologist and phenomenologist Alfred Schutz. Schutz described human commonsensical knowledge of the world as patchy and approximate; nevertheless, Schutz contended that this knowledge was adequate for all practical purposes. Garfinkel developed many of his ideas about commonsensical practices from Schutz's work, but he had the express aim of turning Schutz's observations about knowledge as an abstract entity into the research agenda for his investigation of "knowledge-in-use," as embedded in courses of social action.

Ethnomethodology will continue to play a robust role in sociology because of its unique position with respect to everyday social action and organization. Ethnomethodology's great contribution to social science is the study of the taken-for-granted aspects of ordinary social action as interesting in their own right. This focus emphasizes the importance of actors' processes of practical reasoning in constituting their courses of action. As ethnomethodological studies show, these shared but tacit reasoning practices provide the orderly basis for social action. Ethnomethodology's commitment to studying practical reason as embedded in courses of social action provides sociology with an omnipresent setting within which to study social order as it is produced and reproduced by a society's members.

Bibliography

Atkinson, J. Maxwell. *Discovering Suicide: Studies in the Social Organization of Sudden Death*. London: Macmillan, 1978. A definitive ethnomethodological study of the relationship between statistics of deviance and the phenomena they represent. Focuses on suicide rates as socially constructed phenomena, depending on the definitions and practices of official investigators.

Cicourel, Aaron V. *The Social Organization of Juvenile Justice*. London: Heinemann, 1976. Shows how the determination of juvenile delinquency, and hence the rates of it, depend on the commonsensical reasoning and background knowledge of policing agencies. The analysis that results is socially engaged, demonstrating how the resulting statistics about delinquency rationalize the injustices of the policing practices themselves.

Garfinkel, Harold. *Studies in Ethnomethodology*. Cambridge, England: Polity Press, 1967. Seminal work in ethnomethodology, collecting Garfinkel's early essays. Topics range from how jurors reach their verdicts to the famous case study of "Agnes." These essays are challenging because of Garfinkel's unorthodox thinking and his difficult writing style; nevertheless, they are well worth the effort invested.

Heritage, John. *Garfinkel and Ethnomethodology*. Cambridge, England: Polity Press, 1984. Most complete, detailed, and accessible secondary treatment of ethnomethodology. Traces the field from the influences of Parsons and Schutz on Garfinkel through Garfinkel's *Studies in Ethnomethodology* to a survey of subsequent research by Garfinkel and others.

Jalbert, Paul L., ed. *Media Studies: Ethnomethodological Approaches*. Washington, D.C.: International Institute for Ethnomethodology and Conversation Analysis, 1999.

Nofsinger, Robert. *Everyday Conversation*. Newbury Park, Calif.: Sage Publications, 1991. Brief introduction to conversation analysis intended for university and college undergraduates. Covers the basics of conversation analysis, from basic sequences of talk such as questions and answers to the "turn-taking system" of ordinary conversation, with special focus on how these affect interpersonal relationships.

Pollner, Melvin. *Mundane Reason: Reality in Everyday and Sociological Discourse*. Cambridge, England: Cambridge University Press, 1987. Explains how people sustain their belief in the objective reality of the world and events in it, especially when faced with competing, divergent accounts of those events. Pollner's study of conflicting testimonies in traffic law courts is an elegant elaboration of Garfinkel's studies; also recommended because of Pollner's unusually lucid prose.

Sacks, Harvey. *Lectures on Conversation*. Edited by Gail Jefferson. 2 vols. Oxford, England: Blackwell, 1992. Large compilation of Sacks's demanding lectures, delivered between 1964 and 1972. Sacks stands as one of ethnomethodology's greatest contributors, and his genius and sparkle are abundantly present in these transcribed lectures. Emanuel

Schegloff's lengthy introductions to both volumes are comprehensive, accessible, and unconditionally recommended to readers finding their way through this vast, unique body of work.

Wieder, D. L. *Language and Social Reality*. The Hague: Mouton, 1974. Ethnographic description of life in a halfway house for narcotics offenders that demonstrates how actors use the "convict code" to make sense of social actions in an institutional setting. Wieder's study remains important because it shows how rules retain their character as sense-making resources even in situations of sustained social conflict.

Andrew L. Roth

Cross-References

Cultural Norms and Sanctions; Culture and Language; Dramaturgy; Ethnography; Horticultural Economic Systems; Hunting and Gathering Economic Systems; Knowledge; Microsociology; Sociology Defined.

FAMILY
Functionalist Versus Conflict Theory Views

Type of sociology: Major social institutions
Field of study: The family

*Functionalist and conflict views are sociological theories that explain "how society oper-
ates on a day-to-day basis through its major institutions," one of which is the family. These
two views provide a realistic picture of society. They help explain how a family can be seen
in terms of harmony and stability on the one hand and in terms of conflict and change on
the other.*

Principal terms

DAY CARE: any type of arrangement that is used to provide care, supervision, or education
    for children under age six when parents are at work
DUAL-EARNER FAMILY: family in which both parents are fully employed
EXTENDED FAMILY: household consisting of spouses, their children, and other relatives
FAMILY DAY CARE: child care that is provided at a caregiver's home
INSTITUTIONS: stable social patterns and relationships that result from the values, norms,
    roles, and statuses that govern activities that fulfill the needs of the society; for example,
    economic institutions help to organize the production and distribution of goods and
    services
NUCLEAR FAMILY: unit consisting of a husband, a wife, and their children

Overview

The family is the most basic institution in all societies. Defining the family is, however,
becoming more difficult because of the changes that are taking place in societies, particularly in Western societies. Sociologist Ian Robertson defines the family as "a relatively
permanent group of people related by ancestry, marriage, or adoption, who live together,
form an economic unit, and take care of their young." This definition is being challenged by
some sociologists who argue that family members are not always bound by "legal marriage"
or "adoption." In order to make the definition of a family more flexible and contemporary,
sociologists Mary Ann Lamanna and Agnes Riedmann, in their book *Marriages and
Families: Making Choices and Facing the Change* (1991), define a family as "any sexually
expressive or parent-child relationship in which people—usually related by ancestry, marriage, or adoption—(1) live together with commitment, (2) form an economic unit and care
for any young, and (3) find their identity as importantly attached to the group."

   The study of the family involves several theories, but the functionalist and conflict theories are the two most fundamental. The functionalist view attempts to answer two questions: "What role does the family play in the maintenance of the society?" and "How does the society as a social system affect the family as an institution?" Functionalist theorists, therefore, are interested in the functions that are performed by the family, and there are several of them.

First, the family must regulate sexual behavior. The incest taboo, for example, is an almost universal rule that prohibits sex between close blood relatives. Societies, however, have different family structures and related norms concerning the number of spouses one may have at a time. These family structures include the nuclear family, which limits sexual activity to a married man and his wife only. By contrast, in polygamous families, sexual activity is not limited to one husband and one wife, because such families involve multiple spouses. Second, in order for the society to continue, its members must be replaced. The family, according to the functionalist view, is the most stable social institution and is therefore ideal for the performance of this function. Third, the family, through the process of socialization, nurtures and prepares children to be productive members of society. It equips them with the cultural values and skills necessary for the society to survive continuously. Fourth, family members receive their basic needs, such as emotional and physical care, from their families. In most societies, there are groups or organizations that take up the responsibility of caring for or protecting the members of the society under certain circumstances. The family, however, seems to be the most appropriate of them all, especially regarding daily living in an impersonal environment caused by rapid changes. Fifth, at birth, children inherit their race, ethnic identity, and social class from their families. This function is critical because it affects the life course of each individual. In some cases, one's future may be predicted on the basis of this one factor, especially when parenting styles, socioeconomic factors, and environmental conditions are taken into account.

Finally, families serve an economic function. Prior to the Industrial Revolution, every society's economic system was dependent upon each family, whose task was to produce and consume the goods that were needed, but significant changes have taken place since then. The production of food and other material goods, for example, is no longer the sole responsibility of the family. The family has become more of a consumption unit than a production unit.

In fact, the drastic changes that are related to economic production and consumption are a major concern of the conflict view. In his book *In Conflict and Order: Understanding Society* (1985), sociologist D. Stanley Eitzen wrote:

> The transfer of production out of the household altered family life in two important ways. First, families surrendered functions previously concentrated in the home and took more highly specialized functions. Second, family units became increasingly private, set apart from society by distinct boundaries.

The specialized functions that the family still performs are "those of procreation, consumption, and rearing of children."

Unlike the functionalist theorists, who emphasize stability and harmony among different parts of the family, conflict theorists stress the constant struggle that exists among individuals and interest groups. In marriage and family, the struggle involves such areas as unequal power between men and women, changing traditional gender roles, economic matters, and different interests, values, and goals.

Studies of families continue to show that husbands tend to have more power in decision making even though changes are taking place. Traditionally, husbands, as sole breadwinners, had absolute authority over other family members. Most of their power resulted from the society's emphasis on gender differentiation, which created inequality between men and women. For example, for a long time, women were required to stay home and rear children. The rising cost of living is now encouraging more women to work full time outside the home. Studies show, however, that the wives and mothers who are in the labor force are not necessarily forced to work; they work for various reasons of their own.

The wage gap between men and women shows that inequality still exists even though women's movements have been fighting for equal pay for equal work. For example, 1989 statistics show that women who held full-time jobs earned only 71 cents for every dollar earned by men. The proportion of married women who are in the labor force has been increasing since World War II. In 1940, only 14 percent of married women were in the labor force, but in 1989, as many as 58 percent of married women were in the labor force, and the number is increasing yearly.

Conflict theorists consider this significant change as one of the sources of conflict in the family, since working wives and mothers continue to do more work despite the fact that they are fully employed. Sociologist Arlie Hochschild calls the additional work they do at home a "second shift." The "second shift" practice is likely to put strain on the family. Sometimes it is seen as a source of frustration that may lead to child abuse. Conflict theorists list the problems of child abuse and spouse abuse as examples of power struggles within families.

Applications

The functionalist and conflict approaches to the study of the family show that the society affects the family and, in turn, the family affects the society's social policies. Furthermore, they show that despite attempts to maintain harmony and stability within families, conflict and change seem to be inevitable. According to the conflict theorists, changes are not necessarily always negative, because they also enhance progress. Some of the changes that have occurred within the family are the increased number of women in the labor force, the increased number of families headed by single females, and high divorce rates.

The increased number of mothers with young children in the labor force has created a great need for child day care services. The 1993 *Statistical Abstracts of the United States* analysis shows that more than nine million children under the age of five are in some type of day care facility. The awareness of this need for child day care services has led some women to establish family day care services in their homes. The home day care facility is the most preferred child care service because it provides the children with a family atmosphere. Some such facilities, however, may be unreliable or may not provide quality day care service. Day care centers tend to be large. Children in such facilities may not get the individual attention they need, but they do acquire some of the skills that prepare them for school.

Some people are opposed to the idea of child day care; their belief is that children should be cared for in their homes by their mothers. Others blame women or dual-earner families for the social problems facing young people, such as drugs, teenage pregnancy, and lower school performance. There are disagreements, however, concerning these allegations. Studies of the effects of maternal employment on children show no conclusive differences in development between children whose mothers are working outside the home and children whose mothers are homemakers.

The Family and Medical Leave Act that was passed by the U.S. Congress and signed into law by president Bill Clinton in 1993 is one example that shows the government's attempts to reevaluate past policies and meet the needs of working mothers. This legislation was passed only after much disagreement and many long debates among politicians, the business community, and families. This law requires companies with fifty or more employees to grant an unpaid leave of up to twelve weeks to employees who need time off for the purpose of taking care of a newborn baby or an adopted or seriously ill child. Many people, however, criticize the law because it does not help to solve the problem of day care. Critics of this law argue that most families in low-income brackets cannot afford to lose any of their income, which is already inadequate.

There is a consensus among researchers that the current high divorce rate creates economic crises among families and that women and children tend to suffer most. This knowledge also has compelled the government to respond in support of the families that are affected. The Family Support Act is one such effort. One of the provisions of this act is an automatic withholding of child support from a noncustodial parent's paycheck. The success of this act depends on the cooperation of the economic institutions that employ such parents. Some economic institutions already cooperate with parents through flexible scheduling of work hours. Such an arrangement helps to reduce the role conflict often experienced by parents of young children.

The functionalist view of the family has influenced social workers and therapists to acknowledge that the family is a social system. Therefore, in their work, therapists who counsel individuals with behavior problems such as alcoholism, eating disorders, and other addictions end up treating the whole family as a unit. The idea behind this approach is that some of these problems are rooted in the family. Consequently, the whole family is affected and is in need of help. Child abuse, for example, is done by parents while fulfilling the function of rearing their children. Because studies of families show a high rate of child abuse within families, all states have now established compulsory child-abuse reporting laws.

The conflict view of the family provides insight into other problems that are manifested in the family. The removal of the production function from the family, according to this view, isolated the family from the rest of the community. This isolation and privacy left the family vulnerable to various problems, including domestic violence and divorce. Because of this understanding there are now certain programs that help the abusive parents. One of them is called Parents Anonymous (PA). There is also Alcoholics Anonymous (AA) for those individuals who are addicted to alcohol. These programs provide some ways of helping families cope with the problems that affect them. Indirectly, these programs are an admission that these problems are not only individual problems but also family and societal problems. Sociologist C. Wright Mills considers such problems "public issues."

The conflict over family roles has begun to receive more attention. This has caused some men to realize the need to share housework and child care. In addition, society as a whole is showing increased support for the family.

Context

The changes that followed the Industrial Revolution caused many social problems, which encouraged social scientists to seek answers and solutions to those problems. Sociology as a discipline emerged during this era. Herbert Spencer, a classical sociologist, in his book *Principles of Sociology* (1876, 1882), presented social institutions such as family, politics, and religion as subjects to be studied by sociologists. He compared society to a living organism with interdependent parts that contribute to its maintenance and stability.

The roots of the functionalist approach can be traced back to Herbert Spencer and Émile Durkheim, the French sociologist, who argued that the various parts of society, such as social institutions, have functions that help to maintain the stability of the social system. Some contemporary sociologists, such as Talcott Parsons and Robert K. Merton, expanded this view to include not only functions but also the positive and negative consequences that are experienced when certain parts of the social system are disturbed. In his classic work *Social Theory and Social Structure* (1968), Merton refined the functionalist view of society by making an important distinction between two types of functions: the manifest and latent functions. Manifest functions of the family are expected or intended; latent functions are unintended consequences. Many families today are producing socially responsible children. Others are producing maladjusted children who become members of subcultural groups such as gangs. Certainly, this is an unintended or latent function of the family.

The conflict theory has its origin in the work of Karl Marx, a German classical theorist, and his associates. They considered the main source of social conflict to be the struggles between social classes, such as between those who controlled the means of production and distribution and those who were mere workers. Contemporary conflict theorists such as Lewis Coser and C. Wright Mills have refined conflict theory. These theorists view conflict as being applicable to many situations in which tension is inevitable. For example, there is tension that stems from interaction between groups (parents and children, husbands and wives, and employers and employees, to name a few). Contemporary conflict theorists are concerned with the issues of competing interests and the benefits that arise from special arrangements in society.

In the 1970's and 1980's, many sociologists took it upon themselves to study all facets of family life. Numerous problems that affected the family were researched widely. Sociologists Arlene Skolnick and Jerome H. Skolnick, in *Family in Transition* (7th ed., 1992), put together readings from the works of various sociologists. The important aspect of this book is that it dispels myths about "perfect," stable, harmonious families of the past. It gives a more realistic view of societies and families in the past and in the present. In his book *The Strong Family: Growing Wise in Family Life* (1991), Charles R. Swindoll uses examples from the Bible to show that even centuries ago there were families that were dysfunctional. The fact that such families exist does not mean, however, that the family as an institution is doomed. Such analyses of the family are incentives to continue to strive to create better and stronger families.

Bibliography

Coser, Lewis A. *The Functions of Social Conflict*. Glencoe, Ill.: Free Press, 1956. Examines the concept of conflict and shows that conflict is not necessarily bad. Although it is dated, this is a good book for students who are interested in the study of conflict.

Eitzen, D. Stanley. *In Conflict and Order: Understanding Society*. 3d ed. Boston: Allyn & Bacon, 1985. Discusses important issues that affect societies. In several chapters, the author presents sociological analyses of social institutions, including the family. Both the functionalist and conflict views are integrated in his discussion of the topics. The book is suitable for students in introductory sociology classes.

Lamanna, Mary Ann, and Agnes Riedmann. *Marriages and Families: Making Choices and Facing the Change*. 4th ed. Belmont, Calif.: Wadsworth, 1991. Introductory text on marriage and family focusing on changes and the choices that people have to make, particularly in marriage. Discusses many family-related issues. Theories, research, case studies, and different views on each topic are presented, and pictures are included in each chapter.

Merton, Robert K. *Social Theory and Social Structure*. Rev. ed. New York: Free Press, 1968. Classic work that systematically defines and analyzes contemporary structural-functionalism. It shows how the functionalist perspective is applicable to different situations.

Mills, C. Wright. "The Promise." In *Sociological Footprints*, compiled by Leonard Cargan and Jeanne H. Ballantine. 5th ed. Belmont, Calif.: Wadsworth, 1991. Mills makes a distinction between the personal problems that originate within a person and social problems that arise from the environment. This valuable article may help to change the attitudes of the general public concerning problems that stem from society and tend to trap individuals.

Robertson, Ian. *Sociology*. 3d ed. New York: Worth, 1987. Introductory text systematically presenting concepts, theoretical perspectives, and research methods in sociology. Provides valuable historical information about the origins of sociology and social institutions.

Rubin, Lillian B. *Worlds of Pain: Life in the Working-Class Family*. New York: Basic Books, 1976. Although published in the 1970's, this book remains relevant to today's working-class families. Rubin uses case studies to demonstrate how industrialization affected a large segment of society. The book illustrates some of the conflict theorists' views on the family by showing how economic factors affect people's lives.

Skolnick, Arlene, and Jerome H. Skolnick, eds. *Family in Transition*. 10th ed. New York: Longman, 1999. Articles by various authors showing the diversity of and the changes that are taking place in the family. Every article in this book is easy to read and understand.

Swindoll, Charles R. *The Strong Family: Growing Wise in Family Life*. Portland, Oreg.: Multnomah Press, 1991. Well-written presentation of an optimistic view of the family. Examines the past, present, and future of the family. His analysis of the problems facing the family includes examples of dysfunctional families found in the Bible.

Rejoice D. Sithole

Cross-References

Functionalism; Marriage; Social Groups; Social Stratification: Functionalist Perspectives; Socialization: The Family.

FUNCTIONALISM

Type of sociology: Origins and definitions of sociology
Field of study: Sociological perspectives and principles

Functionalism is a major theory in sociology for analyzing and understanding certain social relationships. This perspective attempts to explain why and how certain social structures work in society by ascertaining their function.

Principal terms

ANOMIE: condition of confusion that exists in both the individual and society because of weak or absent social norms

CONFLICT THEORY: social theory that focuses on tension and strain as a natural state within the social system

DYSFUNCTION: a negative consequence which may lead to disruption or breakdown of the social system

LATENT FUNCTION: unrecognized or unintended consequence

MACROSOCIOLOGY: the level of sociological analysis that is concerned with large-scale social issues, institutions, and processes

MANIFEST FUNCTION: intended or obvious consequences

MICROSOCIOLOGY: level of sociological analysis concerned with small-scale group dynamics

Overview

The sociological agenda throughout much of the twentieth century has been empirically rooted, and this approach has generated an abundance of research facts and figures. Empirical information remains useless, however, unless its meaning is discerned; this is the purpose of a theory. It organizes a set of concepts in a meaningful way by explaining the relationship among them. Theories thus make the "facts" of social life understandable by explaining cause and effect relationships.

Functional theory is one of the central sociological perspectives that is concerned with explaining large-scale social structures and relationships. In other words, it is one of the principal approaches of macrosociology. Functionalists attempt to explain why certain conditions exist in society by trying to ascertain their purpose—their function. This type of approach is used extensively, even dominantly, in all the social sciences as well as in many of the natural sciences, biology in particular. In sociology, the functionalist approach—examining how things work to meet people's needs and to promote social consensus—is contrasted primarily with conflict theory, which emphasizes the struggle and strain among different groups within society.

Sociologists use the functionalist perspective (sometimes called structural functionalism) to explain why social institutions such as the family take on a certain form or structure within a given society. It is assumed that for something to exist it must have a purpose within the social system. The premise underlying this assumption is that if the social institution served to purpose in its existing state it would either change to accommodate new social conditions or would simply cease to exist.

This question of why certain institutions or patterns of relationships exist in society was formulated by the French social philosopher Auguste Comte (1798-1857), who has been called the founder of sociology. Comte developed the basic organic analogy that was extended and popularized by the British sociologist Herbert Spencer (1820-1903), who drew parallels to the theories of the naturalist Charles Darwin (1809-1882). Darwin theorized that, over time, biological species adapt and change to survive as environmental conditions change. Spencer related Darwin's thesis to societies. Spencer's theory states that all the parts of the social system, like the parts of the human body, have a fit or function and connect to the whole; if one part of the system changes, the change will influence other parts of the system to change. Thus, as the family begins to change because of social changes in the environment (for example, the shift from an agrarian society to an industrial society), so too must the other social institutions (political, educational, and religious) change, leading to a realignment of all the social institutions so they all "fit" the new social order.

The functionalist school of sociology has from its inception been concerned with how society adapts and changes. The classic evolutionary view sees changes occurring slowly, allowing for adaptation and realignment of the various interrelated social institutions. A society which changes too rapidly is likely to experience structural misalignment in which parts of the system do not fit snugly together, leading to confusion or anomie for the society's members. Theoretically at least, the component parts of the system will eventually mesh, and the expected harmonious interconnection of social institutions will again be achieved.

This classic evolutionary adaptation of social systems has never posed a problem for functionalists, since such change tends to occur without disrupting the existing social system. More cataclysmic, conflictive forms of change, however, have challenged functionalist explanations because they tend to lead to social disharmony. This problem was addressed in various forms by sociologists from Max Weber (1864-1920) and Émile Durkheim (1858-1917) to Talcott Parsons (1902-1979) and Robert K. Merton (b. 1910).

The concept of viewing even disruptive change as functional may be used as a simplistic though straightforward summation of latter-twentieth century functionalism. Change, whether internal (such as recessions or depressions) or external (war), causes strain, throwing the existing system into a state of disequilibrium. Prolonged strain cannot be endured without the society suffering considerable damage. The destructive impact of prolonged stress on the human body, both physical and mental, has been well documented, and functionalists extend the same premise to society. They see society moving to restore balance or harmony (the "natural" social condition). The restored system, however, may be markedly different from the old. In other words, social change is a natural evolutionary process, and while it may sometimes be painful, it helps the system adapt and adjust to new social conditions; it is therefore functional.

For Parsons, social strain was natural; strain is the painful adjustment which results from society's continued growth, inevitably making each successive social stage more complex than earlier ones. This increased complexity causes tension. Merton took into consideration the idea that not everything which happens in society leads to equilibrium; indeed, Merton points out that certain changes, while beneficial for some, may be dysfunctional for others. Nevertheless, he maintains that these dysfunctions may be beneficial if one distinguishes between manifest functions, which are stated or intended, and latent functions, which are unintended or hidden. Competition provides an excellent example of Merton's thesis. Economic competition is often lopsided, with clear winners and losers, but competition also leads to benefits for the consumer, who gets improved products at reduced cost (latent function). In the process the winner, by building the "better mousetrap," reaps rewards in enhanced profits (manifest function). Yet from the competitive loser's vantage point, competition is seen as dysfunctional, since they did not benefit.

Applications

Functionalism primarily deals with large social units and attempts to understand how these units are interrelated. Functionalists work from a premise that these units strive to maintain a balance: order, equilibrium, homeostasis. As such, the social institution is connected to society and adapts to changes in the social environment. Two examples may be utilized to illustrate this connection. The first traces the normal evolutionary processes of adaption in the social institution of sports; the second examines the more disruptive but functional place of revolutions.

In the preindustrial, agrarian society of the early nineteenth century, sports fit the social environment: fishing, hunting, boating, cockfighting, foot racing, and other activities rooted to the land and water dominated. As the social environment began to change in the mid-nineteenth century, people moved from rural areas and adopted an urban, industrial way of life. Cities had a larger population base from which to draw, so arena and stadium sporting events replaced local sporting activities, giving rise to soccer, football, baseball, and boxing. Spectator sports replaced participatory sports, because industrialization required specialization and people no longer had either the time or talent to devote to sports; however, they did have more disposable income and could pay to see sporting events that had formerly been participatory and free.

As the twentieth century progressed, technological changes prompted adaption in sports. Radio and then television made stadium crowds unnecessary, either to generate income or to reach sports fans. Broadcasting made sports a mass event, no longer confined to particular cities and soon reaching tens of millions of listeners and viewers. Football, as well as most major sports, has been altered by the media; for example, time-outs have increased to allow time for television advertising. The game time has thus been substantially extended. Other sports that have traditionally garnered only a small audience, such as tennis and golf, have received more coverage and risen in prestige, and more amateurs have become interested in the games. In addition, sporting forms which have previously not existed have been developed for television. One example in the late 1980's was a program called *American Gladiators*, in which athletes competed in a staged series of tests of strength and endurance in an atmosphere that was part carnival, part game show.

Sports, then, has changed; it has evolved as social conditions (notably urbanization and technology) have changed, and changes in sports have largely taken place without major disruption in other interrelated parts of the social system. The racial integration of sports has proceeded at a pace that reflects racial integration in other social institutions, such as education, politics, and the military, all of which took their first major strides toward integration during the 1950's. Similarly, the entrance of women into sports, as well as the increased attention paid to women's sports in the 1980's and 1990's, paralleled the general social movement of women as they entered the American workforce and political arena in increasing numbers during this period.

Changes in macropolitics are sometimes less harmonious. Revolutions are extraordinarily disruptive. They typically result in major upheavals and radical changes in all existing institutional arrangements. The American Revolution occurred in 1776; the French in 1789; the Russian in 1917. Germany underwent major political shifts between 1880 and 1910, though not marked by the same degree of violence. In other words, many of the major Western powers experienced radical political reform over a relatively short historical period, moving from monarchy systems to predominantly parliamentary forms of government. Such political "facts" require interpretation. Classic organic functionalism cannot explain this widespread social upheaval because the evolutionary process was not allowed to take its "natural" course. More contemporary forms of functionalism (Parsons, Merton) help in understanding the functional aspect of disruptive change.

The old monarchy systems were rooted in the feudal period, and they were once beneficial. Under the feudal system, the nobility protected the outlying agrarian populace from marauding bands. The peasant paid for this protection by providing the nobility with food and other services. Over time, the monarchy system decayed and became corrupt, providing fewer services for the populace. Ultimately, this resulted in forced change. The revolutions of the eighteenth and nineteenth century that swept Western Europe and North America were the result of corrupt, unresponsive systems of government (those of George III, Louis XVI, and Czar Nicholas in England, France, and Russia, respectively). Disruptive as these periods of strife were, they were necessary (functional) in moving the society from an agrarian monarchy system of government to an industrial and parliamentary one.

The industrial age requires adaptation and change, and entrenched parties in power (such as monarchies) are notoriously resistant to change. Parliamentary systems are thus more functional in the modern age. Great Britain, where the parliamentary system first arose in the aftermath of the English Civil War of the mid-seventeenth century, was the first nation to industrialize and became an early economic world leader. More recently, Japan's powerful monarchy was replaced by a parliamentary system after World War II, and Japan has since taken its place among the world's economic giants. Those countries which have lagged industrially have been totalitarian, most notably the communist governments of China and the former Soviet Union. These governments struggled with the transition to industrialization because changing one aspect of their world, the economic-industrial stratum, requires change in other areas, especially the political. To function in the modern world they have been forced to make concessions; while change has led to major internal strife, such tension is necessary for countries to enter the industrial age.

Context

Functionalist explanations have been used for millennia by a diverse group of philosophers and scientists and have been used by sociologists to explain social conditions since Auguste Comte first coined the term "sociology." This theoretical heritage does not in itself ensure its continued dominance, but it is at the very least a strong indicator of its general historical importance. A number of important sociological perspectives have been developed in the twentieth century, but in a way they are all descendants of the functionalist view—all represent attempts to come to terms with what either functionalists or their critics have seen as weaknesses in functionalist theory. Conflict theory, which came into prominence in the late 1960's and the 1970's, is the most notable example. Moreover, functionalism itself has changed and adapted markedly since its initial formulation by Comte and Spencer.

Particularly since the 1960's, sociological theory has been moved forward significantly by the debate among those espousing various viewpoints; a central debate has been between functionalists and conflict theorists. The historical criticism of functionalism by theorists outside the functionalist tradition is that the theory is too one-sided: It assumes that simply because something exists it must have a function. This assumption has been criticized as being tautological. In the 1960's and 1970's, Marxist theorists also criticized functionalist views as being overly conservative and argued that they tended to be used to support the societal status quo. The criticism that functionalism is one-sided cannot truly be refuted, but it should be pointed out that other sociological perspectives can also be found to possess the same trait. Conflict theory, for example, tends to stress tension, struggle, and social strain to the exclusion of seeing any consensus or harmony in society; if society were as fractious as conflict theory sometimes suggests, it could be argued, peaceful and evolutionary change in society's institutions could hardly take place—as it certainly sometimes does.

It is perhaps most useful to view functionalist and conflict theories not as mutually exclusive but as pointing out each other's weaknesses. Both perspectives are useful in dealing with certain aspects of social structure and social change; they shed light on different dimensions of large-scale social patterns. For this reason, both traditions, as they evolve and adapt to answer criticism, are likely to continue in sociology.

Bibliography

Buckley, Walter. "Structural-Functional Analysis in Modern Society." In *Modern Sociological Theory in Continuity and Change*, edited by Howard Becker and Alvin Boskoff. New York: Dryden, 1957. Early attempt to assess the role of the functional perspective for the second half of the twentieth century.

Merton, Robert. *Social Theory and Social Structure*. Rev. ed. New York: Free Press, 1968. Introduces the key distinction of manifest and latent functions in a chapter of the same name.

Sorokin, Pitirim. *The Sociology of Revolution*. New York: Howard Fertig, 1967. Acknowledges the economic conflict thesis but goes beyond this to show how social institutions are interrelated and to argue that revolution is a necessary and recurring step in maintaining societal equilibrium.

Szacki, Jerzy. *History of Sociological Thought*. Westport, Conn.: Greenwood Press, 1979. Chapter titled "Sociological Functionalism and Its Critics" examines how other theorists see the functionalist perspective.

Timasheff, Nicholas. *Sociological Theory: Its Nature and Growth*. New York: Random House, 1967. Critique of early functionalists, including Comte, Spencer, and the social Darwinists, plus a chapter on modern functionalism.

Turner, Jonathan. *The Structure of Sociological Theory*. 6th ed. Belmont, Calif.: Wadsworth, 1998. Best and most detailed analysis of the difficult theories of Talcott Parsons and Robert Merton. Also assesses the functionalist aspect of other perspectives: neofunctionalism, general systems functionalism, ecological functionalism, and biological functionalism.

White, Harrison, and Cynthia White. *Canvases and Careers: Institutional Change in the French Painting World*. Chicago: University of Chicago Press, 1993. Examines the rise of Impressionism as a dominant art form during the nineteenth century. Though not specifically labeled as a functionalist analysis, their work clearly shows the interconnection of social institutions and how the shift from one school (the Royal Academy) was beneficial for the artists and art patrons.

John Markert

Cross-References

Conflict Theory; Deviance: Functions and Dysfunctions; Education: Functionalist Perspectives; Family: Functionalist Versus Conflict Theory Views; History of Sociology; Religion: Functionalist Analyses; Social Stratification: Functionalist Perspectives; Sociology Defined.

GENDER INEQUALITY
Analysis and Overview

Type of sociology: Sex and gender

Fields of study: Basic concepts of social stratification; Theoretical perspectives on stratification

Gender inequality refers to the distribution of resources within society by gender. This concept describes the relative advantages and disadvantages of men and women in society.

Principal terms

GENDER: socially determined expectations for what it means to be male and female

GENDER ROLES: the socially determined sets of rights and obligations that are associated with being male and female

POWER: ability to affect the behavior of others, with or without their willingness to comply

SEX: biologically determined differences between men and women

STRATIFICATION: system in which individuals or groups are ranked according to their differential access to valued resources in society

Overview

Gender inequality refers to the process by which resources are allocated differentially in society to men and women. Gender is one element in a larger stratification system in which individuals and groups are ranked according to their access to valued resources in society. Stratification occurs in many forms and can be based on social class, race/ethnicity, or age as well as on gender.

A major goal of social scientists has been to explain the nature of inequality between men and women. The types of questions asked and the answers proposed depend on the theoretical perspective that is used. Two major perspectives used to address this issue are the functionalist and conflict perspectives.

One of the major assumptions of functionalism is that society operates much like an organism in that it is composed of a system of interrelated parts, each of which operates in a unique way to contribute to the maintenance of the whole. Another assumption is that the ideal social system is one in which the parts function together to create a state of harmony and balance. An analysis using a functionalist perspective examines the various elements of society and the way in which each part fits into the working of the whole.

The functionalist perspective as it is used to understand gender roles comes from the work of sociologists Talcott Parsons and Robert F. Bales in *Family, Socialization and Interaction Process* (1955). Parsons and Bales wrote that men's and women's roles are complementary; both roles are necessary for the survival of society and the family. They drew upon their work on groups, in which they found that in all small groups two functional leaders emerge: instrumental (goal-oriented) and expressive (integrative). Because of women's biological role in bearing children, it is they who specialize in nurturing and in providing for the emotional well-being of the family. Men, however, provide for their families' survival by serving as breadwinners and by representing their families to the outside world. According to the functionalist perspective, this specialization of tasks is adaptive not only for the family and society but also for men and women themselves.

The functionalist perspective has been criticized for not properly considering that the division of labor by gender leads to a disadvantage for women. Women become isolated in the home and lack access to valued societal resources that would give them power in the broader society and in family life, creating an inherent inequality of opportunity not addressed by functionalists.

Conflict theorists believe that conflict is an inevitable part of social life; they do not portray society as a harmonious system of interrelated parts. Society is composed of individuals and groups that have competing interests and varying amounts of power to promote those interests. The gender role system is one in which men benefit at the expense of women rather than a system of interdependence. A key question for conflict theorists, then, is how and why men maintain that advantage.

One of the earliest conflict theorists to address problems of inequality between men and women was the British social thinker Friedrich Engels. In his book *The Origin of the Family, Private Property, and the State* (1884), Engels drew upon the anthropological knowledge of his time to propose that monogamy came into existence with the advent of private property and that its motivation was to control that property. A primary concern for men was to ensure that property went to their own children by controlling women's reproductive capacity and their sexual activity. The origins of inequality between men and women are related to the emergence of private property.

Women's disadvantage is not confined exclusively to capitalist systems but exists in all types of economies. According to sociologist Rae Lesser Blumberg, it is necessary to examine the role of women in economic production to understand the relative advantages of men and women. If women's labor is strategically indispensable to society, if the kinship system allows women to control property, and if the goods are produced communally for the group rather than for the individual, women have more power in society. This power is expressed in the ability of women to control their own lives, including having control of reproduction and marriage and having power in the community.

According to sociologists Randall Collins and Scott Coltrane, in their book *Sociology of Marriage and the Family: Gender, Love, and Property* (1991), the key to explaining relative power between men and women is the degree to which men and women create their own organizations. Men's superior physical size and strength can be translated into political power in society, which allows them to play a primary role in protecting the community from outside threats. The greater the threat, the more likely men are to create all-male warrior groups that control the weapons in society and maintain political influence over women. In a society in which men also control the inheritance of property and women do not create their own all-female groups, there is little female power. Men's military power affects the type of work that men do and allows them greater control in family life, such as their involvement in marriage politics. The relative power of men and women in society can be predicted by the level of political power commanded by men in society.

Applications

Gender inequality exists in modern American society in several areas, especially in the economy. Overall, women earn lower wages than do men. For example, according to the U.S. Department of Labor, the median weekly wage in 1991 for families maintained by a sole male earner was $404, whereas it was $306 in families in which a female was the sole earner. The median yearly income for women in 1990 was $10,494; the median income for men was $21,147.

There are several reasons that women earn lower wages. Women are segregated in occupations that have lower wages. For example, within the medical field, men are more likely to be physicians and women registered nurses. In 1991, there were 198,000 male physicians and 72,000 female physicians, and 78,000 male nurses and 1,092,000 female nurses. Physicians earn higher wages: 1991 median weekly wages were $994 for physicians and $634 for nurses.

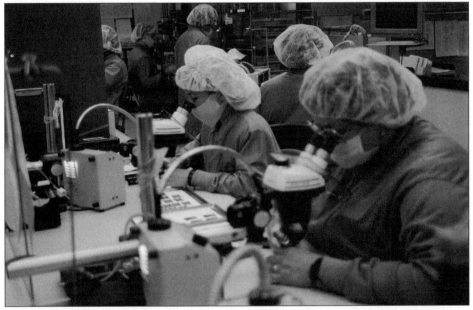

Studies have found that jobs women usually have are lower-paying and of lower status than the jobs men usually have. *(PhotoDisc)*

Women are paid lower wages within occupational categories. For physicians in 1991, the median weekly wages were $1,155 for men and $623 for women, and the median weekly wages for nurses were $703 for men and $630 for women. This discrepancy is partly explained by the fact that women often enter less-prestigious specialties. Women physicians are more likely to specialize in pediatrics and public health than are male physicians, who are more likely to be surgeons. Sociologist Christine Williams, in her book *Gender Differ-*

ences and Work (1989), showed that men who become nurses are less likely to specialize in hands-on care and more likely to move directly into more highly paid administrative positions.

Women also experience a disadvantage in work because of their primary responsibility for the well-being of the family. It is women who usually take time from work to take care of children or elderly relatives. According to the U.S. Department of Labor, married women with a spouse present were more than four times more likely to miss work time for reasons other than illness in 1991 than were married men with a spouse. Women also take time for pregnancy and maternity leave.

Women, at least until recent years, were less likely to have completed higher education. Even though women were more likely to receive college degrees than men in 1990, they were more likely to have taken degrees at lower levels. Doctorates and professional degrees were more likely to be awarded to men. Women also major in fields that pay less well. In 1990, only 8.5 percent of all mathematics degrees were awarded to women, while 72.7 percent of all education degrees were awarded to women. It should be noted that women have made significant gains in higher education. In 1950, 75.7 percent of all college degrees were awarded to men; in 1990, 47.3 percent of all college degrees were awarded to men.

One significant trend that reflects women's economic disadvantage is the feminization of poverty. This refers to one of the fastest growing segments of the poor population: female-headed households. This trend has an especially serious impact on children. In 1991, 57.5 percent of children of age six who lived in mother-only families lived below the poverty level, whereas only 39.5 percent of six-year-old children in married-couple families lived in poverty. The feminization of poverty reflects two separate trends. First, there has been an increase in the percentage of women who are having children outside of marriage. Second, there has been an increase in the divorce rate, along with a continuing trend of mothers maintaining primary custody of the children. Women are raising children without the benefit of a husband's income, and many women do not make enough to support a family on their own. The median income in 1991 of female-head-of-household families was $16,692, compared to a median income of $40,995 in married-couple families.

Economic disadvantages are especially severe for minority women. Minority women have even lower wages than do other women and are more likely to be in low-skill jobs and to be single parents. In 1991, African American families maintained by women had a median weekly wage of $339, compared to a median weekly wage of $401 in families maintained by African American men. The same pattern holds for Hispanic families. The median weekly wage for families maintained by men in 1991 was $462; for those maintained by women it was $343. The median yearly income in 1991 was $11,414 for African American female-headed households and $12,132 for Hispanic female-headed households. This is compared to a median income of $19,547 for white female-headed households. African American and Hispanic women are more likely to have low-birth-weight children and have higher infant mortality rates; they are less likely to receive prenatal care.

The gender system also has disadvantages for many men. For example, men do not live as long as women. Life expectancy at birth in 1990 was 71.8 years for males and 78.8 years for females. Men are more likely to die from risk-taking behavior. For example, the rates of alcohol-induced and drug-induced death are higher for men than they are for women. According to the Centers for Disease Control, in 1990, the rate of drug-induced death was 11.4 percent for men and 3.4 percent for women. The death rates for accidents and suicide are also higher for men than for women. This reflects the fact that in Western culture men are expected to take more risks and be more daring in their behavior, which has a serious effect on health.

Context

The conflict and functionalist perspectives are only two of several sociological approaches that have been used to examine the nature of gender inequality. Functionalism was popular in sociology in the 1950's and the 1960's but has since lost favor and is not as widely used in studying gender inequality as are other approaches. Sociologist Miriam Johnson contends that sociologists have many misconceptions about functionalism and that it can be useful for the study of gender inequality, especially with the addition of the element of conflict in social relations.

Most perspectives on gender inequality fall into the broad category of feminist theory. Feminist theory was first introduced in the 1970's, and in many ways it parallels the women's movement. Feminist theory refers to a general class of theories that are concerned with explaining the relative position of women in society. According to sociologist Janet Saltzman Chafetz in *Feminist Sociology: An Overview of Contemporary Theories* (1988), a feminist theory not only deals with women's issues but also deals with these issues in such a way that the findings have the potential to bring about change in societal gender roles. Chafetz states that a feminist theory has the following characteristics: Gender is the central concern, gender relations are considered to be problematic, and implied in the theory is the notion that gender relations in society can be changed. She also states that feminist theories often focus on the following issues: the causes of inequality, the manner in which gender systems are reproduced, the consequences of gender roles, and the ways in which gender systems are changed.

As is the case with most other sociological theories, feminist theories often focus on one of two basic levels of analysis. A theory may relate to the micro level of social life, which involves the one-on-one interactions that occur between men and women and the way in which gender is reproduced in those interactions. For example, a micro-level theory may examine the way in which verbal and nonverbal communication between men and women mirrors the broader structure of gender inequality in a society.

A macro-level approach examines gender roles at a larger societal level. One example of a macro-level feminist theory is one developed by sociologist Janet Saltzman Chafetz in her book *Gender Equity: An Integrated Theory of Stability and Change* (1990). In this book, Chafetz demonstrates the way in which societal-level variables such as major technological change create economic change, which increases the resources available to women. In combination with other societal conditions, such as the level of political conflict, sex ratio characteristics, and numbers in the working age population, such change can enable women to gain more power in society. Rather than focusing on individual-level variables, in this macro-level approach, the focus is on the characteristics of an entire society.

Bibliography

Chafetz, Janet Saltzman. *Feminist Sociology: An Overview of Contemporary Theories.* Itasca, Ill.: F. E. Peacock, 1988. Contains brief summary of major feminist theories, organized by the type of question addressed. An excellent reference when a brief overview of the entire spectrum of feminist theories is needed.

_____. *Gender Equity: An Integrated Theory of Stability and Change.* Newbury Park, Calif.: Sage Publications, 1990. Proposes a theoretical framework to explain the way in which gender inequality is maintained and reproduced and the levels of change in gender equality.

Collins, Randall, and Scott Coltrane. *Sociology of Marriage and the Family: Gender, Love, and Property.* 4th ed. Chicago: Nelson-Hall, 1995. College textbook rich in theoretical applications, especially for gender. Includes Collins's political theory of gender inequality.

Engels, Friedrich. *The Origin of the Family, Private Property, and the State.* New York: Viking Penguin, 1985. Includes Engels's study of gender inequality and an introduction by anthropologist Eleanor Burke Leacock. The anthropological findings upon which Engels based his theory have changed, but his work is still relevant to the study of gender.

England, Paula, ed. *Theory on Gender, Feminism on Theory.* New York: Aldine de Gruyter, 1993. Contains essays applying mainstream sociological theory to the understanding of gender. Includes Miriam Johnson's essay "Functionalism and Feminism: Is Estrangement Necessary?" Also includes essays applying Marxism, rational-choice theory, and macrostructural perspectives to the understanding of gender.

Ore, Tracy E., ed. *The Social Construction of Difference and Inequality: Race, Class, Gender, and Sexuality.* Mountain View, Calif.: Mayfield, 2000.

Parsons, Talcott, and Robert F. Bales. *Family, Socialization, and Interaction Process.* Glencoe, Ill.: Free Press, 1955. Applies the perspective of functionalism to the understanding of gender and family roles. This influential book is useful for understanding the basic ideas of functionalist theory.

Williams, Christine L. *Gender Differences at Work: Women and Men in Nontraditional Occupations.* Berkeley: University of California Press, 1989. Reports of findings from a study of individuals in nontraditional occupations: men in nursing and women in the Marines. Focuses on how traditional gender roles are reproduced even in nontraditional settings.

Charlotte Chorn Dunham

Cross-References

Gender Inequality: Biological Determinist Views; Role Conflict and Role Strain; Social Stratification: Analysis and Overview; Sociobiology and the Nature-Nurture Debate; Statuses and Roles.

GENDER INEQUALITY
Biological Determinist Views

Type of sociology: Sex and gender
Fields of study: Basic concepts of social stratification; Theoretical perspectives on stratification

Men and women undeniably have certain physical differences. It is a subject of debate whether these biological differences also cause behavioral differences and whether biology, therefore, is one of the causes of sex roles and gender-related social stratification. Biological determinism holds that biology does affect these things, but most sociologists argue against the idea.

Principal terms

BIOLOGICAL DETERMINISM: belief that most human behavior is a result of genetic "programming" rather than learning

ENVIRONMENTAL DETERMINISM: the belief that most human behavior is shaped by learning and other postnatal, environmental influences rather than by hormones and genetics

GENDER: sometimes used as a synonym for the word "sex" in referring to male and female, but usually encompassing social and psychological as well as biological attributes

MISOGYNY: a belief that sex differences are based in biology and are therefore natural and also that women are lesser persons than men

SEX ROLES: social expectations and norms that are different for males than for females

SEX TYPING: differential treatment of individuals based on stereotypes and beliefs about sex and gender differences

SEXISM: discriminatory attitudes or behavior exhibited toward an individual or group based upon stereotypes about sex and gender

SOCIOBIOLOGY: study of the biological and evolutionary underpinnings of social behavior; controversial because its biological determinist assumptions sometimes have political implications, especially regarding gender relations

Overview

Sociologists and other scientists who study human behavior are ultimately engaged in an effort to understand human nature and the nature of human interactions. Biological determinists believe that "human nature" is based in human biology (genetics, evolution, hormones, and physiology) and that there are therefore some kinds of behaviors that are more "natural" than others. Environmental determinists, on the other hand, believe that the complexity and flexibility of the human mind and culture allow people to engage in a diversity of behaviors that have no relationship to biology. They argue that patterns of human behaviors and interactions must be explained by patterns in the environment, especially the human environment (including learning, socialization, discrimination, and oppression). Although almost everyone agrees that both biology and culture are important determinants of human behavior, when discussing particular behaviors, most people tend to agree with one side or the other in what has come to be called the "nature/nurture debate."

Explanation of the widespread existence of gender-related social roles is one of the most controversial issues in this debate. Biological determinists are convinced that the ubiquity of such roles across cultures strongly indicates that there must be a biological basis for them. After all, they would say, it seems to make sense that since women, but not men, can bear and nurse children, women must "naturally" be better than men at child rearing, and that can explain why there are no societies in which child care is primarily the task of men. Using this logic, it is an easy next step to say that women are therefore probably more nurturant than men because of their biology rather than because they are taught to be, and that women are predominant in service roles and careers because they seek out such roles, not because they are relegated to them by prejudice and discrimination. Environmental determinists would counter that most gender differences are a result of the internalization of roles that people are taught through the process of sex typing—the differential treatment of boys and girls based on gender stereotypes—and that to continue teaching these gender roles is a form of sexism.

Generally speaking, biological determinists attempt to explain existing conditions rather than to make predictions or recommendations. The kinds of social conditions claimed to have biological underpinnings are many, including sex differences in aptitudes, interests, and performance; preferences for activities, lifestyles, and career; rates and types of criminal victimization and criminal activity; attitudes and behaviors related to sex, politics, and other social interactions; nurturance, empathy, and other emotions; cooperation, competition, and decision-making styles; and life expectancy and rates and types of mental and physical illness. In many cases, the arguments and data have been extrapolated from studies of nonhuman primates; in other cases, data come from cross-cultural comparisons.

Traditionally, most of the literature in this area attempted to provide proximate explanations for gender differences, that is, explanations about how social and psychological gender differences come about as a result of physical differences (such as hormone levels, body build, and brain chemistry). More recently, however, much of the literature has focused on ultimate explanations—that is, explanations about why sociological, psychological, and even physical gender differences exist in the first place. This newer approach is based on the successes of a field called "sociobiology" in explaining and predicting many attributes of the social organizations and interactions of nonhuman animals. Sociobiologists view every behavior as the result of an evolutionary process which selects only those behaviors that help the individual or species to survive and reproduce. According to this perspective, all behaviors have some adaptive function, and if some behaviors are differentially expressed by the two sexes, then there must be some adaptive, biologically functional reason for that difference. Thus, sociobiologists believe that gender differences exist because evolution designed humans that way.

This is the first time that biological determinists have had the benefit of a theory upon which to draw, and sociobiologists, unlike most biological determinists of the past, are beginning to make predictions about gender differences rather than only trying to explain already known conditions. If tests of these predictions prove to be correct, then biological determinism will gain a bigger following among sociologists. Until that happens, however, most sociologists will continue to believe sociobiology cannot be applied to humans to the extent that it can to nonhuman animals because of the role, neglected by sociobiologists, of cultural influences on behavior. In addition, a number of social scientists reject the sociobiological approach for political reasons.

Applications

The behavioral sex difference that has been most convincingly argued to be at least partly biologically determined is aggressiveness. The strength of this argument is based on the fact that research using many different approaches all converges on the same answer. Cross-cultural studies show that most crime, especially violent crime, is performed by males; most wars, as well as most personal (physical) battles, are fought by males; and boys are much more physically active and physically aggressive than girls across all ages. Studies of nonhuman primates show the same thing, leading scientists to believe that such differences are based in biology rather than in culture. Controlled experiments that manipulate prenatal and postnatal hormones in other animals consistently show that those which experience unusually high levels of masculinizing hormones while in the womb or during other critical periods of development show greater levels of aggressive behavior than normal. Likewise, although researchers cannot randomly assign children to different levels of hormones, data from so-called "experiments of nature" also suggest that it is biology, not rearing, that makes males more aggressive than females.

Unlike studies of aggression, which give fairly certain and consistent results, other studies of sex and gender differences in society are hard to interpret, because the variables involved preclude experimental manipulation and the behaviors and patterns of interest simply do not occur in nonhuman animals. An example of a biological determinist position that is more controversial is the claim that social stratification as it relates to gender is based on the fact that men and women choose different careers and lifestyles rather than on the concept that women are being discriminated against. In the United States, there are many stereotypes about the kinds of jobs that are acceptable for women versus men; women are more likely to be found in jobs that are considered service positions, jobs assisting someone else in a higher position, jobs related to child care or housework, and careers in the arts, while men are more often found engaging in entrepreneurial ventures, in positions associated with power and decision making, in jobs relating to technology or machinery, and in careers in science and math. On the average, the jobs women are most likely to have are lower-paying and of lower status than the jobs men are most likely to have. The reasons behind this stratification are complicated.

Some biological determinists have argued that women are more skilled than men at jobs that involve nurturing (such as child care, elementary school teaching, and nursing) or fine motor skills (such as sewing and typing), and that this superiority explains their overabundance in certain jobs; men, on the other hand, are presumably more skilled at mathematics and jobs involving physical labor, and that is why they are overrepresented in those kinds of jobs. One of the arguments against this interpretation, however, is that it would predict that women would be more common than men in jobs such as surgeon and mechanic, whereas clearly they are not. The counterargument points out that women are selectively more common in low-status, low-paying jobs, no matter what kinds of skills are involved. Cross-cultural studies tend to support this latter view in that in cultures that put different values on jobs than is the case in the United States, women still tend to be found in the lower-status jobs and men in the higher-status jobs; where physicians are high in status, for example, they tend to be men, and where physicians are low in status, they tend to be women. This pattern would suggest that women are being denied access to higher-status jobs solely because of discrimination.

This debate does not end there. Recent studies suggest that as women do break into traditionally male-dominated jobs in American society, those jobs start to lose their high status. The discrimination model would interpret this pattern by concluding either that because women started dominating a certain job, discrimination and the change in the job's status followed, or that when a job starts to decline in status, more women are allowed in. An alternative interpretation, however, consistent with biological determinism, is that women are by nature more cooperative and less competitive than men and that they therefore seek jobs that are less competitive. Thus, as a job started to lose status, it would become less competitive, less attractive to men, and more attractive to women; or, as women joined the ranks of men in a high-status job, the job would become less competitive, men would start to leave, and more women would start to apply. Most sociologists would tend to side with the environmental (discrimination) interpretation, but it could be argued that the two interpretations are equally logical.

Context

The idea that gender differences are based in biology is perhaps as old as humanity itself; it can be found expressed in religion, art, philosophy, and a variety of other areas. Most sociologists, however, prefer to distance themselves from this perspective. One reason for this is that many sociologists believe that biological determinism fosters misogyny; they argue that a commitment to the biological approach springs more from a political desire to "keep women in their place" than from a desire to seek scientific truth.

Misogyny is the belief that women are not only different from men but also somehow lesser than men in a social, spiritual, or political sense. Misogynistic attitudes can lead to discrimination, oppression, and male dominance. For some people, the belief that gender roles are caused by biology implies that no one should attempt to go against those roles or to improve the status of women. This illogical inference easily leads to consequences such as discrimination against women who choose not to have children or follow socially prescribed sex roles, lack of respect toward women in power, and violence toward women when they do not do what men want and expect of them. Most biological determinists argue that they are not condoning discrimination or misogyny; they are seeking only an explanation of current conditions, not a rationale or an ethic to determine what behavior is socially and ethically desirable.

Another argument made against the biological determinist position is based on the assumption that "biology is destiny"—the idea that, since biological sex differences cannot be changed, it is pessimistic to look for biological explanations of gender differences when there might be environmental explanations for those differences. The logic behind this criticism is based on two assumptions: that it is desirable to change some existing gender-based social stratification, and that environmentally caused phenomena are easier to change than those that are biologically caused. The latter assumption, however, is not universally correct; some biologically caused phenomena are easy to change, while some learned or encultured behaviors are quite difficult to modify. Thus, if the goal is to change gender roles and expectations, it is not necessarily more pessimistic to look for biological explanations and solutions than environmental or cultural ones.

A third argument against biological determinism is based on the fear that individuals in power will try to impose their own values on society through biological intervention such as involuntary drug treatment, psychosurgery, selective sterilization and breeding, or even infanticide. Fears of this type are not unfounded, given the many horrible examples of the past hundred years alone. On the other hand, totalitarian leaders who believe in environmental determinism give humankind just as much to fear, as they have implemented equally extreme environmental programs and sanctions, such as torture, brainwashing, and imprisonment. Neither biological determinism nor environmental determinism is, in and of itself, a danger; like any idea, each can be used as a tool or as a weapon.

Bibliography

Archer, John, and Barbara Lloyd. *Sex and Gender*. Rev. ed. New York: Cambridge University Press, 1985. Excellent, balanced summary of gender differences using both the biological and environmental approaches. The book is research oriented but is nevertheless highly readable. Excellent introduction. Extensive bibliography, but not separated by chapters.

Birke, Lynda. *Women, Feminism, and Biology*. New York: Methuen, 1986. Excellent example of a political (feminist) critique of biological determinism; it is very well-written, although it is activist, one-sided, and even angry.

Christen, Yves. *Sex Differences: Modern Biology and the Unisex Fallacy*, translated by Nicholas Davidson. New Brunswick, N.J.: Transaction, 1991. Easy-to-read presentation of the biological approach has twelve chapters, each subdivided into several brief essays summarizing issues related to gender differences. Occasionally a bit one-sided. Only 117 pages, it includes a bibliography for those seeking more of the original research. Originally published in French in 1987.

Durden-Smith, Jo, and Diane deSimone. *Sex and the Brain*. New York: Arbor House, 1983. Study of biological determinism written by women. Presents totally nontechnical synopsis of the research cited by Archer and Lloyd, Christen, and Mitchell, as well as a heavy dose of sociobiology.

Goldberg, Steven. *The Inevitability of Patriarchy*. New York: William Morrow, 1973. This book was extremely controversial when it was written, and although some of its "facts" are now out of date, it remains one of the best examples of a pure biological determinist approach to gender differences.

Goldberg, Steven, and Cynthia Fuchs Epstein. "Is Patriarchy Universal and Genetically Determined?" In *Taking Sides: Clashing Views on Controversial Social Issues*, edited by Kurt Finsterbusch and George McKenna. 6th ed. Guilford, Conn.: Dushkin, 1990. Reprints both sides of a debate published in *Society* magazine in October, 1986. Goldberg argues that the near ubiquity of patriarchy and male dominance makes them, by definition, "natural"; Epstein argues that patriarchy is not inevitable. Both present an excellent case.

Mitchell, Gary. *Human Sex Differences: A Primatologist's Perspective*. New York: Van Nostrand Reinhold, 1981. Twenty-six short chapters, each covering some issue related to sex differences from a primatological viewpoint. Each chapter discusses nonhuman primates and then humans; topics for which there is no similar behavior in nonhumans do not get addressed.

Montagu, Ashley. *The Natural Superiority of Women*. 5th ed. Walnut Creek, Calif.: Alta Mira Press, 1999. Montagu, an anthropologist, wrote this book (first published in 1952) as a counterargument to the prevailing notion of the times that men are the superior sex. Montagu mixes biological and sociocultural arguments in making his case.

Rhode, Deborah L., ed. *Theoretical Perspectives on Sexual Difference*. New Haven, Conn.: Yale University Press, 1990. Written at a more advanced level than the other works cited here, this edited text is more balanced than most books that attack biological determinism in that it includes several different types of arguments. Four chapters specifically address sociobiology.

Ruse, Michael. *Is Science Sexist?* Boston: Reidel, 1981. This book takes its title from one of its ten essays. The author, a philosopher, has written many books on science, especially sociobiology, and has basically concluded that this approach is scientifically legitimate and not fundamentally sexist.

Linda Mealey

Cross-References

Gender Inequality: Analysis and Overview; Role Conflict and Role Strain; Sociobiology and the Nature-Nurture Debate; Statuses and Roles.

HISTORY OF SOCIOLOGY

Type of sociology: Origins and definitions of sociology
Field of study: Basic concepts

Sociology took form as an academic discipline and applied science in the late nineteenth century with the rise of the social and behavioral sciences. Ideas and theories about societal institutions, social structures, and the relation of persons to groups dates to antiquity. The development of American sociology reflects the influence of French, German, British, and American thinkers who evolved from nineteenth century systematizers to twentieth century specialists.

Principal terms

CRITICAL THEORY: school of thought developed in Frankfurt, Germany, during the 1920's that employed the early humanistic ideas of Karl Marx to criticize positivism and scientific Marxism

FUNCTIONALISM: approach that explains social institutions by the functions they provide or the consequences that they yield

PHENOMENOLOGY: approach that emphasizes the socially constructed nature of knowledge, especially knowledge of everyday life

POSITIVISM: view that sociology should model itself in method and theory after the physical sciences and that all knowledge can be hierarchically arranged

QUANTITATIVE METHODS: techniques that attempt to measure in an objective fashion aspects of social structure, social groups, and social opinions; these methods often involve surveys

SOCIOBIOLOGY: influential perspective since the 1970's derived from evolutionary biology and seeking to understand social phenomena through biological, especially genetic, explanations

STRUCTURALISM: orientation that places an emphasis on the relations among social elements rather than on the elements themselves

SYMBOLIC INTERACTIONISM: set of ideas developed at the University of Chicago during the 1920's that emphasized the importance of meaning, language, and learning to take the role of the other in the development of the self

Overview

Sociology is one of the social sciences, along with anthropology, psychology, political science, and economics. It studies the origin and development of human society by examining the social organization and structure of society, its principal institutions (the family, school, religion, politics and government, health care, and economy), collective behavior, and interactions (relations between individuals and between the individual and society). Sociology became a discipline in the late nineteenth century. Previously, ideas and theories about society had been discussed widely in philosophical, political, and theological contexts.

In the nineteenth century, books appeared that offered a systematic approach to the study of society. The emphasis was on the logical and cohesive arrangement of known facts about society combined with a particular philosophical or theoretical orientation. Among the principal thinkers in this "systematics" period of the history of sociology was Auguste Comte (1798-1857), a French theorist sometimes described as the "father of sociology." He coined the term, and he argued for a hierarchical arrangement of the sciences with sociology at the top (a form of positivism). Also influential during this period was Herbert Spencer (1820-1903), a British systematist who authored a three-volume work entitled *Principles of Sociology* (1876, 1882, 1896) in which he reasoned that all societies develop in a similar manner following principles of evolutionary theory.

In addition to the systematically qualitative sociology of the nineteenth century, a quantitative tradition developed. Social statistics on suicides, prostitution, unemployment, and other topics came to be treated as social facts—facts to be explained by societal factors rather than as merely the aggregate of individual behavior. Later, survey research methods for discerning opinions and attitudes were developed, as were techniques to assure the representativeness of the survey sample and to analyze relationships among opinions and demographic data (techniques of statistical correlation). In the latter part of the twentieth century, quantitative methods assumed a major role in sociological research.

Another quality of nineteenth century American sociology was the influence of psychological analysis, resulting in the discipline of social psychology. As developed from the social rather than the psychological end, social psychology has considered the influence of the group on the individual and on those circumstances in which behavior may be unique to social context. The "interactionists" among the social psychologists have emphasized the "meaning" that the situation has to the individual as the determiner of behavior.

By 1905 the American Sociological Society (later the American Sociological Association) was formed. Earlier societies had been formed in France in 1894 and in England in 1903. Professorships, journals, departments, and doctoral programs devoted to the field began to proliferate, although for many years sociology professors often shared a department with anthropologists or scholars in some other social science. The sociological opinions of Comte and Spencer were best represented in the United States by Lester F. Ward (1841-1913), who is regarded as the earliest American systematic sociologist. He distinguished between "pure" and "applied" sociology and thought that social betterment could be brought about by an active scientific process.

Several individuals occupy special positions in the development of sociology. Among them is Émile Durkheim (1858-1917), a nineteenth century French sociologist who helped establish sociology as an independent discipline and science. He is best remembered for his works *De la Division du travail social* (1893; *The Division of Labor in Society*, 1933) and *Le Suicide: Étude de sociologie* (1897; *Suicide: A Study in Sociology*, 1951). In the latter, Durkheim argued, on the basis of suicide statistics from many different countries, that what appeared as individual decision making (taking one's own life) could be better understood in terms of the qualities of the society and times in which one lived. "Social facts" should be explained by social factors, Durkheim believed. Why one particular person takes his or her own life might be explained by psychology, but the overall rate of suicide could not be. Durkheim also wrote other influential works on sociological methods and on the sociology of religion.

Max Weber (1864-1920) was an influential German sociologist who held professorships at various universities. He was plagued by nervous illness, and he died prematurely of pneumonia. His most widely read work is *Die Protestantische Ethik und der Geist des Kapitalismus* (1904; *The Protestant Ethic and the Spirit of Capitalism*, 1930), in which he examined the forces that shaped modern capitalism, particularly the hierarchical institutional and bureaucratic structures. As the title suggests, he argued for the central role of Protestantism, which he believed provided the model for viewing work as a "calling," with its associated aspects of duty and obedience. Hard work, he said, was viewed as rewarded by wealth. In Weber's view, Protestantism "invented" achievement motivation. Weber also made contributions to sociological methodology.

The ideas of Karl Marx (1818-1883) were also influential in sociology. Marx argued for a social basis of consciousness and placed emphasis on social class as a relevant variable in understanding a person's behavior, motivation, and ideology. Marxism rationalized the focus on the social in understanding the behavior of the individual and placed emphasis on the particular historical circumstances. Marx also emphasized the social and political nature of knowledge, a theme that was developed by later twentieth century sociologists. His best works, with those of Durkheim and Weber, are regarded as among the great classics in sociology's history.

Another important sociologist of the nineteenth century was William Graham Sumner (1840-1910), who offered the first American course in sociology at Yale University in 1876 and became known for his work *Folkways* (1907), which treated customs and mores (socially accepted patterns of behavior) from a social Darwinist perspective. He coined the term "ethnocentrism" to describe the preference people have for the viewpoint and folkways of their own group. Albion Woodbury Small (1854-1926) promoted the development of sociology at the University of Chicago, where the first doctoral program was begun in 1893, and in 1895 he founded the first journal in the United States devoted exclusively to sociology, the *American Journal of Sociology*. Charles A. Ellwood (1873-1946) is credited as the founder of sociological social psychology, although Edward A. Ross (1866-1951) was the first sociologist to author a book entitled *Social Psychology* (1908). Ross wrote widely on other sociological topics and was for many years a professor at the University of Wisconsin.

During the 1920's and 1930's, sociology expanded through increased specialization and controversy over method. Some sociologists chose essentially historical methods, others comparative techniques (in which social organization in different cultures might be contrasted), and many others a case-study method focusing on a particular social organization (ranging from a small group, such as a street gang, to an entire small town or city). Still others preferred quantitative methods in which systematic surveys would sample people's beliefs and behaviors. A small number of sociologists emphasized the subjective and meaningful nature of human behavior and tried to employ phenomenological methods.

In Germany the Frankfurt school developed around a group of philosophers and social theorists associated with the Frankfurt Institute for Social Research. Beginning in the late 1920's, they developed systematic criticisms of positivistic theories. The views of the Frankfurt school are termed "critical theory" and reflected a neo-Marxist approach combined with German traditions of reason as contained in the philosophy of Georg Wilhelm Friedrich Hegel. Among the important members were Theodor Adorno, Max Horkheimer, and Herbert Marcuse.

Georg Simmel (1858-1918) was a German philosopher who developed the "formal" school of sociology. He believed that the processes which sociologists study, such as conflict, competition, and the formation of alliances, could be examined independently of the particular contexts in which they occurred (such as schools, churches, and political parties).

The views of George Herbert Mead (1863-1931) were also influential during this period. He taught at the University of Chicago as a philosopher and developed the social behaviorist perspective, which argued that the self is a product of interaction with others. His contributions were mainly to the field of social psychology and the social nature of language, gesture, and mind.

Two leading sociologists who exerted a strong influence following World War II were Talcott Parsons and C. Wright Mills. Parsons was for many years associated with Harvard University and the prewar development of sociology at Harvard, where he chaired the doctoral dissertations of many of the subsequent leaders in the field. Several phases of Parsons's career may be distinguished, but his development of "social systems theory," in which the relationship between the individual and group is understood in terms of the role the person occupies and the social expectations associated with the role, has been enormously influential, especially in social psychology. Mills is best known for his works (such as *The Power Elite*) which describe the ways in which ruling classes exert their influence. His writings were influential not only in academic sociology but also as revolutionary texts for the social unrest in the United States in the 1960's. In the latter decades of the twentieth century, sociology saw an increasing development of subspecialties, an emphasis on quantitative technique, and the influence of European theorists such as Claude Lévi-Strauss, Jürgen Habermas, and Michel Foucault.

Applications

Applications of sociological methods and knowledge have developed over time. The effort to explain suicide is a useful example, for it was one of the earliest undertakings by Durkheim. In his classic 1897 work *Suicide* he used statistics from various countries in an attempt to understand what social facts might account for differences in their suicide rates. While he identified social conditions that made a difference (for example, being unmarried and a Protestant), he noted that such social statistics could not explain the choice of suicide by an individual. To understand the behavior of a particular person, he recommended examining the "personal stamp" evident in the actions associated with the suicide.

His view contrasts with those of the Chicago school of sociology, which, under the influence of Mead during the 1920's, sought a more psychological explanation of suicide rates. In addition to social statistics on suicide, an examination of case studies and personal histories was utilized. These could reveal the meaning of the act of suicide for the individual. An effort was made to understand the actions of particular persons, rather than only the gross differences in rates among countries or subpopulations.

Modern sociologists have criticized the early reliance on governmental statistics in the study of rates of suicide. Instead, they have gathered independent data and analyzed it with statistical techniques called multivariant analysis. Hundreds of possible influences on the decision to take one's own life can be examined, and the degree to which each individually and collectively predicts the choice of death can be precisely quantified. Such studies often involve extensive interviews with persons who knew the deceased, and they may include hundreds of cases of suicide. The mass of data studied, the numbers of persons involved in its collection, and the sophistication of the techniques used in its analysis would have been unimaginable in the late nineteenth century when sociologists first took up the topic.

Context

An extensive history of sociology would need to trace the development of exchange theory and interactionism and examine the perspectives of structuralism, functionalism, positivism, and Marxism. It would also look at the refinement of quantitative techniques, including modern techniques of surveying by telephone, demographic analysis, and increasingly sophisticated statistical techniques. Such a history would also include an examination of the broad nineteenth century ideas (many stemming from the works of Marx and Charles Darwin) that strongly influenced the origins of sociology and continue to affect the discipline. Although evolutionary explanations of social behavior existed before Darwin's watershed work *On the Origin of the Species* (1859), Darwinian evolutionary theory provided a foundation both for social Darwinism and for the field known as sociobiology that developed in the later twentieth century.

Modern sociology has developed a wide range of interests. Some sociologists have devoted their work primarily to theory building and analysis, whereas others have focused on the application of sociological methods in governmental agencies and private industry. The dramatic social changes and violent events that took place in the twentieth century have provided extensive social actions and behavior for sociologists to study. The mass of quantitative data now routinely gathered by modern governments at all levels has provided unending data for sociological examination. Mass culture is transmitted over worldwide communication systems, leading to collective behavior of a magnitude unknown during sociology's formative years. The development of complex social systems, such as the health care industry, and ever-changing technology assures that the methods and theories that sociology has developed over its history will continue to find individual and collective behavior that is in need of study and understanding.

Bibliography

Barnes, Harry Elmer. *An Introduction to the History of Sociology*. Abridged ed. Chicago: University of Chicago Press, 1966. Collection of essays tracing the development of sociology up to World War II. Each chapter focuses on an influential sociologist, most of them twentieth century scholars.

Bottomore, Tom, and Robert Nisbet, eds. *A History of Sociological Analysis*. New York: Basic Books, 1978. Large collection of essays on selected topics in the history of sociology. Emphasis is on themes (such as Marxism, structuralism, and functionalism) rather than personalities.

Manicas, Peter T. *A History of Philosophy of the Social Sciences*. Oxford, England: Basil Blackwell, 1987. Broad discussion of the theoretical and philosophical aspects of the social sciences as they have developed since the nineteenth century, with selected discussion of sociological concepts.

Martindale, Don. *Prominent Sociologists Since World War II*. Columbus, Ohio: Charles E. Merrill, 1975. Study of theorists influential after World War II. Max Weber, Talcott Parsons, C. Wright Mills, and Pitirim A. Sorokin are given extensive coverage.

Maus, Heinz. *A Short History of Sociology*. New York: Philosophical Library, 1962. Approaches sociology geographically by describing developments in North America, Europe, and Latin America, with additional chapters on Great Britain, Germany, Belgium, and Eastern Europe.

Ross, Dorothy. *The Origins of American Social Science*. Cambridge, England: Cambridge University Press, 1991. Places the history of sociology in the United States within the context of the other social sciences, such as anthropology and psychology, as they developed during the late nineteenth century.

Sahakian, William S. *History and Systems of Social Psychology*. 2d ed. Washington, D.C.: Hemisphere, 1982. Lengthy and detailed work that emphasizes the social psychological developments in sociology.

Swingewood, Alan. *A Short History of Sociological Thought*. 3d ed. New York: St. Martin's Press, 2000. A history of sociological ideas, with excellent coverage of Marxism, positivism, functionalism, and structuralism.

Terry J. Knapp

Cross-References

Conflict Theory; Education; Functionalism; Knowledge; Marxism; Protestant Ethic and Capitalism; Religion; Sociology Defined; Symbolic Interaction.

Horticultural Economic Systems

Type of sociology: Major social institutions
Field of study: The economy

Horticultural economic systems are based on cultivation without the use of plows. In preindustrial horticulture, human labor supplies all the energy that goes into cultivation. This imposes some limits; it has supported dense populations and states and still feeds hundreds of millions.

Principal terms

CHIEFDOM: a polity that lacks full-time politicians or bureaucrats; a few individuals, however, control political power and the flow of wealth

MATRIARCHY: a society ruled or otherwise under the control of women, as men rule a patriarchy

POPULATION PRESSURE: a population's demand for resource exploitation—not a simple function of population density, because resources and technology vary; the amount of population pressure that can be absorbed through technological advances is a controversial subject

SETTLEMENT PATTERN: arrangement of habitation

SOCIAL EVOLUTION: regular change from one form of society to another, following general laws or principles; often associated with progress and with progression through a sequence of stages

STATE: polity that includes strong, centralized rule, including a professional bureaucracy that administers it; associated with moderate to high degree of social stratification

SUSTAINABLE: capable of being continued indefinitely without degrading nonrenewable resources

Overview

Many authorities subsume horticulture under agriculture, but others reserve "agriculture" for systems in which draft animals or tractors pull plows and do other tasks. In preindustrial horticulture, the availability of labor limits the size of the operation. For that reason some authors write of horticultural "gardens" but agricultural "fields," although a horticultural landscape can consist of contiguous areas in grain or any crop.

There are relatively "extensive" forms of horticulture—that is, those in which inputs of labor, material, or capital are few—and more "intensive" forms, in which inputs are greater. Preindustrial horticulturists make few energy investments, since they do not exploit the energy of animals in cultivation. The object of intensification is to raise yields. Gains may be in the current season, such as those from drainage.

One of the most widespread forms of horticulture is used extensively: clearing forest or scrub, cropping, then abandoning the area to return to its original cover. Usually clearing is by the "slash and burn" method. Undergrowth and trees are cut and left to dry, then burned. Crops, usually a mixture, are planted through the ashes, after light tillage. The ashes are a source of nutrients and reduce soil acidity. Yields are generally good the first year, but they ordinarily decline the next year. That, and invading weeds, may prompt abandonment, often after one to three years; longer cropping delays the regrowth of woody vegetation unless some care is taken. Occasional variations include leaving the felled vegetation unburned, and *chitemene* cultivation of the Congo-Zambesi watershed in Africa, in which felled scrub is concentrated in small circles before being burned.

A planted tree crop is an occasional alternative to a forest fallow. This is an old technique used in Hokkaido, Japan, southern China, Burma, Malaysia, Papua New Guinea, several parts of West Africa, and Java. If cropping is lengthened or fallows shortened, grasses tend to replace woody growth in the fallows. "Permanent cultivation" results from the elimination of fallows. Grass fallow and permanent cultivation systems, unlike forest fallow systems, are either horticultural or agricultural. Whereas plows are very difficult to use in recently cleared forests, they readily break ground that has been in grass or under cultivation, as do hand tools. Heavy hoes are the tools of choice in Africa; spades in Europe. Wooden digging sticks are used in the Pacific islands, though spades have replaced them in most places.

ore frequent cropping makes horticulture more intensive, first because work goes into a given area of land in more years, and second because inputs usually increase. Grass, no matter how well tilled, grows back, requiring more frequent weeding, though ingenuity helps; for example, the Sudanese *hariq*, a burn of cut grass timed to catch emerging growth, suppresses regrowth for weeks. Harvesting removes plant nutrients, and few soils have reserves to support frequent cropping. Some techniques may improve the utilization of nutrients, such as digging in crop residues, but in the long run cultivators must import nutrients, enhance biological processes that "fix" atmospheric nitrogen (that is, put it into forms that plants can take up), or both.

One solution is to gather dead leaves, grass, and other vegetation from surrounding areas and work it into garden soils. The practice mines the surrounding soils of nutrients but may be sustainable if enough uncultivated land is at hand. Kitchen wastes, animal manures, and human feces are often recycled, usually onto "home gardens," permanently cultivated sites near habitations. Deliberate application of human feces is common in East and South Asia; it is rare in sub-Saharan Africa and scattered elsewhere. Legumes fix nitrogen and can thereby aid intensive horticulture.

"Wet" systems—that is, those in natural wetlands or irrigated areas—are often readily sustainable. Irrigation water brings in variable amounts of nutrients. Rice and taro, a tropical root crop, thrive in shallow, flooded fields; nitrogen-fixing microorganisms are often active in the water, contributing to sustained yields. One way to exploit lands that are permanently or seasonally flooded is to move soil from ditches onto planting surfaces. Such surfaces are known as "island beds" in the Pacific, where they are often low and are used for crops that tolerate waterlogged soils, and as "drained fields" in tropical America, where they are higher and used for diverse crops. The Mexican *chinampas*, or "floating gardens," are an example. Muck and vegetation from the ditches fertilize crops. Another usually sustainable system is "decrue cultivation," on fresh soil left behind by receding floodwaters. On the whole, the settlement patterns of horticulturalists are more like those of agriculturalists than unlike them. One exception is the frequent association of long fallow horticulture with "shifting cultivation," in which the settlement is regularly moved. In some societies it is moved with each clearance of new gardens.

One distinctive social feature of horticulture is a greater role of women in food production (as opposed to food processing) than in plow agriculture. Anthropologists M. Kay Martin and Barbara Voorhies found that women contribute more labor than men in 50 percent of horticultural societies but only 15 percent of agricultural societies. Men contribute the most in 17 percent and 81 percent, respectively. In the remainder the work is equally divided.

Applications

Study of the variety of horticultural systems that exist furnishes knowledge with which to dispel Eurocentric judgments of their "primitiveness." Europeans, when they embarked on colonial expansion, were mainly plow-using agriculturalists and had a developing love of mechanical solutions to practical problems. In the slash-and-burn and other fallow systems of their colonies they saw few implements, and they tended to overlook the environmental knowledge necessary for success. Plants were usually not grown in rows, but in complex, irregular patterns. A system that many observers saw as disorder actually takes advantage of complementary habits of the plants and diverse microenvironments in the clearing.

Contemporary thinking regards horticulture as a viable system in its own right. As economist Ester Boserup has demonstrated, intensive forms of horticulture (or agriculture) readily develop when demand increases, principally because of mounting population pressure. In preindustrial cultivation the use of draft animals for tillage saves labor, but forest fallow systems do not require tillage, and their yields compare quite favorably with those of preindustrial agriculture per unit of labor spent. Horticulture that supports dense populations often, but not always, requires more labor than agriculture to produce the same amount of food. In the right circumstances preindustrial horticulture offers good returns on labor.

Horticulture predominated in the precolonial Americas and the Pacific islands, not out of primitiveness, but because there were no domesticated animals suitable for draft purposes. In most of sub-Saharan Africa, horses do not thrive, and pasture, not generally of good quality, is more in demand for dairy and beef cattle than for draft oxen. Colonial-era depopulation accounts for some of the predominance of long fallow systems in parts of Africa, the Pacific islands, and the Americas; archeology reveals large areas with abandoned intensive systems.

Postwar population growth has strained the capacities of many horticultural systems in developing countries, in many places causing a shift from sustainable to nonsustainable land use. This, plus demand from growing urban markets and pressures to commercialize production, has created a changing social and economic environment, to which many horticulturalists are having trouble adapting.

Agricultural development programs now often build on existing horticultural knowledge, particularly in the tropics. One important example is row intercropping, in which traditional crop mixtures are planted, but in rows. This gives most of the yield advantage gained by the old complex intercropping methods, and it allows tillers, power hoes, and other machinery to pass between rows. Many horticulturalists stand to gain by adopting plows and either draft animals or tractors. Not all horticulturalists are able to become plow agriculturalists, however; many lack capital or enough land of the right kind to repay the investment.

Consequently, much research on horticulture is on sustainable methods to raise yields. Much of the needed agronomic knowledge (for example, concerning the use of chemical fertilizers to maintain soil fertility or the breeding of new crop varieties for higher yields and disease resistance) builds on previous research on larger-scale agricultural operations. Other issues may be peculiar to horticultural operations or—as most workers in the fields describe them—small, "low resource" operations.

One specific agronomic strategy for the development of horticulture, one with great promise for sustainable development in tropical countries, is agroforestry, variously the alternation of tree crops with gardens or the permanent cultivation of mixed gardens of trees and annuals. Both are new versions of old strategies. Trees, because their roots bring up nutrients from lower soil layers that most crop plants cannot reach, can be valuable adjuncts to crops. Harvesting wood for timber, fuel, and other purposes removes nutrients that would be recycled in a forest fallow system, but some is left behind in debris and leaves; in addition, several of the tree species involved fix nitrogen. Mixed gardens of trees and annuals replicate and extend an old strategy mostly used in home gardens in the past. Continuing research focuses on selection and breeding of trees, interrelations with annual crops, and uses for tree products. Despite the antiquity of the basic methods, they are unfamiliar to many potential producers and consumers in target populations, and in many places social and economic research is needed.

"Farming systems research" has grown as an interdisciplinary approach to understanding the diverse agronomic, ecological, and social issues confronting farmers in developing countries, and much of the effort has targeted horticulture. Research teams, which generally include sociologists and other social scientists, explore links among such diverse variables as investment, the division of labor and profits between men and women, market demands, expectations of rewards from proposed changes, and farm ecology, often with the aim of evaluating specific innovations.

Context

The distinction between horticulture and agriculture originated with the Romans, but it was nineteenth century anthropologist Lewis Henry Morgan who made it part of a general model of social evolution. Horticulture, Morgan wrote, originates in the "Upper Status of Savagery"; agriculture comes two stages later, in the "Middle Status of Barbarism."

Friedrich Engels adopted Morgan's scheme of social evolution, which became a part of orthodox Marxist theories of history. A Marxist and feminist writer, Evelyn Reed, in a 1974 book, cited the role that women play in horticulture and revived Morgan's scheme, including the idea that matriarchy preceded patriarchy.

In the 1940's and 1950's, some anthropologists revived social evolutionism, trying to remove such value-laden baggage as labeling cultures "savage." Leslie White proposed that cultural evolution is essentially a process of increasing energy capture, a proposition that has since echoed in some human ecological writing. White did not distinguish between horticulture and agriculture but argued that a system that combines plant and animal husbandry is "superior" to one based on plants alone. Like Morgan, he argued that the transition to plow agriculture would have important societal consequences, though his model is more flexible than Morgan's.

Morgan's premise that horticulture preceded agriculture has some archeological support from regions where both plants and animals were domesticated early, and White's generalizations that keeping animals for draft and other purposes adds to energy capture can hardly be faulted. The case for consistent societal associations, however, is weak. Horticulture has, like agriculture, supported dense populations, including urban concentrations and elites. For example, states and urban civilizations arose in the precolonial Americas and sub-Saharan Africa. The best case for White's energy theory is perhaps early modern England. There, during the "agricultural revolution," both the numbers of livestock and their contribution to agriculture increased in conjunction with increased use of water and power and the burning of coal, processes that led to the industrial revolution.

The most important trait of horticulture to remember is its variety. The absence of plows and animal or tractor power imposes some limits, but those limits are not as great as has often been maintained. Many sociology and anthropology texts still identify horticulture with only its extensive forms, such as slash-and-burn cultivation. To gardeners and agricultural scientists in developed countries, horticulture is something utterly different: ornamental gardens and small vegetable gardens, sometimes orchards and vineyards. In these, the use of small power implements, such as rototillers, may obscure the original distinction between agriculture and horticulture.

Bibliography

Allan, William. *The African Husbandman*. New York: Barnes & Noble Books, 1965. Classic survey of sub-Saharan horticulture, mostly as it was years before population growth strained these systems. Attention is also paid to pastoralism, and a few examples of plow cultivation are included. A geographic perspective, with good information of patterns of settlement and their relation to food production. Good bibliography on colonial era sources.

Collinson, M. P., ed. *A History of Farming Systems Research*. New York: CABI, 1999.

Denevan, William, and Christine Padoch, eds. *Swidden-Fallow Agroforestry in the Peruvian Amazon*. Bronx, N.Y.: New York Botanical Garden, 1988. Good survey in a fairly representative part of the Amazon basin of traditional fallow horticulture and the response to pressures for development. Several contributions exhibit both social and ecological insights. Contrasts sustainable and nonsustainable land use in a fragile environment. The bibliography reflects the interdisciplinary interests of the contributors.

Kidd, Charles V., and David Pimentel, eds. *Integrated Resource Management: Agroforestry for Development*. San Diego: Academic Press, 1992. Probably a better introduction or sampling than some previously published proceedings of agroforestry conferences. An interdisciplinary work with an ecological focus.

Landauer, Kathleen, and Mark Brazil, eds. *Tropical Home Gardens*. Tokyo, Japan: United Nations University Press, 1990. Proceedings of a 1985 conference on gardens of mixed annuals and perennials. Includes reviews of the literature, both global and regional. The dominant perspective is ecological, complemented by the perspectives of economists, sociologists, anthropologists, agronomists, foresters, and others. Broad geographical coverage, with emphasis on Indonesia.

Office of Technology Assessment. *Enhancing Agriculture in Africa: A Role for U.S. Development Assistance*. Washington, D.C.: Government Printing Office, 1988. Besides discussing the U.S. role, this volume surveys the present status of horticulture ("low resource agriculture") among rapidly growing populations. Attention is given to land degradation and conservation measures, and to yield-raising techniques, including crop and livestock improvement, intercropping, agroforestry, aquaculture, transitions to agriculture using draft animals, and sociological issues of tenure and labor.

Poats, Susan V., Marianne Schmink, and Anita Spring, eds. *Gender Issues in Farming Systems Research and Extension*. Boulder, Colo.: Westview Press, 1988. About gender, mostly women's roles in farming systems, but also one of the best introductions to the philosophy and methodology of farming systems research, particularly in the introductory part. Multiple selections on Latin America and the Caribbean, Asia and the Middle East, and Africa, but not on the Pacific nor developed countries. Papers unfortunately tend to be heavy on specialist jargon, much of it gratuitous.

Ruthenberg, Hans. *Farming Systems in the Tropics*. 3d ed. Oxford, England: Clarendon Press, 1980. Mostly about horticulture, this book is strongest on Africa and weakest on the American tropics. Mostly agronomic and ecological, only occasionally sociological, but offers excellent descriptions and illustrations.

Daniel E. Vasey

Cross-References

Ethnography; Ethnomethodology; Hunting and Gathering Economic Systems; Industrial and Postindustrial Economies.

HUNTING AND GATHERING ECONOMIC SYSTEMS

Type of sociology: Major social institutions
Field of study: The economy

A hunting and gathering economy is a mode of subsistence that relies on collecting wild plants and hunting game. Early sociologists used food foraging societies to develop progressive theories of social evolution and social change.

Principal terms

BAND: a grouping of thirty to one hundred individuals who identify with a particular home range and share resources

DIVISION OF LABOR: allocation of economic tasks

DOMESTICATION: a process whereby wild plants and animals are genetically altered by human intervention in order to foster desirable traits

ETHNOGRAPHY: detailed study of a particular society and its culture

FISSION-FUSION SOCIETY: system of flux in which band members fragment into household units when resources are scarce and reunite when resources are plentiful

HORTICULTURE: the cultivation of domesticated seeds that are grown on small plots of land without the use of draft animals or irrigation

HOUSEHOLD: domestic group that cooperates as an economic unit on a daily basis

SEASONAL ROUND: seasonal movement within a ranging area as resources become available

SOCIAL INSTITUTION: pervasive pattern of social relationships with recognized positions or statuses and roles with appropriate social behaviors attached to statuses and roles

Overview

A hunting and gathering economy is a subsistence strategy that depends on the collection of wild plants and animals. As the oldest of human economic institutions, it originated with the beginnings of humankind. Until the domestication of plants and animals, it was the only economic pattern for a period of time that included about 99 percent of human existence. Although a society that "lives off the land" may be distinguished in many ways from one that "cultivates the land," a hunting and gathering economy is still organized around universal economic processes that are involved in the gathering, producing, and distribution of goods and services among individuals. In this endeavor, food-foraging economies also vary among themselves in the resources that are available for consumption, the level of technical skills necessary for individuals to participate in economic processes, the kinds of tools used in conjunction with labor, and the technological complexity that is required for a society to exploit a specific ecological zone.

Until horticulture, or simple farming, was first adopted in the Near East about ten thousand years ago, hunters and gatherers occupied climatic regions around the globe, from the tropical rainforests and coastal areas to the near-deserts and frozen Arctic zones. Yet during this time the human population numbered less than ten million persons, with a population density of one or two individuals per square mile. In certain respects, contemporary hunters and gatherers parallel the lifeways of prehistoric foraging societies, in part because foraging for food requires individuals to live in small groups and to follow a nomadic and flexible lifestyle. Consequently, individuals in food-collecting societies will disperse, or "fission," when resources are scarce and congregate, or "fuse," when resources are plentiful and concentrated.

Contemporary hunter-gatherers are arranged into loosely organized bands of thirty to one hundred individuals who embody what is called a "band-level" society. A band is an autonomous political unit of self-sufficient families or households that share a common foraging range and move about this region in a "seasonal round." Since each family is a well-defined economic unit, households are free to join or leave a band depending on individual preference and procurable resources. In every domestic household, economic labor is strictly divided according to age and sex: Men hunt and women gather, while the old and young are exempt from subsistence activities. Among all contemporary hunting and gathering societies there is little formal leadership beyond the domestic household, little stratification, and an egalitarian decision-making process; above all, there is an abiding "principle of reciprocity," a form of economic exchange that advocates the sharing of foods, goods, and services.

The Andamanese are hunter-gatherers who once inhabited tropical islands on the eastern edge of the Bay of Bengal in Southern Asia. Favored with a moist and warm coastal climate, the Andaman possessed a bounty of natural resources that included wild honey, roots, fruits, seeds, civet cats, wild pigs, large lizards, snakes, and abundant marine animals.

In his ethnography *The Andaman Islanders* (1922), A. R. Radcliffe-Brown describes Andamanese bands as having a production strategy that is associated with a definite ranging area, economic units that are composed of domestic households, and a sexual division of labor that is fairly clearly marked. Adult females in the Andamanese economy are responsible for the gathering of fruits, plants, prawns, and crabs, while adult males are involved in fishing and hunting enterprises. In turn, economic activities are linked with technological skills and tools. Males make and use bows and arrows, adzes, knives, ropes for harpoon lines, and seaworthy dugout canoes, while females make and use digging sticks for harvesting wild plants and fishnets for catching prawns, crabs, and other small fish. On a daily basis, Andaman women also gather firewood, carry water, and prepare the family meal.

While these coastal dwellers practiced no horticulture, the easily obtainable and concentrated coastal resources enabled them to congregate frequently and to spend part of the year in semipermanent settlements. This more sedentary lifestyle is reflected in Andamanese manufactured goods, which are a noticeable departure from those of most hunter-gatherers. For traveling on the water, the Andaman built canoes from hollowed-out logs. They built sturdy settlement huts and produced a variety of durable, bulky goods that included wooden buckets, cups and plates made of seashells, heavy clay cooking pots, and sleeping mats with wooden pillows.

In comparison, the Dobe !Kung are hunter-gatherers who inhabit a hot, semiarid savanna on the edge of the Kalahari Desert in Southern Africa. In this harsh climatic zone, the !Kung are always on the move, and their economic institution is adapted to exploit an enormous variety of widely dispersed resources. In this pursuit of food procuring, the !Kung sexual division of labor recruits males for the hunting of game and females for the gathering of plants.

Richard Lee's ethnography *The Dobe !Kung* (1984) describing !Kung life in the 1960's, depicts !Kung males as highly skilled hunters who will pursue almost anything—from warthogs, porcupines, guinea fowl, antelopes, and leopard tortoise to pythons. Male weaponry includes bows and arrows, spears, knives, hooks, ropes, and occasional use of well-trained dogs for capturing small game that are then speared. While fresh meat is always the prized food, vegetables, fruits, and nuts are the abundant and predictable foods that make up the bulk of the !Kung diet. According to Lee, "the !Kung have an astonishing inventory of over 100 edible plants: 14 fruits and nuts, 15 berries, 18 species of edible gum, 41 edible roots and bulbs, and 17 leafy greens, beans, melons, and other foods: 105 species in all." In the gathering process, Lee reports, !Kung females have exceptional technical knowledge about the growing conditions of wild plants, which they collect by either picking or digging into the soil with a sharpened wooden stick.

In contrast to the Adamanese, the !Kung production strategy depends upon a highly mobile and fluid population with frequent "fission" of the band. This flexible lifestyle is reflected in their provisional dwellings and in the nature of !Kung manufactured goods, which are mostly light, portable items such as sewing materials or fire-making kits that are easily stored and transported.

Applications

Information on the economic systems of hunting and gathering societies is mostly drawn from ethnographic accounts of aboriginal populations such as the Andaman and !Kung who survived into the nineteenth century. During this era, hunter-gatherers still lived in most parts of the globe, although aggressive farmers had already pushed most food foragers into marginal ecological zones where climatic soil conditions made cultivation impractical. Yet even under these limited environmental conditions, hunters and gatherers still managed to assemble successful economic systems that afforded an adequate and reliable food base with only a few cases of hardship documented. The realization that contemporary hunter-gatherers did not fit the stereotype of starving peoples living "nasty, brutish, and short" lives was documented in the classic volume *Man the Hunter* (1968, edited by Richard B. Lee and Irven DeVore), the proceedings of a symposium that brought together seventy-five distinguished scholars in the field.

Since the 1970's, long-term field studies of the adaptive responses of modest, food-collecting peoples living under diverse environmental circumstances have been especially important in providing practical information on how economic systems operate in particular ecological settings. Equally important, extended research has revealed that, despite the variety in adaptive conditions, all food-collecting societies share a core of economic patterns that can serve as an economic baseline by which to compare them with industrialized economies. First, by and large, hunter-gatherers meet their dietary needs with a minimal energy budget, while foods grown in industrial societies are far more costly in energy terms. Second, hunter-gatherers normally preserve their resource base, while industrialized societies normally deplete theirs, suggesting the possibility that demands may soon exceed resources. Third, hunter-gatherers eat well, although they expend minimal labor, have considerable leisure time, and often live long lives with minimum stress and anxiety. Marshall Sahlins, in *Stone Age Economies* (1972), called them "the original affluent society," and Elman Service wrote in "The Hunters" (1966) that "many hunting-gathering peoples are quite literally the most leisured peoples in the world." In comparison, the economic forces in industrialized societies compel individuals to work longer and harder than workers in any past societies, and often create considerable stress and anxiety in the process.

Thus, while industrialization has led to a substantial increase in material benefits, as a practical matter, foraging economies can serve as a corrective yardstick by which to assess potential problems of energy flow, environmental abuse, and the social and emotional consequences of modern subsistence modes. In this regard, Gerhard Lenski, Jean Lenski, and Patrick Nolan considered modes of production from simple hunting and gathering to industrialized societies and concluded in their book *Human Societies* (1991) that "there is no simple one-to-one correspondence between technological advance and progress in terms of freedom, justice, and happiness."

Studying economic systems cross-culturally has also helped sociologists appreciate how social relationships differ among individuals in market economies (in which individuals offer goods for sale to others) and marketless economies (in which goods are not for sale but are exchanged through social mechanisms). In market-dominant economies, gathering, production, and distribution are governed by "market principle" of supply and demand, and economic life is primarily based on private profits. In foraging (marketless) economies, resources are pooled according to a "principle of reciprocity," and economic life is governed by an egalitarian ethic of sharing. In turn, the way goods are exchanged seems to influence other social institutions in a society. For example, societies that have economic institutions in which members have equal rights to resources also have political institutions that uphold what is perhaps the most cherished of Western democratic ideals: the belief that all members of a society are social equals.

Finally, inquiry into a food-foraging lifestyle in which individuals interact with their physical environment on a daily basis is a useful way to assess the potency of economic forces. According to Lenski, Lenski, and Nolan, most variations in human societies can be understood in terms of the differences in habitats and subsistence technologies.

Context

Interest in hunter-gatherers is a longstanding sociological tradition that goes back to the formative years of sociology when nineteenth century evolutionary notions of order, progress, and continuity were used to understand the development of societal types. In England,

Herbert Spencer, in his *Descriptive Sociology* (1873-1881), made extensive use of information collected on foraging societies in an attempt to understand social progress and social change from simple societies to the modern political state. By using standard categories to examine variations in the features of human societies, Spencer attempted to document how social phenomena are interrelated in an effort to develop generalizations about the operation of human societies.

In France, Émile Durkheim focused on change in economic systems in his *De la Division du travail social* (1893; *The Division of Labor in Society*, 1933). In this classic monograph, Durkheim attempted to show how units of a social system are coordinated and how the basis of social solidarity changes as individuals move from simple food-foraging economies to complex state societies. In *Les Formes élémentaires de la vie religieuse: Le Système totémique en Australie* (1912; *The Elementary Forms of the Religious Life: A Study in Religious Sociology*, 1915), Durkheim continued his analysis of progressive social evolution by using data drawn from Australian food foragers to try to uncover the origins of society. While the evolutionary schemes of both Spencer and Durkheim were tainted by a belief that primitive societies, and hunter-gatherers in particular, were savages at the most elementary stages of humanity, both scholars were major figures in helping to legitimate sociology as the discipline concerned with the workings of human societies.

In contemporary sociology, there has been a renewed emphasis on hunting and gathering societies, partly because of a rekindling of interest in evolutionary concepts and a realization that humans evolved in a food-foraging context. For example, many of the physical attributes of human beings, such as upright walking, a large brain relative to body size, language, and a sexual division of labor were all acquired when humans lived solely by food collecting. Additionally, human nutritional requirements, social needs, and even emotional responses to stress and aggression are now being viewed as adaptive responses acquired when humans foraged for food. Thus, despite the fact that the food collectors of the world are rapidly disappearing and this societal type will probably soon vanish, this lifestyle is still an important meeting ground for current economic issues and for its potential importance in providing insights into "human nature" and other legacies acquired during that long historical phase when all humans were nomadic food collectors.

Bibliography

Bettinger, Robert. *Hunter-Gatherers: Archaeological and Evolutionary Theory*. New York: Plenum Press, 1991. Comprehensive overview of the history of research and theory in relation to hunter-gatherers and an overview of contemporary evolutionary and materialist perspectives. For readers who want a greater understanding of the background and conceptual frameworks in hunter-gatherer research.

Bicchieri, M. G., ed. *Hunters and Gatherers Today*. New York: Holt, Rinehart and Winston, 1972. General perspectives on hunting and gathering in eleven contemporary food-collecting societies. Descriptive ethnographies are drawn from all parts of the world and paint a general picture of hunter-gatherer lifeways.

Johnson, Allen, and Timothy Earle. *The Evolution of Human Societies: From Foraging*

Group to Agrarian State. Stanford, Calif.: Stanford University Press, 1987. Uses an evolutionary framework to focus on the developmental sequence of human societies, beginning with food foragers. It also summarizes the evolution of economic behavior in a broad environmental and cultural context.

Lee, Richard. *The Dobe !Kung.* New York: Holt, Rinehart and Winston, 1984. Excellent case study of the !Kung foragers of the Dobe area of northwestern Botswana. Particularly rich in detail and offers the reader a realistic picture of the !Kung as they were living as food collectors in the early 1960's.

Lenski, Gerhard, Jean Lenski, and Patrick Nolan. *Human Societies.* 8th ed. New York: McGraw-Hill, 1999. Takes an evolutionary-ecological approach to understanding the social evolution of human societies. Essentially, these sociologists argue that a society's economic institution usually sets the limits of what is possible for a society and its institutions. It also serves as the prime mover in social change.

Maryanski, Alexandra, and Jonathan Turner. *The Social Cage: Human Nature and the Evolution of Society.* Stanford, Calif.: Stanford University Press, 1992. Looks at "human nature" and the biological foundations of human societies. Essentially, these sociologists argue that when humans abandoned a foraging lifestyle, they began to construct sociocultural cages that infringe on human needs for parity, freedom, mobility, and individualism. This work is one example of the revival of evolutionary thinking in sociology, using food-foraging societies as a baseline for understanding the legacy of humankind.

Radcliffe-Brown, A. R. *The Andaman Islanders.* Cambridge, England: Cambridge University Press, 1922. Based on fieldwork in the Andaman Islands begun in 1906. Radcliffe-Brown is one of the founders of a theoretical approach known as structural-functionalism (or simply functionalism).

Symposium on Man the Hunter (1966, University of Chicago). *Man the Hunter.* Edited by Richard B. Lee and Irven DeVore. Chicago: Aldine, 1968. Classic volume was the result of a conference that brought together seventy-five international hunter-gatherer scholars to discuss the current status of food collectors throughout the world. It resulted in reappraisal of some basic theories of hunting and gathering people.

A. R. Maryanski

Cross-References

Ethnography; Ethnomethodology; Horticultural Economic Systems; Industrial and Postindustrial Economies.

Hypotheses and Hypothesis Testing

Type of sociology: Sociological research
Field of study: Basic concepts

Hypotheses are clear and precise statements that provide tentative answers to research questions. Hypotheses make predictions about the relationship between variables. The predictions are found to be supported or unsupported by empirical testing.

Principal terms

DIRECTIONAL HYPOTHESIS: hypothesis that makes a specific prediction regarding the variables being studied—for example, that television violence increases aggressive behavior in children

EMPIRICAL TEST: defining and measuring variables that can be observed; often includes statistical analysis of the data

NONDIRECTIONAL HYPOTHESIS: hypothesis that does not make a specific prediction regarding the variables being studied, for example, television violence affects aggressive behavior in children

OPERATIONAL DEFINITION: defining of a variable or construct in a specific and concrete way, describing the operations of how it will be observed and measured

PROBABALISTIC CONFIRMATION: confirming or disconfirming a hypothesis using the principles of probability theory

QUANTITATIVE ANALYSIS: analysis performed by obtaining measures that attempt to categorize and summarize observations through the assignment of numbers, then statistically analyzing these numbers

SCIENTIFIC METHOD: method for acquiring knowledge that is characterized by systematic observation, experimentation, experimental control, and the ability to repeat the study

Overview

For any discipline to thrive and grow as a science, it is imperative that good research questions be formulated and answered. The development and testing of hypotheses plays an essential role in the quest for new knowledge. All research questions at some point must be framed as clear and precise statements that can be empirically tested; these statements are referred to as hypotheses.

According to social scientists Chava Frankfort-Nachmias and David Nachmias in their book *Research Methods in the Social Sciences* (1992), a hypothesis possesses four characteristics. First, it is derived from a research question and must be written using clear and precise language. For example, a frequently asked research question is: "Does violence on television cause children to behave aggressively?" For this question to be answered, it first must be framed as a hypothesis. Clear and precise language must be used and definitions must be assigned to a number of conceptual terms such as "violence," "children," and "aggressively." One must specify, for example, whether "violence" refers only to acts of physical aggression directed at others or whether verbal threats and acts such as spitting at another person should be included. Similar problems can be found with the label "children." Specifically, the age group to be included must be decided; it must be clarified, for example, whether a twelve-year-old is a child or an adolescent.

To arrive at a clear hypothesis, terms must be operationally defined so that they can be observed. For example, "violence" could be operationally defined as the number of times a female child hits, kicks, punches, or throws a doll. It would then be possible to categorize how violently a child behaves after viewing a series of violent television programs. An operational definition is established by the researcher not only for the purpose of clarifying what is being measured but also to allow other scientists to repeat the study using the same methods of measuring the variables.

A second characteristic of a hypothesis is that it is value-free. In other words, it should be written as an objective statement that does not reflect the researcher's own personal values and biases. (When a personal belief or preference is inserted, it should be made clear to the reader.) A third characteristic of a hypothesis is that it is specific. Using the example given previously, a hypothesis would need to express the nature of the relationship between watching television and aggressive behavior. Whether viewing violent television increases, decreases, or has no impact on aggressive behavior would need to be spelled out clearly. Most hypotheses are framed in terms of a specific prediction. In this way, a hypothesis can be seen as a tentative answer to a research question that needs verification. The literature frequently refers to this kind of a hypothesis as a directional hypothesis. On the other hand, some hypotheses are specific yet do not predict a particular direction of the relationship between the variables. This type of hypothesis is referred to as a nondirectional hypothesis.

The fourth and last characteristic of a hypothesis is that it must be testable. Once data have been collected, it must be possible to organize or manipulate the data in such a way as to confirm or disconfirm the research hypothesis. In other words, evidence should suggest whether it is probably true or false. The testable nature of the hypothesis is what challenges the researcher to improve methods or find new methods to test the veracity of the hypothesis.

Hypothesis testing is not as clear-cut a process as it may first appear. Testing a hypothesis empirically does not lead to a conclusion that absolutely proves that the hypothesis is either true or false. Rather, it leads to a probabalistic confirmation. To test a hypothesis, a researcher must determine how the variables expressed in the hypothesis will be measured, make the necessary observations, collect the data (which is usually in the form of numbers), and then subject the data to quantitative analysis. The quantitative analysis attempts to summarize the vast array of numbers and then to determine whether the results of the study could possibly have occurred by random chance.

Thus, in most instances, quantitative analysis results in a probability statement in which the following rule applies: If the probability of getting the results of the study by mere random chance factors is found to be extremely rare, then one concludes the results are attributable to the variables of the study and not to chance. The hypothesis would receive either confirmation or falsification in terms of a probabalistic statement.

Applications

One of the benefits of hypothesis testing is that it makes possible the testing of, and therefore the reevaluation of, existing theories. Theories provide the framework within which hypotheses are formulated and tested; their overall organization of ideas makes possible the questions, thoughts, and predictions that go into the creation of hypotheses. In turn, the outcome of experiments that test the hypotheses formulated under these larger theories reflects back on the validity of the theories themselves. Therese L. Baker, a social scientist, in her book *Doing Social Research* (1988), states that hypothesis testing leads to one of three possible outcomes with regard to testing a theory's ability to explain data: confirmation of a theory, modification of a theory, or the overthrow of a theory. Hypothesis testing is a valuable tool for helping sociologists refine the theories that provide the foundation of the discipline.

Hypothesis development and testing can be best understood through example. Judith M. Siegel, a public health specialist, in her article "Stressful Life Events and Use of Physician Services Among the Elderly: The Moderating Role of Pet Ownership," published in the *Journal of Personality and Social Psychology* (1990), attempts to test the following hypothesis: Pet ownership plays a beneficial role during times of high stress for the elderly. Notice that the hypothesis is clear and value-free. Siegel chose an operational definition of "beneficial" as decreasing the number of doctor visits over a one-year period. She defined "high stress" by using an instrument that measures depressed mood (a common by-product of psychological stress). The hypothesis makes a specific prediction involving the variable pet ownership and the expected beneficial outcome during periods of high stress. It is therefore a directional hypothesis. In addition, the hypothesis is testable. Providing that the two measures for stress are accurate measures and that reliable data can be collected on the number of doctor contacts made by a group of elderly persons, the hypothesis can be confirmed or falsified.

The study involved interviewing and following up on a group of more than one thousand elderly respondents (sixty-five years of age or older) for a one-year period. The subjects were assessed as to how much psychological stress they were experiencing on multiple occasions. In addition, they were asked if they owned a pet (37 percent responded "yes") and questioned about their affective attachment to the pet. After controlling for differences among subjects on sex, age, race, education, income, employment status, and chronic health problems, Siegel conducted a quantitative analysis that compared the number of physician contacts between subjects who owned pets and those who did not. The results supported her initial hypothesis by showing that elderly subjects who owned pets had significantly fewer physician contacts during the year than those without pets had. Pets appeared to alleviate and buffer some of the stress their owners were experiencing during difficult times.

Another example of hypothesis testing can be seen in a study by Lee A. Rosen, a behavioral science researcher, and his colleagues entitled "Effects of Sugar (Sucrose) on

Children's Behavior," published in the *Journal of Consulting and Clinical Psychology* (1988). Rosen attempted to test the veracity of a commonly held belief within American society that sugar produces detrimental effects on children's behavior. He began by pointing out that the few controlled studies conducted in this area so far had produced conflicting results. Some indicate that sugar has a detrimental effect on children's behavior, while others show that it does not. Rosen decided to test the following hypothesis: Sugar can have detrimental effects on children's behavior. Using a controlled experimental design, he studied forty-five children over a fifteen-day period. He obtained parental permission, and all the children were instructed that they would be eating breakfast at school. During the first five days, the subjects were randomly assigned into one of three groups. In one group they received a breakfast that contained no sugar (aspartame was used to make the drink sweet)—this was the control condition. A second group received a breakfast that contained 6 grams of sugar (the low-sugar group), and a third group received 50 grams of sugar (the high-sugar group). At no time did the children or those involved in collecting the data ever know how much sugar the children in each group were given. During each subsequent five-day period, the children were placed in a different group.

The children were then observed each day on measures such as fidgeting, change in activity level, active movement, vocalization, and aggression. In addition, they were administered various cognitive and performance measures to test their ability to stay on task. Because the outcome variable "children's behavior" is multifaceted, there was a need for many different indicators. Contrary to commonly held social beliefs about the effect of sugar on behavior, no evidence was found to suggest that sugar causes significant changes in children's behavior. The hypothesis was not supported. Rosen and his colleagues believe that the false stigma attached to the ingestion of sugar could be attributable to spurious correlations made through casual observation. For example, eating large amounts of sugar is often associated with certain activities (such as birthday parties) that may contribute to excited or disruptive behavior.

Context

Social scientists Mark Mitchell and Janina Jolley, in their book *Research Design Explained* (1992), suggest that hypotheses may be generated in a number of ways. One source is intuition, in the form of common sense. The hypothesis mentioned earlier regarding the psychological benefits of owning a pet appears to have originated from intuition. The intuition could have easily come about through casual observations of real-life events. The author of the study could have seen that the elderly, particularly those who have recently lost a spouse, develop a close companionship with a pet. This relationship could in turn help moderate psychological distress commonly experienced by the elderly.

Another rich source for hypotheses is existing theory. Theories not only attempt to summarize a large body of data but also attempt to explain the relationships that exist among many different variables. In general, theories allow for a number of predictions (in the form of hypotheses) to be made about future events. Previous research is also a primary source for developing hypotheses. Perusing the sociological literature via books, journals, indexes, and handbooks enables one to see what previous studies have shown. This allows the opportunity for a skilled researcher to pose hypotheses in areas that have not yet been explored.

Hypothesis testing is a critical component in the process of uncovering new knowledge. In any process of critical inquiry, one must keep in mind that the primary objective is to discover the truth about a particular object of study. It was mentioned earlier that a hypothesis can be seen as a tentative answer to a research question. It remains tentative until it has been tested. Even after a hypothesis has been empirically tested and upheld, it is not guaranteed that the scientific community will automatically embrace it. The confidence and credibility that a hypothesis holds in the eyes of the scientific community are dependent on how the data was collected. The particular methods employed to conduct the study are of central importance. If the methods were weak, then credibility is instantly reduced. In addition to the methodology, the ability of others to replicate the findings is critical. In simple terms, a hypothesis that has been repeatedly found to be true through a number of similar experiments is much more likely to be accepted as true than a hypothesis that has not been replicated.

Bibliography

Babbie, Earl. *The Practice of Social Research*. Belmont, Calif.: Wadsworth, 1999. Comprehensive volume characterized by an informal writing style that explains complex research methods concepts in a way that a novice can understand. A clear description of hypothesis testing can be found.

Baker, Therese L. *Doing Social Research*. New York: McGraw-Hill, 1988. Provides general introduction to the scientific method, including the development and testing of hypotheses. Also contains topics that will help the reader evaluate both good and poor field experiments.

Berg, Bruce L. *Qualitative Research Methods for the Social Sciences*. Boston: Allyn & Bacon, 1989. To understand differences between different types of research strategies used in developing hypotheses, it is necessary to understand the differences between quantitative and qualitative research. This book clarifies that distinction; it also discusses commonly used methods of studying groups of people.

Frankfort-Nachmias, Chava, and David Nachmias. *Research Methods in the Social Sciences*. 4th ed. New York: St. Martin's Press, 1992. Gives many examples of hypotheses; also explains how hypotheses fit in with the overall picture of social science research. In addition, part 4, "Data Processing and Analysis," highlights quantitative analyses that are available to test hypotheses. Some quantitative methods are also touched on.

Rosen, Lee A., et al. "Effects of Sugar (Sucrose) on Children's Behavior." *Journal of Consulting and Clinical Psychology* 56 (August, 1988): 583-589. This research performed a well-controlled study on the effects of sugar on behavior. Although the study has some methodological drawbacks, overall it appears to be one of the best studies done on this topic. An excellent example of hypothesis testing.

Siegel, Judith M. "Stressful Life Events and Use of Physician Services Among the Elderly:

The Moderating Role of Pet Ownership." *Journal of Personality and Social Psychology* 58 (June, 1990): 1081-1086. This article provides an interesting and surprisingly non-technical example of the process of hypothesis testing. The introduction and discussion sections provide a rationale for how pets (particularly dogs) could help moderate stress experienced by their owners.

Singleton, Royce, Jr., Bruce Straits, Margaret Straits, and Ronald McAllister. *Approaches to Social Research*. New York: Oxford University Press, 1988. Well-written text discussing aspects of hypothesis testing in addition to other areas of experimentation such as selecting a research setting, gathering information, how to get into the field, and when a field study should be adopted. Chapter on experimentation can be used to contrast "true" experiments with field studies.

Bryan C. Auday

Cross-References

Causal Relationships; Quantitative Research; Surveys; Validity and Reliability in Measurement.

IMMIGRATION AND EMIGRATION

Type of sociology: Population studies or demography
Field of study: Sources of social change

Studies of immigration and emigration explore the causes of voluntary population move-ments and the effects of these movements on immigrants as individuals and society as a whole. The net migration rate is the difference between the number of immigrants and emigrants and refers to whether a society's population is increasing or decreasing through population movements.

Principal terms

ASSIMILATION: becoming a part of, or absorbed into, the dominant culture

CHAIN MIGRATION: the process in which one immigrant enters a new country and then brings other family members, one after the other

EMIGRATION: leaving one's native country in order to settle in a new country

IMMIGRATION: entering a new country or region with the intent to settle there

MELTING POT THEORY: belief that individuals from various ethnic backgrounds eventually blend into one homogeneous American culture

PUSH/PULL FACTORS: circumstances that force (push) individuals or groups out of their native country or attract (pull) them toward a particular destination

STRUCTURAL FACTORS: economic or political forces that are beyond individual control

Overview

Immigration and emigration are studied by sociologists in a number of different ways; researchers studying demography (population), social stratification, and social mobility are all interested in these phenomena, but they view them from differing perspectives. Demog-raphy examines the characteristics of, and changes in, human populations. To demogra-phers, immigration and emigration are two forms of migration.

Migration is one of the primary processes (alongside fertility and mortality) that affect the size, composition, and distribution of a population. Migration simply consists of the movement of people from one place to another. Migration can be internal (within a country) or international, and both types can have significant impacts. Immigration (the movement into a new country) and emigration (movement from a country) are forms of international migration. The term "net migration rate" refers to the difference between the rate of immigration and the rate of emigration. It is expressed as the number of people per 1,000 who enter or leave an area during one year. Migration may have a number of important effects, such as relieving "population pressure" in crowded areas, spreading culture from one area to another, and bringing groups into contact—and possible conflict.

Sociologists also study the experiences of immigrants in relation to prejudice, discrimination, and social stratification and mobility. They explore the differing experiences of immigrants of differing ethnicities and races; such studies have revealed much about the nature of prejudice and about the disparity between the ideology and the reality of American life. A look at various aspects of immigration to the United States allows an examination of these processes at work in the real world. Over the course of immigration to America, beginning in the sixteenth century (if one excludes the first immigration, the prehistoric migration of the ancestors of the American Indians), most immigrants have come for similar reasons: to escape persecution, to find economic opportunities, and to enjoy the freedoms available in the United States. Yet despite the traditional emphasis on the forces that pushed people out of their countries of origin and the separate forces that pulled them toward the United States, a number of studies, such as David M. Reimers's *Still the Golden Door* (1985), emphasize structural forces—economic and political—that have influenced population movements.

Many studies of immigration to the United States identify two massive waves of immigration between 1820 and 1914. The first decades of the nineteenth century brought increasing numbers of immigrants; 151,000 arrived in the 1820's, nearly 600,000 in the 1830's, more than a million in the 1840's, and 2.3 million in the 1850's. Many were Irish Catholics escaping political persecution and famine and Germans fleeing political upheavals. These "old immigrants" came to cities on the East Coast; some moved inland to the farmlands of the Great Plains.

"New immigrants" were those from eastern and southern Europe who arrived between the 1880's and World War I. This second period of immigration far surpassed the earlier waves in numbers, rising from 788,000 in 1872 to 1,285,000 in 1907. By 1914 nearly fifteen million immigrants had arrived in the United States, many from Austria-Hungary, Italy, Russia, Greece, Romania, and Turkey. The federal Dillingham Commission (1907) regarded this group as poor, unskilled, and mostly male, and its report reinforced prejudices about eastern and southern Europeans. It concluded that these immigrants would be more difficult to assimilate into American society. As the children or grandchildren of immigrants became indistinguishable from other Americans, however, the concept of American society as a "melting pot" into which many nationalities merged into one, took hold.

Often invisible in early immigration studies were the numbers of Africans and Latin Americans who had not come voluntarily to the United States. Africans were forcibly brought to the United States as slaves. Many Mexicans did not technically immigrate but were absorbed into the United States when lands from Texas to California were conquered in the Mexican-American War (1846-1848). These groups needed to adapt to a new nation and a new culture, as did European immigrants, but they faced both discrimination and a lack of understanding about their circumstances. Asian immigrants formed another group that was long invisible in immigration histories. Chinese men were imported as cheap labor to build the railroads in the mid-1800's, and they were expected to leave when their job was done. Many Japanese, Filipino, and Korean immigrants came first to Hawaii as agricultural laborers, and some moved on to California.

Some structural reasons for emigration and immigration have not changed greatly over the last three hundred years. Many individuals have come to North America to escape religious or political persecution. Early refugees in this category included the English Pilgrims and French Huguenots. Later religious groups came from Norway, Holland, and Russia, among them Jews and Mennonites. From the early nineteenth century to the present, immigrants have come because of economic changes in their native lands and opportunities in the United States. The enclosure movement in England and Western Europe, which began in the 1700's, forced many peasants off the land. They sought new land in America. Factories brought ruin to skilled artisans, who came to the United States hoping to open workshops. Many Europeans and Asians also came to escape political turmoil. Revolutions in 1830 and 1848 in Europe, and the Taiping Rebellion in China in 1848, led refugees to seek safety in the United States. Twentieth century upheavals such as World War II, the Cuban Revolution, repression in Southeast Asia, and civil wars in Lebanon and El Salvador have continued to bring refugees to the United States.

Immigrants and refugees have not settled equally in all regions of the United States. Large immigrant communities in California, New York, and Florida have led to the need for government services in many languages. Students in schools speak Vietnamese, Spanish, Korean, Ethiopian, Haitian, and a number of Chinese dialects. Many require courses in English as a second language. Courts need to provide translators, and social service agencies struggle to communicate with many immigrant groups.

Some Americans have responded to foreigners with resentment. Some states and localities have passed laws declaring English to be the only official language. Sociologists studying immigration, however, have found that the large number of immigrants has led to a gradual shift in the population of the United States and its culture. Television stations around the country broadcast programs in many languages. Spanish-speaking markets in particular represent many new business opportunities, and large American companies are beginning to offer advertisements in Spanish.

Applications

Americans have been proud of their heritage of immigration yet ambivalent about immigrant groups who have come to the United States. Federal legislation has expressed the varying reactions of Americans toward immigrants and immigration over time. Before 1820 there were no laws requiring lists of passengers arriving in the United States. Immigrants brought skills and talents that were needed by the new country, and they were welcomed. Non-British immigrants in the early nineteenth century, however, did experience discrimination. Irish Catholics and German immigrants, whose religion or language was different from that of the majority, faced ridicule and were stereotyped as drunkards or dullards. Asian immigrants faced racial prejudice, and Chinese people were eventually barred from immigrating to the United States.

Despite mixed reaction to foreigners, the first federal immigration law was not passed until 1875. In that year prostitutes and convicts were prohibited from entering as immigrants. Additional exclusions for lunatics and idiots were added later.

By the 1880's, increasing immigration from areas outside northern Europe, the closing of the frontier, and increasing urbanization led to attempts to control immigration. Some Americans claimed that southern and eastern Europeans were replacing American stock and that immigration produced a declining birthrate among Americans. Others were more worried about Asian immigrants. The Chinese Exclusion Act of 1882 specifically denied entry to Chinese people, while the Foran Act (1885) made it unlawful for employers to import aliens to perform labor in the United States. This law was aimed at large companies who were importing eastern Europeans to fill low-wage jobs instead of hiring American labor, and it reflected suspicion that immigration caused wages to decline. The Immigration Act of 1917 barred Asians not by nationality, but by excluding geographically any immigrants from East or South Asia.

Immigration to the United States was regulated for most of the twentieth century by the Immigration Act of 1924, which reflected the nation's desire to encourage European immigration and discourage non-Western immigrants. This law established a series of quotas for immigrants from all countries except the Western Hemisphere. Larger quotas were assigned to countries whose citizens were more traditionally identified with the American population. The Immigration and Nationality Act of 1952 tightened the quota system.

A significant change in United States policy toward immigration came with the Immigration and Nationality Act of 1965. This law removed strict quotas and Asian exclusion. Instead, it created preferences for persons with certain skills and gave priority to people with immediate family in the United States. The consequences of this legislation led to greater changes in immigration than were anticipated. By 1974, for example, foreign-born physicians made up 20 percent of all medical doctors in the United States. The "brain drain" from developing countries continued, as scientists, engineers, and scholars sought better conditions and higher salaries in the United States. The law also brought increasing non-European immigration, as family members petitioned to bring relatives from Asia, Africa, and Latin America.

The increasing number of undocumented immigrants in the United States has led to calls for policing the U.S. border with Mexico more efficiently and for penalties for employers of illegal immigrants. Illegal immigrants have been accused of stealing jobs from United States citizens, draining social services, and changing the very nature of American society. In 1986 the Immigration and Control Act attempted to resolve these issues for many illegal immigrants. Those who could show permanent residency in the United States since 1982 could become legal residents. Employers who hired illegal immigrants were to be fined, and additional funds were appropriated for stronger immigration enforcement.

Immigration reforms have continued, showing the changing response of American society over time. The Kennedy-Donnelly Act of 1988 permitted a lottery to provide visas for permanent resident status, and the 1990 Immigration Law raised annual immigration ceilings and ended restrictions on homosexuals, communists, and people with acquired immune deficiency syndrome (AIDS); it also granted safe haven status for Salvadorans. This law was not without opposition from those who feared that disease or undesirable ideas would be spread by immigrants.

Refugees have become an increasingly important part of population movements. Emigra-

Immigrants are often made the scapegoats of society's economic and social problems. *(International Daily News)*

tion from countries experiencing conflict has increased in the twentieth century, and the United States has traditionally thought of itself as a nation receptive to the oppressed. The need to resettle large numbers of eastern European refugees after World War II was recognized by the Refugee Relief Act of 1952. In the 1980's the church-sponsored sanctuary movement broke immigration laws by providing asylum for Salvadorans who feared deportation by immigration authorities enforcing strict refugee policies. The impact of immigration on American society has continued to challenge cherished concepts and ideologies and to highlight prejudices. The idea of the United States as an open door, a place where people from all lands can find a haven, is still shared by many. Since the 1980's, however, this ideal has faced considerable challenges. The large numbers of Central Americans, Asians, and Haitians seeking asylum in the United States has led to tighter controls at borders and interdiction on the high seas.

Context

Immigration studies have focused both on numbers of immigrants and on the circumstances of individual immigrants. Demographers seek to understand the significance of numbers in population movements. Statistics about the net migration rate, for example, indicate the influence of immigration on population growth. For example, during the 1920's, approximately four million immigrants entered the United States, while nearly one million emigrated. The net migration increase was therefore three million. During the Depression years of the 1930's, however, immigration and emigration were nearly equal, and the country experienced no gain in population from immigration.

Immigration studies also seek to understand the changes that occur to individuals and to whole populations. Family ties often become strained when immigrant parents rear children in a strange culture. Some children reject their parents' culture, and many parents cannot understand the pressures their children face in American society. Marriages also undergo stress. Men often come first to the United States, leaving their wives and children behind. While many send money back home, and they often bring their families later, some abandon their families or divorce their wives.

Modern technology has also had an impact on immigration. When the steamship replaced the sailing ship, more immigrants could return home. A percentage of immigrants have always returned to their native lands; some became disillusioned with life in the United States; others returned because they had made enough money to buy land or a shop in their own land. The airplane made international travel faster and cheaper. Modern immigration does not necessarily lead to prolonged separation from one's native land, and this has strengthened ethnic ties.

Nathan Glazer and Daniel Patrick Moynihan, in *Beyond the Melting Pot* (1963), challenged this popularly accepted concept of a melting pot society by focusing on the continuity of ethnic identity. While most immigrants or their families have eventually learned English, become American citizens, and accepted much of the dominant culture, ethnic diversity continues. Many immigrants rely on ethnic assistance. Chain migration was an important part of immigrant strategies. Early arrivals would often pay for the passage of relatives and then find work for them when they arrived. It was not uncommon for an immigrant to leave Ellis Island with a train ticket for a town in Nebraska or Minnesota, where he or she would be met by relatives.

Sociologists have studied many effects of immigration on American society, especially in the form of ethnic networks and organizations. Churches, both Catholic and Protestant, have reflected the national origins of their parishioners. Many immigrants obtain capital to start businesses from family members or banks run by members of their ethnic group. Ethnic identity has also been influential among voting blocs, especially within the Democratic Party.

While some scholarship, particularly since the 1980's, has stressed structural rather than personal reasons for population movements and has challenged the concept of the melting pot, American society has continued to mold immigrants from many nations. At the same time, American society has changed as a result of this immigration.

Bibliography

Daniels, Roger. *Coming to America: A History of Immigration and Ethnicity in American Life*. New York: HarperCollins, 1990. Begins with prehistoric migrations of American Indians and continues through American history, placing immigration in the context of American society. Provides tables on countries of origin, ethnic enclaves, and net migration rates.

Glazer, Nathan, and Daniel P. Moynihan. *Beyond the Melting Pot*. 2d ed. Cambridge, Mass.: MIT Press, 1970. Classic exploration of experiences of African American, Italian, Irish, and Jewish groups in New York City. Argues against the concept of the melting pot by demonstrating continuing ethnic identity and separate communities of these groups.

Johns, Stephanie Bernardo. *The Ethnic Almanac*. Garden City, N.Y.: Doubleday, 1981. Presents statistics and background on immigration arranged by ethnic group; an easy-to-use reference. Provides good illustrations of ethnic contributions to American society and presents examples of various foods brought by different ethnic groups as well as foreign words added to the English language.

Jones, Maldwyn Allen. *American Immigration*. 2d ed. Chicago: University of Chicago Press, 1992. Offers a clear history of immigration from colonists to modern refugees. Recognizes reasons for emigration and includes immigrants from Asia as well as Europe. Addresses issues surrounding immigration legislation, and the second edition includes a discussion of refugee questions in the early 1990's.

Reimers, David M. *Still the Golden Door: The Third World Comes to America*. 2d ed. New York: Columbia University Press, 1992. Focuses on Third World immigration, emphasizing on the post-World War II era. Undocumented immigrants and refugees are included, and their impact on immigration policies is discussed.

Schuck, Peter H., and Rainer Munz, eds. *Paths to Inclusion: The Integration of Migrants in the United States and Germany*. New York: Berghahn Books, 1998.

Thernstrom, Stephan, ed. *The Harvard Encyclopedia of American Ethnic Groups*. Cambridge, Mass.: The Belknap Press of Harvard University Press, 1980. Excellent reference work, covering many topics related to immigration and giving information about immigrant and ethnic groups in the United States. Good statistics.

Vertovec, Steven, ed. *Migration and Social Cohesion*. Northhampton, Mass.: Edward Elgar, 1999.

Yans-McLaughlin, Virginia, ed. *Immigration Reconsidered*. New York: Oxford University Press, 1990. Essays on immigration, approaches to comparative research, and immigrant networks. Includes both sociological and historical perspectives. Raises questions about traditional assumptions regarding immigrant groups, their assimilation, and the relationship between emigration and immigration.

James A. Baer

Cross-References

Cultural and Structural Assimilation; Ethnicity and Ethnic Groups; Race Relations: The Race-Class Debate; Racial and Ethnic Stratification.

INDUSTRIAL AND POSTINDUSTRIAL ECONOMIES

Type of sociology: Major social institutions
Field of study: The economy

In the opinion of many social scientists, industry-based economies in the United States and other countries will be replaced by postindustrial economies in which central importance is assigned to the generation of new knowledge and the storage and transfer of information.

Principal terms

CAPITAL: money or wealth that has been invested in the means of production, including land, factories, and machinery

DEINDUSTRIALIZATION: closing of industrial facilities in one country or region as a result of the movement of capital to other countries or regions or to nonindustrial investments

ECONOMIZING MODE: traditional mode of operation of a corporation in which it seeks to maximize its profit by means of the careful allocation of scarce resources

SOCIAL CLASS: group within society with a specific social status and problems which is recognized as such by members of other classes

SOCIOLOGIZING MODE: effort on the part of a corporation to identify the true needs of society and to derive income from meeting them in a rational way

STRUCTURAL DIFFERENTIATION: notion that as institutions increase in size and in the complexity of the functions that they perform, they necessarily form specialized subsystems with distinct responsibilities

Overview

Industrial societies are a relatively recent development in the history of civilization. Prior to the eighteenth century, the vast majority of human activity in any part of the world was devoted to extracting the necessities of life from nature, at first by hunting and gathering, then by agriculture, mining, and fishing. In preindustrial society, the highest status and political power were associated with the ownership of land. Between the aristocracy of landowners and a lower class of agricultural workers and domestic servants, a rudimentary middle class of merchants and skilled tradesmen existed.

The beginning of industrial society is generally associated with the Industrial Revolution, which is sometimes taken to have begun with the invention of the steam engine at the beginning of the eighteenth century. The steam engine offered an almost limitless source of energy, far in excess of that available from human or animal muscle. Readily available energy made possible the concentration of production in factories and the specialization of labor, which made possible increased productivity. New occupations developed: semiskilled workers who were needed to tend the new machines took their place at the top of the working class, and engineers, the designers and refiners of the means of production, became new members of the middle class. Financing the growth of industry required the development of capitalists, wealthy individuals who could provide the initial funds needed for production machinery. Capitalists could accumulate wealth more quickly than could landowners, who relied on agriculture and thus formed a wealthy upper middle class that was excluded from the aristocracy more by tradition and style of life than by lack of wealth.

In the United States, the principal economic trends between the end of the Civil War and

One consequence of the Industrial Revolution was the concentration of jobs in urban factories, such as this 1890's shoe factory. *(Library of Congress)*

the end of the twentieth century caused a shift of the working population first from agriculture to manufacturing and then from manufacturing to the service sector. The departure of workers from agriculture was a consequence of improved agricultural productivity, resulting from the development of farm machinery, chemical fertilizers, and crop-management techniques. Growth in manufacturing resulted from an influx of workers into urban areas and the exploitation of coal energy and petroleum and hydroelectric power. At the outset of the twentieth century, industrialization received additional stimulus from the development of electric power transmission technology, which allowed energy to be transmitted over long distances, and of the assembly line, a production strategy introduced by Henry Ford, which allowed workers to increase their output by several times.

The demands of military production during World War II brought about the increasing automation of factories, eliminating jobs for many semiskilled workers. As other nations recovered from the war, their production capabilities became comparable with those of the United States, luring investment away from American plants. With improved communication and transportation, resulting in part from computer technology, increasing numbers of corporations turned to globally integrated manufacturing, in which as much of the factory work as possible was done in countries with much lower wages than the United States. The growth of the industrial sector slowed to a point at which economists began to speak of the deindustrialization of the United States. At the same time, the service sector grew quickly enough to absorb most of the increase in the working population. By 1960, more Americans worked in the service sector than in industry and agriculture combined.

For many social analysts, the growth in the service sector, and particularly in the number of teachers, professors, scientists, social scientists, and technical specialists, marked the transition to a postindustrial economy based on the growth of knowledge and new technologies for the storage and transmission of information. In contrast to industrial society, in which trial and error was the principal means of innovation and engineers played a key role in industrial development, in the postindustrial society primacy is given to theoretical knowledge and the elucidation of basic scientific principles as providing the major source of innovation. In the postindustrial society, the key individuals in the production of goods are no longer the capitalists who control the flow of investment, but the expert managers needed to coordinate global production and sales. These experts view themselves as practitioners of a learned profession rather than as competing businessmen, and they exchange information freely with each other and with university scholars and government specialists. They are less driven by the profit motive and more concerned with making a positive contribution to society. The government comes to play an increased role as a stabilizer of the economy, patron of research, and stimulator of innovation.

It is noteworthy that the shifts from an agrarian economy to an industrial economy and from an industrial economy to a postindustrial economy both involved the principal technology of the emerging sector reducing labor requirements. Thus, the farm machinery produced in the early stages of the industrial period and the synthetic fertilizers produced during the latter stages did much to increase the productivity of agriculture, making it possible for an ample food supply to be produced by a very small fraction—less than one-twentieth—of the working population. Likewise, the development of the science of self-regulating systems and electronic computer technology made possible the automation of factories and the globalization of production, which reduced the need for American industrial workers.

Applications

The concept of an emerging postindustrial society is most often associated with Harvard University professor Daniel Bell, who, in a series of essays and in the widely noted *The Coming of the Postindustrial Society* (1973), traced the demographic evidence for the change in American society and examined in some detail the sociology of the growing class of knowledge workers.

The early years of the Industrial Revolution were harsh indeed from the standpoint of the workers. Pay was low, the hours were long, and child labor was common. The German economist and historian Karl Marx, author with Friedrich Engels of *Manifest du Kommunistischen Partei* (1848; *The Communist Manifesto*, 1850), predicted increased class conflict between the proletariat, or industrial working class, and the capitalist class until, by force, the basis for a new and more just society was established. According to Marx, all other social classes would be absorbed into the proletariat as the relentless drive to accumulate capital drove wages even lower. According to Bell, the goal of a more just society will be achieved in the postindustrial society through the activity of a distinct social class—that of scientists and social scientists in government, industry, and the educational establishment.

As late as 1900, farmworkers outnumbered factory workers, and white-collar service occupations accounted for less than one-fifth of the workforce. By 1940, there were twice as many farmworkers as factory workers and more than a third of the work force was in white-collar occupations. By 1968, white-collar and other service workers approached 60 percent of the work force. In that year there were 2,800,000 teachers in the United States, about a million professional engineers, and nearly 500,000 scientists. By 1980, more than 45 percent of the work force in the United States was directly concerned with the generation and transmission of information.

In a sense, the origin of the present-day knowledge industry can be traced to the founding of the first scientific societies and the first published scientific journals in the sixteenth century. As measured by the number of journals, the growth of this social group has been phenomenal throughout the Industrial Revolution and to the present day. By 1800, some one hundred scientific journals had been established; by 1850, one thousand; and by 1900, ten thousand. By 1950, some three hundred periodicals were devoted to the publishing of brief abstracts of the scientific papers to be found in tens of thousands of journals. The astonishing growth of the scientific literature reflects a remarkable process of specialization, itself an excellent illustration of the sociological principle of structural differentiation, which states that as a social institution becomes larger and confronts a more complex task, a specialization of function develops within the institution. As scientific knowledge has grown, the subject matter has been organized into a vast array of specialties and subspecialties so that individual scientists remain able to identify and follow developments that are pertinent to their own work. The integration of scientific and, more generally, academic specialists into government and industry has grown steadily since World War II.

Bell asserts that the increasing importance of knowledge workers—that is, scientists and others who are concerned with basic or theoretical knowledge in the postindustrial economy—implies an expanded role for government in assuring the smooth functioning of society. By the middle of the twentieth century, the U.S. government had already accepted a regulatory role in the economy in the interests of preventing the more extreme effects of the business cycle. The increased role of the government also results from the centrality of theoretical knowledge in the postindustrial society. Because the advances in production and the stable operation of business are tied to the application of fundamental scientific and economic principles, all industries have a stake in the advancement of fundamental knowledge. Corporations will not, however, be willing to invest a substantial amount of resources in the development of new knowledge that will benefit themselves and competitors equally, so they prefer to see public funds devoted to this purpose. The government thus must become the principal patron of research and postgraduate education. Bell further predicted a transition in corporate behavior from an economizing mode, in which the corporation tries to maximize its income, regardless of the consequences, to a sociologizing mode, in which corporations value their contribution to the well-being of society as well as their ability to increase profits, since the scientific and technical workers would have less concern with personal wealth and more concern with seeking to see their knowledge applied to benefit society.

The notion of a postindustrial society has its critics. Many writers have preferred to use the term "information society" instead of the term "postindustrial society" to indicate the importance of the growing group of occupations, from librarian to computer scientist, concerned with the storage and use of information, without implying a deemphasis on manufacturing. Others question that a healthy information society can exist apart from the control of production facilities. The intense global economic competition of the 1980's and 1990's has engendered a new emphasis on production and a concern about the cost-to-benefit ratio of pure scientific research but has not slowed the development of new information technologies.

Context

Colleges were established in colonial America primarily to prepare the sons of landowners to take their places as leaders of society and to guarantee a supply of clergymen adequate to meet the needs of a growing population. The role of education as a potentially productive force in the U.S. economy began to be recognized at the time of the Civil War. In 1861, the Massachusetts Institute of Technology opened; it was the nation's first engineering school. In 1862, Congress passed the Morill Act, granting the income from the sale of a substantial portion of land in each state to create a college for "agriculture and the mechanical arts." Johns Hopkins University, founded in 1876, was the first institution to emphasize the generation of new fundamental knowledge through research and the first to establish graduate programs in individual academic disciplines for scientists and other scholars. The first university-level business school, the Wharton School, opened in 1881.

Before World War II, universities and industry coexisted with relatively little interaction except for the hiring of university graduates by corporations. Those who completed advanced academic work generally became professors or teachers. Industries depended on engineers and individual inventors for innovation, which was often the result of a tedious process of trial and error, as was the case in the invention of the electric light, the telephone, and the phonograph. The war, however, placed demands on industry which led to new modes of interaction between industries, universities, and government. War plants demanded new levels of production that made it necessary to recruit scientists and mathematicians from university faculties as expert consultants. The Manhattan Project, which developed the first atomic bombs, demonstrated the value of theoretical knowledge in a unique way. The government committed vast resources to the project based on the calculations of physicists that such a weapon could be constructed. So little of the actual explosive material required was available that there was no question of developing bombs by trial and error. Instead, the results of a very limited number of experiments had to be combined with fundamental scientific principles to design a bomb that would work the first time. Among subsequent inventions based on advances in scientific theory are those of the transistor, the laser, and the integrated circuit.

At the close of the war, Vannevar Bush, who had been director of the wartime Office of Scientific Research and Development, led a campaign to establish a government agency, the National Science Foundation, to continue government support of basic scientific research. In the influential essay "Science: The Endless Frontier," Bush set forth the rationale for continued support of basic scientific research by the United States government as a source of continuing innovation for industry.

The foundation, established in 1950, quickly established a program of federal grants to universities to support basic research and also provided direct financial support to students doing advanced work in science. The government also established a number of national laboratories, to be operated by universities and industrial firms, intended to support the development of nuclear energy for military and peaceful purposes, while the armed forces developed their own programs of grants to universities to fund basic and applied research with potential military applications. Thus began a pattern of interdependence of industry, government, and universities which vastly increased the number of scientists and engineers who were available to participate in a postindustrial economy.

Bibliography

Bell, Daniel. *The Coming of the Post-Industrial Society: A Venture in Social Forecasting.* New York: Basic Books, 1973. Influential book documenting the shift of American workers from the agricultural and industrial sectors to the service sector, arguing that economic activity in the resulting postindustrial society will be more consciously directed toward the benefit of society as a whole.

Cohen, Stephen S., and John Zysman. *Manufacturing Matters: The Myth of the Post-Industrial Economy.* New York: Basic Books, 1987. Despite their book's subtitle, the authors have little disagreement with Bell about the demographic and economic trends. They do disagree with him, however, about the role of scientists and other knowledge specialists in the economy, and they believe that a stronger manufacturing sector is needed for economic health.

Dordick, Herbert S., and Georgette Wang. *The Information Society: A Retrospective View*. Newbury Park, Calif.: Sage Publications, 1993. Updates the demographic information cited by Bell and attempts to show that progress toward an information-based postindustrial society is occurring on a worldwide basis.

Feigenbaum, Edward, Pamela McCorduck, and H. Penny Nii. *The Rise of the Expert Company*. New York: Vintage Books, 1988. Describes how one aspect of information technology, the "expert system program," is changing the decision-making process in many companies. It provides an interesting illustration of how knowledge can be preserved and marketed as a commodity.

Frenkel, Stephen J. *On the Front Line: Organization of Work in the Information Economy*. Ithaca, N.Y.: ILR Press, 1999.

Donald R. Franceschetti

Cross-References

Capitalism; Horticultural Economic Systems; Hunting and Gathering Economic Systems; Workplace Socialization.

INDUSTRIAL SOCIOLOGY

Type of sociology: Major social institutions
Field of study: The economy

Industrial sociology focuses on the study of people in relation to work—how their viewpoints and actions are shaped by different forms of work organization and cultural patterns. Answers to these questions help to explain the conditions that affect job satisfaction, workplace relationships, and organizational efficiency.

Principal terms

ACTIONS: actual, visible behavior, as distinct from attitudes or feelings

HIERARCHY: organizational system of graded positions, from high to low, that considers such factors as authority, prestige, and income

INCENTIVES: material (such as pay and benefits) and nonmaterial (such as interesting work) rewards for staying with an employer, working harder, or taking more training

MOTIVATION: desire to strive for available incentives; motivation can range from very high to very low

PRODUCTIVITY: amount of goods produced, or services provided, in relation to the work hours used; fewer hours and more production equals higher productivity

RELATIONSHIPS: nature of the ties (which may be trusting or wary, cooperative or hostile) among persons in the same hierarchical level and across levels

WORK ORGANIZATION: organization whose members earn a living by their actions in it, in contrast to voluntary organizations such as social clubs

WORK SATISFACTION: person's overall positive or negative outlook on a specific job and work setting

Overview

The roots of industrial sociology lie in the writings of economist Adam Smith, philosopher Karl Marx, efficiency expert Frederick Taylor, and the industrial researchers Fritz Roethlisberger and William Dickson. Though these analysts' views sometimes clashed, their concerns became the central theme of industrial sociology. Smith's *The Wealth of Nations* (1776) explained that specialized, repetitive tasks in a division of labor sharply increase productivity but that workers' mental health suffers. In *Das Kapital* (1867; *Capital: A Critique of Political Economy*, 1886), Marx noted that people's natural inclination to enjoy work and to do it voluntarily is stifled by the necessity of working for others' profits while following orders. Taylor's *Scientific Management* (1911) emphasized that economic incentives overcome humans' normal preference for working less. In *Management and the Worker* (1939), Roethlisberger and Dickson proposed that employees' attitudes and actions are influenced by the social setting of the workplace; productive workers are the result of membership in friendly work groups and managers who listen to personal and work problems.

A wide range of topics are now found in industrial sociology—for example, occupational mobility, income distribution, gender and race discrimination in workplaces, how people get jobs, the meaning of work, labor unions and labor relations, work and family, work organization in other countries, and historical study of work. While this list offers some idea of the breadth of industrial sociology, there are core issues which persistently hold attention. Repetitive work, for example, may damage psychological well-being, including self-esteem. If this is true, can work be organized differently without causing productivity losses? Perhaps by stimulating a "natural" inclination to work—if indeed there is such a predisposition—work could be structured so that motivation is not tied to material incentives. How important are economic incentives in the motivational picture? How do employees assess their present jobs, and what is meant by a "good" job?

These are questions which much of the research in industrial society investigates. In one form or another, these issues reflect the important puzzles of work life raised by the earlier analysts. Definitive conclusions have eluded researchers.

While all industrial sociologists might not agree, most think that lifelong repetitive work does affect self-esteem in a negative way. The sense of self among workers with repetitive jobs is less favorable than among persons with more challenging tasks. An industrial hierarchy allocates many rewards at various levels, among which are judgments of worth that affect workers' own beliefs. Unskilled or semiskilled workers can be trained to do enriched (more complicated) tasks, but—especially for small firms—training costs often look very high to employers, and the productivity gains may not seem sufficient to be worth the investment. The issue of incentives is closely linked to what most people mean by a "good" job. Generally, good jobs provide more advantages by offering larger amounts of a variety of rewards (ranging from pay and vacations to interesting work). Put another way, higher positions in the hierarchies of the work world are attractive for three reasons: They confer a measure of social importance, offer less routinized work, and provide financial rewards (and therefore, security). Sociologists debate what would happen if work were voluntary and not required for survival, but most doubt that humans are born with an urge to work.

Closely related to these questions is the issue of job satisfaction, the single most researched topic by industrial sociologists. Thousands of studies have been devoted to it. A large share (two-thirds or so) of employed men and women, it turns out, are either very satisfied or somewhat satisfied by their jobs. In *The State of the Masses* (1986), sociologists Richard Hamilton and James Wright reviewed numerous surveys conducted over many years. They point out that when respondents do register their dissatisfaction, most frequently it involves economic factors such as fears of unemployment or losing income to inflation. Moreover, while high overall, satisfaction is lower among younger (under thirty years old) workers and among black employees. Researchers have also examined the association between work attitudes and actions. A persistent and important finding is that job satisfaction and job behavior are only weakly related or even not related at all. Nevertheless, two behaviors—being absent from one's job or looking for another—are consistently associated with dissatisfaction.

Because of the increased entry of other nations' goods into the United States market and the importance of exports for the U.S. economy, in the 1980's industrial sociologists began to take a closer look at foreign companies' practices. They wondered whether there were methods that Americans could learn in order to improve quality and productivity. Japanese firms gained attention for their widespread and successful use of quality circles (QCs), small groups of production workers that meet for about an hour weekly. On the basis of their hands-on experience and investigation of a problem, detailed suggestions are offered by QCs for improving quality and productivity in their own work area.

As noted by sociologist Robert Cole in *Strategies for Learning* (1989), Japanese companies formed QCs in the mid-1950's and greatly benefited. This inspired a growing number of U.S. companies to install similar groups, sometimes called "workers' participation" programs or "employee involvement groups." Other industrial sociologists compared Japanese and U.S. employees. In *Culture, Control, and Commitment* (1990), James Lincoln and Arne Kalleberg found that work satisfaction was higher among U.S. workers, as was commitment to the organization. Yet Japan's high product quality and productivity is impressive, so Lincoln and Kalleberg concluded that attitudes and actions are separate facets of work life. These sorts of studies examine the basic questions of work, though from a global perspective in keeping with the contemporary economic interdependence of the United States with other nations' economies.

Applications

The research findings of industrial sociology have various applications. They are used in the education of managers, for example, especially in gaining the MBA (master of business administration) degree, in on-site research or consulting focused on business problems, and in the education of sociology and other undergraduate and graduate students regarding work matters.

Industrial sociology has made a major contribution to the education of MBA students. As future managers, their understanding of the human dimension in the workplace is an important educational matter. This has been aided by integrating industrial sociologists' research and ideas into business education. To illustrate, Rosabeth Kanter's *Men and Women of the Corporation* (1977) is a widely read analysis of women's difficulties in gaining acceptance and advancement in the male-dominated business world. Kanter argues that without government intervention, neither women nor other minorities will make much headway in increasing their proportions of executive posts beyond a token representation. Robert Jackall's *Moral Mazes* (1988) is often assigned reading. His study of managers reveals in detail how the pressures of daily business decisions can lead to expedient solutions while deflecting moral judgments. An employee's goal of trying to please the boss, Jackall reports, has the potential to stimulate ethically dubious actions. David Halle, in *America's Working Man* (1984), demonstrates in his case study of a chemical plant that workers may keep cost-cutting and time-saving steps in the production process a secret. This gives them extra time to relax and prevents others, above them in the hierarchy, from using that information to demand more production. These are only a few examples of the types of sociological research that contribute to MBA programs and thus challenge future managers to consider solutions to these serious issues.

Researching and consulting are closely allied, since many problems require close analysis before advice can be offered. Kanter illustrates this role of industrial sociology. Kanter's _The Change Masters_ (1983) explains why firms have difficulties in changing their ways of doing things and offers ways to overcome the difficulties. The cases explored in this book were researched by Kanter, and the firms discussed in it sought her counsel. Her advice revolves around the idea that rigid hierarchies obstruct problem solving by delaying decisions, inhibiting information about problems from reaching top levels of the hierarchy, and not tapping information that is available at lower levels of the organization. Both the pace and quality of decisions can be improved by, as much as possible, sending decisions to be made down to those persons most directly involved with a problem—in short, by integrating employees into decision-making processes. William Ouchi studied Japanese companies and then wrote _Theory Z_ (1981). It summarizes the core of his advice as a highly respected consultant to U.S. companies. Japanese companies, he comments, create a climate in which everyone has a sense of belonging. Members trust the company to look out for its employees' interests, and the company trusts the employees to do their best for the firm. While mutual trust and loyalty take time to develop, they pay off for companies as well as employees. Ouchi recommends that U.S. firms also take this road.

Most industrial sociologists are employed by universities and colleges as teachers of undergraduate or graduate students. The theories and findings of this area of sociology are thus passed on to students who will have the opportunity to apply in their jobs what was learned in the classroom. Here, too, an internationalist, as well as historical, outlook is encouraged. For example, a portion of a course in industrial sociology might examine a number of large-scale comparative work organization issues. Topics could include discussing the types of economic systems that are most productive and provide the most job security. When and why labor unions were formed, and the conditions that strengthen and weaken unions, could also be examined. Knowledge of these sorts of materials provides a larger context for understanding current work issues. Sensitizing students to workplace issues, providing new perspectives from which to view problems, offering methods of empirical investigation, and indicating findings to date are major tasks for industrial sociologists.

Context

Industrial sociology began to emerge as a distinct subfield of sociology in the late 1930's. For a decade, economic depression had hit the United States, pushing unemployment up and pulling companies' earnings down. Not surprisingly, productivity was a concern. Roethlisberger and Dickson's research, published in _Management and the Worker_, was aimed at ways to increase productivity. Others had attempted this earlier, with emphasis on the economic factors of base pay, piece rates, and job security. The data reported by Roethlisberger and Dickson, however, created new possibilities. They placed the social elements of work organization at the center of attention: norms, values, sentiments, listening, talking, groups, and methods of supervision all became important. This fresh approach attracted sociologists, stimulating them to extend industrial research and theory. The subfield of industrial sociology was beginning to surface.

By the 1950's there were university courses called "industrial sociology." Industrial sociology was also sharing parts of its focus on work with several other academic specialties: another subfield of sociology that studies complex organizations, industrial psychology, an area termed "organizational behavior" in business schools, and "labor studies" courses in industrial relations departments. Industrial sociologists themselves held opposing views of such work issues as the conditions that lead to higher productivity. The target of industrial sociology has expanded, from concern with production industries to any sort of work, including service providers and government organizations. Industrial sociology had become comprehensive, with ample room for diverse research and many different perspectives.

Bibliography

Applebaum, Herbert. *The Concept of Work: Ancient, Medieval, and Modern*. Albany: State University of New York Press, 1992. Describes clearly what people at various points in time thought about work and what they actually did. Applebaum takes the reader from Greece and ancient Rome to the Middle Ages and then into modern times, in each instance providing historical background. Focuses on Europe and the United States.

Erikson, Kai, and Steven Vallas, eds. *The Nature of Work: Sociological Perspectives*. New Haven, Conn.: Yale University Press, 1990. Collection of the research and views of leading analysts of work. The essays deal with such topics as alienation from work, labor in concentration camps, how work affects personality, and the size and uses of the "irregular economy" (cash transactions for legal or illegal services or products to avoid taxes or arrest). Broad-ranging and very readable.

Frenkel, Stephen J. *On the Front Line: Organization of Work in the Information Economy*. Ithaca, N.Y.: ILR Press, 1999.

Gillespie, Richard. *Manufacturing Knowledge: A History of the Hawthorne Experiments*. New York: Cambridge University Press, 1991. Account of famous social science experiments intended to explain what motivates employees to work harder. Though the findings were long accepted in sociology, their validity has become controversial; Gillespie describes the debates. Absorbing and thought-provoking book that is exceptionally well written.

Halle, David. *America's Working Man*. Chicago: University of Chicago Press, 1984. Describes how chemical plant workers protected their jobs by letting management know that only experienced workers could actually keep the plant running, since the formal written procedures were incomplete. Halle reports what really goes on, and why, when labor and management are suspicious of each other.

Hodson, Randy, and Teresa A. Sullivan. *The Social Organization of Work*. 2d ed. Belmont, Calif.: Wadsworth, 1995. Good introduction to industrial sociology. Topics covered include methods of analysis, work and family, job satisfaction, labor unions, work in manufacturing and in services, work at different levels of hierarchies, and consequences of the global economy.

Juravich, Tom. *Chaos on the Shop Floor*. Philadelphia: Temple University Press, 1985. The data for this study of a factory are Juravich's experiences while working there. Through his observations, one learns of the rigid hierarchy that governs production. Even when equipment or materials are faulty, a situation which is quickly obvious to the workers, no one higher up listens. This nicely crafted book indicates that production would benefit from listening to workers.

Wardell, Mark, Thomas L. Steiger, and Peter Meiksins, eds. *Rethinking the Labor Process*. Albany: State University of New York Press, 1999.

Womack, James P., Daniel T. Jones, and Daniel Roos. *The Machine That Changed the World*. New York: Rawson Associates, 1990. Major worldwide study of the automobile industry explaining how faster methods for designing cars, fewer workers needed to build them, and speedier and more quality-driven production have changed the nature of this industry, which serves as a model for other sectors of the U.S. and other economies. The authors present their findings and projections in clear language.

Curt Tausky

Cross-References

Capitalism; Industrial and Postindustrial Economies; Protestant Ethic and Capitalism; Workplace Socialization.

KNOWLEDGE

Type of sociology: Origins and definitions of sociology
Field of study: Sociological perspectives and principles

Sociology of knowledge is the field of sociological theory that studies how human knowledge—especially knowledge used in everyday life—is created and maintained in the course of social life. The field seeks to explain how a society organizes its culture into certain categories and passes them from one generation to the next.

Principal terms

INSTITUTIONALIZATION: process by which people develop habitual patterns of behavior and categories of thought that make social relations orderly and predictable

LEGITIMATION: justification or explanation created by members of the social group to maintain the habitual patterns and categories that have been reified in their society

LIFE-WORLD: world of daily life along with the corresponding knowledge needed to exist in it; a world and knowledge shared by members of a society or social group

REIFICATION: process by which habitual patterns of behavior and categories of thought are apprehended by members of society as if being external to them and having a life of their own

SOCIAL CONSTRUCTION: ability of human groups to create and maintain the knowledge in their cultural heritage

TYPIFICATION: shared idea about a relationship or a category that focuses on its generic characteristics

Overview

Sociology of knowledge is the field of sociological theory concerned with the social construction and maintenance of everyday knowledge. To sociologists of knowledge, the world that is shared by all members of a group, the life-world, is filled with routines that determine how those individuals perceive and categorize things and relations around them. The life-world is a human construction; it is created by the group yet it acts upon the group as if it has a "life of its own."

According to sociologists of knowledge, the physical world, the empirical reality, is related to but distinct from the social world, the life-world. Whereas reality in the empirical world consists of relationships between variables which lead to natural consequences (for example, the physical process leading to rain), the social world apprehends that reality through the meanings and interpretations that the social group adds to it (a group may deem rain to be the result of God's will, an imbalance in the bow of the heavens, or a blessing from mother earth).

Sociologists of knowledge are interested in documenting how the influence of social location or social context affects the way groups perceive reality and build their knowledge of everyday life. To these scholars, external events cannot be completely explained by the ideas of any group because that group always perceives those events through the eyes of its collective tendencies and habits. In adapting to a certain environment, the group develops categories of thought and habitual patterns of behavior that delimit the way it further relates to the empirical world. People are not generally aware that they construct the social world in which they live. They tend to take the world "out there" for granted. Because knowledge of it is transmitted from one generation to the next, the life-world seems to have a life of its own. Its components seem prearranged, standing on their own, independent of "observers."

Sociologists of knowledge, however, argue that the reality that human beings encounter is always influenced and guided by their social location or context. In order to survive and adapt to their environment, humans create both material and ideal products: technologies to deal with the acquisition of food and shelter, laws to regulate disputes, and values to instill a sense of group solidarity. Those patterns of behavior and categories of thought are institutionalized, thereby becoming the way of life of a group. They are typifications—recipes for dealing with life situations such as being a spouse, buying a television, taking a test, and so on.

Once institutionalization takes place, the categories and patterns of behavior become expected and therefore seem to "act upon" the individual members of the group. The typifications seem to acquire an external force. To be able to live in social groups, individuals adopt this shared world of knowledge and pass it on from one generation to the next. That is the process known to sociologists of knowledge as reification—the process by which the cultural creations of a group are perceived by the group as a part of the overall reality, as "the way things are." To maintain reification, groups create systems of ideas that justify or legitimate "the way things are."

In the life-world, the stock of available knowledge provides the means to interpret the past and present and to help determine the shape of things to come. Thus, middle-class individuals may be socialized into a lifestyle of tastes quite different from those of upper-class people, members of a certain ethnic group may perceive reality in terms that are quite different from those of another ethnic group, and Protestants may celebrate a different set of life events from the ones celebrated by Hindus or Muslims.

Sociology of knowledge was brought to the English-speaking world by Karl Mannheim and Alfred Schutz. Mannheim developed his work in England; Schutz lived in the United States. Given the spread of Marxism in Europe after World War II, Mannheim's work centered on the function of ideology in society. His work redefined ideology as not simply the collective thought of an opposing group (as when the British pointed to German war propaganda as ideology while ignoring their own propaganda or calling it something else), but as the whole of any group's collective thought. Mannheim suggested that all human thought is socially located and therefore influenced by social context. He also argued, however, that certain groups are more capable of transcending their own narrow position than others are. According to him, in the process of interacting with other groups, a group may change and alter its ideological stand to better manage the compromises, coalitions, and conflicts that arise in everyday life.

Mannheim's work was heavy with political preoccupation as a result of the conditions under which the author was writing. It was only with the work of Alfred Schutz that sociology of knowledge lost its political edge and became a field involving the study of everyday life. Born in Vienna, Schutz immigrated to the United States in 1938. He joined the faculty of the New School for Social Research. Free from the political struggles in Europe, Schutz was able to dedicate his sociological analysis to the study of everyday life. Perhaps his most important contribution to sociology of knowledge was the change in the focus of the field. To him the task was no longer the debunking of political discourse but the study of modern life in general. Schutz introduced sociology of knowledge to American sociologists in the book *The Phenomenology of the Social World* (1967). He argued that the world of daily life (the life-world) is not private, but intersubjective. In this shared world there is a stock of knowledge passed from one generation to the next that provides individuals with parameters to guide their lives and to fit in society. The life-world is composed of typifications that are partly shared by individuals, depending on the groups to which they belong in a given society. To Schutz, only a small part of an individual's knowledge is derived from personal experience. Much of what people use in everyday life comes from assimilating the typifications accepted by their groups. The less one knows of a situation, the more likely one is to use the generalizations shared by one's group to categorize it.

In the work of two of Schutz's students, Peter L. Berger and Thomas Luckmann, sociology of knowledge gained its most mainstream presentation in American sociology. Quite familiar with the current American sociological schools of thought of their time, Berger and Luckmann used Schutz's ideas and a blend of Durkheimian, Weberian, and Marxian synthesis to expand the focus of the field to the study of modern society at large. Their book, *The Social Construction of Reality* (1966), discusses modern society as objective and subjective reality. In other words, they explain how categories of thought and habitual patterns of behavior are constructed by members of society and then gain a life of their own, acting upon and restricting the lives of their creators. It was through Berger and Luckmann's book that the discussions of institutionalization, reification, and legitimation were brought into mainstream sociology in the United States.

Applications

The insight that knowledge is always determined by the social context has helped sociologists to be better equipped to study social life without assuming that all individuals are free and disinterested in apprehending reality. One application of such knowledge comes in the realm of politics. For example, conditions that may be tolerable for the group in power may be intolerable for those being oppressed. For example, Martin Luther King, Jr., wrote a letter from his jail cell in Birmingham, Alabama, explaining to the white clergy of the town why the black leadership could not wait for "gradual" reforms. To the white ministers, who had not experienced prejudice and discrimination, the Christian duty was to "render unto Caesar" and wait for slow change. To the black ministers, who, along with their congregations, suffered harsh discrimination, the Christian call was to fight injustice to bring about drastic change.

James Montgomery Flagg, the creator of "Uncle Sam," perhaps the most enduring propaganda image of the twentieth century. *(National Archives)*

The determination of knowledge by context is also outlined by sociologist Karl Mannheim in his book *Ideology and Utopia* (1936). Written on the eve of World War II, the book documents how the vested interests of different political groups—liberals, conservatives, and radicals—make it difficult for them to agree on a common definition as to the causes of any social problem, to develop a common strategy on how to solve it, or to share similar motivations for addressing the problem. Furthermore, Mannheim shows that the group in power at any given time tends to sustain the status quo and determines what is and is not politically feasible.

Mannheim argues that all points of view in politics are partial, because historical totality (the whole of the life-world) is always too comprehensive to be grasped. Since the points of view of liberals, conservatives, and radicals emerge from the same general social context, and since their partial views represent slices of the whole picture, understanding the totality of politics means seeking a synthesis—finding different ingredients from all three points of view that will produce a balanced, relatively realistic view of the whole. In other words, since in practice various groups will always highlight or emphasize certain truths at the expense of others, it is left to the body of professionals who analyze opinion-making (those in academia or the news media, for example) to help the population see the truth amidst the propaganda.

Another application of the sociology of knowledge is seen in a book discussing Third World development, Peter L. Berger's *Pyramids of Sacrifice* (1976). Sociology of knowledge is used by Berger to demonstrate how the major economic models used to bring development to Third World countries (capitalism and socialism) exact a steep price from those nations without delivering on their promises. This occurs because the models are created by cliques of politicians and intellectuals who are likely to ignore the insights of local meanings, knowledge, and context. Failing to take into account local everyday knowledge, capitalism and socialism both demand that Third World nations sacrifice for the promises of a more equitable and safe future that never seems to arrive. Berger suggests that any policy directed toward development needs to take into account local knowledge to be successful.

Berger uses the examples of Brazil and China to show how both models (capitalist and socialist) are willing to sacrifice one or more generations for the sake of creating a developed nation. The problem is that both sets of sacrifices are justified by the imported theories; they structure life in such a fashion that both Brazilian and Chinese populations act as if such definitions were the only true possibility and had a life of their own in determining the steps needed for economic development.

Insights from the sociology of knowledge are also applied to the study of religion. Sociologists of knowledge study religion as both a social product and a contributor to the maintenance of everyday knowledge. In the book *The Sacred Canopy* (1967), Berger argues that human beings create religion by projecting certain characteristics cherished by their group onto the gods they worship. Those characteristics give the gods a feeling of familiarity that makes them appear as if they have a life of their own. Once the religious community accepts the gods as having a life of their own (existing independently from the group), it comes to believe that the gods are capable of establishing the kind of behavior that is acceptable or unacceptable among individuals in the religious community. Berger discusses how, after reification, the religious beliefs of a religious community legitimate the way of life of its individual members and reinforce their shared image of the gods.

Context

As a field of sociological theory, sociology of knowledge is a product of European scholars, specifically of the German academic world of the 1920's. During the period between the two world wars, there was a dramatic rise in radical politics in Germany. Fascists and communists fought for the heart and soul of the country. Ideological pamphleteering, rhetoric, and propaganda escalated on both sides. For German scholars of the period, the question of ascertaining the truth and clarifying the amount of distortion in the claims of political fashions was more than theoretical speculation.

Sociology of knowledge was heavily influenced by the work of historian Wilhelm Dilthey. Dilthey argued that social truth is always situational, that the way one looks at human events is relative because it depends on one's social location. Living in Germany during its surge of ideological nationalism, Dilthey believed that certain ideas have the upper hand on reality because of the social forces that validate them in the eyes of the social group in a given historical period.

Max Scheler, a sociologist at the University of Cologne and one of Dilthey's students, was responsible for the application of Dilthey's historical approach to sociological analysis. Following Dilthey's insights, Scheler created a sociological field that he called *Wissenssoziologie* ("sociology of knowledge"). To separate fact from fiction, reality from political propaganda, Scheler claimed that the two realms—the realm of the ideal and the realm of the real—exist in parallel but are not totally identified. In the end, empirical reality regulates the conditions for the appearance of certain ideas and ideologies in history. In his opinion, it was sociology of knowledge's basic task to isolate and identify the connection between the "real" and the "ideal."

Scheler claimed that external events are not the unfolding of ideologies in the real world (such a claim would be made by the Nazi Party later on, arguing that its platform was the fulfillment of Germany's manifest destiny). Rather, he said, ideologies have a greater or lesser chance of unfolding in the presence of certain external events. Scheler also called attention to the power of ideology in everyday life by showing how, because it precedes the individual, human knowledge (be it in the form of values, ideas, or ideologies) it appears to be the natural way of looking at the world. The creation in Germany of the Nazi youth corps and the commitment of its participants to the Nazi Party confirmed Scheler's theoretical insight.

Bibliography

Berger, Peter L. *Pyramids of Sacrifice*. Garden City, N.Y.: Doubleday, 1976. Applies concepts from sociology of knowledge to the study of politics and social change, specifically to their relationship to Third World development. He compares the promises of the two main economic models—capitalism and socialism—and views their results, respectively, in Brazil and China.

_____. *The Sacred Canopy: Elements of a Sociological Theory of Religion*. Garden City, N.Y.: Doubleday, 1967. Applies the insights from sociology of knowledge to the study of religion in modern life. The book addresses specifically the problem of maintenance of religious beliefs in a society in which religion no longer seems to have a central role.

Berger, Peter L., and Thomas Luckmann. *The Social Construction of Reality*. New York: Doubleday, 1967. Expands on Alfred Schutz's work, bringing sociology of knowledge into the study of modern society in general. The book discusses the processes of institutionalization, reification, and legitimation as well as their functions in modern society.

Mannheim, Karl. *Ideology and Utopia.* New York: Harvest/HBJ, 1936. First work in sociology of knowledge published in English. Although a political study, the book contains many of the field's sociological insights. The last chapter is Mannheim's own description of sociology of knowledge as a field of study.

Meja, Volker, and Nico Stehr, eds. *The Sociology of Knowledge.* Northhampton, Mass.: E. Elgar, 1999.

Schutz, Alfred. *The Phenomenology of the Social World.* Evanston, Ill.: Northwestern University Press, 1967. Major work in the field of sociology of knowledge. Contains the seeds of all the major concepts and insights developed later by others.

H. B. Cavalcanti

Cross-References

Education; Ethnomethodology; History of Sociology; Microsociology; Religion; Sociology Defined; Values and Value Systems.

LABELING AND DEVIANCE

Type of sociology: Deviance and social control
Field of study: Theories of deviance

According to labeling theory, deviance is defined by society when a generally accepted rule or custom is violated. Thus, the term "deviance" represents a value judgment that is applied to individuals who do not conform to a social norm. Such labels generally carry negative and lasting connotations that may profoundly influence persons to whom they are applied.

Principal terms

DEVIANCE: in labeling theory, this term refers to a value judgment by society for behavior that violates social rules or expectations

RULE-BREAKING: violation of a social rule, whether it is an explicit or implicit rule

SOCIAL CONTROL: all practices and forces that are designed to maintain social order and conformity within society

SOCIAL NORMS: rules and expectations for acceptable behavior within society

SOCIAL REACTION: another term for labeling; it stresses the view that deviance is more of an "audience effect" than a characteristic of the offender

STIGMA: intense social disapproval and alienation that follow the assignment of deviant status

Overview

Labeling theory explains deviance in terms of a violation of social norms or rules that is followed by social disapproval and sanctions. In this view, particular acts themselves are not deviant; rather, acts become deviant when society declares them unacceptable. Thus, deviance is in the eyes of the beholder. Deviance is a social value judgment that is passed upon those individuals who do not conform to social norms.

The labeling theory of deviance is based on two assumptions. First, for someone to be called "deviant," that person must have broken a rule. Rules generally refer to the social norms and expectations for acceptable behavior. These rules, or norms, may be explicitly formulated, as in the case of laws and regulations. Many social rules, however, are implicit, since they are not clearly articulated. Norms about interpersonal behavior, such as facing a person to whom one is speaking and maintaining fairly consistent eye contact, are examples of implicit rules in society. Rule-breaking per se is not sufficient for defining deviance according to the theory. If the rule violation is undetected, then no label will be assigned to the violator, and therefore he or she will not qualify as deviant. For example, an individual who cheats on income taxes will not be declared a criminal if the fraud is not detected. The second component of the labeling theory of deviance focuses on the reaction of society to the rule-breaking. If a social norm violation is noticed, it becomes defined as deviance (the perpetrator is labeled "deviant"), and this label leads to social disapproval and a host of other negative consequences. This emphasis on the negative social reactions to norm violations is reflected in the other term used in reference to the labeling theory of deviance: social reaction theory.

The basic premises of labeling theory were clearly articulated by sociologist Howard S. Becker in his influential book *Outsiders: Studies in the Sociology of Deviance* (1963):

> Social groups create deviance by making the rules whose infraction constitutes deviance, and by applying those rules to particular people and labeling them as outsiders . . . deviance is not a quality of the act the person commits, but rather a consequence of the application by others of rules and sanctions to an "offender." The deviant is one to whom that label has successfully been applied; deviant behavior is behavior that people so label.

In their original formulations, labeling theorists stressed that deviants do not form an identifiable homogeneous group; instead, deviants are simply individuals who have been publicly labeled as having violated social conventions and subjected to various forms of reprimand. A multitude of labels exist in society to categorize specific types of norm violations: "Criminality" is used for behavior that violates laws, "perversion" is assigned to behavior that does not conform to norms for sexual behavior, and "drunkenness" applies to alcohol usage that society considers excessive. Labels also exist for violations of minor social norms, such as "obnoxious," "crude," and "ignorant."

The ultimate purpose of labeling individuals as deviant is social control or pressure to conform to the norm (pressure to become "normal"). The social control function begins with the assignment of an undesirable label which is associated with social disapproval and stigma. For some forms of deviance, more intrusive social interventions are employed, such as incarceration or hospitalization. Sociologist Thomas J. Scheff provides illustrations of these ideas in his book *Being Mentally Ill: A Sociological Theory* (1984). According to Scheff, a minor norm violation may result in the person being labeled "odd," but more serious violations or a recurrent pattern may lead to a diagnosis of "mental illness." Once this label is used, society reacts to the "deviant" based on traditional stereotypes of mental illness or insanity. As Scheff notes, a label and its associated stigma are very resistant to change; the terms "mental patient" and "former mental patient" both carry negative and lasting connotations in society.

Labels may exert effects on those to whom they are assigned. A person assigned a particular label may accept and enact the assigned role. A person declared "crazy" may ultimately act crazy because it is expected; the label becomes a self-fulfilling prophecy. The initial rule violation has been called primary deviance; secondary deviance occurs when the deviant label is accepted by the "offender" and becomes incorporated into the individual's self-concept and social identity. In this view, secondary deviance represents the deviant accepting, enacting, and fulfilling the assigned label.

In sum, a person who violates social norms tends to be viewed as "deviant" and is subjected to subtle or overt pressure to conform. If the person resists the pressure and demands of society, stigmatization and social alienation generally follow. Finally, some of the labeled individuals enact a deviant role, leading to a deviant career and to more long-term social condemnation and stereotyping.

Applications

Labeling theory has been applied to a variety of social problems, including crime, mental illness, physical disabilities, drug abuse, and racial prejudice. The theory has been particularly influential in challenging many accepted views of mental illness. Scheff noted that classifying behavior as abnormal can only occur within the context of the standards of a particular society. In his view, cultural relativism applies to mental illness: What is normal in one culture may be abnormal in another. Presumed signs or symptoms of mental illness are just as easily described as normal behavior depending on the setting, persistence of the behavior, existing stereotypes, and—most important—the presence of observers. An individual's behavior is more likely to be explained as mental illness if it violates some norm, is persistent, matches existing cultural stereotypes of insanity, and is observed by others. This is particularly true if the audience is composed of persons who accept the concept of mental illness. Scheff sought to develop, in his own words, "a theory of mental disorder in which psychiatric symptoms are considered to be labeled violations of social norms and stable 'mental illness' to be a social role."

A dramatic illustration of these principles was provided by psychologist David Rosenhan. Rosenhan and several colleagues presented themselves for admission at different psychiatric hospitals in the United States. All participants masked their true identities and initially complained of hearing voices, but otherwise they exhibited no signs of distress. Once hospitalized, the "pseudopatients" behaved cooperatively and normally, never referring again to the voices. In every instance, the pseudopatients were labeled mentally ill, typically schizophrenic. The deception was never discovered by the mental health professionals or staff. (Ironically, the only people who expressed suspicion were the "real" patients.) Rosenhan and colleagues were kept in hospitals for an average of nineteen days before being discharged. During their hospital stays, even the most innocuous behavior displayed by the participants was commonly interpreted as pathological by hospital staff (boredom, for example, was reported by staff as "anxiety"). When finally discharged, the pseudopatients were usually described as "improved," with the implication that they still suffered from mental illness.

Labels are very resistant to change. Once a person has been diagnosed as mentally ill, he or she will frequently be subjected to a lifetime of social alienation. The stigma of mental illness is powerful and lasting, as evidenced by associated prejudice and discrimination in employment, social status, and general relationships. Aspiring politicians have lost or had to withdraw from elections when it was discovered that they had previously received treatment for psychiatric problems. Once a person has been labeled mentally ill, he or she may be subtly rewarded for playing the part and punished for attempting to return to a conventional role in society.

Results such as those of Rosenhan and others have been used to criticize accepted concepts of mental illness. The antipsychiatry movement was born because of opposition to the negative consequences of psychiatric labels. Even prominent psychiatrists, such as Thomas Szasz, have ardently criticized existing views of mental illness. According to Szasz, what is referred to as mental illness could more accurately be called "problems in living." According to him, the notion of mental illness should be abandoned, since it is a myth. The term "mental illness" is simply used to describe the behavior of those considered to be different. Consistent with basic principles of labeling theory, Szasz argued that the concept of mental illness is merely an effort to persuade nonconforming individuals to modify their behavior and beliefs in a socially desirable direction, another illustration of social control.

Although these criticisms have influenced terminology and practices in psychiatry, they have not revolutionized the field. Positive influences have included the abandonment of some stigmatizing terms (such as "moron" and "idiot," which were formerly official terms to describe mental retardation), systematic efforts to increase the reliability of psychiatric diagnoses, and legislation to prevent discrimination against individuals purely on the basis of their having received a label of mental illness. Proponents of psychiatric diagnoses have also pointed to possible flaws in Rosenhan's study. One criticism is that psychiatrists would naturally assume that someone seeking admission to a psychiatric hospital suffers from mental illness. After all, with the exception of Rosenhan and colleagues, well-adjusted individuals do not seek psychiatric treatment or complain of hearing voices.

Critics of the labeling perspective on mental illness also note that some behaviors, such as murder and suicide, are virtually universally recognized as deviant or abnormal. Proponents of the psychiatric model have argued that psychiatric problems exist independently of labels and cultural definitions. For example, a person could be instructed to fake a medical illness, such as migraine headache, and could ultimately receive a diagnosis of and treatment for the condition. This does not prove, however, that migraine headaches do not actually exist and that physicians fabricate stigmatizing labels. Finally, being labeled mentally ill does not inevitably lead to negative consequences. Some patients benefit from treatment and lead productive lives in spite of having previously received a particular psychiatric label.

Context

Labeling theory represents one of the major theories of deviance in sociology. One of the original theories of deviance was offered by Émile Durkheim, who was concerned with the function that deviance serves in a society. According to Durkheim, deviance occurs in all societies and serves several positive purposes. Deviance helps consolidate cultural values and social norms. Identifying and punishing violations of laws and social norms emphasizes what is acceptable and "normal." In this way, violations increase solidarity and cohesion in society by drawing attention to deviant behavior and its consequences. Societal responses to deviance foster unity and conformity. Deviance may also serve as a catalyst for social change; when a large number of people violate a particular norm, society at large may be forced to reconsider and modify that norm.

Another major theory of deviance is the conflict perspective. Two basic components of this theory are social inequality and relative power. Social norms and laws are formulated by the powerful elements of society, generally the wealthy upper socioeconomic class.

These norms and laws are designed to maintain the status quo, and anyone who challenges or violates the norms will be branded a "deviant." Social inequality is manifested in the fact that powerless groups, the lower socioeconomic class and minorities, are more likely to be classified as "deviant." For the same violation, a powerless person is more likely to be considered deviant than a powerful person. Therefore, according to conflict theory, the inequality in wealth and power in society shapes norms and laws to maintain the power structure. The powerless and those who threaten the system are stigmatized to maintain this uneven balance.

Labeling theory was a leading influence in the study of deviance in the 1970's and remained the conventional wisdom for nearly a decade. Although it has lost much of its preeminent status in sociology, few other theories have received the wide acceptance labeling theory once had. It is widely recognized that definitions of abnormality or deviance vary considerably across cultures. Further, the potentially damaging nature of labels is better understood. The study of mental illness has greatly benefited from labeling theory. Most comprehensive discussions of diagnosis and psychiatric labels include cautionary discussions about the dangers of labeling.

It seems unlikely that any single sociological theory of deviance will explain the diversity of phenomena that "deviance" comprises. The theories are complementary, however, in that they account for different aspects of the phenomena in question. The unique contribution of labeling theory is its focus on social value judgements and on how these may exacerbate existing problems.

Bibliography

Becker, Howard S. *Outsiders: Studies in the Sociology of Deviance*. New York: Free Press, 1963. Classic presentation of the labeling theory of deviance. Applies labeling theory to several nonconforming practices, including marijuana smoking.

Goode, Erich. *Deviant Behavior*. 5th ed. Englewood Cliffs, N.J.: Prentice-Hall, 1997. Introductory text on the sociology of deviance, summarizing theories of deviance and applying them to drug use, sexual deviations and variations, criminal behavior, and mental illness.

Macionis, John J. *Sociology*. 3d ed. Englewood Cliffs, N.J.: Prentice-Hall, 1991. Popular introductory text that offers an overview of the foundations of sociology, deviance, social life, social inequality, social institutions, and social change.

Robertson, Ian. *Sociology*. 3d ed. New York: Worth, 1987. Popular introduction to the field of sociology. Theories of deviance and applications are summarized in several contexts.

Scheff, Thomas J. *Being Mentally Ill: A Sociological Theory*. 2d ed. New York: Aldine, 1984. Standard labeling theory text in which the principles are applied to mental illness. Scheff presents the theory in nine propositions and reviews relevant research findings.

Schur, Edwin M. *Labeling Women Deviant: Gender, Stigma, and Social Control*. Philadelphia: Temple University Press, 1983. Gender issues are discussed in the context of labeling theory. The author notes cultural stereotypes and their detrimental effects on women in a male-dominated culture.

Szasz, Thomas. *The Myth of Mental Illness*. Rev. ed. New York: Harper & Row, 1974. Psychiatrist's controversial but influential book on the use of mental illness labels to promote conformity in society. Applies author's views to the practice of psychotherapy, which he describes as a secular religion.

Richard D. McAnulty

Cross-References

Cultural Norms and Sanctions; Cultural Transmission Theory of Deviance; Deviance: Analysis and Overview; Deviance: Functions and Dysfunctions; Structural-Strain Theory of Deviance.

LEGITIMACY AND AUTHORITY

Type of sociology: Major social institutions
Field of study: Politics and the state

Authority is the legitimate use of power. Authority and legitimacy depend on societal norms, values, and beliefs. For this reason, ruling elites always try to influence mass beliefs and values in order to maintain the legitimacy of the institutions they control and thus reinforce their authority.

Principal terms

AUTHORITY: power that is exercised legitimately
BELIEFS: shared ideas about what is true
LEGITIMACY: belief that some particular use of power is right or proper
NORMS: shared rules and expectations about behavior
POWER: ability to control or influence the acts of others
SANCTIONS: rewards and punishments for conforming to or violating norms
VALUES: shared ideas about what is good and desirable

Overview

Although scholars frequently relate the concept of authority to the phenomenon of government, the concept appears in all associations and not merely in governmental circles. Every association in a society has its own structure of authority. Organization creates authority. Where there is no organization, there is usually no authority, and vice versa. Similarly, the idea of legitimacy has always had a particular association with the state. In this case too, however, the notion has been extended to the study of leadership, hierarchy, and management in social units of all kinds, especially organizations. Sentiments of legitimacy arise even in social situations in which ties are intimately affective and dependency is great (as in the relationships of children and parents).

According to the renowned sociologist Max Weber, authority originates from one of three forms of legitimacy: traditional, rational-legal, and charismatic. Traditional legitimacy is based on established beliefs in the sanctity of family rights, which are passed down from one generation to another, and the moral need to obey leaders. In the case of rational legitimacy, which is usually based on laws and on recognized legal regulations, authority is formally conferred by general designation of the interested group on a given person. In modern societies, this is the most common form of authority, and its source is the rule of law. Modern governments, industrial societies, and bureaucratic structures all derive their authority from rational legitimacy. Charismatic legitimacy is based on the voluntary and spontaneous submission of the masses to the rule of persons who are endowed with extraordinary personal heroic qualities. By virtue of these qualities, such persons are deemed capable of accomplishing great, and even miraculous, things. For that reason, they are sometimes perceived as having been appointed by God. They operate beyond the boundaries of legitimacy.

Usually, there is a shared conception of a legitimate order arising from a network of social relationships, which, in turn, guarantees the legitimacy of the persons in formal organizations who help to maintain that order through the exercise of authority. To help the designated persons accomplish their tasks, their positions are backed by power, including the threat of, or the actual use of, physical force. Not all power, however, is legitimate: A carjacker who forces one to turn over his or her car at gunpoint is exercising power, not authority. The representative of a financial institution who repossesses a car because the owner failed to pay, however, is exercising authority. Thus, what clearly distinguishes authority from power, coercion, and force is legitimacy. In this respect, legitimacy is a sentiment whereby people feel morally obligated to submit to power that is perceived to be valuable and conforms to the general will of the society.

The right to exercise authority—that is, the right to make decisions and enforce them—is attached to offices, and this right receives the support of all those who belong to the organization and who conform to its norms. The person who is subjected to an order by a competent authority has no alternative but to obey. Through a system of procedures, roles, and relationships defined by coercive social rules, a society's system of government becomes a means of controlling behavior. Coercive social rules (norms, beliefs, values, laws, and conventions) have the following two features: First, they are prescriptive—that is, they require people to behave in a particular way; second, they are backed or enforced by an effective form of social sanction or pressure. Social norms legitimate the use of force by defining it as correct, appropriate, or permissible although, inasmuch as people believe the institutions in which power is vested to be legitimate, the use of force will hardly be required. If people begin to question the legitimacy of the institutions, however, and perceive their laws, rules, and decisions to be unjust and improper, then they may no longer feel morally obligated to abide by them. Institutional power will then rest not on constituted authority but on sheer force alone. In such cases, governments rely on repression by police or military forces to exercise power over their populations.

Applications

No government can survive for long without authority. This much celebrated concept, many people believe, is threatened in modern society. Over the years, it has become fashionable to say that authority is in difficulty, in crisis, and in decline. The arguments and reasons given for this analysis vary. In *Authority Revisited* (1984), Roland J. Pennock quotes Hannah Arendt as saying that authority has vanished from the modern world. In Samuel Huntington's view, the problem stems from an overemphasis on egalitarianism. The fabrics of social institutions (family, school, state, and church) are all said to have been affected by this decline of authority. Authoritative offices are increasingly challenged by those who are subject to them and increasingly burdensome to those who occupy them. Others have traced this decline to times past, putting the blame on Martin Luther, who they claim destroyed the power of religion by means of his attack on the Church, and Thomas Hobbes, who attacked tradition in his writings. According to Max Weber, religion and tradition are the two most ancient sources of legitimate authority. Nevertheless, in spite of this pessimism, the general consensus is that authority is still very much alive.

In its application, the concept of authority (and hence that of legitimacy), may sometimes be confusing. In his book *The Social Order* (1970), Robert Bierstedt contends that authority is sometimes confused with two other phenomena, namely, "competence" and "leadership." In the first case, a person may be described as "an authority" on a given subject, such as baseball, classical music, radioactivity, or Shakespeare. In this sense, authority is related to influence rather than power. This kind of authority has nothing to do with legitimacy or obligation. It is a recognition of competence that induces people voluntarily to accept the opinions of those who have excelled in their specialized fields of endeavor. According to Bierstedt, people voluntarily respect the competence of others, whereas authority requires submission. Authority requires an office or a status, whereas leadership does not. The police officer, the judge, and the monarch represent authority because they are all backed by legitimate power, but all three may lack leadership qualities. Paradoxically, when an order or a command is said to be issued by a "competent authority," in the etymological sense, it does not imply that the authority is competent, but that it is legitimate. Thus, people will obey the (unreasonable) command of a superior whose authority they recognize and disobey the (reasonable) command of one whose authority they question. In other words, superior knowledge, superior skill, or superior competence may sometimes be irrelevant in the exercise of competent authority. One who commands may be no wiser than those who obey.

The second phenomenon with which authority is sometimes confused is leadership. Ironically, Bierstedt singles out Max Weber, one of the greatest and most influential of all sociologists, as being largely responsible for this confusion. This confusion derives from Weber's classification of charisma as a source of legitimate authority. It is the view of many others, however, that charisma is a form not of authority but of leadership (although leadership qualities more often than not allow an individual to rise to a position of authority). Leadership depends on the personal qualities of the leader. Authority, however, need not involve a personal relationship of any kind. In a military establishment, for example, thousands of men are sent on a mission even though they may not know the officer who is responsible for the orders. Thus, in a leadership relationship, the person is basic; in an authority relationship, personal identity is irrelevant. An authority relationship is one of superordination and subordination; the leadership relationship is one of dominance and submission. No one is required to follow a leader. An organization whose members wish it to survive must create authority where initially there was leadership. The leader who has been instrumental in establishing the organization may eventually be indisposed or may quit. Unless his or her role has been institutionalized, such a contingency might jeopardize the health of the organization. After his or her status as been institutionalized, the leader may even be deposed from his or her position of authority and a successor named without damage to the organization.

What, then, sustains the authority that is exercised by the military officer over his troops?

Why does a subordinate obey a superordinate when he disapproves of the command? Why does an inferior obey a superior whom he or she may dislike or may never have met? Technically, both the superordinate and the subordinate recognize that they are operating in a status relationship and that personal sentiments have no relevance to the exercise of authority. Thus, ideally, the army officer or foreperson or judge is required to exercise the same kind of authority over a sibling that he or she does over an enemy. In the ideal case, the exercise of authority is supposed to be wholly impartial, objective, impersonal, and disinterested. Any exercise of authority, however, depends upon the willingness of officials and the public to respond positively to commands or rules. In other words, ultimately, the official relies on the existence of goodwill. The single policeman exercising his authority in a crowd is assuming, especially under normal circumstances, that, with due respect for his badge, the crowd will allow him to exercise that authority. Effective authority thus depends on cumulative, individual acts of compliance or confidence, with those in positions of authority acting on the assumption that the requisite compliance will be forthcoming. The ultimate reason that people submit to authority is that it is supported, sanctioned, and sustained by the group it serves.

Context

The concepts of authority and legitimacy existed long before the birth of nation-states. Eminent philosophers dating back to the times of Plato, Aristotle, and Socrates attempted to conceptualize them. Even so, placing these two concepts in their right context has been a strenuous and an ongoing process. They have both generated controversies, partly as a result of their theoretical foundations. It is assumed, for example, that force that is not consented to or perceived as being right cannot constitute a legitimate form of authority. In practice, however, conventional wisdom has increasingly demonstrated that only a very thin line separates "force" from "legitimate authority." Initially, Max Weber presented the two concepts in a very antithetical way; that is, he proposed that both concepts are opposites in every sense except that legitimate authorities can use coercive force. It has been proved by tradition on numerous occasions, however, that coercive force can and does play a part in helping to create legitimacy, especially the rational-legal form of legitimacy. It often happens that structures of authority that we subsequently legitimated originate in force. On several occasions, following a coup or revolution (sometimes bloody), the successful government has been tolerated and, eventually, if not immediately, accepted as legitimate. In other words, force itself may well be a value that governs perceptions of legitimacy.

How, then, does a government become legitimate? Civil legitimacy can be obtained through the expression of the general will. The concept of the general will describes the moral values and political aspirations that are shared by the members of a community and to which the policies of its government must broadly conform if that government is to be considered legitimate. Bases of legitimacy are thus values within a particular society that govern perceptions that authority patterns are rightly constituted and therefore are worthy of support. People may accept a government as legitimate because they believe that it is well grounded and justifiable, when in fact it is not. Sometimes it happens that what people believe to be a sound foundation may turn out to be unacceptable at a later date. When that happens, new criteria of legitimacy are applied. At one time, the American colonists considered British rule to be legitimate and acceptable. After a period of grievances without redress, however, they came to believe that the government was no longer legitimate, so they disregarded its authority, revolted, and established their own government. Modern constitutional government makes one characteristic of civil legitimacy clear: Governmental offices are ordered by trust rather than exercised by dominion. This characteristic is expressed in the institution of periodic elections. In a democracy, more often than not, elections are expressions of the general will of the majority. There is, in fact, an analogy between legitimacy and voting. One presumably votes for a party (or a candidate) because one considers it (or him or her) worthy of support, and people accord legitimacy to an authority pattern for the same reason. Thus, the electoral procedure serves as a means of legitimizing the assignment of a person to an office of authority. In recent times, however, popular elections have become so predominant a criterion of legitimacy that almost every nation (including totalitarian ones) feels obligated to pay lip service to the institution of elections.

Bibliography

Bierstedt, Robert. *The Social Order*. 3d ed. New York: McGraw-Hill, 1970. Still useful work that treats topics in a logical, rather than a random, order. Simplifies the study of the concepts of legitimacy and authority and is highly recommended.

De George, Richard T. *The Nature and Limits of Authority*. Lawrence: University Press of Kansas, 1985. Attempt to put into perspective what authority is, what its forms are, which of its functions can be justified, and when it should be challenged or resisted. It also deals extensively with the issue of legitimacy. Very easy to comprehend and thus appropriate for beginners.

Eckstein, Harry, and Ted Robert Gurr. *Patterns of Authority: A Structural Basis for Political Inquiry*. New York: John Wiley & Sons, 1975. Proposes a relatively different approach by equating political analysis with the study of authority patterns in any and all social units. Provides a rationale, concepts, methods, illustrative data, and theoretical justifications for further systematic research into the subject.

Edmundson, William A. *Three Anarchical Fallacies: An Essay on Political Authority*. New York: Cambridge University Press, 1998.

Pennock, Roland J., and John W. Chapman, eds. *Authority Revisited*. New York: New York University Press, 1984. Effectively an update of Carl J. Friedrich's *Authority* (1958). Addresses a wide variety of issues, including the concepts, perspectives, and contexts of authority. Suitable for the advanced reader.

Raz, Joseph. *The Authority of Law*. Oxford, England: Oxford University Press, 1979. Deals extensively with the concept of legitimacy and provides comprehensive analysis of the justification of authority.

Olusoji A. Akomolafe

Cross-References

Bureaucracies; Cultural Norms and Sanctions; Democracy; Power Elite.

Looking-Glass Self

Type of sociology: Socialization and social interaction
Field of study: Interactionist approach to social interaction

Self-identity can be significantly shaped by an individual's perceptions of the views that others have of him or her. To this extent, individuals conceive of themselves in terms of how they think they are "mirrored" in others' minds. In turn, people's personalities mirror the evaluations that they imagine are occurring in the minds of others. The "looking-glass self" is a metaphor for this phenomenon.

Principal terms

CONJUNCTIVE SENTIMENTS: feelings that create bonds and connectedness, as opposed to disjunctive sentiments

HUMAN NATURE: features, characteristics, and tendencies of people, especially as they are considered as a whole species

INTERNALIZE: to make something (as a belief) a part of oneself and of one's mental makeup and nature

OBJECTIVITY: seeing things as they are; evaluating things accurately and fairly rather than subjectively

ROLE: part played in society; a social function

SELF-CONCEPT: personal identity; the collection of ideas that one has about oneself and one's nature

SOCIAL INTERACTION: mutual involvements of people in society

SOCIALIZATION: process of learning and internalizing appropriate attitudes, behaviors, and values so that one has an identity and can function in society and perform various social roles

SUBJECTIVITY: having to do with opinion; a mental or personal reality that is biased or otherwise lacking in objectivity

SYMBOLIC INTERACTIONISM: a school of thought in sociology that stresses the importance of interpersonal social experiences in shaping one's personal identity

Overview

In his book *Human Nature and the Social Order* (1902), the pioneering American sociologist Charles Horton Cooley introduced, somewhat incidentally, the term "looking-glass self." This metaphor has since become a standard concept in American sociology—with a larger meaning than Cooley himself first implied or envisioned, and with important implications in psychology, ethical studies, theories of child rearing, and other fields. Cooley meant by this term that to some degree individuals develop their identities or self-concepts, and come to understand and define themselves, by considering the ideas and reactions that they think others have about them—especially others who seem significant in their lives. Thus, in the process of socialization, which is especially critical at the earlier stages of life but is always occurring, people mold their natures and personalities and assume their roles in response to their reactions to the other people in their social contexts. In that sense, according to Cooley, one's "self" may be said to "mirror" social aspects that are outside oneself; it reflects society itself in many individualized ways. The concept actually implies an interacting pair of mirrors. First one imagines oneself pictured (and judged) in the mind of another; then one mirrors in one's mind those judgments that one imagines, thus regulating one's behavior and partially defining oneself.

What is "reflected" in the mirror of one's own mind includes the value systems, self-definitions, and judgments of others in the surrounding society. In this view, one's self-development does not necessarily depend upon objective social realities; rather, it comes about because one perceives or conceives of others' responses in certain ways. Thus the feedback that one *thinks* one is getting from society may actually be more important than any objective reality outside oneself. As sociologist George J. McCall and J. L. Simmons summarized Cooley's theory in 1966, "our imaginations of self reflect our interpersonal concerns." Patricia R. Jette, writing in *The Encyclopedic Dictionary of Sociology* (1986), says that the "looking-glass self" theory distinguishes three separate components that contribute to the development of self: the responses of others to the individual; the individual's perception of what these responses are, were, or might be (which may differ from the actual responses); and the individual's patterned internalizing of these perceived responses so that they become parts of his or her self-concept and behavioral makeup. In this latter stage, the individual molds a self that reflects the social surroundings and people in it—as she or he has subjectively perceived them.

Noting the precise way in which Cooley first used his term can help one to apply it with its original subtleties. In *Human Nature and the Social Order*, the term occurs in the chapter entitled "The Meaning of 'I,' " one of two chapters about "the social self." Cooley makes clear, in proposing the term "looking-glass self," that it is not intended as an absolute definition of the nature of the self but is merely one "very large and interesting" category in which the self (or the "I") is defined by its social surroundings. According to Cooley's original language, one imagines oneself appearing in some other mind, and then "the kind of self-feeling one has is determined by the attitude . . . attributed to that other mind. A social self of this sort might be called the reflected or looking-glass self."

Cooley goes on to quote an anonymous verse couplet: "Each to each a looking-glass/ Reflects the other that doth pass." Thus Cooley's first use of the term suggests that, in any social interaction, each of two minds is a mirror: that of a self-conscious person, and that of another person who is a reacting "mirror." In real life, one can imagine some interchanges, especially among social peers, as working both ways, in a balanced fashion—with each person simultaneously being both a self-conscious actor and an evaluating judge. Young people in the earlier stages of socialization, however, or people lacking in social power, would be most likely to function in the self-conscious roles, while those who are older, more powerful, or more authoritative would be most likely to be the self-assured "judges" whose opinions matter enough for the other person to take them into account and allow them (perhaps unconsciously) to govern behavior.

Social psychologists such as Tamotsu Shibutani emphasize the importance of Cooley's ideas in the socialization process. In Shibutani's view, the "looking-glass self" means simply that "each person's orientation toward himself is a reflection of the manner in which he is treated." Cooley noted what Read Bain confirmed in the 1930's—that children know other people as objects, and call others by name, before they sense themselves as separate entities. Many experts agree that children see themselves as recipients of action before perceiving themselves as actors. Therefore, their evolving natures as active selves acquiring personalities will be likely to mirror the way they have been treated by others; they first gain self-identity from social interaction.

Cooley's metaphor, like any analogy, embeds both the merit of vividness and the danger of distortion. Though McCall and Simmons call Cooley's looking glass a "somewhat clouded" concept, the term is commonly used by sociologists to help explain certain aspects of the process by which all people achieve their identities, regulating and in effect fine-tuning and modulating them as they go. Most sociologists grant that Cooley's idea contains an important truth.

Applications

The generalized examples that Cooley used when he first mentioned the looking-glass self in 1902 are good beginning points for illustrating how the concept works in real life. Cooley suggests, first, that as we pass a real mirror and "see our face, figure, and dress" reflected, we are naturally interested, and we are either pleased or not, depending on whether what we see measures up to what we would like to see. Similarly, when we meet another person, we readily imagine ourselves as mirrored in that person's mind—"our appearance, manners, aims, deeds, character, friends, and so on." In the next step, we find ourselves imagining what that other person's judgment of our "reflected" selves may be. The third stage triggered by this sequence is a reflective feeling in ourselves "such as pride or mortification" when we conceive of this judgment.

Cooley himself admits that the metaphor of the looking glass is not adequate to explain the second of these three components—that is, the subjective evaluation of the onlooker. The nature and role of the onlooker is strategic in any such hypothetical situation, because one will be concerned about the onlooker's evaluation only if that person seems somehow significant. Assuming the onlooker's importance in one's life, Cooley says, one will be ashamed to seem reticent if one knows the onlooker is straightforward; one will not want to seem cowardly if one knows the onlooker is brave; and one will hesitate to appear gross if one knows the onlooker is refined. One may, in a certain social situation, boast to one onlooker about how one made a sharp business deal, but with some other person whom one perceives as having different social values one might try to hide the very same fact. In these senses, then, the outside mirror of the onlooker's mind actually determines the nature of one's social self, generating one's behavior and role in a given setting.

Though Cooley's examples do not imply that the whole of anyone's self is determined by the process of such interactions, one can see how—generally speaking, from earliest childhood onward—one is likely to shape oneself to fit what one anticipates to be the expected judgments of those with whom one is dealing. In individual situations throughout life, even after one's identity is rather fully formed, one tends to adopt the contextual roles that one thinks of as suitable when mirrored in the minds of others. Thus in one's grandmother's living room or at a church service, one may in effect be one person, while at a basketball game one may reveal an entirely different self; this is role-playing behavior. Proud parents may discuss their children freely with other parents, but, with some degree of consciousness, they may refrain from mentioning their children when talking to someone who is childless—or who has recently lost a child in a car accident. In these cases, the looking glass of social surroundings and audience shapes one's perceived identity.

Although Cooley illustrated only interchanges between two adults and did not specifically explore the implications that his concept has for childhood socialization, the looking-glass self helps to explain early identity development: A young child tends to become a combination of the features that are approved and desired in society. Society always puts pressure on individuals to conform to its values and judgments in order to receive approval; thus humans—who generally seek acceptance and want to be well thought of—shape their social actions according to the signals they get from the social mirror into which they are always looking. Since children tend to internalize what they encounter outside themselves and to act as if it were valid and true, it is clear that those who are treated as worthwhile entities have a better chance of becoming socially productive than those who are treated with abuse or disregard. The development of negative self-concepts as children discourages individuals from acting later as if they have positive contributions to make to society.

Context

Sociology, which studies patterns of human behavior in social contexts, became a recognizable discipline in the nineteenth century, although many predecessors—writers and theorists in various fields—anticipated its main concerns. As a general social science it is less specialized than, say, economics or law. In some of its focuses it parallels the interests of psychology; this is true of its interest in the nature of the self—personal identity, the self-concept, the nature of the "I" in society. Cooley was addressing this subject when he first mentioned the looking-glass self.

Cooley's idea, in fact, seems to be as much a psychological concept as a sociological term, since it comments on the workings of an individual mind. It has particular implications for studies of such psychological phenomena as repression (the exclusion from consciousness of socially unacceptable desires or impulses) and sublimation (the redirection of primitive urges, such as sex, toward goals that are "higher" or socially favored). These terms, however, seem more compatible with ian psychoanalytic theory than with Cooley's sociology. As Shibutani points out, Cooley tended to be mainly interested in "conjunctive sentiments," whereas Austrian doctor and psychiatrist Sigmund Freud often focused on "disjunctive sentiments" in the childhood years that had negative effects on personality. Still, both Freud and Cooley "in their theories of the formation of personal idiom . . . stressed the importance of adjusting to particular people" and especially to a "significant other."

Psychological behaviorists, who focus on the reality of external actions and who stress stimulus-response interactions, might adapt Cooley's concept, but Cooley was not a behaviorist, and he thought that behaviorism omitted much of the "mystical" nature of human beings. Cooley's original explanation of the looking-glass self notably includes the workings of a mind and implies some degree of consciousness, choice, and social control—aspects that behaviorists deemphasize or deny.

Theoretical sociology in the twentieth century has tended in three major directions: conflict theory, structural-functional theory, and symbolic interaction theory. Cooley's ideas, including the looking-glass self concept, fit best into the last of these categories. Conflict theory, influenced by Karl Marx, interprets social change in terms of underlying conflict (such as economic inequities); structural-functional theory emphasizes the balancing process by which ma-

The concept of the "looking-glass self" owes much to the psychoanalytical theories of the Austrian physician Sigmund Freud, the founder of modern psychiatry. (*Library of Congress*)

jor social institutions interact; and symbolic interaction theory stresses various patterns of social communication and their meanings and values. While Cooley is an important early figure in the interactionist movement, the major figure is George Herbert Mead, who incorporated various ideas put forward not only by Cooley but also by the progressive educational philosopher John Dewey and the pragmatic philosopher William James. Symbolic interactionism not only entered mainstream sociology but also has influenced areas of psychology, psychiatry, and cultural anthropology. Ideas about the self, role-playing, and the social grounding of self-evaluation are central to symbolic interactionism, which emphasizes that individual identity develops and has meaning only in the contexts of a social environment and human interconnectedness.

Throughout most of Western history, the idea of human nature was discussed separately from the idea of social order, and often human nature was viewed as a theological topic. The position of such sixteenth century Protestant thinkers as John Calvin, for example, was that human nature was basically evil and needed salvation to reform it before society could ever be improved. The eighteenth century Swiss-French theorist Jean-Jacques , by contrast, tended to see human nature as innately good and suggested that humans are corrupted by their social contacts and institutions. Cooley's theories were generally important because they linked ideas about human nature and about society inextricably together. Cooley's famous phrase on this point is, "Self and society are twin-born." The discipline of sociology generally assumes this idea to be true.

Like other sociologists of his era, Cooley spoke of the human species collectively but seldom examined varieties of social organization other than his own. Thus critics note that his ideas have an American bias, presuming white, Anglo-Saxon, Protestant (WASP) values. Cooley believed in social progress, and he had faith that change was directional—evolutionary or progressive—rather than cyclical. He hoped that sociology, including his own research and study, could contribute to social progress, and he listed methods for social reform. Because Cooley took an idealistic, humanistic, and liberal stance, he opposed those who wanted sociology to be more scientific. Sociologist Roscoe Hinkle has called his position "sociological romanticism." In general, Cooley's statement that "the imaginations [that] people have of one another are the solid facts of society" not only summarizes the central idea of his looking-glass self theory but also epitomizes many of his other notions about social interaction.

Bibliography

Billington, Rosamund, Jenny Hockey, and Sheelagh Strawbridge. *Exploring Self and Society.* Basingstoke, England: Macmillan, 1998.

Cooley, Charles Horton. *Human Nature and the Social Order.* New York: Charles Scribner's Sons, 1902. Reprint. New York: Schocken Books, 1964. Introduces the term "looking-glass self." Arguing that what is called "human nature" has no reality independent of the social order that an individual human identity mirrors, Cooley assumes an American, democratic context and supports a value system that in retrospect appears to be white, Anglo-Saxon, Protestant, and liberal. Preface (1930) by George Herbert Mead evaluates Cooley's "contributions to American social thought."

_____. *Social Organization: A Study of the Larger Mind.* New York: Charles Scribner's Sons, 1909. Reprint. Schocken Books, 1967. Here Cooley shows himself the moralist, discussing the false conflict (as he sees it) between selfish individuals and the larger society. Cooley argues that each self exists only as a member of all and that, as he says, "We must improve as a whole." Philip Rieff's introduction provides a helpful context and background.

_____. *Social Process.* Carbondale: Southern Illinois University Press, 1966. First published in 1918, this work develops Cooley's theories of social change, ideas which have been given less attention than his interactionist ideas about the development of personality. Helpful introduction by Roscoe C. Hinkle gives an overview of Cooley's ideas and evaluates his importance as a sociologist.

Healy, Mary Edward. *Society and Social Change in the Writings of St. Thomas, Ward, Sumner, and Cooley.* Westport, Conn.: Greenwood Press, 1972. Analysis of Cooley's ideas about the self and socialization in the context of the larger topic of social change and in relation to other theorists. Emphasizes Cooley's philosophical aspects and notes that he acknowledged himself to be more philosopher than scientist. First published in 1948.

McCall, George J., and J. L. Simmons. *Identities and Interactions.* New York: Free Press, 1966. In incidental ways these sociologists incorporate Cooley's ideas into their own generalized views. They underplay the concept of the looking-glass self, however, by calling Cooley's mirror "somewhat clouded."

Shibutani, Tamotsu. *Society and Personality: An Interactionist Approach to Social Psychology.* Preface by Barry Glassner. New Brunswick, N.J.: Transaction Books, 1987. Study of how personalities develop from interactions between people and their social contexts. Cooley's name and theories recur more frequently than any others, except those of Sigmund and George H. Mead. Integrates Cooley's ideas with those of many theorists.

Roy Neil Graves

Cross-References

Dramaturgy; Microsociology; Significant and Generalized Others; Statuses and Roles; Symbolic Interaction.

MARRIAGE TYPES

Type of sociology: Major social institutions
Field of study: The family

Marriage in its various forms is an important sociological topic because what a society thinks about marriage influences what it thinks about sex roles, gender, the family, and happiness. To understand a culture, it is important to understand its preferences regarding marriage.

Principal terms

ENDOGAMY: practice of marrying within a particular group to which one belongs
EXOGAMY: practice of marrying outside a particular group to which one belongs
GROUP MARRIAGE: marital relationship in which two or more individuals share two or more spouses
MARRIAGE: union between two or more individuals that is usually meant to be permanent, is recognized legally or socially, and is aimed at founding a family
MONOGAMY: marital relationship in which an individual has only one spouse at a time
POLYANDRY: marital relationship in which an individual has more than one husband at a time
POLYGAMY: marital relationship in which an individual has more than one spouse at a time; sometimes used to mean "polygyny"
POLYGYNY: marital relationship in which an individual has more than one wife at a time

Overview

Marriage is an extremely widespread institution that occurs in virtually every known culture. Marriage, unlike cohabitation, usually involves a commitment to a permanent union. This commitment is recognized by law or custom. Marriage generally occurs between individuals of opposite sexes, but some cultures recognize same-sex marriage. For example, Cheyenne Indians could take a same-sex partner as a "second wife."

By marrying, one assumes certain rights and duties, which vary from culture to culture. In the Nayar culture of India, the husbands of a marriage do not have any obligations toward the children of the marriage; the wife's family provides for the children. In Western culture, however, the husband is expected to provide for the offspring of his marriage. Different kinship systems may result in different sets of marital rights and duties, but one marital right that is almost universally recognized is the right to have sexual relations with one's spouse or spouses.

Marriage is a means to legitimize both sexual relations and the children who result from them. Sociologist William Graham Sumner noted in *Folkways* (1960) that marriage, as an ongoing relationship, is important as a means of taking care of children and educating them.

Some cultures regard marriage as necessary to fulfill a duty to family or tribe. Many African societies believe that dead ancestors are reincarnated in new children. Having children is thus regarded as necessary for letting the ancestors live and even for one's own rebirth.

In a variety of cultures, some people marry for economic or political reasons. Small clans, for example, may need to "trade brides" in order to increase the labor pool available during seasonal harvests, and marriages to form political alliances between European countries are well documented. At the same time, in many cultures people marry because they love other people and want to spend their lives with them in a socially recognized and respected manner.

According to ethnographer George Murdock's *Atlas of World Cultures* (1981), the preferred form of marriage differs widely from culture to culture. Monogamy, in which an individual is married to only one other individual at a time, is the preferred form in Europe and in the areas of the world settled by Europeans. In these areas, other forms of marriage have been regarded as less civilized, but monogamous marriages in which the partners set up a separate household from their relatives are the preferred form of marriage in only about 12 percent of the 563 cultures studied by Murdock. Polygamy, in which an individual has more than one spouse at the same time, is a popular marital arrangement in Africa, East Asia, and the Pacific Ocean region. Polygamous marriages in which partners reside apart from their other relatives are preferred in about 36 percent of the cultures studied by Murdock. Murdock classifies as extended families 44 percent of the cultures studied. Since extended families are groups of related families that are living together, this category leaves it unclear whether the members of these families are practicing monogamy, polygamy, or both.

Polygamy has two forms: polygyny and polyandry. In polygyny, an individual has two or more female spouses at the same time. In cultures where the women are laborers, it may be economically beneficial for a man to have more than one wife. In other cultures, having many wives may be a status symbol, a means of showing off one's wealth. In polyandry, an individual has two or more male spouses at the same time. Polyandry is rare, appearing in no more than 1 percent of the cultures studied by Murdock. Poverty is one motivation for polyandry. If there is a tax on houses in which married women reside, poverty-stricken brothers may share a wife.

Different cultures have different practices concerning the selection of mates. In India, many marriages are arranged by parents, and the parents are likely to consult an astrologer about whether a prospective match will be auspicious. In contrast, in the United States, individuals generally select their own mates. Selection is not based on astrology, but on love, physical attraction, and compatibility, among other things.

Both the Indian system of marriage and the American system of marriage have traditionally been endogamous. Endogamy is the practice of marrying within one's own group. Traditionally, in India's caste system, one is born into a caste and is expected to marry within that caste. To marry someone from a lower caste is regarded as polluting the higher caste member and may cause that person to be ostracized. Beyond the middle of the twentieth century in the southern United States, there were laws against marriage between partners of different races.

Generally, the custom of marriage within one's own group does not allow marriage within one's own immediate family. The incest taboo against marriage between parents and their children and marriage between siblings is fairly universal. The Ptolemaic dynasty in Egypt provides an exception. Regarding themselves as gods, the Ptolemies could not marry non-gods, so they married each other. Cleopatra was the product of twelve generations of marriages between siblings.

The incest taboo is one basis for the practice of marrying outside a particular group to which one belongs. The particular kinship system in place in a culture determines who is covered by the incest taboo. Some traditional Africans regard cousin marriage as incestuous, but Arabic Muslims do not.

Applications

The only legal form of marriage in the United States is monogamy. In the nineteenth century, Mormons practiced polygyny and defended their practice as a matter of religious freedom. In *Solemn Covenant: The Mormon Polygamous Passage* (1992), historian B. Carmon Hardy documents the national outcry that arose against the Mormons. Polygamy was castigated as a barbarous threat to Western civilization. Americans who believed in the superiority of Western culture regarded polygamy as a throwback to the instability and disorder of non-Western cultures. Mormon polygyny would not be tolerated, and in 1890 the U.S. Supreme Court upheld the decision to outlaw polygamy in the United States.

Traditionally, American marriages have been patriarchal. In the twentieth century, however, American marriages have become more egalitarian. More American women are playing an active role in family decision making. In addition, traditional gender roles for women have shifted from homemaking to both homemaking and working outside the home. Between 1977 and 1988, the number of American children with working mothers increased from 48 percent to 60 percent. Many working mothers experience conflict between their work roles and their family roles, and as a result have no children or fewer children.

American divorce rates are among the highest in the Western world. The expectation is that at least half of all first marriages will end in divorce. Major reasons for divorce include alcohol or drug abuse, conflicts over gender roles, value differences, sexual incompatibility, and marital infidelity. Most divorced people remarry; second marriages, like first marriages, end in divorce more than 50 percent of the time.

In the latter third of the twentieth century, the old idea of monogamy as having one mate for life is no longer the norm in the United States. Many Americans seem to be practicing serial monogamy, in which one has one mate at a time but one mate after another. Some people regard this system of marriage as a modified form of polygamy, since it involves having more than one spouse during a lifetime.

Unlike American culture, many other cultures approve of having more than one mate at a time. In *Facing Mount Kenya* (1965), anthropologist Jomo Kenyatta described the practice of polygyny among Kenya's Gikuyu (Kikuyu) people. According to Gikuyu custom, the larger the family, the better it is for the man and the tribe. With more wives, a man can have more children. A man is expected to provide male children to help with the defense of the tribe and female children to have and to rear further children. Upon marrying, one's primary duty is to reproduce. A key Gikuyu belief is the larger the family, the happier the family.

There is no limit on the number of wives a Gikuyu may have. In the early twentieth century, Gikuyu men averaged two wives, but some men, because of poverty, had only one wife. A wealthy man might have as many as fifty wives. Each wife has her own hut in the husband's compound, and each wife is assigned a plot of land to cultivate. The husband provides labor for all and allocates collectively owned resources. The wives take turns cleaning the husband's hut, cooking for him, and doing other chores around the compound.

According to Kenyatta, the wives do not resent sharing a husband with one or more other women. In fact, once the first wife becomes pregnant, she may actually encourage her husband to marry again so that there will be someone to do the chores after she has given birth.

In preparation for a polygynous way of living, the Gikuyu learn from an early age to share. Males are taught early that they should be able to love many women, and females are taught to share, too. To avoid jealousy among wives, a husband sets up a schedule of lovemaking visits to their huts. In the evenings, when the husband has male visitors from his age group, the wives are expected to visit with them in the husband's hut as a sign of group solidarity. If a visitor has traveled far and will spend the night, a wife may openly invite him to stay in her hut. Because sharing is emphasized, the husband is not supposed to object. The unity of the age group is partly the result of a mutual concern for collective enjoyment.

At the same time, a woman caught receiving a male visitor secretly in her hut is subject to harsh penalties. This kind of adultery is rare, however, since there are socially acceptable means of accomplishing the same end. Repeated adultery, barrenness, and impotence are grounds for divorce among the Gikuyu.

Another kind of multiple-mate marriage is polyandry, in which a woman has more than one husband at a time. According to anthropologist Peter, prince of Greece and Denmark, polyandry may be rare worldwide, but it was the predominant form of marriage in Tibet prior to the Chinese communist occupation in 1950.

Fraternal polyandry, in which brothers marry one wife and live together, was the preferred form of polyandry. Tibet's harsh natural environment made survival difficult, and polyandry was one way to keep the population down. Another reason for polyandry was the desire to avoid dividing family property. A Tibetan custom was that when children married, they would take over the parents' property. If the children took different wives, the parents' property would have to be divided—something that could have made survival more difficult.

The Tibetan family was patriarchal. It was expected that the wife would be subject to her husbands. The head of the family was not the eldest man, but the most influential man or the first-wed man in case the men did not all marry the woman at the same time. The men made some agreement about when they could have intercourse with their wife. The wife appeared to have little, if any, say in the matter.

Jealousy was not something that men in such marriages could afford. Preserving family unity was more important because it seemed necessary for survival in Tibet's difficult natural environment. The emphasis on family unity helped the men suppress jealousy and also made divorce rare.

Context

As early as the eighteenth century European Enlightenment, French philosophers dreamed of discovering laws of society that were similar to the laws of physics. Aware that different societies had different forms of marriage, Charles-Louis Secondat, baron de La Brède et de Montesquieu, was still confident that there were social laws that could explain the differences. He, along with Jacques Turgot, postulated evolutionary stages through which societies travel. While European society was regarded as the most evolved, there was great interest in finding out more about the other stages on the evolutionary ladder. This led nineteenth century researchers to theorize about the nature of the first social arrangements. Were they loosely organized groups of individuals or families? What was their political structure? What form of marriage came first on the evolutionary ladder?

In the late nineteenth century, in *The Origin of the Family, Private Property, and the State* (1985), Friedrich Engels claimed that group marriage came first and gradually developed into monogamous marriage. Engel's evidence for his claim was primarily linguistic; he noted that among the Iroquois Indians, one's father's brother was also called "father." He believed that the only way to explain this linguistic usage was to regard it as reflecting an earlier form of marriage—group marriage. Many scholars have criticized this reliance on language, however, noting that the language used by the Iroquois might just have been a polite form of address rather than a residual trace of group marriages.

If group marriage did come first, however, what eventually led to monogamy? In group marriages, paternity could be difficult to determine, so descent would have been traced through the women. In these circumstances, women also would tend to have more political power. All this would have changed when men, as owners of cattle, became more wealthy and more powerful than women. Men would have wanted to leave their property to children who were indisputably their own. Thus, according to Engels, the accumulation of property and the concern over its inheritance led to monogamy. Many scholars have pointed out, however, that monogamy might have arisen from changes in sexuality or ideology instead of changes in economics.

However monogamy came to be, Engels claimed that it was designed to establish the man's supremacy in the family. The woman became the man's subject—his servant and sexual property. While her sexual freedom was abolished, the man's was only lessened. In effect, there was monogamy *only for women*. The resulting tension between husband and wife was similar to that found between classes in society, and liberation was called for in both situations. Engels questioned whether monogamy was the best form of marriage, especially for women. His work has influenced many feminists, but he painted monogamy at its worst; it is possible for monogamous unions to be based on fairness, love, and mutual respect. Critics of monogamy may insist that it does not lead to personal fulfillment for either women or men. While this may be true for some, 90 percent of Americans believe that a monogamous marriage is an important part of a good life. Predictions of the demise of monogamy seem premature.

Twentieth century social scientists have continued their interest in cross-cultural studies of marriage, but they have been less concerned with how marriage began and evolved than with how marriage is related to socioeconomic conditions, ethnicity, individual personality, place of residence, the status of women, gender-role expectations, and ideas of gender and family.

Bibliography

Engels, Friedrich. *The Origin of the Family, Private Property, and the State*. New York: Viking Penguin, 1985. Originally published in 1884, this work is a good example of Marxist attempts to explain social changes in terms of economic changes.

Hardy, B. Carmon. *Solemn Covenant: The Mormon Polygamous Passage*. Urbana: University of Illinois Press, 1992. Chapter 2 of Hardy's work is entitled "Civilization Threatened: Mormon Polygamy Under Siege." It gives an interesting account of the national campaign against Mormon polygamy.

Kenyatta, Jomo. *Facing Mount Kenya*. New York: Vintage Books, 1965. Himself a Gikuyu and the future first president of independent Kenya, Kenyatta gives an insider's view of most aspects of Gikuyu culture. He shows how easy it can be for an outsider to misinterpret a culture. First published in 1938.

Murdock, George Peter. *Atlas of World Culture*. Pittsburgh: University of Pittsburgh Press, 1981. Compares 563 cultures in terms of twenty-seven categories, including family organization. Concluding chapter summarizes findings in tables. Valuable for anyone interested in cross-cultural comparisons.

Peter, prince of Greece and Denmark. "The Tibetan Family System." In *Comparative Family Systems*, edited by M. F. Nimkoff. Boston: Houghton Mifflin, 1965. Prince Peter's article on Tibetan polyandry is thorough and interesting. His dissertation, *A Study of Polyandry* (Mouton, 1963), is an extended, detailed study of various systems of polyandry.

Strong, Bryan, and Christine DeVault. *The Marriage and Family Experience*. 7th ed. Belmont, Calif.: Wadsworth, 1998. Popular introductory text taking an interdisciplinary approach to marriage. Includes chapters on sexuality, gender roles, parenting, and the meaning of marriage.

Sumner, William Graham. *Folkways*. New York: New American Library, 1960. Originally published in 1906, Sumner's important cross-cultural study includes separate chapters on sex mores, the marriage institution, and incest.

Vander Zanden, James W. *The Social Experience*. 2d ed. New York: McGraw-Hill, 1990. Introductory sociology text covering the basic topics of sociology in clear, lively, and focused prose.

Westermarck, Edward. *A Short History of Marriage*. New York: Humanities Press, 1968. Although Westermarck sometimes seems to have an ethnic bias, his book is an important resource, containing separate chapters on endogamy, exogamy, monogamy and polygamy, and polyandry and group marriage.

Gregory P. Rich
Lanzhen Q. Rich

Cross-References

Family: Functionalist Versus Conflict Theory Views; Role Conflict and Role Strain; Social Stratification: Functionalist Perspectives; Socialization: The Family.

MARXISM

Type of sociology: Social change
Field of study: Theories of social change

Marxism is a system of inquiry that focuses on the different types of societies associated with different modes of production. Marxist analysis examines the structural inequality that limits every historical society, particularly capitalist society; it explores the prospects for attaining a form of society that would restore creativity and freedom to all human beings.

Principal terms

ALIENATION: the loss of human beings' creative powers when these are controlled and exploited by others

CAPITALISM: mode of production and associated form of society based on the market and private ownership of the means of production

CLASS: group formed by unequal social relations of production and distinguished by differences in property ownership and control of the labor process

HEGEMONY: process by which an economically dominant class establishes political and cultural control of a society

HISTORICAL MATERIALISM: precise term for "Marxism," a system of thought that emphasizes change in modes of production and the societies associated with them

LABOR: essential human capacity for creative, purposive, and cooperative action to satisfy needs and form societies

MODE OF PRODUCTION: patterning of the activities and relationships of human beings as they engage in labor to satisfy their needs and wants

REVOLUTION: transformation of political, economic, and social structures in which a dominant class loses power

Overview

Marxism is a system of thought and inquiry based on the work of Karl Marx (1818-1883), a social theorist and revolutionary, and his coauthor, Friedrich Engels (1820-1895). Marx's central premise is that human nature is characterized by the capacity for creative and purposive action—"labor"—that has effects in the establishment of institutions and the accumulation of material culture. When agriculture enabled human beings to produce a surplus of food, conflicts arose in society over these products and over control of the labor process, initiating a process of social differentiation and growing inequality.

Human societies thus moved from a stage of equality ("primitive communism") to a succession of historical societies characterized by structures of inequality and exploitation. In the Mediterranean region and Europe, this sequence includes the slavery-based societies of the ancient world, feudalism, and capitalism. Each social formation (or type of society) is structured by its specific relations of production as well as by its specific form of the "forces of production": the way human beings organize activities, knowledge, and material objects to confront the problems of survival. These two elements—the forces and relations of production—are together called the "mode of production." In turn, the mode of production gives shape to the political and cultural institutions of each type of society. This conception has led to the erroneous view that Marx was an "economic determinist"; Marx, however, emphasized that the mode of production in all social formations is not a self-regulating mechanism external to society but a set of relationships between human beings, a social institution.

Early twentieth century editorial cartoon conveying the image of capitalists amassing their wealth by exploiting poor workers—a concept central to Marxist thought. (*Library of Congress*)

Marx focused his analysis on capitalism, the mode of production and type of society that rose to global dominance by the middle of the nineteenth century. Capitalism is a mode of production in which the means of production are owned privately and economic decisions are made by private firms in response to the market mechanism; the capitalist's motivation for production is realizing a profit from exchange value, and not the criterion of use value. To Marx the structure of capitalism was based on the relationship between capitalists (owners of the means of production and buyers of labor power) and wage laborers (who do not own the means of production and are therefore constrained to sell their labor power in order to make a living). In precapitalist modes of production, the subordinate classes were coerced into producing a surplus for the dominant classes, but in capitalism this unequal and exploitive relationship is masked by the fact that workers freely consent to sell their labor power to capitalists at prevailing wage rates. Workers produce goods whose exchange value is greater than workers' wages, so when the goods are sold at their exchange value, capitalists realize "surplus value." Surplus value is the form in which capitalists appropriate a surplus from workers without resorting to the coercion typical of slavery and serfdom.

On the one hand, capitalism is a system of inequality and exploitation; on the other hand, it contains a promise of freedom from scarcity and exploitation because of the enormous potential of the forces of production it generates. Under the pressure of relentless competition among capitalists, technological innovation soars and thus makes conceivable a future without scarcity and exploitation. In this future, each individual would be able to recognize his or her unique talents and potentials. All would cooperate in sustaining life, a task made easy by the intelligent use of machinery, and the division of labor would disappear, eliminating the narrow specialization that reduces labor under capitalism to a monotonous routine. Marx's vision of the future is one of freedom. As he wrote in *Manifest du Kommunistischen Partei* (1848; *The Communist Manifesto*, 1850), the future could consist of "an association, in which the free development of each is the condition for the free development of all." This future cannot be realized within the framework of capitalist institutions of private ownership, production for profit, and wage labor. For example, automation in the capitalist economy eliminates jobs and thus has a disastrous effect.

Capitalism, according to Marxist views, continues to consign most people to alienated conditions of labor and condemns a majority of the globe's population to poverty, despite its enormous technological dynamism. The potential locked within capitalism can only be realized when the system is replaced by socialism and ultimately by communism—that is, when institutions of ownership and political power are brought into line with the possibilities inherent in the forces of production. To Marx, in sharp contrast to utopian socialists, this transformation cannot come about by an act of will and imagination; it can only begin to take place in the most developed capitalist countries and only through the action of the working class organized as conscious agent of such a transformation. Marx commented that human beings make history, but not in circumstances of their own choosing. In other words, the future is formed in the dialectic of acting Subject (the working class as agent) and determined Structure (the most advanced forms of capitalism).

Marx's writing spanned four decades and produced fifty volumes of published works; as he matured as a theorist, he moved from philosophical concepts to analysis of economic structures. He responded to historical changes and events of the nineteenth century—the revolutions of 1848, European colonial expansion, the U.S. Civil War, the Paris Commune, and the spread of industrialization. Friedrich Engels published theoretical writings that have also become part of the essential outline of Marxism. Thus, they left a huge and complex legacy of social theory that has been divided, added to, and debated by generations of theorists and revolutionaries.

Applications

Applications of Marxist theory to revolutionary practice are distinct from applications of Marxist inquiry to questions in the social sciences; only the latter will be reviewed here. Since the end of the nineteenth century, many sociologists who are not Marxists have tried to answer the questions Marxists raise. Since the 1960's, the influence of Marxism on sociology has expanded; Marxist views of capitalism and class structure have influenced many subfields of sociology, especially "macrosociology"—the study of whole societies and global processes.

One subfield that has been deeply influenced by Marxism is the study of class structure and stratification. Beginning with German sociologist Max Weber, many non-Marxist sociologists have engaged in "a debate with Marx's ghost," offering a looser definition of class and paying more attention to status and political power as independent dimensions of inequality. Marxist sociologists continue to emphasize ownership of enterprises, purchase of labor power, and control of production processes as hallmarks of class dominance. They have carried out studies of capitalist class structure with attention to new strata and contradictory class positions. Closely related inquiries examine the way in which class inequality is reproduced from generation to generation; Marxist theory has become a major explanatory perspective in the sociology of education, through studies of schools and the interaction of school culture with working-class cultures of students.

A second major area of application is the study of work under capitalism. A number of scholars, both Marxist and non-Marxist, have observed workplaces, labor markets, and the effects of technology on work. Much of this research has been guided by the notion of "alienation" as a characteristic of work under capitalism, in which neither the labor process nor the product is controlled by workers.

A third application of Marxist theory appears in studies of the relationship between the state and society. In most capitalist societies, the state is not the "night watchman" posited by laissez-faire ideology but takes an active part in economic regulation, social services, and infrastructure development. Both Marxist and non-Marxist scholars explore conditions under which the state expanded its functions to intervene in the capitalist economy. Another area of political sociology informed by Marxism is analysis of the form of states in terms of class structure. Marxist theory has also influenced the study of revolutions and types of societies that emerge after revolutions. Barrington Moore and Theda Skocpol are two social theorists whose work has been influenced by Marxist inquiries into the relationship of state and society. A fourth area of sociology in which Marxist theory is influential is in the analysis of global inequalities. Dependence theory and world systems theory look at the global capitalist economy as an integrated and uneven whole and analyze processes within it, especially international flows of capital and labor, the social impact of economic cycles, and unequal relationships between developed core countries and the weaker periphery.

Marxism has an impact on culture theory, the analysis of cultural representations. In this field, which spans sociology and the humanities, Marxism is in a dialogue with feminist, psychoanalytic, and linguistic theories. One of the most influential concepts is Marx's "commodity fetishism." A fetish is an idol made by human beings who then worship their own creation as a divine force. Marx uses the term "fetishism" to refer to an analogous process of mystification in capitalist society: The capitalist economy is formed by relationships between human beings, who then misconstrue and misrepresent their own creation as an omnipotent, compelling, external, alien "thing" that has power over them. Ongoing social relations between living people are misexperienced as relationships between dead objects, between prices of commodities following supposedly immutable "laws of supply and demand." The concept of fetishism guides culture theorists who document how social relations are represented as fixed and natural things rather than as products of interaction and discourse.

Context

Marxism as a theory in the social sciences has changed in response to global economic, political, and social change. It began as an effort to understand capitalism, and its concepts are continually developing to account for changes in capitalism itself. After Marx's death, Marxists in Europe and North America formed a network of socialist parties called the Second International. Its theorists tended to emphasize the structural side of the transition to socialism, the increasing instability of the capitalist economy. Vladimir Ilich Lenin, Russian revolutionary, offered an alternative model: In his theory of imperialism, he pointed to the global nature of capitalism and posited that socialist revolution could begin in the periphery rather than in the developed center of the capitalist system. He emphasized the shift from industrial to finance capitalism and proposed a new role for the party, as a vanguard organization that must take initiative in capturing and transforming the state. With the Bolshevik Revolution in Russia (1917), Western socialist parties split into socialist and communist parties, with the latter committed to the Leninist model. The revolution touched off a major split in Marxist theory. In the Soviet Union, Marxist thought had to legitimate state practice and leaned heavily toward emphasizing the role of the party and the subjective or "voluntarist" side of historical transformations. In the West, Marxist theory engaged in dialogues with varieties of non-Marxist thought and shifted back and forth between emphasis on consciousness and emphasis on structure.

Two major currents of Marxism that developed before World War II continue to influence both Marxist and non-Marxist sociology. Antonio Gramsci (a theoretician of the Italian Communist Party) has had a lasting impact on sociology by introducing the concept of "hegemony"—the process whereby the economically dominant class translates economic power into political and cultural dominance. He analyzed the role of intellectuals in supporting or challenging hegemony. His work is particularly relevant to developed capitalist societies in which the system appears to hold the allegiance of large parts of the working class. Before it was dispersed by the onset of Nazism in Germany, the Frankfurt Institute explored theoretical connections between Hegelian Marxism and the growing body of psychoanalytic thought. A lasting influence of this milieu is the writing of Walter Benjamin, whose analysis of cultural production underlies most work—non-Marxist as well as Marxist—in the culture theory that emerged in the 1980's and 1990's.

One can trace a shift away from issues of consciousness back to issues of structure beginning with the work of Leo Huberman, Paul Baran, and Paul Sweezy in the United States in the late 1950's and 1960's. Baran and Sweezy analyzed the emergence of monopoly capitalism—capitalism associated with giant corporations, an interconnection of capital and government, and a reduction of free market competition. Ernst Mandel's work also explores the capitalist economy in the later twentieth century. At a more philosophical level, French structural Marxists (most notably, Louis Althusser) tried to remove the Hegelian influence in Marxism and to replace it with a model of societies as determined structures that owed much to Émile Durkheim in sociology, to Ferdinand de Saussure in linguistics, and to Jacques Lacan in psychoanalysis.

Althusser's theory of social formations even converged with contemporary functionalist sociological theory. Meanwhile, more concrete studies were done by Serge Mallet and Andre Gorz on new technical and managerial strata and by Harry Braverman on capitalist management practices that deskill workers. Braverman has had a strong influence on sociological studies of the impact of computerization and technology on the labor force. In the postcolonial era, Marxists returned with renewed energy to issues of imperialism; they updated this concept with the analysis of dependency in "underdeveloped nations," showing how these regions were caught up in an unequal global capitalist system. These trends coincided with the upsurge of the New Left, with hopes for a worker-intellectual alliance in France and Italy in the late 1960's, and with the accession to power of revolutionary forces in Vietnam and elsewhere.

As prospects for these movements faded and European communism as well receded after electoral victories in the 1970's, Marxism found itself increasingly in a dialogue with non-Marxist culture theory, feminism, and poststructuralist and postmodernist thought. Some Marxists repudiate the notion of the "postmodern," emphasizing the continuity of capitalism; others (such as Frederic Jameson) theorize that new "postmodern" forms of culture do indeed accompany advanced capitalism. This dialogue was accelerated by the collapse of socialist systems in Eastern Europe and the Soviet Union; the evident difficulties in creating viable socialist societies have forced Marxist thought back into a reflection on agency and discourse.

Marxism is above all a challenge to capitalist hegemony in the economy, in politics, and in social theory. As long as capitalism remains the prevailing form of society, Marxism exists as the expression of an alternative vision of the human future as well as an ongoing mode of inquiry into the structure of capitalist society.

Bibliography

Burawoy, Michael, and Theda Skocpol, eds. *Marxist Inquiries: Studies of Labor, Class, and States*. Chicago: University of Chicago Press, 1982. Research articles that address questions raised by Marxism, illustrating the impact that Marxist thought has on contemporary sociology. Some essays are technical, but Burawoy's introduction is a good overview.

Engels, Friedrich. *The Origin of the Family, Private Property, and the State*. New York: Viking Penguin, 1985. Classic exposition of the history of these institutions, first published in the nineteenth century. Discussion of the family is of continuing interest to feminists.

Howard, Dick, and Karl Klare, eds. *The Unknown Dimension*. New York: Basic Books, 1972. Essays reviewing European Marxist social thought of the twentieth century, with clear expositions of the ideas of major theorists.

McLellan, David. *The Thought of Karl Marx*. London: Macmillan, 1971. Explains the basic ideas of Marx; the material is treated in chronological order and in terms of major concepts. The exposition is accompanied by excerpts from Marx's writings. Excellent organization.

Marx, Karl. *Selected Writings*. Edited by David McLellan. Oxford, England: Oxford University Press, 1977. Definitive one-volume collection of Marx's writings, exemplary for comprehensiveness, chronological order, and the length and representativeness of the selections.

Zeitlin, Irving. *Ideology and the Development of Sociological Theory*. 6th ed. Englewood Cliffs, N.J.: Prentice-Hall, 1994. Places Marx and Engels within the history of sociology, showing how sociological theory developed in the "debate with Marx's ghost."

Roberta T. Garner

Cross-References

Capitalism; Class Consciousness and Class Conflict; Conflict Theory; Education: Conflict Theory Views; Social Stratification: Marxist Perspectives.

MEDICAL SOCIOLOGY

Type of sociology: Major social institutions
Field of study: Medicine

Medical sociology is an area of study that focuses on the social aspects of the causes and effects of health and illness within society. In doing so, medical sociologists attempt to explain the complex relationships between social characteristics and the development, treatment, and curing of illness; they also analyze the organization of health care.

Principal terms

DEVIANCE: behavior that violates social norms
FUNCTIONALISM: view that society is composed of a set of interrelated parts that must maintain a balance to work together
PRESTIGE: social honor given to a person based on the social role the person occupies
SOCIAL NORMS: rules of acceptable social behavior defined by a social group
SOCIAL ROLE: pattern of behavior defined by the expectations of the ways individuals behave in particular social situations

Overview

Medical sociology is the study of the social facets of health and illness. It applies sociological principles to the study of topics such as the organization of health care, the socialization of health professionals, sociocultural responses to illness, the nature of the patient-practitioner relationship, and other health-related subjects. Sociologist Robert Straus suggested in 1957 that medical sociology could be divided into two subcategories representing two different approaches to studying similar phenomena. The first he called the sociology of medicine. This category comprises the application of basic sociological theories and principles to the study of medical issues. The sociology of medicine represents an academic pursuit indicative of a basic research approach designed to gain better understanding and insight as to how the health care system operates. The second category is sociology *in* medicine, which includes those who work in medical environments attempting to use sociological principles to help solve medical or patient care problems and represents an applied research approach.

For example, one medical sociologist examining the patient-practitioner relationship might view the interaction between the patient and the physician as an example of the ways people of different status behave in a particular situation. Understanding how patients and physicians deal with one another should provide greater insight into, and understanding of, the ways in which members of society interact in general. This approach is indicative of the orientation of the sociology of medicine. Another medical sociologist may study the relationship between a patient and a physician to understand better what methods of communication work well and which ones result in a breakdown in communication. By better understanding the nature of the interaction in this manner, the sociologist hopes to improve the level of communication between the patient and the practitioner. This approach exemplifies the orientation of sociology in medicine.

Medical sociologists traditionally have been employed primarily in sociology departments in universities. They can also be found in schools of public health, medical schools, health administration programs, and allied health profession programs. Nonacademic medical sociologists are employed by federal, state, and local agencies as well as by health care consulting organizations. In either case, they may adhere to either or both of the approaches to medical sociology, although academic medical sociologists tend to adhere to the sociology of medicine approach, whereas medical sociologists in nonacademic positions tend to subscribe to the sociology in medicine approach.

What adherents to both approaches have in common is their search for the causes and consequences of health and illness. As the field of medicine continues to advance at a staggering rate, medical sociologists are confronted by a widening array of outcomes of progress. Each new technological innovation has ramifications for people involved in the health care system, both as patients and as providers of care. Medical sociology strives to provide coherent analyses and explanations of these effects.

Applications

The medical sociological perspective has been applied to every aspect of health, illness, and the delivery of health care. Perhaps the most important application is in analyzing and assessing the nature of the patient-practitioner relationship.

The results of research conducted by medical sociologists are used to gain a keener understanding of how the health care system works and how social factors affect the ways in which individuals interact with different components of the system. Sociologist Talcott Parsons, in his book *The Social System* (1951), developed and presented his view of the social nature of the relationship that develops between a patient and a doctor. As a functionalist, Parsons conceived of society as consisting of interrelated parts. Every member of society occupies multiple social statuses, each with sets of expected behaviors known as roles. For society to continue running smoothly, every member must fulfill his or her role obligations. Those failing to fulfill their roles are considered deviant by society. Deviant behavior is potentially disruptive to the social system and must therefore be controlled.

Illness temporarily prevents people from fulfilling the tasks and obligations associated with their roles. To maintain social order, Parsons maintains, the sick individual must assume a new role, which he termed the sick role. The sick role, like every other social role, comes complete with a set of tasks and obligations that the individual is expected to fulfill. First, the sick individual must recognize that being ill is undesirable and must try to get well. Second, the individual is obligated to seek technically competent help. (To Parsons, technically competent help takes the form of a physician.) The third obligation is that the sick individual must comply with the treatment prescribed by the physician. In return for meeting these obligations, the individual occupying the sick role is granted two exemptions. First, the individual is exempted from responsibility for his or her own illness. Second, the individual is temporarily exempted from performing his or her normal roles. The collective goal of this process is to return the sick individual to his normal roles as quickly as possible.

At the same time, physicians occupy a professional status which also has a set of role expectations. First, the physician is expected to act in the patient's best interests rather than in his or her own interests. Second, he or she must be guided by established rules of professional behavior. These rules represent ethical guidelines that the physician is expected to follow during the course of treatment. Third, the physician is expected to apply a high degree of skill and knowledge to solve the patient's health problems. Finally, the physician must be objective and emotionally detached when dealing with the patient. In return for fulfilling these role expectations, the physician is accorded the following three privileges. First, the physician is granted access to personal and emotional intimacy with the patient. Second, the physician is granted "practice autonomy," or the freedom to practice competent medicine in the way the physician sees fit. Third, physicians are granted professional dominance; that is, only licensed physicians can practice medicine in American society.

When the people occupying these roles interact, the outcome is, according to Parsons, predictable. Because Parsons views illness as a subset of deviant behavior, it is logical that the physician must, as part of the professional role, assume the responsibility for controlling the patient's behavior. This aspect of the patient-practitioner relationship mandates that the physician be in control. That is, the physician has the power in the relationship and the patient, by the definition of the sick role, must obey. Parsons argues that the power in the relationship shifts from the patient to the physician for three reasons. First, physicians have a high level of prestige in Western society. Second, the physician is assumed to have the expertise that the patient needs and wants in order to regain health. Finally, the patient is dependent on the physician because he or she lacks the knowledge that a competent physician possesses. The combination of the second and third reasons results in a "competence gap": a wide gap between what the patient and the physician know about medicine and between their respective levels of expertise.

The Parsonian view of the patient-practitioner relationship is considered to be the traditional sociological perspective. More recently, however, medical sociologists Marie R. Haug and Bebe Lavin, in their book *Consumerism in Medicine: Challenging Physician Authority* (1983) and in other research on the topic, present a different view of the patient-practitioner relationship. Haug and Lavin view the patient as a consumer of health care rather than as a deviant. Given this consumerist perspective, the patient is seen to have every right to question the physician and challenge physician authority when necessary, and the patient need not blindly obey the physician's directives. Therefore, the consumerist model is in direct opposition to the traditional Parsonian view of the patient-practitioner relationship.

One assumption of this perspective is that patients have become more intelligent about their own health and about health care in general. The proliferation of medical self-help books and magazines, the coverage of medical advances in newspapers, and television coverage of a wide range of health care issues have all served to educate patients. This increased level of education, in turn, has made the patient less dependent on the physician. In other words, the wide competence gap that Parsons believed is the basis for the shift of power to the physician has narrowed considerably. This narrowing of the competence gap, according to Haug and Lavin, has shifted the power back to the patient (or consumer).

The emergence of the patient as consumer is part of the more general societal consumerist movement. Since the 1960's, consumers have achieved greater power. Proponents of the consumerist approach in health care believe that the patient, like any other customer, is entitled to the type and quality of service he or she wishes. Therefore, rather than blindly accepting the physician's authority, the consumerist patient wants and deserves an equal voice in the development of a treatment plan.

The consumerist approach to the patient-practitioner relationship continues to grow among patients. In general, older patients still consider the physician to be the sole power broker in the relationship; younger patients are demanding and receiving greater input regarding how the relationship will operate. The results of sociological research on the nature of the patient-practitioner relationship have helped social scientists to understand better the nature of social interaction and have provided guidance in building better relationships between patients and their doctors.

Context

In his book *Medical Sociology* (1980), medical sociologist Minako K. Maykovich describes the development of the field of medical sociology as an evolutionary process involving the merging of medicine and sociology. This process can be viewed as flowing through three distinct stages. The first, known as the embryonic stage, covers the historical period through the Renaissance. During this stage, both medicine and sociology were indistinguishable from religion, which formed the basis of human attempts to explain daily occurrences. During the divergent stage (the seventeenth through the twentieth centuries), medicine and sociology began developing as separate disciplines. (Medicine began developing much earlier than sociology, which did not appear until the late nineteenth century.) It was not until the mid-twentieth century, during the convergent stage of development, that the melding of medicine and sociology occurred. Most of the converging process occurred in the United States. Thus, historically speaking, medical sociology is a relatively recent phenomenon. As medical sociologist William C. Cockerham notes in his book *Medical Sociology* (1989), medicine was not the sole factor in the development of medical sociology:

> What prompted sociologists to organize medical sociology as an area of sociological inquiry in its own right was neither medicine nor biology, but the realization that medical practice represented a distinct segment of society with its own unique social institutions, social processes, occupations, problems, and behavioral settings.

Although some work in the area appeared during the first half of the twentieth century, medical sociology was viewed as more of an interest than a discipline. In 1955, however, the Committee of Medical Sociology was formed by the American Sociological Association (ASA). This served as the first step toward legitimizing medical sociology as a separate and distinct field of study. The ASA formally recognized and added the Section on Medical Sociology to its complement of specialty sections in 1959. The following year, a separate ASA-sponsored quarterly publication, the *Journal of Health and Social Behavior*, became the official journal of the section and still serves as a primary source of the most recent research in the field.

The Section on Medical Sociology has grown steadily since its inception. In the early 1990's it had more than 1100 members, and, as Cockerham pointed out, "one out of every ten American sociologists is a medical sociologist." Research on every aspect of the field increases daily. As Cockerham has declared, "the position of medical sociology itself is very healthy."

Bibliography

Armstrong, David. *An Outline of Sociology as Applied to Medicine*. 3d ed. London: Wright, 1989. Short, easy-to-read book highlighting key topics covered by medical sociologists.

Brown, Phil, ed. *Perspectives in Medical Sociology*. Belmont, Calif.: Wadsworth, 1989. Forty-five articles on topics central to the field of medical sociology. Articles are divided into five parts and thirteen sections. Most traditional aspects of the field are covered, and several newer areas of interest are highlighted.

Cockerham, William C. *Medical Sociology*. 4th ed. Englewood Cliffs, N.J.: Prentice-Hall, 1989. Good introductory text overviewing the field of medical sociology. What differentiates this book from other generic medical sociology texts is its public health approach.

Haug, Marie R., and Bebe Lavin. *Consumerism in Medicine: Challenging Physician Authority*. Beverly Hills, Calif.: Sage Publications, 1983. Thorough analysis of the role of consumerism in the American public health care system. The topic is reviewed from both the patient and physician perspectives.

Jonas, Steven. *An Introduction to the U.S. Health Care System*. 4th ed. New York: Springer, 1998. Useful introduction to the way health care is delivered in the United States. Each chapter ends with two to three pages of relevant references.

Maykovich, Minako K. *Medical Sociology*. Sherman Oaks, Calif.: Alfred, 1980. Introductory text on medical sociology. Its unique feature is the application of general theoretical orientations to research in health care. Somewhat dated, but provides excellent analysis of the historical development of medical sociology.

Parsons, Talcott. *The Social System*. Glencoe, Ill.: Free Press, 1951. Outlines Parsons's functionalist perspective on the nature of social order and disorder. Recommended primarily for those with advanced knowledge of sociology, as the book is often difficult.

Raffel, Marshall W., and Norma K. Raffel. *The U.S. Health System: Origins and Functions*. 3d ed. New York: Wiley, 1989. Provides a concise history of the development of health care in the United States.

Straus, Robert. "The Nature and Status of Medical Sociology." *American Sociological Review* 22 (April, 1957): 200-204. This article outlines the differences between sociology in medicine and the sociology of medicine.

Wolinsky, Fredric D. *The Sociology of Health: Principles, Practitioners, and Issues*. 2d ed. Belmont, Calif.: Wadsworth, 1988. Provides an excellent overview of the field of medical sociology. It is recommended for those with little or no background in the field.

Ralph Bell

Cross-References

Culture of Poverty; Deviance: Functions and Dysfunctions.

Microsociology

Type of sociology: Origins and definitions of sociology
Field of study: Sociological perspectives and principles

Microsociology involves the study of how people act and react in small-group settings; it may be contrasted with macrosociology, which is concerned with the study of large-scale social processes and institutions. For example, microsociology has examined social inter-action in the family and in the classroom.

Principal terms

BEHAVIOR: how individuals overtly act in the presence of others; includes verbal expression

DEVIANCE: violation of a group norm

GROUP: two or more individuals who are part of a defined membership and who meet regularly to achieve a specific goal

GROUP NORMS: standards of behavior, thought, and values that exist within a particular group

GROUP PROCESSES: dynamics of interaction, behavior, norms, roles, sanctions, and expression which typify the workings of a group

GROUP VALUES: ideas held by group members about what is most desirable for the group as a whole; ideas may differ, but they involve notions about what the group is and should become

ROLE: behavior expected of a person with a particular status in a group; identified by a related cluster of behavioral norms

SANCTION: reward or punishment which shapes behavior and reinforces norms and roles

Overview

The sociology of the late nineteenth and early twentieth centuries focused primarily on the study of large-scale phenomena such as large groups, major social institutions, and even entire societies. Sociologists sought to develop theories that would account for how social institutions—such as the state, the family, religion, and education—function to meet people's needs, how societies change over time, and how conflict within society is created and resolved. This large-scale approach is often termed "macrosociology." Macrosociology might examine, for example, the functions of education in society, the relationship between class and religion, or the causes and effects of social stratification (the domination of some groups by others in a hierarchical arrangement). The two major perspectives that have dominated macrosociological analyses are functionalism and conflict theory.

In the twentieth century, a new approach developed as a number of sociologists became intrigued by the interactions of individuals in small-group settings. This approach became known as "microsociology," which is concerned with studying (often through direct obser-vation) how people act in real-life, face-to-face situations. A considerable amount of microsociological study has centered on educational interaction, as between teachers and students in the classroom, but microsociology has been applied to the study of small-group processes as they occur within many social frameworks and institutions.

Interest in the study of small groups grew as sociologists came to grasp the workings of societies and to recognize the interrelationship between the individual and the many groups in which he or she participates. Sociologists became interested in identifying and understanding the processes that typified the workings of small groups, including the interconnectedness between the growth of the individual and the growth of the group. This interest involved the work of psychologists, social psychologists, and sociologists; all brought the viewpoints of their respective disciplines to bear on investigation and interpretations of group phenomena.

It was the methodologies of social psychologists, particularly symbolic interactionists (who believed that behavior results from interactions constructed by the self) led by George Herbert Mead and Herbert Blumer, that laid the conceptual and methodological foundations for the domain of microsociology. These new methods were important for the development of this new subdiscipline and for the implications it had for sociology in general. The use of experimentation, in which certain variables were controlled among two or more groups and then compared, became a popular method of understanding how change occurs. Borrowed from anthropologists, the use of participant observation, in which the researcher acts as a member of a group and records its rules, norms, and other processes as they are lived, became recognized as a credible means of achieving understanding of group function. The social survey, used in conventional sociology, and the collection of life histories, borrowed from history, were also implemented as means of obtaining knowledge about groups. While seen as controversial by conventional sociologists, these methodologies provided new kinds of data that were rich with possibility. Ensuing research suggested that certain fundamental features exist among all groups. The identification of these features provided an important foundation for guiding subsequent small-group research and analysis.

One of the first features that emerged concerned order. Researchers found that interpersonal behavior among members is ordered and could be detected fairly easily in act-by-act sequences. Further, it was found that phases of disorder are systematically followed by phases of order and that situational factors affect the development and nature of that order. For example, the resignation of a leader might stop all activity and cause confusion (disorder). Almost immediately, however, individuals would act to restore order by appointing a new leader or by distributing tasks among group members.

A second feature essential to interaction systems is the distribution of action among members. Researchers found that patterns tended to develop related to one's rank within the group; with few exceptions, interaction tended to occur toward higher ranks. Although attempts to devise formulas to calculate and predict the direction and frequency of interaction were not particularly successful, the discovery of patterns and of the influences of such factors as members' roles, group goals, and subgroup formations proved invaluable to understanding both the nature and predictability of group phenomena.

The size of the group was found to affect both the nature and quality of interaction within the group. The quality of participation was found to decrease with increased group size.

Similarly, increased group size allows for less inhibition among members. Further, regardless of the formal organizational structure of a group, a systematic pattern of interaction among members was always found.

The concept of group emotion emerged as another important feature of group relations. Theodore M. Mills and other sociologists found that, instead of suppressing their individual needs, desires, and feelings, individuals' combined emotional states were affected by the emotional states of others. They also affected the group as a whole. Further, the structures or kinds of group emotions were found to variously affect the function of the group. For example, a group operating from respect and autonomy is more likely to be loyal, creative, and risk-taking, whereas one operating from fear is likely to be more edgy and stagnant. Overall, the growth of the group is either enhanced or inhibited by the structure of group emotion.

The presence and fluidity of norms in groups were identified as another feature central to group process and analysis. In his pioneering work with Edward Shils, *Toward a General Theory of Action* (1951), sociologist Talcott Parsons identified several areas addressed by group norms: the nature and significance of relationships among group members, the kinds of feelings identified with normative roles, and individual significance based upon personal characteristics or role performance. Parsons's work permitted the comparison of groups along these norm domains, thus enriching understanding of how they are learned and maintained, how they evolve, how they influence group interactions, and how they are modified based on group needs.

One of the more prolific and influential of interactionist researchers was Erving Goffman. In the preface to his 1971 text *Relations in Public*, he identified the importance of conducting research on small groups as well as the interrelatedness of these central features. To illustrate, Goffman presented an analysis of games and compared them with social systems in his essay "Fun in Games," included in his 1961 publication *Encounters: Two Studies in the Sociology of Interaction*. As an initial aspect of analysis, Goffman considered what he called "rules of irrelevance." Games involve a focused interaction in which participants effectively agree to establish and submit to rules of recruitment, membership, and play; to limits on overt hostility; and to certain divisions of labor. For the duration of the event, participants adhere to certain rules that are not of the "real" world, while rejecting—or viewing as irrelevant—others under which they might ordinarily serve. Goffman was also intrigued with players' abilities to transform any place or object, of any quality or condition, into a valued and functional field or field piece, again ignoring conventional rules for the duration of the game. Further, roles and norms for games tend to be explicitly defined and strongly enforced. Regardless of the personality of the individual coming to the game, the role and behavioral conventions required to play are readily adopted by participants.

Goffman was also intrigued that these rules about procedures, roles, and norms tell players what to treat as real in a particular game situation. As such, rules represent constructs of expression and interpretation which generate events that are meaningful in the context of the game, and around which entire worlds are built. It is the individual's capacity to engage in this matrix of possible events to create a world different from all others that Goffman found most intriguing. Goffman's work, which spanned two decades, created conceptual frameworks that have continued to contribute to the richness and diversity of small-group research.

Applications

As knowledge from these studies accumulated, sociologists became more involved in researching groups in particular settings. Howard L. Becker's study of deviance, best represented in *Outsiders* (1963) and *The Other Side* (1964), demonstrated that deviance is a social condition that exists only because others value their own norm expectations so much that they are compelled to force others to comply with them.

Similarly, using case studies and autobiographies, Erving Goffman exposed the personal pain and coping strategies of many individuals who found they were unable to conform to standards deemed by society as "normal." In *Asylums: Essays on the Social Situation of Mental Patients and Other Inmates* (1961) and *Stigma: Notes on the Management of Spoiled Identity* (1963), Goffman addressed the life situations of the mentally ill, people with physical disabilities, drug addicts, prostitutes, and the incarcerated. He analyzed the intricate system of communication that leads to stigma and rejection as well as the dynamics that each encounter or interaction brings with it. Those who are able choose to pass as normal as often as possible; the stutterer speaks only when required, for example, and the prostitute lives and shops in neighborhoods apart from her work territory. Goffman's research generated concrete understanding of the nature and impact of these coping strategies, the different sets of rules to which individuals try to conform, and the personal and interpersonal conflict people experience. Further, Goffman provided unparalleled analysis of how primary societal institutions work to establish and maintain roles, norms, and sanctions, as well as how they institutionalize labeling and discrimination. Understanding these dynamics has enabled the human and Civil Rights movements initiated in the 1960's and regenerated in the 1990's to work effectively toward removing the stigma, and therefore the discrimination, associated with being different.

By the 1970's, microsociological perspectives and research were developed to the extent that they became the preferred method for exploring process and policy. With the racial integration of education in the 1960's and curricular reforms involving women and minorities beginning in the 1970's, schools became primary sites for conducting microsociological explorations. As discrepancies in academic achievement became evident, patterns that related differential achievement to the race, class, and gender of students became established. Researchers were then faced with the challenge of explaining the processes responsible for these outcomes.

One of the most significant findings emanating from this research involved the work of sociologist Ray Rist, who conducted extensive explorations of classroom phenomena. Rist identified a series of processes, beginning with teachers' expectations and differential treatment of certain students, which—when maintained consistently over time—tended to shape students' self-perceptions, achievement motivation, and subsequent academic performance. Various mechanisms, such as tracking, ability grouping, the use of standardized test scores, and counseling, were found to be aiding in the institutionalization of different allocations of educational opportunity. As schools renewed reform efforts in the mid-1980's, the significance of these studies dramatically affected their efforts. As a result, the governors of all fifty states pledged to abolish tracking. Ability grouping has been modified, and awareness courses have been incorporated into the staff development of teachers and counselors.

Context

Claude-Henri de Rouvroy (comte de Saint-Simon) and August Comte are credited with founding sociology as a discipline in the early nineteenth century. Initial sociological explanations of societal formation involved either a functionalist (or structuralist/function-alist) approach or a conflict theory approach. Sociologists Max Weber, Talcott Parsons, and Émile Durkheim were foremost in developing and using functionalist theory. Analysis was based on determining how various institutions meet societal needs. Major premises of this theoretical interpretation included societal balance and consensus.

Karl Marx, Georg Simmel, and Ralf Dahrendorf were among the principal theorists who used a conflict perspective to analyze and explain societal organization and conditions. Central to conflict theory is the idea that different groups in society are in conflict with one another over economic resources and the availability of wealth and power. In this domination-subordination model, the masses are viewed as generally oppressed and exploited by the elite for their own gains.

As sociologists came to understand the nature of social classes, attention was turned to the study of the smaller groups that exist within larger societies. A recognized dichotomy between the individual and smaller groups of membership became recognized as a tension that was connected in intricate ways with the larger institutions or societies to which individuals belong. Sociologists began making connections between the stability or deterio-ration of societies and the situations, actions, and reactions of individuals within those groups.

One theorist and researcher who was instrumental in facilitating this shift was social psychologist George Herbert Mead, one of the most influential social psychologists of the early twentieth century. Mead worked from the premise that behavior is the result of one's concept of the self, which is constructed through interaction. Mead's work at the University of Chicago, which became known as symbolic interactionism, dominated the thinking and research regarding small-group research for several decades. In the 1930's, after Mead's death, Herbert Blumer, also of the Chicago school, became the intellectual leader and representative of symbolic interactionism. Blumer was largely responsible for establishing symbolic interaction as a respected, sociologically grounded field in social psychology (as opposed to experimental social psychology). The validity of the methodology used by symbolic interactionists laid a foundation for those sociologists who were interested in further exploration of individuals and the groups to which they belonged.

By the mid-twentieth century, sociologists Kurt Lewin, Talcott Parsons, Edward Shils, Jacob Moreno, Robert Freed Bales, and others had given new direction to the study of groups through their uses of the experimental method in laboratory situations, through applying observation techniques to small groups and communities, and through developing interaction theory. The definition of groups as miniature social systems enabled sociologists to apply conventional sociological concerns and analyses to small groups. They found that, as in large groups, members of small groups needed to find ways to meet the group's goals, to maintain group solidarity, to meet members' needs, and to adapt to the various situations that confronted the group. The discovery that, although each group is unique, all confront these same kinds of problems allowed sociologists to benefit from the rapid development of small-group theory and research.

Between the 1950's and 1970's, training laboratories were established, and training groups were popularized to assist individuals in developing and using their understanding of group process and social change. The conducting of research on small groups expanded from industrial, governmental, and social agencies to families and schools. Major works began bridging the gap between social psychological theory and actual analysis of class-rooms.

Much of this new research was influenced by social psychologist Robert Freed Bales. In his book *Personality and Interpersonal Behavior* (1970), Bales provided a shift of focus to more systematic methods of gathering and quantifying information about the interaction that occurs among group members. Bales devised a method of factor analysis that involved statistical calculations that would indicate, among twenty-seven types of group roles and their related value directions, those most typical of each group member. The development of microsociological principles along with systematic and qualitative research established the field as an important contributor to the discipline of sociology.

Bibliography

Bales, Robert Freed. *Personality and Interpersonal Behavior.* New York: Holt, Rinehart and Winston, 1970. Readable, though lengthy, text providing insight into transition from symbolic interactionist research to legitimization of observation.

Becker, Howard S. *Outsiders: Studies in the Sociology of Deviance.* New York: Free Press, 1963. Provides in-depth presentation and application of deviance theory. While the role of the dance musician of Becker's study is dated, the analysis represents a cornerstone of deviance theory, and Becker's discussions of deviance and the moral entrepreneur are enlightening for both the lay and professional reader.

Blumer, Herbert. *Symbolic Interactionism: Perspective and Method.* Englewood Cliffs, N.J.: Prentice-Hall, 1969. A classic for scholars, this clearly written text is essential for the serious student who is interested in knowing one of the most significant early works in microsociological research and theory. Blumer provides a thorough discussion of the essence of symbolic interactionism, its implications for other disciplines, and several applications of the method.

Cahill, Spencer E., comp. *Inside Social Life: Readings in Sociological Psychology and Microsociology.* 2d ed. Los Angeles: Roxbury, 1998.

Collins, Randall, ed. *Three Sociological Traditions: Selected Readings.* Rev. and expanded ed. New York: Oxford University Press, 1994. Part 3 of this book provides an excellent overview of microsociology through representative works of Cooley, Mead, Blumer, Mehan and Wood, and Goffman.

Goffman, Erving. *Stigma: Notes on the Management of Spoiled Identity*. Englewood Cliffs, N.J.: Prentice-Hall, 1963. Demonstrating early use of ethnomethodology in small-group research, presents analyses and alternatives for those individuals in society that suffer from being stigmatized. Enlightening and virtually uncompromised by time; particularly relevant in times when tensions between different peoples are unabated.

Knorr-Cetina, K., and A. V. Cicourel. *Advances in Social Theory and Methodology: Toward an Integration of Micro- and Macro-Sociologies*. Boston: Routledge & Kegan Paul, 1981. Variety of perspectives on development of microsociology and its relation to macrosociology. Includes papers on social reconstruction, inherited disorders, law, and space analysis examined from microsociological perspectives. Suggested for those who have achieved a sound grasp of microsociological method and conceptual treatments.

Mills, Theodore M. *The Sociology of Small Groups*. Englewood Cliffs, N.J.: Prentice-Hall, 1967. Useful for providing a survey of thought and research in microsociology. Includes a brief history and detailed descriptions of the various concepts, processes, and research techniques used. The book's strength lies in the many examples used to illustrate small-group research techniques and principles.

Slater, Philip. *Microcosm: Structural, Psychological, and Religious Evolution in Groups*. New York: John Wiley & Sons, 1966. Combines ian analysis and microsociological theory to address the concepts of independence, boundary awareness, and leader goals among groups. Several chapters are particularly useful in understanding the application and development of microsociology.

Denise Kaye Davis

Cross-References

Conflict Theory; Dramaturgy; Functionalism; History of Sociology; Social Groups; Sociology Defined; Symbolic Interaction.